CHALLENGES
AND
RENEWALS

Jacques Maritain

CHALLENGES
AND
RENEWALS

Selected readings edited by
Joseph W. Evans and Leo R. Ward

UNIVERSITY OF NOTRE DAME PRESS
Notre Dame & London

COPYRIGHT © 1966, UNIVERSITY OF NOTRE DAME

NOTRE DAME, INDIANA

LIBRARY OF CONGRESS CATALOG CARD NUMBER: 66-14626

MANUFACTURED IN THE UNITED STATES OF AMERICA

39,606

FOREWORD

Jacques Maritain has a profound sense of tradition—man's past is something very *living* for him. Also, he holds that there is in fact a *philosophia perennis*—a philosophy that embodies, let us say, the deepest convictions on which the civilization of the Christian West was established, and whose most articulate formulation he finds in the thought of St. Thomas Aquinas. Maritain has been inspired throughout most of his life by the principles of St. Thomas—*Woe to me if I do not Thomistize,* he wrote in one of his early books. He re-assures those who are scandalized by such a fact and such a frank avowal, by saying: ". . . the telephone and the radio do not prevent man from still having two arms, two legs, and two lungs, or from falling in love and seeking happiness as did his faraway ancestors. Besides, truth recognizes no chronological criteria, and the art of the philosopher is not to be confused with the art of the great dressmakers."

But Maritain is quick to add that this perennial philosophy is also eternally young and always inventive, and involves a fundamental need, inherent in its very being, to grow and renew itself. However, he explains that whereas progress in the sciences of phenomena, where the "problem" aspect is so characteristic, takes place chiefly by *substitution* of one theory for another, progress in philosophy, where the "mystery" aspect is predominant, takes place chiefly by *deepening insight.* Besides, the different philosophical systems, however ill founded they may be, constitute in some way, in their totality, a virtual and flowing philosophy, overlapping contrary formulations and unfriendly doctrines and carried along by the elements of truth they all contain. If, therefore, there exists among men a doctrinal organism entirely supported by true principles (and, as we have seen, there is for Maritain such a doctrinal organism), it will incorporate—more or less tardily, due to the laziness of its defenders—it will progressively realize within itself this virtual philosophy, and this will thereby, and in a proportionate degree, take on form and organic arrangement.

Laziness has never been much of a temptation for Jacques Maritain. As Wallace Fowlie has said, "he is a man who knew and accepted his vocation very early," and his tireless labors and ascetic discipline of life have been such as to provoke the admiration of all lovers of truth. He has written more than fifty philosophical books, and has contributed countless articles to the leading philosophical journals of the world. In them he has come to grips with many of the most challenging problems that have been confronting twentieth-century man, and there is in his work a powerful renewal of the *philosophia perennis*. It seems to us that this renewal itself constitutes quite a challenge to all who take ideas seriously.

Our purpose is to bring together in one volume many of Maritain's most challenging insights and renewals in the different areas of philosophy. The book does not supersede, rather we intend it to complement, our earlier book *The Social and Political Philosophy of Jacques Maritain: Selected Readings*. We have provided brief "situating comments" for each of the six divisions.

We wish to thank Professor Maritain for his helpful suggestions; and also Reverend Theodore M. Hesburgh, C.S.C., President of the University of Notre Dame, for his friendly interest and encouragement.

Joseph W. Evans
Leo R. Ward

The Jacques Maritain Center
University of Notre Dame
May, 1966

ACKNOWLEDGMENTS

The editors wish to thank the publishers listed below who hold the English and American rights to the indicated materials, for their cooperation in making this book possible.

The Archabbey Press, Latrobe, Pennsylvania, who hold the English language rights for Chapter 7, "The Pre-Philosophical Knowledge of God" from *Man's Approach to God*.

Bollingen Foundation, New York, who hold the English language rights for the United States for Chapter 2, "The Pre-Conscious Life of the Intellect" from *Creative Intuition in Art and Poetry;* Chapter 15, "Creative Intuition and Poetic Knowledge" from *Creative Intuition in Art and Poetry.*
The Harvill Press Ltd., London, hold the rights for the British Commonwealth.

The Bruce Publishing Company, Milwaukee, who hold the English language rights for Chapter 11, "Moral Evil and the Eternal Plan" from *God and the Permission of Evil.*

Fordham University Press, New York, who hold the English language rights for Chapter 5, "About Christian Philosophy" from *The Human Person and the World of Values*, edited by Balduin V. Schwarz.

Geoffrey Bles, Ltd., London, who hold the English language rights for Chapter 1, "The Philosophy of Nature" from *Science et Sagesse.* (Originally published in France by Librairie Éditions Labergerie.)

Harper & Row Publishers, Inc., New York, who hold the English language rights for Chapter 9, "The 'Sixth Way'" from *Approaches to God;* Chapter 10, "The Approach of the

Practical Intellect to God" from *Approaches to God;* Chapter 13, "Natural Law and Moral Law" from *Moral Principles of Action: Man's Ethical Imperative,* edited by Ruth Nanda Anshen.

Librairie P. Téqui, Paris, who hold the English language rights for Chapter 14, "The 'Natural' Knowledge of Moral Values" from *Neuf leçons sur les notions premières de la philosophie morale.*

The Macmillan Company, New York, who hold the English language rights for the United States for Chapter 16, "The Human Person and Society" from *Scholasticism and Politics.* Geoffrey Bles, Ltd., London, hold the rights for the British Commonwealth.

Princeton University Press, who hold the English language rights for Chapter 8, "God and Science" from *On the Use of Philosophy.*

Random House, Inc., New York, who hold the English language rights for Chapter 3, "The Human Subjectivity" from *Existence and the Existent.*

Sheed & Ward Inc., London and New York, who hold the English language rights for Chapter 6, "The Intuition of Being" from *Sept leçons sur l'être et les premiers principes de la raison spéculative.* (Originally published in France by Librairie P. Téqui.)

Charles Scribner's Sons, New York, who hold the English language rights for the United States for Chapter 12, "The Impact of Christianity on Moral Philosophy" from *Moral Philosophy;* Chapter 18, "Spurious and Genuine Philosophy of History" from *On the Philosophy of History;* Chapter 19, "The Law of Two-Fold Contrasting Progress" from *On the Philosophy of History;* Chapter 20, "Magical and Rational States in Human Thought and Culture" from *On the Phi-*

losophy of History; Chapter 21, "Man and the Human Condition" from *Moral Philosophy.*
Geoffrey Bles, Ltd., London, hold the rights for the British Commonwealth.

The University of Chicago Press, Chicago, who hold the English language rights for Chapter 17, "Church and State" from *Man and the State.*

CONTENTS

I

Theory of Knowledge

The point to be emphasized in Maritain's theory of knowledge is his defence and critical elucidation of different ways of knowing reality. He sees the richness and inexhaustibility of the material real as requiring that the mind let fall on it different noetic glances, each of which reveals a different universe of intelligibility. First, there is the universe of mobile being, *or of being imbued with mutability. This constitutes the sphere of the knowledge of nature, and itself calls for both an empiriological analysis, i.e., a spatio-temporal analysis oriented toward the observable and measurable (science of nature), and an ontological analysis, i.e., an analysis oriented toward the being and intelligible structure of things (philosophy of nature). Secondly, there is the universe of* quantity as such, *which constitutes much of the sphere of mathematics. Finally, there is the universe of* being as being, *which constitutes the sphere of metaphysics.*

One of Maritain's primary aims has been to give philosophy of nature its epistemological charter, as opposed to many Thomists who would have it eclipsed by metaphysics

*and as opposed to those scientists who think the only sub-
ject capable of providing exact and demonstrable knowledge
is that which is sense-perceivable and can be submitted to
methods of experimental and mathematical analysis. His
study of biology and his reading of modern physicists made
clear to him that scientists discover in nature problems which
go beyond the experimental and mathematical analysis of
sensory phenomena. It also convinced him that the conceptual lexicon of the scientist is radically different from
the conceptual lexicon of the philosopher. Whence his emphasis on the need for and the prerogatives of both an
ontological and an empiriological analysis of the sensible
real. Whence also his elaboration of a theory of physico-
mathematical knowledge relating to the epistemological type
which Scholastics called "intermediary sciences"* (scientiae
mediae), *sciences which straddle the physical and the mathematical order and have more affinity with mathematics than
with physics as to their rule of explanation and yet at the
same time are more physical than mathematical as to the
terminus in which their judgments are verified.*

*Maritain sees the human mind as having another life than
that of its conscious logical tools and manifestations: "there
is not only logical reason but also, and prior to it, intuitive
reason." There is, indeed, not only the Freudian unconscious
of instincts, tendencies, complexes, repressed images and
desires, and traumatic memories; there is also a spiritual unconscious or preconscious, the preconscious of the spirit.
The acts and fruits of human consciousness and the clear
perceptions of the mind—in other words the universe of concepts, logical connections, rational discursus, and rational
deliberation—emerge in the last analysis from the hidden
workings of this preconscious life of the spirit; but there
also emerge from them many genuine knowings and many
affective movements which remain more or less on the edge
of the unconscious. Among such knowings are various kinds*

of knowledge by inclination or knowledge through connaturality, notably these three: poetic knowledge, the "natural" or pre-philosophical knowledge of moral values, and mystical knowledge.

Maritain's most important writings in this area are

CREATIVE INTUITION IN ART AND POETRY

THE DEGREES OF KNOWLEDGE

PHILOSOPHY OF NATURE

QUATRE ESSAIS SUR L'ESPRIT DANS SA CONDITION CHARNELLE

RÉFLEXIONS SUR L'INTELLIGENCE ET SUR SA VIE PROPRE

SCIENCE AND WISDOM

THE PHILOSOPHY OF NATURE*

I

The debate between philosophy and the sciences reduces to a central problem: that of the philosophy of nature. Should there be a philosophy of nature distinct at one and the same time from metaphysics and from the special sciences? What are its characteristic features, its nature and definition, its spirit? As these questions are of a rather technical order, the aridity of the exposition which they demand will be excused. They are not easy, because they reach us charged with historical implications and associations. Is not the philosophy of nature what Aristotle called physics? Did not "physics" cover, for the ancients, the whole domain of the sciences of nature? Is not the overthrow of the Aristotelian explanations of the phenomena of nature also the overthrow of the whole of Aristotelian physics—and hence of the philosophy of nature? And thus, ought not the place of physics in Aristotle's sense be occupied still today by physics, but by physics in the sense of Einstein, Planck, and Louis de Broglie, or, more generally, by the ensemble of the sciences of the phenomena of nature—what the modern world calls Science? Such are the connections and liaisons of memory involved in the theoretical questions I propose to consider.

These questions are not easy; they are fundamental ones. We need not hesitate to affirm that they have an importance of the first rank for human wisdom. We must not neglect the problem of the philosophy of nature. Of all speculative wisdoms it is the humblest, the nearest the senses, the most imperfect. It is not

* *Science et Sagesse* (Paris: Labergerie, 1935), pp. 67–122.

5

even a wisdom in the pure and simple sense of the word; it is wisdom only in the order of mobile and corruptible things. But this is precisely the order that is most proportioned to our nature as a thinking being. This wisdom, which is not even purely and simply wisdom, is the first that offers itself to us in the progressive and ascending movement of our reason. And that is why it has so much importance for us—precisely because it is at the lowest rung of the ladder of φιλία τῆς σοφίας.

Through what sources can the real enter within us? There are but two, one natural, the other supernatural: the senses, and the divine Spirit. If it is a question of the lights which come down from heaven, it is not metaphysics which is primary, but rather the highest and purely spiritual wisdom—the wisdom by which we open ourselves and by which something enters into us according to the gift of grace. And if it is a question of the lights which come up from the earth, it is likewise not metaphysics which is primary, but rather an inferior wisdom bound to sense perception and strictly dependent on experience, because it is through the senses that we open ourselves onto things, and that something enters into us, according to our natural mode of knowing.

Metaphysics lies halfway between. It does not open directly, as the Platonists held, on an intuition of divine things. The intuition with which it deals is at the summit of the process of visualization or abstraction which starts from the sensible. Metaphysics is in itself and formally independent of the philosophy of nature, being superior to the latter and ruling it. But materially, and *quoad nos*, it presupposes the philosophy of nature, not of course in its achieved state, but at least in its first positions.

II

How are we to conceive the first moments of speculation on nature, as evidenced, for example, in the history of the Pre-Socratics? The intelligence is made for being, and ours must seek it in corruptible things. It seeks Being, and, doing so, its glance falls on the sensible flux of the changing singular, on unseizable Becoming. What a deception! Heraclitus and Parmenides are scandalized, each in his own way. Plato, too, and he turns away from this deceiving flux. With him the intelligence turns back to a world of essences separated from things, and thus ends in a metaphysics of the *extra-real,* conceived in the image of mathematics. And so we have the sketch of a metaphysics. But what about a philosophy of nature? There is not, there cannot be, a philosophy of nature in a system like that of Plato. The sensible world is delivered over to opinion, to δόξα.

But with Aristotle we have the genius of the West safeguarding among us intellectual respect for the being of the things we touch and see. His metaphysics is a metaphysics of the *intra-real.* It snatches from the very heart of sensible things the pure intelligibility of *being,* which it disengages as *being* and divests of the sensible. If this is so for metaphysics, it is because the intelligibility of things is not transcendent but immanent in them.

Henceforward, before attaining in the things of nature *being as being* and its pure metaphysical intelligibility, the intelligence can and must seize in them an intelligibility invested in the sensible. It can and must know, not with mere opinion, but firmly and demonstratively, those very things our eyes see: these things are no longer *maya,* but an object of science. A scientific knowledge, a *savoir* properly speaking, a philosophy of the sensible universe, of change, of movement, of becoming, is possible, so far as centers and bonds of intelligibility are invested in the moving itself and as such. The philosophy of nature, Φυσική, is founded.

These matters have become very commonplace for us. But at the time they were first discovered, how thrilling, how full of promise they were for the human spirit! At the origin of European science and philosophy lies Aristotle's act of intellectual courage, which surmounted the temptation to discouragement and the deception practiced on the intellect by the subterfuge of becoming and by the contradictions of the first philosophers.

The way things are organized in Aristotle's thought is well known. The theory of the three degrees, or the three generic orders, of abstractive visualization[1] has become classic in the schools. At the first degree, the mind knows an object which it

1. The substance of this doctrine is found in Aristotle; the Scholastics only made explicit its notional vocabulary. Cf. Aristotle, *Anal. Post.,* I, 28; *Phys.,* II, 2; *De Anima,* I, 1, *in fine.*

has disengaged from the singular and contingent moment of sense perception, but whose very intelligibility implies a reference to the sensible. This first and lowest degree of scientific abstraction is precisely the degree of physics, of the philosophy of nature. It embraces the field of the *sensible real*. Above it is the degree of mathematical abstraction, where the mind knows an object whose intelligibility no longer implies intrinsic reference to the sensible, but to the imaginable. This is the domain of the mathematical *praeter-real*. And finally, at the highest degree of intellectual visualization, at the metaphysical level, the intelligibility of the object is free of any intrinsic reference to the senses or to the imagination. This is the field of the *trans-sensible real*.

Thus, not only did Aristotle found physics, but at the same stroke he brought to light the very important difference which distinguishes it from metaphysics. The division of the three orders of abstraction is an analogical division. The three orders are not part of the same genus; they constitute fundamentally different genera. They are not piled one above the other in the same generic line; there is a true *noetic* heterogeneity between them. That is why St. Thomas teaches, in his commentary on the *De Trinitate* of Boethius, that in the metaphysical order we need not be brought back, as to the term in which our judgments are verified, either to the senses or to the imagination; in the mathematical order, our judgments are realized in the world of the imagination, not of the senses; and in the physical order, the judgment is realized in the world of sense itself. And that is why, he adds, it is a sin against the intellect to wish to proceed in the same way in the three fields of speculative knowledge.

Physics or philosophy of nature constitutes, with the experimental sciences of nature adjoined to it, a universe of intelligibility essentially distinct from the metaphysical universe. This distinction must be regarded as fundamental, because it relates to the first intuitions of being. We can seize *being* intuitively, either *as being*, i.e., disengaged in all its intelligible purity and its universality, or *as immersed in the sensible* and particularized in the specific diversity—this or that being—of the world of becoming. This distinction is bound up with the very birth of the philosophy of nature.

But this capital truth was paid for dearly by the ancients, by Aristotle himself and by the mediaevals, at the price of a serious sin of intellectual haste. We cannot say that the ancients were incurious about the detail of phenomena, but they had not seen that this detail requires its own science, specifically distinct from the philosophy of nature. The philosophical optimism of the ancient world, which moved so quickly to sometimes very hypothetical explanations of phenomena, saw philosophy and the experimental sciences as one and the same knowledge. All the sciences of the material world were subdivisions of one, single, specific science which was called *philosophia naturalis,* and to which it belonged to explain both the substance of bodies and the rainbow or snow-crystals. And it was the same with Descartes. We may say that for the ancients the philosophy of nature absorbed all the sciences of nature, that analysis of the ontological type absorbed all analysis of the empiriological type.

III

At the end of the revolution inaugurated by Descartes and Galileo, we meet an exactly opposite error, which was the price paid for great scientific advances. I have just said that the ancients absorbed the sciences of nature into the philosophy of nature. The moderns were to end up by absorbing the philosophy of nature into the sciences of nature. A new discipline, of inexhaustible fecundity, was to establish its rights. But this discipline, which is not a wisdom, was to supplant wisdom—both the *secundum quid* wisdom of the philosophy of nature and the wisdoms superior to it.

Below the plane of metaphysics, in the world of the first order of abstraction, an obscure drama between physico-mathematical knowledge and philosophical knowledge of sensible nature was enacted: its consequences have been capital for metaphysics itself and for the intellectual climate of modern man. This drama involved two principal moments: in the first, physico-mathematical knowledge was taken for a philosophy of nature, for *the* philosophy of nature; in the second, it excluded all philosophy of nature.

The first moment lasted two centuries, from the epoch of Galileo and Descartes to that of Newton and Kant. Prepared by the researches of the great Scholastics of the fourteenth and fifteenth centuries, announced and so to speak prophesied by Leonardo da Vinci and by certain thinkers of the Renaissance, a new mechanics, a new astronomy, and a new physics triumphed, at the beginning of the seventeenth century, over the explanations of the detail of phenomena taught on the same subject matters in the name, alas, of the philosophy of Aristotle. A new epistemological species, a conceptual equipment of a new type was then installed in human thought, consisting above all in the making of a mathematical reading of the sensible.

One may say that this science, which has had such great successes during the last three centuries, consists in a progressive mathematization of the sensible. Its success has been especially significant in physics. The *noetic* type to which it corresponds was not unknown to the ancients, but they had only unearthed it in very restricted and particular fields, such as those of astronomy or harmony or geometric optics. They had noted, however, that here in any event was what they very rightly called an intermediate science, a *scientia media*. According to the principles of Aristotle and St. Thomas such a knowledge must be regarded as *formally* mathematical, because its rule of analysis and deduction is mathematical; and as *materially* physical, because it is physical reality that it thus analyzes by number and measurement. St. Thomas, moreover, observes in his commentary on the second book of Aristotle's *Physics* that these *scientiae mediae*, though formally mathematical, are nevertheless more physical than mathematical, because their term, the term in which judgments in them are verified, is sensible nature.

Thus one starts from and returns to sensible reality, sensible and mobile being as such—but in order to decipher it rationally by dint of the intelligibles which are the object of the science of extension and number; not therefore to know it in its ontological aspect, but in its quantitative aspect. This is how the new type of knowledge sets out to interpret the whole field of the phenomena of nature. It is clear that this is not a philosophy of nature, but quite simply a mathematics of nature.

If we have an accurate idea of what essentially constitutes this physico-mathematical knowledge, we can understand what great folly it was for the decadent Scholastics to oppose it, as if it were a philosophy of nature opposed to their philosophy. But it was also great folly for the moderns to ask of such a knowledge the last word about the physical real, and to regard it as a philosophy of nature opposed to that of Aristotle and the Scholastics. Thus, this great epistemological tragedy was based on a misunderstanding. The problem posed itself in the same way for the Scholastics and for their adversaries—and in an erroneous way. For both of them it was a question of choosing between the old philosophy of nature and the new. Now in one case there was a philosophy of nature, and in the other a discipline which can never be a philosophy of nature: two knowledges which do not hunt on the same terrain, and which consequently are perfectly compatible with one another.

But a mathematical interpretation or reading of the sensible can obviously be made only with the aid of the fundamental notions of mathematics, that is to say, of extension and number, and also of movement (for though movement is not in itself an entity of the mathematical order, it is an indispensable intrusion of physics into mathematics when the latter is applied to nature). Thus from the moment one takes physico-mathematical knowledge of nature for a philosophy of nature, and asks of it an ontological explanation of the sensible real, it is clear one tends inevitably towards a mechanist philosophy. The rigorous mechanism of Descartes was thus—and it is this that condemns it as philosophy—a remarkably servile adaptation of philosophy to the dynamic state of the sciences and of scientific research in his time.

There we have then physico-mathematical knowledge erected into a philosophy of nature. At the same stroke it becomes (because of the natural place the philosophy of nature—as the lowest type of wisdom—inevitably occupies in the organic structure of human wisdom) the first center of organization of the whole of philosophy; and it is around this philosophy of nature confused with physico-mathematical science that metaphysics will be constructed. Thus we can understand how metaphysics has been turned from its course, from the seventeenth century onwards. All the great systems of classical metaphysics that have been developed from Descartes onwards have posited as the first key to the system of our philosophical knowledges a so-called philosophy of nature which was the mechanist hypostasis of the physico-mathematical method.

But a second moment was to follow, a moment which began with the nineteenth century and still continues.

It was apparent from the beginning, and after several vain attempts at an integral materialism it became more and more clear, that the things of the soul and even—in spite of Descartes— of organic life, are irreducible to mechanism. Descartes knew it well, and that is why he paralleled his absolute mechanism for the world of bodies with an absolute spiritualism for the world of thought. This dualism, in spite of many efforts, has never been surmounted. And this is not a good sign for a knowledge which claims to be a philosophy.

On the other hand, Kantian criticism has shown that the science of phenomena brings with it no instruments capable of discovering for us the thing-in-itself, the cause in its ontological reality. Kant saw very well this incapacity of experimental science's equipment to pass on to metaphysics, or more generally to ontology, to philosophical knowledge. His error consists in his having falsely generalized this partial view—for he, too, idolized the science of his time—and in his having built on this his philosophy of knowledge.

Finally, and above all, this science itself, with the progress of time, became gradually more conscious of itself and its procedures. This law of *prise de conscience* is a general law of all spiritual activities, but, because man is not a pure spirit and even thinks more often than not in the senses, it takes considerable time for this law to exert itself. We need not be surprised that physico-mathematical science took three centuries to discover its own nature—the definition of which, as we have noted above, had already been traced by the old wisdom of Aristotle and St. Thomas. So science became little by little more conscious of itself and of its procedures. And by this very fact it freed itself of the philosophical or pseudo-philosophical matrix imposed by mechanism. In becoming conscious of itself it perceived more and more that it was not a philosophy.

What was the result of these three facts? Physico-mathematical knowledge of nature, which in the seventeenth and eighteenth centuries had been taken for an ontology and a philosophy of nature, was reduced little by little to its true proportions; so that in the nineteenth century it became expressly what it already was without knowing it—a science of phenomena as such.

At the same time this liberation from philosophical preoccupations and pretensions, which was initiated by physics under the impulse of mathematics, was extended to the whole empiriological domain, even to the sciences of phenomena which do not yet allow, or which never can allow, a mathematical reading. Thus was set up—on its own account and according to its own proper law—the universe of that science which is in no sense a wisdom, not even *secundum quid*. Such a differentiation in itself represents considerable progress. But this progress had its other side; it was paid for at a price. The sciences in question claimed knowledge of nature *for themselves alone*. Thus it came about that, as the result of a long historical evolution, intellectual positions were reversed. While for the ancients ontological analysis and ontological explanation absorbed everything, even the sciences of phenomena themselves, into a philosophical interpretation, now on the contrary it is empiriological analysis which absorbs everything and claims to be a substitute for a philosophy of nature. Physico-mathematical science is no longer taken for a philosophy of nature, as it was in the seventeenth century, but it continues to occupy the place of a philosophy of nature. First of all it was confused with it, and then it replaced it.

I would now like to indicate briefly two remarkable consequences of this eclipse of the philosophy of nature in favor of the natural sciences: one consequence concerning science itself, and the other concerning metaphysics.

So far as science is concerned, one might say that the self-awareness it achieved, in the philosopher (and also, thanks especially to the philosopher, in the scientist), became falsified and strained in the nineteenth century from the very fact that in taking the place of the philosophy of nature it tried to define

itself as a counter-philosophy. Henceforth it had to do violence
to itself so as to exist not only for itself but also in opposition to
philosophy and in the place of philosophy, setting itself abristle
with means of defense and epistemological pretensions foreign
to its nature, so as to protect the place it occupied against an
eventual counter-offensive of philosophy. Thus was born the
positivist schema of science: which is in the process of being
destroyed before our eyes by the phenomenologist movement in
Germany, the epistemological criticism of Meyerson in France,
and finally, the crises and the progress of science itself, especially
of physics.

So far as metaphysics is concerned, it is quite clear that the
advent of criticism and positivism could not annihilate the natural aspiration of the mind towards first philosophy. Metaphysics
was to attempt to put forth some new branches. But under what
conditions? The lesson of history is singularly clear.

After the failure of the great post-Kantian idealist systems (in
which, we must not forget, a great amount of work in the philosophy of nature—the romantic *Naturphilosophie*—was bound
up with the work in metaphysics and suffered the same fate)
and after the failure of the partial and timid French attempts
at a speculative metaphysics founded on psychological introspection, in the manner of Victor Cousin or Maine de Biran, what
do we find? There is no longer any philosophy of nature; the
whole field of the knowledge of sensible nature is abandoned to
the sciences of phenomena, to empiriological knowledge. Philosophers try to set up a metaphysics, it is true; but much more
influenced than they think by positivism, they dare not even conceive the possibility of an ontology of sensible nature completing
empiriological knowledge. There is no longer any philosophy of
nature. Well, then, there is no longer any speculative metaphysics!

There is no longer anything but a reflexive metaphysics: either
reflexive and openly idealist like that of M. Brunschvicg, looking
for spirituality in the consciousness of the work of scientific discovery, in which the spirit goes beyond itself endlessly; or else
reflexive and occultly idealist like that of Husserl and of many
of the neo-realists; or else reflexive and inadequately realist like
that of Bergson, who seeks within physico-mathematical science

a metaphysical stuff which that science does not know, and which is discovered only in the intuition of pure change;[2] or tragic-reflexive like so many contemporary systems of metaphysics in which, especially in Germany, the mind tries to recover the sense of being and of existence in the drama of moral experience or of the experience of anguish.

Suppress the philosophy of nature and you suppress metaphysics as speculative knowledge of the highest mysteries of being naturally accessible to our reason. Here we have a case of causal involution: *causae ad invicem sunt causae*. Metaphysics is necessary for the constitution of a sound philosophy of nature, which is subordinate to it; but inversely a sound metaphysics can be constituted only presupposing a philosophy of nature which serves as a material basis. The very nature of our mind is involved in this. As we have immediate contact with the real only through our senses, a knowledge of the pure intelligible, a knowledge situated at the highest degree of natural spirituality, cannot reach the universe of immaterial realities, if it does not first get a hold on the universe of material realities. And it cannot grasp this universe, hunt out its proper object in it, if a knowledge of the intelligible mingled with or overshadowed by the sensible is held to be impossible—i.e., a knowledge, inferior in spirituality, which first of all attains the being of things so far as it is imbued with mutability and corruptibility, and which thus prepares, announces, and prefigures metaphysical truth in the shadows of this first degree of philosophical knowledge. Without a philosophy of nature to which the natural sciences are subordinated while it itself is subordinated to metaphysics, without a philosophy of nature which maintains contact between philosophical thought and the universe of the sciences, metaphysics has no tie with things and can do no more than turn vainly back upon the knowing and willing mind itself. In the order of material and dispositive causality, the wisdom *secundum quid* of the philosophy of nature—taken in its first positions, at least—is a *condition* for

2. With regard to Bergson it should be added that his direct objective was perhaps more in the order of the philosophy of nature than in that of metaphysics.

speculative wisdom, pure and simple (in the natural order), that is, a condition for metaphysics.

Inversely, without a philosophy of nature which transmits, so to speak, the regulations from above to the world of the sciences of phenomena, metaphysics can no longer exercise its function of *scientia rectrix* with regard to these sciences. It remains without efficacy either to orientate towards a knowledge of wisdom whatever in the sciences of phenomena aspires to, without attaining, an intellectual grasp of the real as such; or to judge and delimit the sense and direction of whatever in the sciences of phenomena undergoes the higher regulation of mathematical entities. The immense and powerful body of scientific activities, the marvellous undertaking of the experimental and mathematical conquest of nature by the human spirit, is abandoned, without superior direction or light, to empirical and quantitative law, entirely separated from the whole order of wisdom. It hurries along into the future, dragging after it men who no longer know anything of speculative wisdom or practical wisdom.

IV

Thus it would be quite futile to try to evade the problem of the philosophy of nature. We must face this problem squarely and try to treat it doctrinally, for its own sake. Here, too, questions confront the metaphysician of knowledge. Should there be a philosophy of nature distinct from the sciences of the phenomena of nature? (This is the question *an sit.*) And in what exactly does it consist? (This is the question *quid sit.*) A whole volume would be necessary to treat them fully. I shall only indicate in the briefest possible way the conclusions I believe we ought to reach.

To reply to the first question we must distinguish—at the first level of abstractive visualization, in the order of knowledge of the sensible real—two ways of constructing concepts and of analyzing the real: the analysis we have already called *ontological*, and the analysis we have called *empiriological*. In the first case we have to do with a resolution that is *ascendant* toward intelligible being, in which the sensible plays an indispensable role, but one wherein it is in the service of intelligible being. In the second case we have to do with a resolution that is *descendant* towards the sensible, towards the observable as such. Not, of course, that the mind ceases then to refer to being, for that is quite impossible: but being enters the service of the sensible, of the observable, and especially of the measurable. It becomes an unknown assuring the constancy of certain sensible determinations and of certain measurements, or the value of certain *entia rationis* founded *in re*.

In one case one seeks to define by ontological characteristics, by the constitutive elements of an intelligible nature or essence, however obscurely this essence may sometimes be attained. In the other case, one tries to define by possibilities of observation and measurement, by "effectuable" physical operations: here the permanent possibility of sense verification and measurement plays for the scientist the same role as essence does for the philosopher.

Once this distinction is understood, it is easy to understand that knowledge of the empiriological kind, that is to say, the sciences of the phenomena of nature, asks to be complemented by a knowledge of the ontological kind, that is to say, a philosophy of nature. For these sciences actually imply, as Meyerson has shown so well, an ontological tendency and reference—which they do not satisfy. They aim at being (as real), but they distrust it (as intelligible) and fall back upon sensible phenomena, so that in order to constitute themselves according to their pure epistemological type, they are in a certain sense obliged to go counter to the intellect's inclination.

The sciences of phenomena thus bear witness to the fact that nature is knowable and that they know it only in an essentially unsatisfying way. In this measure, then, they ask to be complemented by another knowledge of the same sensible universe, an ontological knowledge, to wit, the philosophy of nature. Not only do we say that the sciences deepen and quicken the intellect's desire to pass to more profound or higher truths, as the philosophy of nature itself quickens the intellect's desire to pass on to metaphysics, but we also say that as knowledge ordered to a certain term the experimental sciences ask to be complemented. They ask to be complemented, not, of course, as to their own rule of explanation, as to the formal object which specifies them, but as to the term in which they issue, which is the sensible real. This sensible real, as mutable and corruptible, is known in an essentially unsatisfying way with the sole help of the lexicon proper to empiriological knowledge. Therefore, this knowledge must be complemented by another which, likewise at the first level of abstractive visualization, will attain to the very intelligibility of the mutable and corruptible real.

But the inverse is equally true. The philosophy of nature asks to be complemented by the experimental sciences. It does not by itself alone give us a complete knowledge of the real in which it terminates, that is, of sensible nature. For by its very structure, this knowledge of the ontological kind—and this the ancients did not see too well—must renounce any claims to explain the detail of phenomena or to exploit the phenomenal riches of nature. From this point of view we may say that the great modern scientific movement since Galileo freed philosophy and ontological knowledge from a host of tasks which it had assumed and which really did not belong to it.

Is not the philosophy of nature already wisdom, though in an inferior way and only in a given order? All wisdom is magnanimous and does not concern itself with the material detail of things—in this sense it is poor and free, like all that is truly magnanimous. And this particular wisdom that is the philosophy of nature is *obliged* to poverty. The fact is that the essence of material things generally remains hidden from us—I mean in its ultimate specific determinations. It is on these ultimate specific determinations that empiriological knowledge bears, blindly, it is true, and without discovering them in themselves, as is only to be expected of a science that is not philosophy. And yet the philosophy of nature demands this non-philosophical knowledge in order that the term in which its judgments are realized may be attained in a sufficiently complete manner. For the term in which it issues is sensible reality, and sensible reality is not only corporeal substance, time, space, vegetative and sensitive life, and so forth; it takes in the whole specific diversity of things.

The fact that the philosophy of nature thus asks to be complemented by the experimental sciences is a very remarkable sign that they both belong to the same generic sphere of knowledge, that they both relate (though by very different titles) to the first level of abstraction. And it is a very remarkable sign that the philosophy of nature is fundamentally distinct from metaphysics. Metaphysics does not ask to be complemented by the sciences of phenomena; it dominates them, is free of them.

Let us turn now to the second question: in what does this philosophy of nature consist, according to definitions more rigorous than those we have used up till now, and in the light of Thomistic principles?

The Thomists reply, with Cajetan: it is a knowledge whose proper object is *the moving,* mutable being as mutable—being, therefore, being analogous and permeating all generic and specific diversifications (and this is why it is a philosophy), but not being as being, or being in its proper intelligible mystery, which is the object of the metaphysician. The object of the philosophy of nature is being viewed under the conditions of indigence and division which affect it in that universe which is the material universe, being viewed according to the mystery peculiar to becoming and mutability, to the movement in space whereby bodies interact, the movement of generation and substantial corruption which is the deepest mark of their ontological structure, the movement of vegetable growth wherein is manifested the ascent from matter to life. But we have need of further precisions. We have already remarked that the ancients did not distinguish, or they distinguished very inadequately, the philosophy of nature and the sciences of nature. Warned by the progress of these sciences, we must stress this distinction, but without forcing it. What ought we to say on this subject? It seems to me that two points of doctrine must be brought to light. In the first place, the philosophy of nature belongs to the same degree of *abstractio formalis,* or abstractive visualization, as the sciences of nature; and that is why, as I remarked above, it is fundamentally distinct from metaphysics. In the second place, however, it differs from the sciences of nature in an essential and specific way.

The philosophy of nature belongs to the same (generic) degree of abstraction, to the same (generic) sphere of intelligibility, as the sciences of nature. And this means precisely that like the sciences of nature it has to do with an intelligibility which is not pure, an intelligibility which intrinsically implies and vests itself in the primitive data of sense perception to which the human mind is subject. The text of St. Thomas I have already cited, on the essentially diverse ways in which the three parts of speculative knowledge proceed, is quite clear on this point. But I would like to insist on it a little more.

I would like to insist on what could be called the paradox of ontological analysis at the first degree of abstractive visualization, or the paradox of intelligible being as it is attained by the philosophy of nature. Consider the intelligible objects of the first order of visualization. In themselves and as intelligibles they are obviously not the object of a sense operation. My eye never perceives the quality "color" as my intelligence thinks it. But yet these objects humble the intelligence in the sense that data received through sense perception are necessarily included in their very intelligibility. Color, as an intelligible, does not fall under the senses. Thus an angel, too, has an idea of color; and yet it does not derive it through senses. But for man it is impossible to understand the notion of color without reference to sense experience. A blind man will never have the *idea* of color.

And that is why, parenthetically, Descartes hated ideas of the first order of abstractive visualization. He refused them all objective value and all explanatory value because they are not pure notions such as he believed mathematical notions to be, in spite of the latter's link with the imagination. He wanted to make physics a knowledge intrinsically free of the senses; he even demanded that it have a pure intelligibility, which, as a matter of fact, lacked purity from the start, because it was a geometric intelligibility. It was in this way that he made science specifically one—by brutally telescoping the distinct and hierarchized worlds which constitute it.

Thus ontological analysis at the first degree of abstractive visualization cannot liberate itself from the sensible given; it definitely rests upon it. And this is true even of the highest notions of this order, such as the notions of form and matter, of soul and body. Compare notions such as those of form and matter, soul and body—I have deliberately chosen the highest and most philosophical—which belong properly to the philosophy of nature, with metaphysical notions such as those of act and potency, essence and existence. In both cases the mind tends toward intelligible being, seeks to grasp intelligible being; but there is none the less an essential difference in intelligibility.

In the case of the concepts proper to the philosophy of nature, the sensible is not only, as with all our concepts, the source of the idea; it remains irremediably bound to the idea. The notion of soul cannot be conceived without the notion of body; they are correlative notions, since the soul is the substantial form of the body. We cannot conceive the notion of body without the notion of organism—*caro et ossa;* we cannot conceive the notion of organism without the notion of qualitative heterogeneity; and we cannot conceive the notion of qualitative heterogeneity without that of sensible properties. And thus we arrive at color, resistance, hardness, etc., which we cannot define except through an appeal to sense experience.

On the other hand—and this is another aspect of the same paradox—ontological analysis at the first degree of abstraction, the ontological knowledge of the philosopher of nature, honors sense perception more than does empiriological knowledge and expects more from it.

In the philosophy of nature, sense-intuition is itself assumed into the mind's movement towards intelligible being; its value as knowledge, its *speculative* value, enters into maximum play. When the philosopher deals with the humblest sensible reality, color for example, he does not do so by measuring a wavelength or an index of refraction, but by referring to his sight-experience and seeking therein the designation of a certain nature, of a certain quality whose specific intelligible structure is not revealed to him. Thus he respects this sense-experience; it brings him a content which as sensible is no doubt not itself intelligible, but which as sensible has a speculative value just the same. And it is thanks to this obscure speculative value which he respects in the sense, that he can turn the data furnished by the sense to the service of the imperfect intelligibility of an object of knowledge. The lived experience of the sense is respected for its own proper knowledge-value, however inferior it may be.

In empiriological knowledge and especially in physico-mathematical knowledge, on the contrary, it is highly noteworthy that the sense serves only to collect information furnished by instruments of observation and measurement, and that it is refused, so far as possible, any knowledge-value properly so-called, any obscure seizure of the real. How could it be otherwise in that lifeless universe without soul or flesh, without qualitative depth—the universe of abstract Quantity mistaken for Nature? Descartes had his reasons for reducing sense perception to a mere subjective warning, exclusively pragmatic.

Aristotle, on the other hand, regarded the act of seeing as the prime example of the joy of knowing. Here we have from the outset two fundamentally opposed attitudes of mind, and one may be permitted to observe that Aristotle's is the only really human one. The true philosophy of nature honors the mystery of sense perception; it knows that this perception takes place only because the immense cosmos is activated by the First Cause whose motion passes through all physical activities so as to make them produce, at the higher reach where matter awakens to *esse spirituale*, an effect of knowledge on an animated organ. Wherefore the child and the poet are not wrong in thinking that in the light of a star coming to us across the ages, the Intelligence who watches over us signs to us from afar, from very far. It is highly instructive to observe here that the renaissance in Germany of the philosophy of nature, due to the phenomenological movement, brought forth on the part of Mme. Hedwig Conrad-Martius, and of Plessner and Friedmann, for example, a great effort to reinstate sense-knowledge. This is not the place to pass judgment on the particular results of this effort. But to my mind, its very existence bears witness to a fundamental need intrinsic to the philosophy of nature, and too often neglected by modern Scholastics.

And so we come to the second of the two points mentioned above. How is the philosophy of nature distinguished from the sciences of nature? The considerations we have already proposed show clearly that the philosophy of nature differs from the sciences of nature in an essential and specific way.

What is the ultimate principle for the specification of the sciences? Thomist logicians answer that it is the typical mode according to which the definitions are formed: *modus definiendi.*

If this is so, it is clear that in the generic sphere of intelligibility of the first order of abstraction, the notions and definitions resulting from empiriological analysis, wherein everything is primarily resolved in the observable, and, on the other hand, the notions and definitions resulting from ontological analysis, wherein everything is primarily resolved in intelligible being—it is clear that these notions and definitions answer to specifically distinct kinds of knowing. The conceptual vocabulary of the philosophy of nature and that of the natural sciences are typically different. Even if they happen to be expressed in the same words, the mental word or concept signified by the same word is formed in a typically different way in the two cases. The philosophy of nature differs specifically from the natural sciences.

Now let us try to reach a more precise definition, along the lines of Thomist epistemology. I will spare the reader the apparatus of technical distinctions that are basic here, and will only say that as I understand it the philosophy of nature ought to be defined as follows: (1) the "intelligibility-appeal" (*ratio formalis quae*) to which it answers, is mutability: it bears on mutable being as mutable—*ens sub ratione mobilitatis;* (2) its objective light (*ratio formalis sub qua*) is an ontological mode of analysis and conceptualization, a way of abstracting and defining which, though having an intrinsic reference to sense perception, aims at the intelligible essence. And it is for this reason that it differs specifically from the natural sciences.

Thus the philosophy of nature has for its object, in all the things of sensible nature, not the detail of phenomena, but intelligible being itself *as mutable,* that is, as capable of generation and corruption; or again, the differences of being it can decipher —aiming at the intelligible nature but without sacrificing sense data—in the world of ontological mutability.

It is here that we should note the spirit and method of the philosophy of nature. I will touch on one aspect of this question.

It goes without saying that the philosophy of nature must use facts that are themselves philosophical, that is, established and judged in the proper light of philosophy. For a fact can give only what it contains, and philosophical conclusions can be drawn only from premises or facts which themselves possess philosophical value. Ordinary observation, when philosophically criticized, can already furnish many facts of this kind.

But what must be the relationship between the philosophy of nature and scientific facts? Two errors need to be carefully avoided.

A first error consists in asking philosophical criteria of *brute* scientific facts. By a brute scientific fact I mean a scientific fact which has not been *treated* philosophically. As long as they are illumined only by the light which first made them discernible in the real and utilizable by the scientist, these facts have interest only for the scientist, not for the philosopher. The scientist has the right to forbid the philosopher to touch them, the right to claim them for himself alone. It is an illusion to think that a philosophical dispute can be settled by an appeal to scientific facts on which no philosophical light has been cast. That, it seems to me, is Father Descoqs' error in his book on hylomorphism.*

The second error would be to reject scientific facts, to try to construct a philosophy of nature independent of them, and to maintain it isolated from the sciences. Now note that this is an inevitable tendency if the philosophy of nature is confounded with metaphysics. Then one will want to give to the philosophy of nature the same freedom with regard to the detail of scientific facts that is proper to metaphysics.[3] In reality, one will not have a metaphysics of the sensible, but one will run the risk of having a metaphysics of ignorance.

---

* P. Descoqs, *Essai critique sur l'hylémorphisme* (Paris: Beauchesne, 1925) [Editors].

3. This does not mean that metaphysics can ignore the sciences. But if it must keep contact with them (which it does normally through the philosophy of nature), this contact is not for the sake of the argumentation proper to the metaphysician, but rather for his general information—for the knowledge of the world and the scientific imagery which, on the side of dispositive or material causality, constitute a vital expanse, as it were, for his thought.

The truth is that the philosopher must make use of scientific facts on condition that these facts are philosophically judged and interpreted; thanks to which, philosophical facts already established will be confirmed, or other philosophical facts will be discovered. By bringing scientific facts into contact with philosophical knowledge already acquired elsewhere and with the first principles of philosophy, one can draw from them an intelligible content that can be handled by philosophy.

But then, if it is true that the philosophy of nature needs to be complemented by the sciences and to draw confirming and enlightening philosophical facts from the material of scientific facts, must it not accept as a consequence a certain law of aging and renewal? Certainly not a substantial change! There is a substantial continuity between the philosophy of nature as it appeared to Aristotle and as it appears to us. But it has undergone many changes along the way, many agings and many renewals. So that insofar precisely as knowledge it is much more dependent on time than is metaphysics.

We have here a sign of the difference in their formal objects and formal values. A treatise in metaphysics, if it be pure (but in fact it always contains allusions to the state of the sciences when it was written, to the opinions of men, etc.), can span the centuries. But how long can a treatise in experimental physics or biology last? Twenty years, ten years, two years, the life-span of a horse, of a dog, of the larva of a cockchafer. And a treatise in the philosophy of nature? Well, at the maximum it can last a man's lifetime—and this provided that its successive editions, if it have them, be periodically brought up to date. For a treatise in the philosophy of nature must necessarily have intimate contact with the sciences of phenomena, and these sciences are subject to much more rapid renewal than is philosophy.

V

We have been speaking of the philosophy of nature considered as an abstract epistemological type. But we may add that today we are witnessing a sort of renaissance of the philosophy of nature. This renaissance parallels the retreat of the positivistic conception of science. Biologists are coming to understand that the methods of purely material analysis leave them with the pieces in their hands. As Goethe put it, only life itself and the spiritual tie is lacking—*fehlt leider nur das geistige Band*. And they are beginning to turn expressly to philosophy for the ultimate understanding, for *Verstehen*, of the living organism. I only need to mention the works of Hans Dreisch, which have done so much towards this new orientation of biology, and the more recent works of Buytendijk, Hans André, Cuénot, and Rémy Collin.

The magnificent achievements in physics—due to Lorentz, Poincaré, and Einstein, on the one hand, and to Planck, Louis de Broglie, Dirac, and Heisenberg, on the other—have renewed and stimulated in this science the sense of the ontological mystery of the world of matter. We find significant evidence of this in the philosophical preoccupations of Herman Weyl, of Eddington, and of Jeans.

The great disputes and discoveries in modern mathematics concerning axiomatic method, the transfinite and the theory of number, the continuous and the transcendent geometries, are in need of a philosophical classification, of which, to my mind, we have only a still quite uncertain beginning in the works of Russell and Whitehead, or of Brunschvicg. On the philosophical side, the ideas of Bergson and Meyerson in France, and of the phenomenologists in Germany (of Max Scheler, notably), on the one hand, and the Thomist revival, on the other, have prepared the ground for a resumption of research relating to an ontological knowledge of the sensible real. Whether or not this research will be directed toward a solidly based philosophy of nature depends upon the activity of Thomists.

We must be on guard here against what I have elsewhere termed "dangerous liaisons"* and the temptation to too easy a spirit of concord, in which the essential distinction between the lexicon of empiriological knowledge and that of ontological

---

* See *The Degrees of Knowledge*, new translation (New York: Charles Scribner's Sons, 1959), pp. 186–192 [Editors].

knowledge would be disregarded. This danger is especially to be feared in what concerns the relation of the philosophy of nature with the physico-mathematical sciences. For, as we have already observed, these latter in their most highly conceptualized theoretical parts reconstruct their universe by means of mathematical beings of reason (*entia rationis*) founded *in re,* myths or symbols which as such cannot be brought into continuity with the real causes that are the object of the philosopher's consideration.

But this being granted, we must also note the very significant affinities which make modern science, despite the vast areas of shadow that still darken it, more synergic with the Aristotelian-Thomistic philosophy of nature than was ancient or medieval science. We will not speak of the sciences of life, where the demonstration of this thesis would be only too easy. The Cartesian conception of the world-machine and of matter identified with geometric extension, the Newtonian conception of an eternal framework of space and time independent of the world, the infinity of the world, the pseudo-philosophical determinism of the Victorian physicists—all these dogmas have had their day. Contemporary scientists' ideas on mass and energy, the atom, mutations due to radioactivity, the periodical table of elements, and the fundamental distinction between the family of elements and that of solutions and mixtures, dispose the mind (dispose, I say, for to have anything more all these materials would have to undergo a properly philosophical treatment) to restore to their full value the Aristotelian notion of *nature* as radical principle of activity, the notion of *substantial mutations* which is the foundation of the hylomorphic theory, and the notion of an *ascendant order* of material substances much richer and more significant than ancient physics ever surmised.

Looking upon our world wherein all is in motion, more so in the invisible atom than in the visible stars, and wherein motion is the universal mediator of interaction, the philosopher sees it as wholly pervaded and, as it were, animated by that sort of participation of the spirit in matter which we call *intentionality.*

Its hierarchy has been reversed: the atomic world and not the celestial spheres is now the basis of time. The center of the physical world is no longer the sublunary globe surrounded by the

eternal rotating of divine and incorruptible bodies. Rather, it is
the human soul, living its corporal life on a tiny precarious planet,
that is the center, not material but spiritual, of this world.

And this world is a world of contingence, of risk, adventure,
irreversibility; it has a history and a direction in time. Little by
little the giant stars grow smaller, are consumed, and burn themselves out. For billions of years an enormous, original capital of
dynamism and energy has been tending toward equilibrium,
using itself up, spending itself lavishly, bringing forth marvels in
its rush toward death. The principle of entropy has been much
abused by philosophers, but yet one has the right to note in it
the deep meaning which accords so well with Aristotle's philosophical, not astronomical, notion of time: *quia tempus per se
magis est causa corruptionis quam generationis.* And one also has
the right to point out how the natural exception which the least
of living organisms makes to the law of the degradation of
energy (which applies, however, to the whole universe of matter)
marks most significantly the threshold where something weight-
less, endowed with a singular metaphysical destiny and called
"soul," pierces its way into matter and inaugurates therein a
new world.

Modern science confirms in its own way and with admirable
precisions that great insight of Thomist philosophy of nature
which sees in the universe of non-living and living bodies an
aspiration and an ascent, from one ontological degree to another,
toward forms of increasingly complex unity and individuality, and
of increasing interiority and communicability at the same time: in
fine, towards that which in the vast universe no longer signifies
a part but a whole itself, a consistent universe open to others
through intelligence and love. Such is the *person,* who is, as
St. Thomas says, the most perfect being in all of nature.

In deciphering the picture of the material universe given to
it by the sciences of phenomena, the philosophy of nature discerns therein, at the heart of what might be called the tragedy
of prime matter, an immense movement of response—at first
indistinct, then stammered, and finally becoming, in the human
being, a word—of response to another Word which the philosophy
of nature does not know. It is metaphysics that will know it. By

casting philosophical light upon the universe of the sciences, the philosophy of nature discerns therein an intelligibility which the sciences themselves cannot reveal to us. Disclosing, in sensible being known as mutable, analogical traces of the more profound realities and truths which are the proper object of metaphysics, the philosophy of nature, a wisdom precarious and *secundum quid,* exercises already at the first degree of abstractive visualization, in the generic sphere of intellection nearest to the senses, the ordering and unifying office of wisdom. Indispensable mediator, it brings into accord the world of the particular sciences, which is inferior to it, and the world of metaphysical wisdom, which holds sway above it. It is there, at the very base and outset of our human knowledge, at the very heart of the sensible and changing multiple, that the great law of the hierarchical and dynamic organization of knowledge, on which the good that is intellectual unity depends for us, first comes into play.

The Pre-conscious Life of the Intellect*

Art Bitten by Poetry Longs to be Freed from Reason

1. I have insisted, in the preceding chapter,** that art is rooted in the intellect. Art is a virtue of the practical intellect; art is, and especially the fine arts are, to a considerable degree more intellectual than prudence: art is the very virtue of working reason. Now we are faced with a paradox, a fact which seems diametrically opposed to this contention: namely, the fact that modern art—I mean in its finest achievements, as well as in its deepest trends—modern art longs to be freed from reason (logical reason).

It is, of course, easy, too easy, to relate this fact to a much more general phenomenon, conspicuous enough indeed: what the French philosopher Blanc-de-Saint-Bonnet called the progressive weakening of reason in modern times. Then one would say, with some people inspired by a bitter zeal, that modern art suffers from the same general weakening of reason, or (and this would be perhaps a little more relevant) that modern art, being surrounded on all sides, and threatened, by modern reason—a so-called reason as afraid of looking at things as it is busy digging in all the detail around them, and as fond of illusory explanations as it is insistent in its claim to recognize only statements of fact, the reason of those who believe that poetry is a substitute for science intended for feeble-minded persons—modern art has

---

* *Creative Intuition in Art and Poetry* (New York: Pantheon Books, 1953), pp. 71–100.
** *Ibid.*, Chapter II [Editors].

endeavored to defend itself by seeking refuge in irrationalism.

Yet such an explanation would fall short of the mark and remain extraneous to the issue. For the yearning for liberation from reason of which we are speaking is in reality a phenomenon very much deeper and more significant. It has to do with a typical aspiration of art in its own line and inner life, in so far as it has become conscious of itself during the last century to an unprecedented degree, and has found, at the center of this self-awareness, poetry, naked and wild poetry. Modern art has been bitten by poetry. And that is the very cause of its estrangement from reason. I am not trying to discuss now what poetry is. I am only concerned with the effects that poetry produces.

Shall I try to describe, in a brief and, to be sure, oversimplified manner, the process, normal in itself and extraordinarily illuminating for the philosophy of art, which the evolution of modern art has enabled us to contemplate? I would say that all is appendent to the fact of art's becoming more and more fully aware—of its *freedom* with respect to everything which is not its own essential law—of the necessity which binds it to *master* everything which is not its own creative and engendering virtue—and of the kind of *loyalty to truth* which is required from the artist, and which is loyalty to his own singular vision. The formulas I just used have been the occasion for a swarm of inept claims and sickening commonplaces. They remain true in themselves.

I would also say that the process in question is essentially a process of liberation or enfranchisement, but liberation or enfranchisement of that intrinsic impulse, one with the nature of art, which requires it to *transform* the things it uses. For just as the art of the craftsman, while watching the natural properties of the materials it uses, deprives these materials of their natural form (I mean the form which wood is possessed of in trees, or metals in the mines of the earth) in order to bring them into a form born out of his mind, so the art of the painter or the poet, while watching the natural appearances of the realities of the world, deprives these realities of their own natural form and beauty, and the instruments of the mind of the age-old patterns of operation established by the common use of men, in order to produce a work invested with a new form and beauty born out of the artist's soul. Liberation and transformation, therefore, keep pace with one another.

Now it seems to me that three principal steps might be discerned in the evolution of modern art, especially modern painting and poetry.

First, it endeavors to free itself from nature and the forms of nature. It transforms nature, not only by carrying to extremes the law of deformation of natural appearances which painting has always brought into play, but also by causing another universe of forms and relations between forms—disclosing a deeper reality, more akin to our dreams, angers, anguish, or melancholy —to arise from nature in art's own fabric of colors or of words. And in great artists this in no way implies any contempt for or divorce from nature. They rather steal from nature its own secrets of poetry.[1]

The second step is liberation from and transformation of language, I mean rational language. Rational language is not cut out to express the singular, it is burdened with social and utilitarian connotations, ready-made associations, and worn-out meanings, it is invaded by the inevitable insipidity which results from habit. So it does not only interfere with poetry, it perpetually sidetracks it and makes poetry say something other than what

---

1. One of these secrets, for instance, is irregularity. "If one examines the most famous plastic or architectural productions from this point of view, one quickly perceives that the great artists who created them, careful to work in the fashion of that nature whose respectful pupils they did not cease to be, took good care not to violate her fundamental law of irregularity. One realizes that even works based on geometric principles, such as St. Marco, the little house of Francis I in the Cours la Reine, as well as the so-called Gothic churches, contain no perfectly straight line, and the round, square, and oval forms that one finds, which it would have been easy to make exact, never are exact. . . ." Renoir, project of a manifesto (1884), in *Artists on Art* (New York: Pantheon Books, 1945), p. 321.

"Ars imitatur naturam in sua operatione," St. Thomas said (*Sum. theol.*, I, 117, 1).

As regards the "fundamental law of irregularity," Renoir's observations on the workings of nature may be complemented by Baudelaire's remarks on beauty: "Ce qui n'est pas légèrement difforme a l'air insensible, d'où il suit que l'irrégularité, c'est-à-dire l'inattendu, la surprise, l'étonnement sont une partie essentielle et la caractéristique de la beauté." *Fusées*, XII, in *Journaux intimes*, ed. van Bever (Paris: Crès, 1919).

poetry wants to say. The same observation can be made with regard to that intelligible discursus—organizing together, according to the accustomed patterns of the pleasure of the eyes or the ears, the movements of the design or the sounds of the melody—which is the rational language of painting and music. Why should we be surprised by the fact that modern artists struggle to free themselves from rational language and its logical laws? Never did they pay more attention to words, never did they attach greater importance to words: but in order to transfigure them, and to get clear of the language of discursive reason. Joyce creates with all the words of the earth a new language conveying an intelligible sense, but intelligible to himself alone. As a rule the other searchers conceal the logical or intelligible sense in a language made up of images, to the evocation of which the words are dedicated. The Impressionists and Neoimpressionists on the one hand, Cézanne, Gauguin, van Gogh on the other, are also more concerned than ever with the elements of the painter's language, its "words"—but in order to discover a new pictorial language liberated from that intelligible external consistency, that immediate rational legibility of visible aspects which was still present even in the drawings of a William Blake. Be it a poem or a painting, the work speaks: it speaks no longer in terms of logical reason.

Thus art enters the regions of obscurity. *"Je suis obscur comme le sentiment,"* I am obscure as feeling is, Pierre Reverdy said. This darkness grows deeper when we arrive at the third step in the process. Then art endeavors to get free from the intelligible or logical sense itself. Think of certain poems of René Char or Henri Michaux, Hart Crane or Dylan Thomas, or of certain cubist canvases. The work, more eager than ever to communicate an invaluable content, speaks no longer, as it were, seems mute. It strikes us at the heart through forbidden ways. Is it true that the logical sense has disappeared? No, that's impossible. But the logical sense has been digested, so to speak, by the poetic sense, it has been broken up, dislocated, to subsist only as a kind of variegated matter of the poetic sense. The poetic sense alone gleams in the dark. This poetic sense, which is but one with poetry itself, is the inner, ontologic entelechy of the poem, and gives it its very being and substantial significance. "It is in no way identical with the intelligible sense, as the soul of a man is in no way identical with his speech, and it is inseparable from the formal structure of the poetic work: whether the work is clear or obscure, the poetic sense is there, whatever becomes of the intelligible sense. The poetic sense is substantially bound to the form, immanent in the organism of words, immanent in the poetic structure as a whole."[2] In modern art it demands to be definitively freed, at any cost.

The process I just described is a process of liberation from conceptual, logical, discursive reason. Though it may entail accidentally a general disregard for the intellect, and a suicidal attitude of contempt for reason, it is by no means, in its essence, a process of liberation from reason itself, if it is true that reason possesses a life both deeper and less conscious than its articulate logical life. For reason indeed does not only articulate, connect, and infer, it also *sees;* and reason's intuitive grasping, *intuitus rationis,* is the primary act and function of that one single power which is called intellect or reason. In other words, there is not only logical reason, but also, and prior to it, intuitive reason.

> . . . whence the soul
> Reason receives, and reason is her being,
> Discursive or intuitive.[3]

Coleridge invoked the authority of Milton to confirm his own views on reason's intuitivity.[4] He might also have invoked the authority of Aristotle.[5]

---

2. Raïssa Maritain, "Sens et Non-sens en poésie," in *Situation de la Poésie* (Paris: Desclée De Brouwer, 1938), p. 14.

3. *Paradise Lost,* Book V, 486–88.

4. *Biographia Literaria,* Chapter X.

5. "If, then, the states of mind by which we have truth and are never deceived about things invariable or even variable are scientific knowledge, practical wisdom, philosophic wisdom, and intuitive reason, and (as concerns the perception of the first principles) it cannot be any of the three (i.e., scientific knowledge, practical wisdom, or philosophic wisdom), the remaining alternative is that it is *intuitive reason* that grasps the first principles." Aristotle, *Nicomachean Ethics,* Book VI, Chapter 6, 1141a 2–8 (trans. W. D. Ross). Here "intuitive reason" means a particular *habitus* (the primary one) of the intellectual power—the *intellectus principiorum.*

Already in the domain of speculative knowledge, science, and philosophy, intuitive reason is fundamentally at work: any demonstration finally resolves into first principles which are not demonstrated, but seen; and any discovery which really reveals a new aspect of being is born in a flash of intuitivity before being discursively tested and justified. But when it comes to poetry, the part of intuitive reason becomes absolutely predominant. Then, as our further analyses will show, we are confronted with an intuition of emotive origin, and we enter the nocturnal empire of a primeval activity of the intellect which, far beyond concepts and logic, exercises itself in vital connection with imagination and emotion. We have quit logical reason, and even conceptual reason, yet we have to do more than ever with intuitive reason—functioning in a nonrational way.

In all that I have just said, moreover, about the yearning for liberation from logical reason, I have tried, quite inadequately, I fear, somehow to disengage the pure meaning of the task progressively accomplished in the laboratories of modern poetry. It is an ideal line that I have tried to follow. In actual fact, the greatest among modern artists, though deeply involved in the general movement, never made for the extremes. They freed themselves from logical reason in the sense that they transformed the use of logical reason, not in the sense that they abolished it.

2. A process like the one we are discussing is of course full of serious dangers. The undertaking was heroical, it was paid for at the price of many casualties. The process took place, moreover, in a variety of ways, quite different in quality, in which genuine and spurious trends were in mutual contact, and sometimes intermingled. Now, to pursue our analysis, I should like to distinguish between three main lines of orientation, which, it seems to me, have passed, like arrows, through the whole process in question.

There has been a direction—the right one—which pointed straight to poetry itself. In the process of transforming nature, language, and the logical or intelligible sense, everything was directed, as to the final end, to the poetic sense itself: in other words, to the pure, free, and immediate passage, into the work, of the creative intuition born in the depths of the soul. Let us think, for instance, of the artistic lineage composed of such men as Rouault and Chagall,[6] Satie or Debussy, Hopkins, Apollinaire, Hart Crane, Reverdy, T. S. Eliot, St.-John Perse (I name only the most significant), not to speak of the great originator, Baudelaire.

Another direction has pointed, I would say, to the pure creativity of art. The emphasis had shifted to something which was

6. Both of them are genuine primitives, though in manner thoroughly different, for Rouault is close to the inspiration of Romanesque art, and Chagall's roots plunge into age-old Jewish inspiration.

May I be permitted to quote here a passage of an essay on Rouault which I wrote twenty-nine years ago [1924]. "A philosopher could study in him the virtue of art as in the pure state, with all its exigencies, its mysteries, its fierce self-restraint. If he wounds many people by reactions lacking gentleness, if he protects himself against all modes of subjection with meticulous and vigilant violence, with umbrageous and proud independence, it is to maintain in himself this virtue in its integrity. He likes to repeat after Poussin: 'We are making a mute art,' and while boiling always with a confused flood of thoughts, while possessing an exquisite sense of the beauty of the old masters and while finding sometimes the most significant sayings (*drawing*, he said, *is a jet of the spirit on the alert*) he never explains himself, letting his work alone defend itself, respecting his art to such a point that he does not wish to touch it by words. Obstinate in his furrow, he cannot be classed in any school. His painting, so human and expressive, has a purely plastic eloquence, with nothing literary in it. His love of rare materials, which could have led him astray in endless research, his human preoccupation, and his taste for satire which could have diverted him toward anecdote—these he has not suppressed but dominated by his art, which, by triumphing over them, has become all the more pure and the more robust. Seeing ahead of him, after his *Child Jesus among the Doctors*, the easiest and most profitable future, he broke his moorings and scandalized his first admirers by entering the *dark night* of which he did not see the end, but where he felt his energies would be purified. . . . He was obeying a necessity of growth, stronger than he. Prostitutes, clowns, judges, shrews, it was himself that he sought; I mean his own interior accord in the universe of form and color. He has found himself, but that is a trail that one must blaze alone. . . . He has a horror of an artificial order reconstituted by mechanical or imitative means; he has always felt himself claimed by a certain spiritual order linked to an exquisite measure, to fleeting nuances that have to be discovered from within. . . . Like his admirable landscapes, his religious work has many surprises in reserve, even for those who have long followed his work. . . . If a painter belongs, like the one in question here, to the family of the very great, it is by reason above all of his *poetics*. In every canvas of Rouault, the forms fill out the space—a unique space, arisen for itself—with a mysterious necessity akin to that with which the natures of a universe fill out their boundaries. But not by virtue of abstract recomposition is this accomplished. It is by the effect of a creative emotion provoked far down in the soul by the irritation of an infallibly sensitive eye and a

not the absolutely central element, yet was still essential. The creative power of the human spirit craved after pure creation—jealous, as it were, of God, Who was tactless enough to create before us. Poetry, and great poetry, was attained and seized upon but, so to speak, in addition, in a supererogatory manner. Let us think of Picasso. That's why he pushed forward along so

profound imagination." "Revue Universelle," 1924; reprinted in *Frontières de la Poésie* (Paris: Rouart, 1935); *Art and Poetry* (New York: Philosophical Library, 1943), pp. 25–29.

On Chagall, Raïssa Maritain writes: "[In his etchings inspired by the Bible] one sees that a genuine primitive demands little of nature (though he loves her with an ever young tenderness, and a mystical love) and much of himself; little of realism and much of transposition, or of what we call today abstraction, which is nothing but the upsurge of new forms mysteriously akin to natural forms, and rich with the spirit of the artist of whom they are born. And doubtless this is but one with the exigencies of art, if Baudelaire was right in saying that 'the first business of an artist is to substitute man for nature, and to protest against her,' but it is true above all of the great primitives who, under the thrust of their interior world, abtract from the natural universe, spontaneously, universal forms endowed with inexhaustible significance. . . . I asked him what had struck him in Impressionist, 'Fauves,' Cubist painters, when he first came into contact with their works in Paris—'Their realism,' he immediately answered with sorrow. . . . He does not avoid natural forms; he does not fly from them, on the contrary he makes them his own through the love he bears them, but by the same token he transforms and transfigures them, brings out and draws from them their own surreality, finding there the symbols of joy and life in their purified essence, their spiritual soul. . . . Surrealism came close to being called *surnaturalism,* in the person of its first representative. But the angels of a Sacred Vocabulary did not permit it. . . . Chagall's surrealism has both a spiritual and a plastic character. With no preconceived idea, through his art's magic, through the liberation of his internal world, Chagall has created forms signifying a spiritual universe entirely his own, whose traits cannot be found to such a degree in any other painter of our time. It was said of Rouault that he is the painter of original sin. But the universe created by Chagall is in ignorance of sin, hatred, and discord; he utters grace and joy, fraternity and love. The suffering of the world is also present, under the signs of a grave and melancholy contemplation; but the symbols of consolation are always near at hand. . . . A painting by Chagall is a tranquil, poised countenance; it is a presence which imposes itself even upon those who are deaf to poetry's voice. But to those who hear are told, not voluntarily, but through the very power of this art, a thousand dreams and mysteries which are, so to speak, the secret network of the arterial tree of the work: they secure life, and they express life, the ineradicable images of childhood, the wishes of the heart, the joy of the eyes." *Chagall ou l'Orage enchanté* (Geneva-Paris: Editions des Trois Collines, 1948), pp. 126–127, 46–49, 94, 98, 83.

many different ways of approach.[7] Yet pure creation is not possible to man. Some inner content, received from elsewhere, is necessarily present. Picasso now gives expression to a bitter and desperate detestation of the world of today (after all, his distorted human faces are perhaps our true likeness, when we are seen by the angels). And contemporary abstract painting falls short of releasing a world of pure self-sufficient forms; it cannot help conveying symbolic meanings, only in a barer—and poorer—manner.

And there has been still another direction—an aberrant one, this time—which means in reality, despite all high ambitions, a diligent effort toward self-deception. For, here, the direction has been reversed; the supreme goal is neither the deliverance of the poetic sense nor even pure creation, but man's self-research through poetry. Narcissism was the beginning—entailing a search either for the subjective enjoyment of the poetic state itself (let us think of Rimbaud—a certain aspect of Rimbaud) or (let us think of Gide) for the bursting forth of a free or gratuitous act with no countenance, and of a power of choosing without making a choice, or (let us think of Mallarmé) for the elaboration of a pure and perfect artifact mirroring only the void, and exercising through the words a power of magic to transmute reality, at least as it exists in the souls of men. Then, narcissism gave place to a kind of Prometheism. Finally we had Surrealism, in which the meaning and direction of the impulse in question were revealed in full. With Surrealism the entire dynamism of deviated poetry tends, in the last analysis, to the liberation of the omnipotence of man or the conquest of infinity by man through the powers of unreason.

3. I think that particular attention should be paid to Surrealism, by reason of its exceptional significance for all the problems we are dealing with. I am interested in the Surrealists because there are real poets among them, and because I remember how they were able to awaken to poetry and to threaten with destruction some young people, now dead, who were among the most

7. And that's also, perhaps, why, as he put it, "in my case a picture is a sum of destructions."

purely gifted and the most imperiled in a period still capable of what Rimbaud called the *combat d'esprit*. First of all I have a respect, not for Surrealist bombast and sophistry, but for Surrealism as a spiritual phenomenon—of considerable intensity, in which we see high qualities of the spirit fall from above, and poetry fated to doom cast its last secret flame at the boundaries of death.

I do not intend to embark on a full discussion of this phenomenon. It is enough for my purpose to observe that with Surrealism we have no longer simply a process of liberation from conceptual, logical, discursive reason. We have a process of liberation from reason, absolutely speaking; a deliberate and systematic craving to deny the supreme autonomy of a power which is spiritual in nature, to reject everywhere and in every respect both the control of conscious reason and, even in its preconscious life, the superior intuitivity of the intellect, and to let loose the infinite powers of the irrational in man—with a view to setting free the *Übermensch* in man. This rejection of reason, this total breaking with reason, not only in its conceptual and discursive life but absolutely, marks the essential limit which separates Surrealism from all the other currents I previously mentioned.

André Breton's texts are quite significant in this regard.[8] In the definition of Surrealism offered by him, the "absence of any control exercised by reason" is central, as well as the "pure psychic automatism"—which means a total release, entirely screened from any guiding activity of intelligence, of the wild powers of the unconscious and of an imagination *separated* from the intel-

---

8. A few significant texts of his on surrealism and automatism:

André Breton, *Manifeste du Surréalisme* (Premier Manifeste; Paris: Sagittaire, 1924): "Je crois à la résolution future de ces deux états, en apparence si contradictoires, que sont le rêve et la réalité, en une sorte de réalité absolue, de *surréalité*, si l'on peut ainsi dire. C'est à sa conquête que je vais, certain de n'y pas parvenir mais trop insoucieux de ma propre mort pour ne pas supputer un peu les joies d'une telle possession."

(Let us note at this point Heraclitus' saying, Fragment 89, Diels: "Those who are awake have a common world, but those who sleep turn aside, each into his own particular world.")

Ibid., "Surréalisme, n.m. Automatisme psychique pur par lequel on se propose d'exprimer, soit verbalement, soit par écrit, soit de toute autre manière, le fonctionnement réel de la pensée. Dictée de la pensée, en

lect. "Automatic writing," therefore, becomes the ideal "limit toward which Surrealist poetry must tend."

Here we are faced with a basic illusion. For automatism "unbinds that which had been brought to the unity of life by concentration," and by that brooding repose of the soul which we call in French *recueillement*. [9] Automatism does not produce freedom, but only dispersion. Separated from intellectual light, the automatic life of the unconscious is fundamentally unable to reveal anything really *new*. To the extent to which there is genuine poetry in Surrealist poets, they fall short of their own dogma, and obey despite themselves the secret music of intelligence.

Yet Surrealism in reality tends to aims which are quite other than poetry. As Breton put it, it leaves aside "any aesthetic" as well as any "moral concern." The aim is to express "the real functioning of thought." This, at first glance, seems to be a sort of scientific aim, psychological in nature. In reality, such a formula is rather an esoteric one, and conveys infinitely larger ambitions; it points to a kind of prophetic revelation of the magic powers involved in human "thought" as bound to the cosmic whole. Yet, in any case, whether we have to do with experimental science or with gnosis, the aim is beyond the province of poetry. Or else, if they say that poetry has no province of its own, and is as universal as "thought," then poetry dissipates in the whole, and loses its identity.

As a matter of fact, poetry has become for Surrealists a mere instrument of prospecting, it has been made subservient to all

---

l'absence de tout contrôle exercé par la raison, en dehors de toute pré-occupation esthétique ou morale."

Les Pas perdus (Paris: N.R.F., 1924): "Je n'attends encore de révélation que de lui [de l'automatisme]. Je n'ai jamais cessé d'être persuadé que rien de ce qui se dit ou se fait ne vaut hors de l'obéissance à cette dictée magique."

Point du jour (Paris: N.R.F., 1934): "L'écriture 'automatique' ou mieux 'mécanique,' comme eût voulu Flournoy, ou 'inconsciente' comme voudrait M. René Sudre, m'a paru toujours la limite à laquelle la poésie surréaliste doit tendre."

With Paul Eluard, "Notes sur la Poésie," in *La Révolution surréaliste* (Paris: G.L.M., 1936): "Le poème est 'une débâcle de l'intellect.'"

9. Cf. Raïssa Maritain, "Sens et Non-sens en poésie," in *Situation de la Poésie*, p. 27 (new edition: 1947, p. 28).

spiritual ambitions of man, it has been required to provide man with deceptive and flashy substitutes for science, metaphysics, mysticism, sanctity. All that poetry is permitted to be is a hungry void, an altogether empty poetic perceptiveness, which satisfies itself *outside*, with the pseudo miracles offered by chance or sorcery. We might expect as much: because poetry, in reality, is an end in itself, and an absolute.[10] And for Surrealism there is and there must be no end in itself, and no absolute, except man himself in his possibilities of development.

MANIA FROM BELOW AND MANIA FROM ABOVE: THE PLATONIC MUSE

4. The Surrealists have had no composers. They have had painters, and good painters. Some particularly interesting observations may be made about these Surrealist painters. (I mean orthodox Surrealist painters clinging to Breton's group and ideology;[11] Miró, for instance, whose forms moving free have such freshness, is not a Surrealist, any more than Calder. Gargallo, who disclosed through the suggestions of the void a new poetry of sculpture, owed nothing to Surrealism.)

First, the Surrealist painters have restored in full the most baneful and antipoetic tenet of academicism, against which every genuine art, and modern art for its part, has waged war, namely the primacy of the *subject* represented. Now of course it was not a question of the beauty of this subject, but of its mysterious horror. The great trick was to represent things devised both to captivate the eyes and to wound and shatter at the same time the heart of the spectator, to disorganize him and destroy something in him, to catch him in a trap, by means of a certain mon-

10. That is why, in the nature of things, that absolute which is poetry (in the line of the free creativity of the intellect) tends of itself to make man more thirsty for *the* Absolute—the first Poet, the creator of being.

11. "Surrealism" is, in itself, a quite apt word. But the great contemporary painter who best deserves the name, Chagall (as, among the old masters, Hieronymus Bosch), belongs in no way to the Surrealist school. See supra, p. 37, last part of note 6.

strous contrivance suddenly revealed in the spectacle. Such a
procedure, in which all the mystery, instead of deriving from
the creative process itself, is demanded of the pictured subject,
is the exact opposite of the nature-transforming expression of a
creative vision. And in this return to the primacy of the subject
represented, we have but a token of that displacement of poetry,
transferred to the outside world, of which I spoke a moment ago.

After that, we must observe that the Surrealist painters made
use of an extremely clever and reasoned-out art. With them we
are very far from automatic writing and from that pure automatism which allegedly reveals the real functioning of thought. They
know all the tricks and recipes of technique. Well, if our remark
is true that Surrealism provides them only with an empty poetic
perceptiveness mistaken for poetry, what will occur when they—
anyway, those who have not received the gift of poetry on their
own account—happen to fall out with the Surrealist group and
Surrealist illusionism? They will simply appear as they are,
shrewd craftsmen—sometimes doing their worst: Chirico, whom
André Breton lauded to the skies as a revealer of deepest poetry
and metaphysical emotions, has now dedicated himself to awful
academic and pseudoclassical painting. I hope that Dali will not
meet with the same adventure, thanks to the resources of his
talented and well-calculated eccentricity.

In any case what I should like to retain is the fact that these
madmen are crafty artisans. Here we are faced with a particular
instance of that element of imposture and quackery which is so
deep-rooted in Surrealism. Surrealism simply lies to us when it
pretends to break with reason in the very field of art properly so
called, or of *technè* in the Platonic sense: just as we lie to ourselves when we wish to think that *poièsis* proceeds in a rational
way, and does not break with the measures of conceptual, logical,
or discursive reason. For at this point we must recognize the
importance of the task achieved by Surrealism in calling attention
to many *invidiosi veri* which the rationalist bias of our everyday
dealings, our classical teaching, our industrial civilization, and
our moral prudery would prefer us not to see. The Surrealists
were right in unmasking the part (not principal, but real indeed)
played by the working of the automatic or animal unconscious

in the soul of the poet, and in emphasizing (as others had done before them) the longing for the world of the marvelous, the availability of sensitiveness to all the allurements of chance, the congeniality with the irrational, in short the element of madness which inhabits him. As William Blake put it:

> All Pictures that's Painted with Sense and with Thought
> Are Painted by Madmen, as sure as a Groat;
> For the Greatest the Fool is the Pencil more blest,
> And when they are drunk they always paint best.

(That's perhaps why the pencil of our dear Utrillo is less blest, now that he is a teetotaller.) "Great wits," Dryden had said, "are sure to madness near allied."[12] And Novalis, in much deeper terms: "The poet is literally out of his senses—in exchange, all

---

12. "Absalom and Achitophel," Part I, 163. The interpretation of this line offered by Poe—"By 'great wit,' in this case, the poet intends precisely the pseudo-genius to which I refer" and which is "but the manifestation of the abnormal predominance of some one faculty over all the others."(*Fifty Suggestions*, XXIII, in *Complete Works* [New York: The Lamb Publishing Co., 1902], Vol. IX)—is more than questionable.

What Poe has in mind here is that requirement of unity and integrity in the poet which we shall stress in the next chapter. He also lays claim (thinking of himself, probably) to the possibility of "universal or even versatile geniuses," and to the right of the poet to pursue scientific studies; and he insists "that the highest genius—that the genius which all men instantaneously acknowledge as such, which acts upon individuals as well as upon the mass, by a species of magnetism incomprehensible but irresistible and never resisted—that this genius which demonstrates itself in the simplest gesture, or even by the absence of all; this genius which speaks without a voice and flashes from the unopened eye, is but the result of generally large mental power existing in a state of absolute proportion, so that no one faculty has undue predominance."

In all this one can but agree with him. And who would not approve of his impatience with the popular notion of the poet as an abnormal scatterbrain, and of "genius" as "the state of mental disease arising from the undue predominance of some one of the faculties"? "The works of such genius are never sound in themselves, and, in especial, always betray the general mental insanity."

But Poe misses the real point, which has to do with that element of "madness from above" which comes from the free and intuitive creativity of the intellect and imagination starting in the spiritual unconscious, above logical reason, and has nothing to do, except accidentally, with psychological unbalance or "mental disease." Poe's and Baudelaire's desperate pretension to make logical and calculating reason the supreme creative power in poetry was but a process of defense to mask and counterbalance the inner splits

comes about within him. He is, to the letter, subject and object at the same time, soul and universe."[13]

5. This element of madness Plato had seen before the Surrealists, and forcefully brought to light. They invoke him on this score, though in reality he is at the opposite pole from them.

The famous passages from the *Phaedrus* and the *Ion* about the poets have such lyrical brilliance that we risk not paying sufficiently serious attention to their significance in the systematic context of Plato's philosophy. For Plato the concept of the Muse is bound to passion, mania and madness, childlike play, and unconsciousness. He never tires of praising mania, or that enthusiasm which abolishes reflection and logical thought, as the finest gift of the gods to mortal beings. So there is no blame involved in his emphasis on the ignorance of poets, or in the lines of the *Apology* asserting that poets speak much and say fine things, but understand nothing of what they say.[14] And he expresses a firm and reasoned-out conviction of his own, founded on his very dialectics, when he says that the poets are possessed and out of their senses, and carried along by passion and madness, that common sense is the greatest obstacle to poetry, and that neither concepts nor logic nor rational knowledge have any part in it. And not only the poets, but their listeners also, not only the poem, but also the delight and the contact with beauty that it brings to us, depend on an inspiration superior to reason; so that, for Plato, any effort of rational criticism remains inadequate if only rational, and necessarily presupposes the intuitive reception, in the unconscious of the soul, of the magnetic power conveyed by the poem. "The stone Euripides calls magnet," as he puts it in the *Ion*,

they suffered, and to protect in themselves that supremacy of the intellect for which these superior minds had an invaluable feeling, but which they mistook for the supremacy of logical reason—whereas it is that of intuitive reason and creative intuition. By this fact they risked misleading or confusing us in our notion of poetry. There would be no more detrimental situation for modern poetry than to be caught between madness from below—a simple release of the automatic unconscious—and rationalistic self-consciousness as a process of compensation. These points, which I only mention here in passing, are elucidated in the central chapters of this book [*Creative Intuition in Art and Poetry*], Chapters IV and VII.

13. Novalis, *Schriften*, ed. Kluckhohn (Leipzig: Bibliographisches Institut, n.d.), Vol. III, p. 349.

14. *Apology*, 22.

"does not only attract iron rings, but it also gives them the power of attracting other rings as the stone itself does. . . . In the same way the Muse herself inspires the artists, and through their inspiration others are enraptured and the line of the inspired is produced. . . . One poet is suspended from one Muse, another from another; he is said to be 'possessed'. . . . From these primary rings, the poets, others are in turn suspended, some attached to Orpheus, some to Musaeus, from whom they derive inspiration."[15]

When I said, a moment ago, that Plato was at the extreme opposite of Surrealism, I had two things in mind. First, contrary to Surrealism, poetry, for Plato, is appendent to a supreme end which is beauty; poetry conveys here below, and gives a body to, beauty, and beauty dwells in a world infinitely superior to man, the world of separate ideas, nay more, the world of the divine, where the Beautiful and the Good and the Wise and the True are united in harmony. Beauty, a sense-perceptible participation in which or a shadow of which human art affords us, is an absolute, a divine attribute, and it is because of its very transcendence that it requires madness from the poet, who is not concerned with truth, as the philosopher is, or with the just and the good, as the legislator is, but only with the beautiful (as reflected upon our shadowy world). Secondly, by the same token, the madness of the poet is madness from above, not from below. For there are various sorts of madness. Madness divides into human and divine madness, Plato explains in the *Phaedrus;* and divine madness into inspiring, mystical, poetic, and erotic madness. In the *Timaeus*, he tells us that because the desiring part of the soul is filled, night and day, with phantasms and fancies, the Maker of the world has planned for this, and put divination at the disposal of men, so that it becomes possible to improve this inferior part of ours, and bring us into contact with truth. Hence it appears, he goes on to say, that God gave inspiration to human unreason. Thus the poet is brought into contact with transcendent and divine truth, as descending to us in the specific line of sense-seducing beauty. Through mania, friendship between gods and men has become possible. And the madness of the poet reveals to us, not the "real functioning of thought," but

15. *Ion,* 534, 536.

our kinship with eternal things. That is why "a poet is a light and winged thing, and holy,"[16] and "a tender and untamable soul,"[17] which is seized hold of by the mania that proceeds from the Muses.

So the Platonic and the Surrealist notions of poetry are divided from one another, and diametrically opposed, as a philosophy of absolute transcendence is divided from and opposed to, a philosophy (Hegelian in its roots) of absolute immanence. Yet the fact remains that, like the Surrealists, though for opposite motives, Plato totally separates poetic inspiration from reason. The myth of the Muse signifies that the source of poetry is separate from the human intellect, outside of it, in the transcendent eternal fatherland of subsisting Ideas. A conception which is akin, in the realm of art, to the Averroistic conception of the separate Intellect in the realm of knowledge, and which is responsible for that detestable idealism which has for so long spoiled the theories of philosophers on beauty. And by virtue of this total separation between poetic inspiration and reason, the poets, for Plato as for Surrealism, simply belong to unreason. They got a good proof of this when Plato—executing another operation of dialectical division, and sacrificing that beauty of which poets are capable, and which they make into a seducer, to that justice which the legislator makes into the goddess of the city—drove Homer and his fellow madmen out of the state.

Here we meet, to be sure, with Plato's humor and his ironical ambiguity.[18] He spoke, moreover, to people who knew what's

16. *Ibid.*, 534.
17. *Phaedrus*, 245. I think that in this passage ἄβατον (literally "untrodden") is better rendered by "untamable" than by "virgin" as is usually done.
18. Is not the purpose of the *Republic* to offer a picture of the ideal requirements of reason—carried to the absolute—in matters of government? I cannot help thinking that, given such a purpose, Plato delivered himself over to an intoxication of pure logic all the more readily as, at the same time, knowing that his picture was merely ideal, he indulged in laughing at assertions made purposely extreme which he most seriously proffered and actually held to be true on the level of that pure logic. Hence a kind of transcendent irony. Thus it is, I think, that in the third Book (309) he reproaches the poets for infringing upon that privilege of lying, which belongs only to the rulers of the city. I would like to surmise that the same kind of irony may be found in the *Laws*.

what, and we may question the irrevocable character of an exclusion performed with all the appearances of a lovers' row. But, after all, what has been ironically put forward to play a trick on the reader, must be seemingly accepted to the letter, to play a trick on the writer. Let us, then, accept in this way the notion that, although the mania of poets is divine, the only beauty they are able to provide the city with is sense-appealing beauty, moving in our earthly shadows and fond of lies, so that their mania finally makes them a nuisance for religion and morality, and for the order of the city: on this again we see Plato and the Surrealists in a sort of agreement. Either it is a duty for the good conscience and the good city to expel poetry, or it is a duty for poetry to disintegrate the good conscience and the good city.

Platonic dialectics succeeded in dividing; it was unable to unite. The sin of Platonism is separation, and a separatist conception of transcendence. Plato, however, did not manage totally to divide, as perhaps he would have wanted, poetry and art, *poièsis* and *technè*, from one another. But in distinguishing the one from the other, he did human thought an invaluable service, for which he is owed singular gratitude. "You know," he wrote in the *Symposium*, "that the word *poièsis* means many things: for every activity causing a passage from non-being to being is *poièsis*, so that the works produced by any kind of art are *poièseis*, and the workmen who achieve them are all *poiètai* or makers. You know, nevertheless, that they are not called *poiètai*, poets, rather they have other names; and only that portion of the whole *poièsis* (in the general sense of art) which is separated from the rest and is concerned with music (*mousikè*) and melodic measures, is called poetry, and those who share in its possession are called poets."[19] *Music*, thus, in Plato's vocabulary, does not mean only music, but every artistic genus which depends on the inspiration of the Muse. And he perceived that all the fine arts are the realm of *Mousikè*, and are appendent to poetry, which quickens painting or architecture as well as poetry in the strict sense of the word.

As to the madness of poets, I would say that Plato conceptu-

19. *Symposium* (Discourse of Diotima), 205.

alized what he felt about it in the too absolute perspectives of his system—but what he felt about it proceeded from the experiential awareness of a true lover of poetry. There is in the poet an element of madness (which of itself is in no way pathological, though of course it may happen to accompany really morbid states);[20] he obeys an all-conquering instinct which is free from and extraneous to logical and conceptual reason. Ben Jonson reminds us that according to Aristotle himself, "there has been no great creative mind without a mixture of madness. Nor is the mind capable of anything grand, or of speaking above other men, if it is not stirred by some superior motion."[21] In point of fact this is a sentence attributed to Aristotle by Seneca.[22] Yet Aristotle's *Poetics* tells us, in more moderate but no less significant terms, "Hence it is that poetry demands a man with a happy gift of nature, or else one with a strain of madness in him."[23] And the *Rhetoric:* "Poetry is a thing inspired";[24] and the *Eudemian Ethics:* "As in the universe, so in the soul, God moves every-

20. The illuminating pages which Bergson wrote on the "deep-rooted mental healthiness" that is characteristic of great mystics, and the nervous disturbances which may nevertheless develop sometimes in them, but which are merely accidental with regard to mysticism, apply also, *mutatis mutandis*, to poets and poetry. "The truth is that these abnormal states resembling morbid states, and sometimes doubtless very much akin to them, are easily comprehensible, if we only stop to think what a shock to the soul is the passing from the static to the dynamic, from the closed to the open, from everyday life to mystic life. . . ."

The obscure depths of the soul are stirred in the poet. "We cannot upset the regular relation of the conscious to the unconscious without running a risk. So we must not be surprised if nervous disturbances and mysticism sometimes go together; we find the same disturbances in other forms of genius, notably in musicians. They have to be regarded as merely accidental. The former have no more to do with mystical inspiration than the latter with musical." Henri Bergson, *The Two Sources of Religion and Morality* (New York: Holt, 1935), pp. 217–18.

21. "Nullum magnum ingenium sine mixtura dementiae fuit. Nec potest grande aliquid, et supra caeteros loqui, nisi mota mens." Cf. Ben Jonson, *Discoveries* (1641)—"how differs a poeme from what wee call poesy?"—in *The Great Critics*, ed. J. H. Smith and E. W. Parks, rev. ed. (New York: Norton, 1939), p. 263.

22. *De tranquillitate animi*, XV, 16.

23. Aristotle, *Poetics*, Chapter 17, 1455 a 33–34.

24. *Rhetoric*, III, 7: ἔνθεον γὰρ ἡ ποίησις."

thing. The starting point of reasoning is not reasoning, but something greater. What, then, could be greater even than knowledge and intellect but God? . . . For this reason, those are called fortunate who, whatever they start on, succeed in it without being good at reasoning. And deliberation is of no advantage to them, for they have in them a principle that is better than intellect and deliberation. They have inspiration, but they cannot deliberate. . . . Hence we have the melancholic men, the *dreamers of what is true*. For the moving principle seems to become stronger when the reasoning power is relaxed."[25] Not Romantic authors alone thought of the poet as a "dreamer of what is true," a man moved by "some breath, as it were, of insanity"[26] or frenzy.[27]

> Lovers and madmen have such seething brains,
> Such shaping fantasies, that apprehend
> More than cool reason ever comprehends.
> The lunatic, the lover, and the poet
> Are of imagination all compact. . . .[28]

6. Is there, then, any truly philosophical solution to the debate of reason and poetry; is it possible to show that, in spite of all, poetry and the intellect are of the same race and blood, and call to one another; and that poetry not only requires artistic or technical reason with regard to the particular ways of making, but, much more profoundly, depends on intuitive reason with regard to poetry's own essence and to the very touch of madness it involves? The truth of the matter is neither in the Surrealist inferno, nor in the Platonic heaven. I think that what we have to do is to make the Platonic Muse descend into the soul of man, where she is no longer Muse but creative intuition; and the Platonic inspiration descend into the intellect united with imagination, where inspiration from above the soul becomes inspiration

25. *Eudemian Ethics*, Book VII, Chapter 14, 1248 a 26–1248 b 2 (trans. J. Solomon).
26. Cicero, *De Oratore*, II, 46.
27. Plutarch, *Symposiacs*, I, 5.
28. *A Midsummer Night's Dream*, V, i.

from above conceptual reason, that is, poetic experience.

This is the very subject of this book.* Here I should like only to outline the general philosophical framework needed for our considerations—in other words, to establish a first preliminary thesis, which paves the way for our further research, and which deals with the existence in us of a spiritual—not animal—unconscious activity.

It is difficult to speak of this problem without discussing a whole philosophy of man. We risk, moreover, being misled by the words we use. I would observe especially that the word *unconscious,* as I use it, does not necessarily mean a purely unconscious activity. It means most often an activity which is *principally* unconscious, but the point of which emerges into consciousness. Poetic intuition, for instance, is born in the unconscious, but it emerges from it; the poet is not unaware of this intuition; on the contrary it is his most precious light and the primary rule of his virtue of art. But he is aware of it *sur le rebord de l'inconscient,* as Bergson would have said, on the edge of the unconscious.

My contention, then, is that everything depends, in the issue we are discussing, on the recognition of the existence of a spiritual unconscious, or rather, preconscious, of which Plato and the ancient wise men were well aware, and the disregard of which in favor of the Freudian unconscious alone is a sign of the dullness of our times. There are two kinds of unconscious, two great domains of psychological activity screened from the grasp of consciousness: the preconscious of the spirit in its living springs, and the unconscious of blood and flesh, instincts, tendencies, complexes, repressed images and desires, traumatic memories, as constituting a closed or autonomous dynamic whole. I would like to designate the first kind of unconscious by the name of *spiritual* or, for the sake of Plato, *musical* unconscious or preconscious; and the second by the name of *automatic* unconscious or *deaf* unconscious—deaf to the intellect, and structured into a world of its own apart from the intellect; we might also say,

* *Creative Intuition in Art and Poetry* [Editors].

in quite a general sense, leaving aside any particular theory, *Freudian unconscious.*[29]

These two kinds of unconscious life are in intimate connection and ceaseless communication with one another; in concrete existence they ordinarily interfere or intermingle in a greater or less degree; and I think, never—except in some rare instances of supreme spiritual purification—does the spiritual unconscious operate without the other being involved, be it to a very small extent. But they are essentially distinct and thoroughly different in nature.

7. It is not necessary to think of those high levels in spiritual life which are the domain of contemplation, of supernatural mystical experience, achieved beyond concepts through connaturality of love; or of that perfect freedom of which St. Paul speaks and in which the "sons of God" are moved by the Spirit of God in a manner which transcends the measures of reason.[30] Nor is it necessary to think of the way in which the disciples in Emmaus recognized Christ when He broke the bread, or of that state of perfect prayer which occurs, according to the Fathers of the Desert, when a man does not even know that he is praying;[31] or even of the natural mystical experience of a Plotinus or of Indian

---

29. This distinction between spiritual unconscious and automatic unconscious is altogether different from Jung's distinction between the *personal* and the *collective* unconscious—both of which are part of the spiritual unconscious inasmuch as they enter the sphere of the preconscious life of the intellect or the will, and are thus spiritualized, and both of which are part of the automatic unconscious inasmuch as they are shut up in a merely animal world, separate from the life of the intellect and the will.

Be it noted that, as will be pointed out infra (*[Creative Intuition in Art and Poetry]* Chapter IV), all the sensitive powers of the soul (which are not "spiritual" in nature) and especially the imagination are involved in the spiritual unconscious, in so far as they participate in the preconscious life of the intellect or the will. The spiritual unconscious pertains primarily to the spiritual powers of the soul, but extends to the other.

30. They are given *eagle wings* to *run* and walk as men still living upon this earth, John of St. Thomas says in relation to Isaias 40:31. (*Les Dons du Saint-Esprit*, trans. Raïssa Maritain [Paris: Téqui, 1950], p. 6.) So they have become winged rational animals.

31. Cassian, *Coll.*, IX, Chapter 31. Did not Degas say, "Only when he no longer knows what he is doing does the painter do good things"? *Artists on Art*, p. 308.

wise men, in which supreme intellectual concentration is attained
by means of the void, and through the abolition of any exercise of
conceptual and discursive reason.[32]

Nor is it necessary to think of the perception of, and delight
in, beauty, which draws tears from the eyes of a man who does
not know what has come about in his mind; or of all the examples
of intuitive, nonconceptual knowledge that Bergson took pleasure
in enumerating.

It is enough to think of the ordinary and everyday functioning
of intelligence, in so far as intelligence is really in activity, and
of the way in which ideas arise in our minds, and every genuine
intellectual grasping, or every new discovery,[33] is brought about;
it is enough to think of the way in which our free decisions, when
they are really free, are made, especially those decisions which

32. Recent studies in natural mysticism have opened a new and particu-
larly fertile field of philosophical research. See in this connection Olivier
Lacombe, "Sur le Yoga indien," *Etudes Carmélitaines,* October, 1937; *idem,*
"Un Exemple de mystique naturelle: l'Inde," *Etudes Carmélitaines,* October,
1938; Jacques Maritain, "L'Expérience mystique naturelle et le Vide,"
Chapter III of *Quatre Essais sur l'Esprit dans sa Condition charnelle* (Paris:
Desclée De Brouwer, 1939); Louis Gardet, "Recherches sur la mystique
naturelle," in *Jacques Maritain, son oeuvre philosophique* (a symposium;
Paris: Desclée De Brouwer, 1948); *idem,* "Mystique naturelle et mystique
surnaturelle en Islam," *Recherches de Science religieuse,* XXXVII (1950)
no. 2; Lacombe, "La Mystique naturelle dans l'Inde," *Revue Thomiste,*
1951, no. 1; Gardet, "La Mystique avicennienne," Chapter 5 of *La Pensée
religieuse d'Avicenne* (Paris: Vrin, 1951); *idem,* "Un probléme de mystique comparée; la mention du Nom divin dans la mystique musulmane,"
Revue Thomiste, 1952, no. 3—Olivier Lacombe and Louis Gardet are
preparing a general survey of the subject, under the title *Mystique naturelle,
l'Expérience du Soi.*

33. The case of scientific discoveries, new ideas, or solutions that suddenly emerge from the unconscious (as was experienced by Poincaré and
Gauss for instance) is well known and particularly striking. Let us quote
here the significant testimony of Marston Morse: "The first essential bond
between mathematics and the arts," he writes, "is found in the fact that
discovery in mathematics is not a matter of logic. It is rather the result
of mysterious powers which no one understands, and in which the unconscious recognition of beauty must play an important part. Out of an infinity
of designs a mathematician chooses one pattern for beauty's sake, and
pulls it down to earth, no one knows how. Afterwards the logic of words
and of forms sets the pattern right. Only then can one tell someone else.
The first pattern remains in the shadows of the mind." Marston Morse,
"Mathematics and the Arts," *The Yale Review,* summer, 1951, pp. 607–608.
—And again: "Mathematics is the sister, as well as the servant of the arts

commit our entire life[34]—to realize that there exists a deep non-conscious world of activity, for the intellect and the will, from which the acts and fruits of human consciousness and the clear perceptions of the mind emerge, and that the universe of concepts, logical connections, rational discursus and rational deliberation in which the activity of the intellect takes definite form and shape, is preceded by the hidden workings of an immense and primal preconscious life. Such a life develops in night, but in a night which is translucid and fertile, and resembles that primeval diffused light which was created first, before God made, as Genesis puts it, "lights in the firmament of heaven to divide the day from the night" so as to be "for signs, and for seasons, and for days and years."

Reason does not only consist of its conscious logical tools and manifestations, nor does the will consist only of its deliberate conscious determinations. Far beneath the sunlit surface thronged with explicit concepts and judgments, words and expressed resolutions or movements of the will, are the sources of knowledge and creativity, of love and suprasensuous desires, hidden in the primordial translucid night of the intimate vitality of the soul. Thus it is that we must recognize the existence of an unconscious or preconscious which pertains to the spiritual powers of the human soul and to the inner abyss of personal freedom, and of the personal thirst and striving for knowing and seeing, grasping and expressing: a spiritual or musical unconscious which is specifically different from the automatic or deaf unconscious.[35]

and is touched with the same madness and genius." *Ibid.*, 605. "The creative scientist lives in the 'wildness of logic' where reason is the handmaiden and not the master. I shun all monuments which are coldly legible. I prefer the world where the images turn their faces in every direction, like the masques of Picasso. It is the hour before the break of day when science turns in the womb, and, waiting, I am sorry that there is between us no sign and no language except by mirrors of necessity. I am grateful for the poets who suspect the twilight zone." *Ibid.*, p. 612.

34. Cf. J. Maritain, *Existence and the Existent* (New York: Pantheon Books, 1948), pp. 53–54.

35. It is not surprising that Freudian "explanations"—which deal only with the automatic unconscious, whose part in art and poetry, significant as it may sometimes be, is accidental, and which ignore completely what is essential, the spiritual unconscious—prove to be particularly unfortunate in this domain (as well as in the religious domain): a failure which has been

When man seeking for his own inner universe takes the wrong road, he enters the internal world of the deaf unconscious, while believing he enters the internal world of the spirit, and he thus finds himself wandering in a false kind of self-interiority, where wildness and automatism mimic freedom. Such was the adventure of the Surrealists. I cannot help remembering this passage written long ago by G.-H. von Schubert, at the time of German Romanticism. The poet, he said, in whom does not arise the passionate desire "to rejoin the essential unity, in the contemplation of the external spectacle as well as in the grasping of the obscure data of the innermost world" yields almost necessarily "to another movement, akin to enthusiasm, which carries man along toward the abyss. Like Phaeton, man's freakish egotism wants to seize hold of the chariot of God: he has endeavored to make himself that inner enthusiasm which God alone can create."[36]

THE ILLUMINATING INTELLECT AND THE PRECONSCIOUS ACTIVITY OF THE SPIRIT

8. Before finishing, I should like to propose some philosophical elucidation of a little more technical nature. The notion of the psychological unconscious was made into a self-contradictory enigma by Descartes, who defined the soul by the very act of self-

disclosed by Jung in relation to art, by Malinowski in relation to the origin of morals and the theory of primitive patricide which, as Roland Dalbiez says (La Méthode psychanalytique et la Doctrine freudienne [Paris: Desclée De Brouwer, 1936]; English trans.: Psychoanalytical Method and the Doctrine of Freud [New York: Longmans, 1943]), belongs to the realm of romantic anthropology.

Raymond S. Stites has clearly stressed this basic inadequacy of psychoanalytical theories of art in sifting Freud's own pseudoscientific fancies about Leonardo ("A Criticism of Freud's Leonardo," in College Art Journal, summer, 1948). In the important studies he has pursued for years on Leonardo, and which will appear soon in a book to be entitled The Psychology of Leonardo da Vinci, Mr. Stites has been especially concerned with the role of the unconscious (the prescience, as Leonardo put it) in artistic activity. Such erudite researches provide philosophy with a remarkable confirmation of the fundamental distinction between the automatic unconscious and the spiritual unconscious.

36. Gotthilf Heinrich von Schubert, Geschichte der Seele; in Albert Béguin, L'Âme romantique et le Rêve (Marseille: Cahiers de Sud, 1937), Vol. I, p. 224.

consciousness. Thus we must be grateful to Freud and his predecessors for having obliged philosophers to acknowledge the existence of unconscious thought and unconscious psychological activity.

Before Descartes, the human soul was considered a substantial reality accessible in its nature only to metaphysical analysis, a spiritual entelechy informing the living body, and distinct from its own operations; and this, of course, made a completely different picture. The Schoolmen were not interested in working out any theory about the unconscious life of the soul, yet their doctrines implied its existence. What Thomas Aquinas teaches about the structure of the intellect seems to me especially significant in this regard. The question does not have to do with poetry, but, on the contrary, with abstract knowledge and the birth of abstract ideas. But for that very reason we find there basic views about the spiritual preconscious of the intellect, which can be utilized later on with respect to poetry.

The intellect, as perennial philosophy sees it, is spiritual and, thus, distinct in essence from the senses. Yet, according to the Aristotelian saying, nothing is to be found in the intellect which does not come from the senses. Then it is necessary to explain how a certain spiritual content, which will be seen and expressed in an abstract concept, can be drawn from the senses, that is, the phantasms and images gathered and refined in the internal sensitive powers, and originating in sensation. It is under the pressure of this necessity that Aristotle was obliged to posit the existence of a merely active and perpetually active intellectual energy, νοῦς ποιητικός, the intellect agent, let us say the Illuminating Intellect, which permeates the images with its pure and purely activating spiritual light and actuates or awakens the potential intelligibility which is contained in them. Aristotle, moreover, added few and sometimes ambiguous indications about the Illuminating Intellect, which he only described as superior in nature to everything in man, so that the Arab philosophers thought that it was *separate*, and consequently one and the same for all men. The Schoolmen anterior to Thomas Aquinas also held it to be separate, and identified it with God's intellect. It was the work of St. Thomas to show and insist that, because the human person is an ontologically perfect or fully equipped agent, master of his actions, the Illuminating Intellect cannot be separate, but must be an inherent part of each individual's soul and intellectual structure, an inner spiritual light which is a participation in the uncreated divine light, but which is in every man, through its pure spirituality ceaselessly in act, the primal quickening source of all his intellectual activity.

Now the process of formation of intellectual knowledge is a very complex process of progressive spiritualization. For the act of intellectual vision can only be accomplished through the identification of spiritual intelligence with an object brought itself to a state of spirituality in act. The Illuminating Intellect only activates, it does not know. The intellect, on the other hand, which the ancients called *intellectus possibilis*, because it is first and of itself a *tabula rasa*, only in potency with respect to knowing and to the intelligible forms it will receive—the knowing intellect, in order to know, must be actuated, and shaped, by what is drawn from the images, and the images are imbued with materiality. Thus, at a first step, the intelligible content present in the images, and which, in the images, was only intelligible in potency (or capable of *being made capable* of becoming an object of intellectual vision), is made intelligible in act in a spiritual form (*species impressa*, impressed pattern), let us say, in an intelligible germ, which is received from the images by the intellect, under the activation of the Illuminating Intellect. But still this is not enough to know. It is necessary that the intelligible content drawn from the images should be not only intelligible in act, or capable of becoming an object of intellectual vision, but intellected in act, or actually become an object of intellectual vision. Then it is the intellect itself, which, having been impregnated by the impressed pattern or intelligible germ, vitally produces —always under the activation of the Illuminating Intellect—an inner fruit, a final and more fully determined spiritual form (*species expressa*), the concept, in which the content drawn from the images is brought to the very same state of spirituality-in-act in which the intellect-in-act is, and in which this now perfectly spiritualized content is seen, is actually an object of intellectual vision.

9. The reader will excuse me for this brief and rather chill irruption of Scholastic lecturing. For, in the views of Thomas Aquinas I just summarized on the structure of our intellectual activity, some points seem to me to be of basic interest for our purpose. There are two things in this structure of our intellectual activity which play an essential role: the Illuminating Intellect and the intelligible germ or impressed pattern. And philosophical reflection is able to establish, through the logical necessities of reasoning, the fact of their existence, but they totally escape experience and consciousness.

On the one hand, our intellect is fecundated by intelligible germs on which all the formation of ideas depends. And it draws from them, and produces within itself, through the most vital process, its own living fruits, its concepts and ideas. But it knows nothing either of these germs it receives within or of the very process through which it produces its concepts. Only the concepts are known. And even as regards the concepts, they cause the object seen in them to be known, but they themselves are not directly known; they are not known through their essence, they are known only through a reflective return of the intellect upon its own operations; and this kind of reflective grasping can possibly not occur. There can exist unconscious acts of thought and unconscious ideas.

On the other hand, and this is the fundamental point for me, we possess in ourselves the Illuminating Intellect, a spiritual sun[37] ceaselessly radiating, which activates everything in intelligence, and whose light causes all our ideas to arise in us, and

---

37. The image of the sun, in Thomas Aquinas' vocabulary, was reserved for the Uncreate Intellect. Yet we can use it with respect to the *intellectus agens* without prejudice to the fact that its light derives from the supreme Sun, the Uncreate Intellect.

On the universally activating part played by the Illuminating Intellect in human intelligence, see my book *Les Degrés du Savoir* (Paris: Desclée De Brouwer, 1932), p. 244, note 1. For Thomas Aquinas the role of the Illuminating Intellect is in no way limited to the process of abstraction and formation of ideas; the Illuminating Intellect is rather the *activator* of intelligence in all its operations. We have a clear sign of this in St. Thomas' teaching (*q. disp. de Anima*, a. 15, ad 9; *Sum. contra Gent.*, III, 45) that the intellect agent will continue to activate and illumine the intellect in *souls separated from the body* (in which there is no longer any process of abstraction).

whose energy permeates every operation of our mind. And this primal source of light cannot be seen by us; it remains concealed in the unconscious of the spirit.

Furthermore, it illuminates with its spiritual light the images from which our concepts are drawn. And this very process of illumination is unknown to us, it takes place in the unconscious; and often these very images, without which there is no thought, remain also unconscious or scarcely perceived in the process, at least for the most part.

Thus it is that we know (not always, to be sure) what we are thinking, but we don't know how we are thinking, and that before being formed and expressed in concepts and judgments, intellectual knowledge is at first a beginning of insight, still unformulated, a kind of many-eyed cloud which is born from the impact of the light of the Illuminating Intellect on the world of images, and which is but a humble and trembling inchoation, yet invaluable, tending toward an intelligible content to be grasped.

I have insisted upon these considerations because they deal with the intellect, with reason itself, taken in the full scope of its life within us. They enable us to see how the notion of a spiritual unconscious or preconscious is philosophically grounded. I have suggested calling it, also, musical unconscious, for, being one with the root activity of reason, it contains from the start a germ of melody. In these remarks, on the other hand, we have considered the spiritual unconscious from the general point of view of the structure of the intellect, and with regard to the abstractive function of intelligence and to the birth of ideas. It was not a question of poetry. It was even a question of the origin and formation of the instruments of that conceptual, logical, discursive knowledge with which poetry is on bad terms. Well, if there is in the spiritual unconscious a nonconceptual or preconceptual activity of the intellect even with regard to the birth of the concepts, we can with greater reason assume that such a nonconceptual activity of the intellect, such a nonrational activity of reason, in the spiritual unconscious, plays an essential part in the genesis of poetry and poetic inspiration. Thus a place is prepared in the highest parts of the soul, in the primeval translucid night where intelligence stirs the images under the light of the Illuminating Intellect, for the separate Muse of Plato to descend into man, and dwell within him, and become a part of our spiritual organism.

THE HUMAN SUBJECTIVITY*

THE SUBJECT (SUPPOSITUM)

1. Precisely because of the existentialism (existentialist intellectualism) of Thomist philosophy, the notion of subject plays a capital part in it; we may even say that subjects occupy all the room there is in the Thomist universe, in the sense that, for Thomism, only subjects exist, with the accidents which inhere in them, the action which emanates from them, and the relations which they bear to one another. Only individual subjects exercise the act of existing.

What we call *subject* St. Thomas called *suppositum*. Essence is *that which* a thing is; suppositum is *that which* has an essence, *that which* exercises existence and action—*actiones sunt suppositorum*—*that which* subsists. Here we meet the metaphysical notion which has given students so many headaches and baffles everyone who has not grasped the true—the existential—foundation of Thomist metaphysics, the notion of *subsistence*.

We are bound to speak of this notion of subsistence with great respect, not only because of the transcendent applications made of it in theology, but because, in the philosophical order itself, it bears witness to the supreme tension of an articulated thought bent on seizing intellectually something which seems to escape from the world of notions or ideas of the intellect, namely, the typical reality of the subject. The existential subject has this in common with the act of existing, that both transcend the concept or the idea considered as the terminus of the first operation of

* *Existence and the Existent* (New York: Doubleday, Image Books, 1956), pp. 70–91.

mind or simple apprehension. I have tried to show in an earlier section** how the intellect (because it envelops itself) grasps in an idea which is the first of its ideas, that very thing, the act of existing, which is the intelligible (or rather the super-intelligible) proper to the judgment, and not to simple apprehension. Now we are no longer dealing with the act of existing but with that which exercises that act. Just as there is nothing more commonplace in language than the word "being" (and this is the greatest mystery of philosophy) so there is nothing more commonplace than the "subject" to which in all our propositions we attribute a predicate. And when we undertake a metaphysical analysis of the reality of this subject, this individual thing which maintains itself in existence, this supremely concrete reality, and undertake to do justice to its irreducible originality, we are forced to appeal to that which is most abstract and most elaborate in our lexicon of notions. How can we be astonished that minds which are fond of facility should regard as so many vain Scholastic refinements and Chinese puzzles the elucidations in which Cajetan and John of St. Thomas show us that subsistence is distinct both from essence and from existence, and describe it as a substantial mode? I concede that the style of their dissertations seems to carry us very far from experience into the third heaven of abstraction. And yet, in reality their aim was to form an *objective notion* of the *subject* itself or the suppositum, to reach objectively, within the ontological analysis of the structure of reality, the property which makes the subject to be subject and not object, and to transcend, or rather exceed in depth, the whole universe of objects.

When they explain that an essence or a nature, considered strictly, cannot exist outside the mind as an object of thought, and that nevertheless individual natures do exist, and that, consequently, in order to exist, a given nature or essence must be other than it has to be in order to be an object of thought, that is to say, it must bear in itself a supreme achievement which adds nothing to it in the line of its essence (and consequently does not enrich our understanding by any new note which qualifies it),

** *Ibid.*, pp. 32–35 [Editors].

but which *terminates* it in that line of essence (closes or situates it, constitutes it as an *in-itself* or an inwardness face to face with existence) in order that it may take possession of this act of existing for which it is created and which transcends it;[1] when they explain in this fashion *that by which,* on the plane of reality, the *quod* which exists and acts is other than the *quid* which we conceive, they attest the existential character of metaphysics, they shatter the Platonic world of pure objects, they justify the passage into the world of subjects or supposita, they rescue for the metaphysical intellect the value and reality of subjects.

2. God does not create essences to which He can be imagined as giving a last rub of the sandpaper of subsistence before sending them forth into existence! God creates existent subjects or supposita which subsist in the individual nature that constitutes them and which receive from the creative influx their nature as well as their subsistence, their existence, and their activity. Each of them possesses an essence and pours itself out in action. Each is, for us, in its individual existing reality, an inexhaustible well of knowability. We shall never know everything there is to know about the tiniest blade of grass or the least ripple in a stream. In the world of existence there are only subjects or supposita, and that which emanates from them into being. This is why ours is a world of nature and adventure, filled with events, contingency, chance, and where the course of events is flexible and mutable

---

1. Cf. the *Further Elucidations On the Notion of Subsistence* which I wrote for the new translation of *The Degrees of Knowledge* [New York: Charles Scribner's Sons, 1959]. Here are some excerpts from this essay:

"The *esse,* is perceived quite precisely—even as in their own order intellection and volition—as an *exercised* act, exercised by the thing or the existent subject, or as an activity in which the existent itself is engaged, an energy that it exerts. Existence is therefore not only received, as if by *esse* essences were pinned outside nothingness like a picture hung on a wall. Existence is not only received, it is also *exercised.* . . . But to *exercise* existence something besides the bare essence is necessary, namely, the supposit or person. *Actiones sunt suppositorum,* actions are proper to supposits, and especially and above all the act of exercising existence. In other words, to exercise existence the essence must be completed by subsistence and thus become a supposit. . . . Since existence by its very notion demands, as we have just seen, that it be not only received but exercised, and since this exigency, pertaining as it does to the existential order, places us outside and beyond the order of essence, it must be said that (substantial) essence or nature can *receive* existence only

whereas the laws of essence are necessary. We know those subjects, we shall never get through knowing them. We do not know them as subjects, we know them by objectizing them, by achieving objective insights of them and making them our objects, for the object is nothing other than something of the subject transferred into the state of immaterial existence of intellection in act. We know subjects not as subjects, but as objects, and therefore only in such-and-such of the intelligible aspects, or rather *inspects*, and perspectives in which they are rendered present to the mind and which we shall never get through discovering in them.

As we pass progressively to higher degrees in the scale of beings we deal with subjects of existence or supposita more and more rich in inner complexity, whose individuality is more and more concentrated and integrated, whose action manifests a more and more perfect spontaneity, from the merely transitive activity of inanimate bodies to the occultly immanent activity of vegetable life, the definitely immanent activity of sentient life, and the perfectly immanent activity of the life of the intellect.[2] At this last degree the threshold of free choice is crossed, and therewith the threshold of independence properly so-called (however imperfect it be) and of personality. With man, liberty of spontaneity becomes liberty of autonomy, the *suppositum* becomes *persona*, that is, a whole which subsists and exists in virtue of the very subsistence and existence of its spiritual soul,

by *exercising* it, which it cannot do as long as it remains in its own essential order. In other words, it can receive existence only on condition of being drawn at the same time from the state of simple essence and placed in an *existential state* which makes of it a *quod* capable of exercising existence. This *state* which completes, or rather surcompletes the essence—not at all in the line of essence itself, but in relation to a completely other order, the existential order—and permits the essence (henceforth supposit) to *exercise* existence is precisely subsistence. . . .

"So the proper effect of subsistence is to place the individual nature in a state of *exercising existence*, with the incommunicability proper to the individual nature. . . . This is the promotion onto a new plane of the incommunicability which defines singularity. Subsistence renders the essence (become supposit) capable of existing *per se separatim*, because it renders an individual nature (become supposit) capable of exercising existence."

2. Cf. J. Maritain, *De Bergson à Thomas d'Aquin* (Paris: Paul Hartmann, 1947), Chapter VI ("Spontaneity and Independence").

and acts by setting itself its own ends; a universe in itself; a microcosm which, though its existence at the heart of the material universe is ceaselessly threatened, nevertheless possesses a higher ontological density than that whole universe. Only the person is free; only the person possesses, in the full sense of these words, inwardness and subjectivity—because it contains itself and moves about within itself. The person, St. Thomas says, is that which is noblest and highest in all nature.

SUBJECTIVITY AS SUBJECTIVITY

3. By sense or experience, science or philosophy, each of us, as I said a moment ago, knows the environing world of subjects, supposita, and persons in their role as objects. The paradox of consciousness and personality is that each of us is situated precisely *at the center* of this world. Each is at the center of infinity. And this privileged subject, the thinking self, is to itself not object but subject; in the midst of all the subjects which it knows only as objects, it alone is subject as subject. We are thus confronted by subjectivity as subjectivity.

I know myself as subject by consciousness and reflexivity, but my substance is obscure to me. St. Thomas explains that in spontaneous reflection, which is a prerogative of the life of the intellect, each of us knows (by a kind of knowledge that is not scientific but experimental and incommunicable) that his soul exists, knows the singular existence of this subjectivity that perceives, suffers, loves, thinks. When a man is awake to the intuition of being he is awake at the same time to the intuition of subjectivity; he grasps, in a flash that will never be dimmed, the fact that *he is a self*, as Jean-Paul said. The force of such a perception may be so great as to sweep him along to that heroic asceticism of the void and of annihilation in which he will achieve ecstasy in the substantial existence of the *self* and the "presence of immensity" of the divine Self at one and the same time—which in my view characterizes the natural mysticism of India.[3]

3. Cf. J. Maritain, *Quatre essais sur l'Esprit dans sa condition charnelle* (Paris: Alsatia, 1956), Chapter III ("Natural Mystical Experience and the Void").

But the intuition of subjectivity is an existential intuition which surrenders no essence to us. We know *that which* we are by our phenomena, our operations, our flow of consciousness. The more we grow accustomed to the inner life, the better we decipher the astonishing and fluid multiplicity which is thus delivered to us; the more, also, we feel that it leaves us ignorant of the essence of our self. Subjectivity *as subjectivity* is inconceptualizable; is an unknowable abyss. It is unknowable by the mode of notion, concept, or representation, or by any mode of any science whatsoever—introspection, psychology, or philosophy. How could it be otherwise, seeing that every reality known through a concept, a notion, or a representation is known as object and not as subject? Subjectivity as such escapes by definition from that which we know about ourselves by means of notions.

4. Yet it is known in a way, or rather in certain ways, which I should like briefly to enumerate. At the very beginning and above all, subjectivity is known or rather felt in virtue of a formless and diffuse knowledge which, in relation to reflective consciousness, we may call unconscious or preconscious knowledge. This is knowledge of the "concomitant" or spontaneous consciousness, which, without giving rise to a distinct act of thought, envelops in fact, *in actu exercito,* our inner world so far as it is integrated into the vital activity of our spiritual faculties.[4] Even for the most superficial persons, it is true that from the moment when they say *I,* the whole unfolding of their states of consciousness and their operations, their musings, memories, and acts, is subsumed by a virtual and ineffable knowledge, a vital and existential knowledge of the totality immanent in each of its parts, and immersed, without their troubling to become aware of it, in the diffuse glow, the unique freshness, the maternal connivance as it were, which emanates from subjectivity. Subjectivity is not known; it is felt as a propitious and enveloping night.

There is, secondly, a knowledge of subjectivity as such, imperfect and fragmentary of course, but in this instance formed and actually given to the mind, and which is thrown into relief by what St. Thomas calls knowledge by mode of inclination, sym-

4. Cf. J. Maritain, *De Bergson à Thomas d'Aquin,* pp. 160–61.

pathy, or connaturality, not by mode of knowledge. It appears before us under three specifically distinct forms: (1) practical knowledge, which judges both moral matters and the subject itself, by the inner inclinations of the subject. I mentioned this some pages back in connection with moral conscience and prudence;* (2) poetic knowledge, in which subjectivity and the things of this world are known together in creative intuition-emotion and are revealed and expressed together, not in a word or concept but in a created word;[5] (3) mystical knowledge, which is not directed towards the subject but towards things divine, and does not of itself issue in any expression, but in which God is known by union and by connaturality of love, and in which this very love that becomes the formal means of knowledge of the divine Self, simultaneously renders the human self transparent in its spiritual depths. Let the mystic reflect an instant upon himself, and a St. Theresa or a St. John of the Cross will show us to what extent the divine light gives him a lucid and inexhaustible knowledge of his own subjectivity.

But in none of these instances is the knowledge of subjectivity as subjectivity, however real it be, a knowledge by mode of knowledge, which is to say, by mode of conceptual objectization.

5. In none of these instances is it philosophical knowledge. It would be a contradiction in terms to seek to make a philosophy of that sort of knowledge, since every philosophy—like it or not—proceeds by concepts. This is the first point to which the consideration of subjectivity as subjectivity draws our attention, and it is a point of capital importance. Subjectivity marks the frontier which separates the world of philosophy from the world of religion. This is what Kierkegaard felt so deeply in his polemic against Hegel. Philosophy runs against an insurmountable barrier in attempting to deal with subjectivity, because while philosophy of course knows subjects, it knows them only as objects. Philosophy is registered whole and entire in the relation of intelligence to object; whereas religion enters into the relation of subject to subject. For this reason, every philosophical religion, or every philosophy

* *Existence and the Existent,* pp. 59 ff. [Editors].

5. Cf. Jacques and Raïssa Maritain, *Situation de la poésie* (Paris: Desclée De Brouwer, 1938).

which, like Hegel's, claims to assume and integrate religion into itself, is in the last analysis a mystification.

When philosophy, taking its start in the being of things, attains to God as the cause of being, it has then, thanks to ana-noetic knowledge,[6] rendered the divine Self an object of philosophical knowledge expressed in concepts. These concepts do not circumscribe the supreme reality presented by them. On the contrary, that divine reality infinitely overflows the banks of conceptual knowledge. But philosophy knows thereby, or ought to know, that the reality thus objectized "through a glass, darkly," is the reality of a transcendent Self inscrutable in its being and its goodness, in its liberty and its glory. And all the other intelligent *selves* who know it, from the instant that they do know it, owe to it, as their first duty, obedience and adoration. St. Paul blamed pagan wisdom for not recognizing that glory of God of which it was in fact aware. But in fact, to recognize that glory is already to adore it. It is something to know that God is a transcendent and sovereign Self; but it is something else again to enter oneself and with all one's baggage—one's own existence and flesh and blood—into the vital relationship in which created subjectivity is brought face to face with this transcendent subjectivity and, trembling and loving, looks to it for salvation. This is the business of religion.

Religion is essentially that which no philosophy can be: a relation of person to person with all the risk, the mystery, the dread, the confidence, the delight, and the torment that lie in such a relationship. And this very relationship of subject to subject[7] demands that into the knowledge which the created subjectivity has of uncreated subjectivity there pass something of that which

6. Cf. J. Maritain, *Les Degrés du savoir* (Paris: Desclée De Brouwer, 1932), pp. 432–47; *The Degrees of Knowledge* (1959), pp. 218–26.

7. Is it necessary to explain that when we employ the word "subject" in speaking of God, we do not do so in the sense in which this word signifies receptivity as regards forms or accidents (for in this sense God is obviously not a "subject"; cf. *Sum. theol.*, I, q. 3, a. 6 and 7), but in the sense in which, as the moderns employ it, the word signifies subsistence and Self? In this circumstance the word "subject" is like the word "hypostasis," which has a similar etymology and which is predicated formally-eminently of God (cf. *Sum. theol.*, I, q. 29, a.3).

the latter is *as subjectivity,* or in the mystery of its personal life. Whence all religion comports an element of revelation. Therefore in the true faith it is the First Truth in Person which makes known to man the mystery of the divine subjectivity: *unigenitus filius, qui est in sinu patris, ipse enarravit.*[8] This knowledge is still "through a glass, darkly," and therein the divine subjectivity is still objectized in order to be grasped by us. But this time it is in the glass of the super-analogy of faith,[9] in concepts which God Himself has chosen as His means of speaking to us about Himself—until at the last every glass falls away and then we know truly as we are known. Then shall we truly know the divine subjectivity as subjectivity in the vision in which the divine essence itself actuates our intellect and transports us in ecstasy within itself. While awaiting this state, the connaturality of love gives us, in apophatic contemplation, a dim sort of substitute and obscure foretaste of such a union.

6. Generally speaking, to *situate* the privileged subject which knows itself as subject in respect of all other subjects, which it knows as objects, to situate the self, that thinking reed in the crowd of thinking reeds, sets a singular problem. Each of us is able to say with Mr. Somerset Maugham: "To myself I am the most important person in the world; though I do not forget that, not even taking into consideration so grand a conception as the Absolute, but from the standpoint of common sense, I am of no consequence whatever. It would have made small difference to the universe if I had never existed."[10] This is a simple remark; but its implications are very wide.

Being the only subject which is a subject for me in the midst of a world of subjects which my senses and my intelligence can know only as objects, I am at the center of the world, as we observed a moment ago. With regard to my subjectivity in act, I *am* the center of the world ("the most important person in the world"). My destiny is the most important of all destinies.

8. John I: 18.
9. Cf. J. Maritain, *Les Degrés du savoir,* pp. 478–84; *The Degrees of Knowledge* (1959), pp. 241–44.
10. W. Somerset Maugham, *The Summing Up* (New York: Literary Guild of America, 1938), § 5.

Worthless as I know myself to be, I am more interesting than all the saints. There is me, and there are all the others. Whatever happens to the others is a mere incident in the picture; but what happens to me, what I myself have to do, is of absolute importance.

And yet, as regards the world itself, from the most obvious "standpoint of common sense," I know perfectly well that "I am of no consequence whatever" and that "it would have made small difference to the universe if I had never existed." I know that I am one of the herd, not better than the rest, worth no more than the rest. I shall have been a tiny crest of foam, here one moment, gone in the twinkling of an eye, on the ocean of nature and humanity.

These two images—of myself and of my situation in respect of other subjects—can positively not be superposed. These two perspectives cannot be made to coincide. I oscillate rather miserably between them. If I abandon myself to the perspective of subjectivity, I absorb everything into myself, and, sacrificing everything to my uniqueness, I am riveted to the absolute of selfishness and pride. If I abandon myself to the perspective of objectivity, I am absorbed into everything, and, dissolving into the world, I am false to my uniqueness and resign my destiny. It is only from above that the antinomy can be resolved. If God exists, then not I, but He is the center; and this time not in relation to a certain particular perspective, like that in which each created subjectivity is the center of the universe it knows, but speaking absolutely, and as transcendent subjectivity to which all subjectivities are referred. At such time I can know both that I am without importance and that my destiny is of the highest importance. I can know this without falling into pride, know it without being false to my uniqueness. Because, loving the divine Subject more than myself, it is for Him that I love myself, it is to do as He wishes that I wish above all else to accomplish my destiny; and because, unimportant as I am in the world, I am important to Him; not only I, but all the other subjectivities whose lovableness is revealed in Him and for Him and which are henceforward, together with me, a *we,* called to rejoice in His life.

7. I am known to other men. They know me as object, not as

subject. They are unaware of my subjectivity as such; unaware not merely of its inexhaustible depth, but also of that presence of the whole in each of its operations, that existential complexity of inner circumstances, data of nature, free choice, attractions, weaknesses, virtues perhaps, loves and pains; that atmosphere of immanent vitality which alone lends meaning to each of my acts. To be known as object, to be known to others, to see oneself in the eyes of one's neighbor (here M. Sartre is right) is to be severed from oneself and wounded in one's identity. It is to be always unjustly known—whether the *he* whom they see condemns the *I*, or whether, as occurs more rarely, the "he" does honor to the "I." A tribunal is a masquerade where the accused stands accoutered in a travesty of himself, and *it* delivers his acts to be weighed in the balance. The more the judges stray from the crude outward criteria with which formerly they contented themselves, and strive to take account of degrees of inner responsibility, the more they reveal that the truth of him whom they judge remains unknowable to human justice. Interrogated by such a tribunal, Jesus owed it to Himself to remain silent.

I am known to God. He knows all of me, me as subject. I am present to Him in my subjectivity itself; He has no need to objectize me in order to know me. Then, and in this unique instance, man is known not as object but as subject in all the depth and all the recesses of subjectivity. Only God knows me in this wise; to Him alone am I uncovered. I am not uncovered to myself. The more I know of my subjectivity, the more it remains obscure to me. If I were not known to God, no one would know me. No one would know me in my truth, in my own existence. No one would know me—*me*—as subject.

What this comes to is that no one would render justice to my being.[11] There could be no justice for me anywhere. My exist-

11. " 'You're tying yourself up more and more,' said the Head Waiter. 'If we're to believe you, we've got to keep forgetting what you said before. . . .'
" 'It's impossible to defend oneself where there is no good will,' Karl told himself, and he made no further answer. . . . He knew that all he could say would appear quite different to the others, and that whether a good or a bad construction was to be put on his actions depended alone on the spirit in which he was judged." Franz Kafka, *Amerika* (New York: New Directions, 1946), p. 174 (English translation by Edwin Muir).

ence would be immersed in the injustice of the knowledge of me possessed by all the others and by the world itself; and in my own ignorance of myself. But if there is no justice possible with regard to my being, then there is no possible hope for me. If man is not known to God, and if he has the profound experience of his personal existence and his subjectivity, then he has also the experience of his desperate solitude; and the longing for death—more than this, the aspiration to total annihilation, is the sole spring that can gush forth within him.

Finally, to know that I am known as subject in all the dimensions of my being is not only to know that my truth is known, and that in this knowledge justice is done me; it is also to know that I am *understood*. Even though God condemn me, I know that He understands me. The idea that we are known to Him who scrutinizes the loins and the heart dissolves us at first in fear and trembling because of the evil that is within us. But on deeper reflection, how can we keep from thinking that God Who knows us and knows all those poor beings who jostle us and whom we know as objects, whose wretchedness we mostly perceive—how can we keep from thinking that God Who knows all these in their subjectivity, in the nakedness of their wounds and their secret evil, must know also the secret beauty of that nature which He has bestowed upon them, the slightest sparks of good and liberty they give forth, all the travail and the impulses of good will that they drag from the womb to the grave, the recesses of goodness of which they themselves have no notion? The exhaustive knowledge possessed by God is a loving knowledge. To know that we are known to God is not merely to experience justice, it is also to experience mercy.

8. In any case, what I should like to say is that our acts are tolerable to ourselves only because our consciousness of them is immersed in the obscure experience of subjectivity. Our acts are hatched in it as in a nest where everything, even the worst rendings and the worst shames, connives with us to emanate from us in the unique freshness of the present instant that we are living. They bathe in that maternal atmosphere emanating from subjectivity, of which I spoke earlier. There is nothing which crushes us so much as our own acts when, forgotten and then

one day evoked by some relic of past time, they pass to the state of objects, separated from the living waters of subjectivity. Even if they were not specifically evil, we are no longer sure that they were good and that some unknown illusion or hidden impurity had not tainted them—those strangers who fling themselves upon us like the dead come forth from within to bring doubt and death to us.

It must be one of the natural features of the state of damnation that the subject, not seeing himself in God, and therefore not seeing his whole life in the eternal instant to which everything is present, all his good and evil acts come back upon him in the sterile endlessly questioning light of the memory of the dead, like enemy objects wholly detached from the actual existence in which subjectivity is definitively set, in the solitude of its ill will which renders its own past a separate thing for it.

But when the subject reaches his end and sees himself in God and in divine eternity, all the moments of his past life are known to him in the actuality and the presentness of the instant in which they were lived, and all his acts (even the evil, now not only forgiven but leaving no spot nor shadow) are known as emanating presently out of the freshness of subjectivity, now itself become trans-luminous. And in the virtue of the vision in which his intelligence possesses the *Ipsum esse subsistens* he knows not only himself and all his life in a sovereignly existential manner, but also the other creatures whom in God he knows at last as subjects in the unveiled depth of their being.

THE STRUCTURE OF THE SUBJECT

9. To objectize is to universalize. The intelligibles in which a subject objectizes itself for our mind are universal natures. It is in relation to the individuality itself of the subject (which the intelligence is not capable of grasping directly); in relation to its subjectivity as subjectivity, as something unique and singular, incommunicable and unconceptualizable, and in relation also to the subject's own experience of its own subjectivity, that objectization is false to the subject and that, known as object, it

is unjustly known, as we have already observed. On the other hand, in relation to its essential structures, the subject is in no wise betrayed when it is made object. The objectization which universalizes it and discerns in it intelligible natures, makes it known by a knowledge destined doubtless to continue to deepen, but not one that is in any sense unjust. Such a knowledge does no violence to the truth of the subject, but renders that truth present to the mind.

The subject, or suppositum, or person has an essence, an essential structure. It is a substance equipped with properties and which is acted upon and acts by the instrumentality of its potencies. The person is a substance whose substantial form is a spiritual soul; a substance which lives a life that is not merely biological and instinctive, but is also a life of intellect and will. It is a very simple-minded error to believe that subjectivity possesses no intelligible structure, on the ground that it is an inexhaustible depth; and to conceive of it as without any nature whatsoever for the purpose of making of it an absurd abyss of pure and formless liberty.

These observations allow us to understand why many contemporary philosophers, while they talk of nothing but person and subjectivity, nevertheless radically misunderstand those words. They remain lightheartedly ignorant of the metaphysical problem of that *subsistence* concerning which something was said in a preceding section. They do not see that personality, metaphysically considered, being the subsistence of the spiritual soul communicated to the human composite, and enabling the latter to possess its existence, to perfect itself and to give itself freely, bears witness in us to the generosity or expansivity of being which, in an incarnate spirit, proceeds from the spirit and which constitutes, in the secret springs of our ontological structure, a source of dynamic unity and unification from within.[12]

Because analysis wearies them, they are ignorant of what the proper life of the intelligence consists in, and in what the proper

12. Cf. J. Maritain, *La Personne et le Bien commun* (Paris: Desclée De Brouwer, 1947), p. 34; *The Person and the Common Good* (New York: Charles Scribner's Sons, 1947), p. 31; paper: Notre Dame: University of Notre Dame Press, 1966, p. 31.

life of the will consists. They do not see that, because his *spirit* makes man cross the threshold of independence properly so-called, and of self-inwardness, the subjectivity of the person demands as its most intimate privilege communications proper to love and intelligence. They do not see that, even before the exercise of free choice, and in order to make free choice possible, the most deeply rooted need of the person is to communicate with *the other* by the union of the intelligence, and with *others* by the affective union. Their subjectivity is not a *self*, because it is wholly phenomenal.

10. I have already cited St. Thomas's aphorism, that the whole root of liberty is established in the reason. What reveals subjectivity to itself is not an irrational break (however profound and gratuitous it may be) in an irrational flow of moral and psychological phenomena, of dreams, automatisms, urges, and images surging upwards from the unconscious. Neither is it the anguish of forced choice. It is self-mastery for the purpose of self-giving. When a man has the obscure intuition of subjectivity, the reality, whose sudden invasion of his consciousness he experiences, is that of a secret totality, which contains both itself and its upsurge, and which superabounds in knowledge and in love. Only by love does it attain to its supreme level of existence— existence as self-giving.

"This is what I mean: Self-knowledge as a mere psychological analysis of phenomena more or less superficial, a wandering through images and memories, is but an egotistic awareness, however valuable it may be. But when it becomes ontological, then knowledge of the Self is transfigured, implying intuition of Being and the discovery of the actual abyss of subjectivity. At the same time, it is the discovery of the basic generosity of existence. Subjectivity, this essentially dynamic, living, and open center, both receives and gives. It receives through the intellect, by superexisting in knowledge. It gives through the will, by superexisting in love; that is, by having within itself other beings as inner attractions directed towards them and giving oneself to them, and by spiritual existing in the manner of a gift. And 'it is better to give than to receive.' The spiritual existence of love is the supreme revelation of existence for the Self. The Self,

being not only a material individual but also a spiritual personality, possesses itself and holds itself in hand in so far as it is
spiritual and in so far as it is free. And to what purpose does it
possess itself and dispose of itself, if not for what *is better*, in
actual existence and absolutely speaking, or to give of itself?
Thus it is that when a man has been really awakened to the sense
of being or existence, and grasps intuitively the obscure, living
depth of the Self and subjectivity, he discovers by the same token
the basic generosity of existence and realizes, by virtue of the
inner dynamism of this intuition, that love is not a passing
pleasure or emotion, but the very meaning of his being alive."[13]

By love, finally, is shattered the impossibility of knowing another except as object. I have emphasized this impossibility above
at length and noted that it directly concerns the senses and the
intellect. To say that union in love makes the being we love
another *ourself* for us is to say that it makes that being another
subjectivity for us, another subjectivity that is ours. To the degree
that we truly love (which is to say, not for ourselves but for the
beloved; and when—which is not always the case—the intellect
within us becomes passive as regards love, and, allowing its concepts to slumber, thereby renders love a formal means of knowledge), to this degree we acquire an obscure knowledge of the
being we love, similar to that which we possess of ourselves; we
know that being in his very subjectivity (at least in a certain
measure) by this experience of union. Then he himself is, in a
certain degree, cured of his solitude; he can, though still dis-
quieted, rest for a moment in the nest of the knowledge that we
possess of him as subject.

13. Cf. J. Maritain, "A New Approach to God," in *Our Emergent Civilization*, ed. by Ruth Nanda Anshen (New York: Harper & Brothers, 1947), pp.
285–86. By permission of the publishers.

4

NATURAL MYSTICAL EXPERIENCE AND THE VOID *

I CLASSIFICATION OF KNOWLEDGE THROUGH CONNATURALITY

This study is in the philosophical order. I have tried to arrange in some sort of synthetic schema the principal elements of interpretation and classification which it seems possible to me to propose concerning this difficult subject of natural mystical experience and the void. The background for this endeavor consists of the historical and experimental data which have seemed to me most significant in my random reading over the years, and of the reflections which I have long pursued concerning the distinction to be made between the typical forms of knowledge through connaturality. I shall first sum up the results at which I have thus been able to arrive. I think it better not to weight the exposition down with the texts and documents which might illustrate it, since this matter is amply familiar to all who have been interested in the Oriental mystics. I trust that the deliberately skeletal aspect of this study will be forgiven me, in view of the fact that in my own thought it merely *proposes* certain lines of investigation, and far from pretending to supply exhaustive solutions, belongs rather to the realm of inquiry and of hypothesis for research.[1]

May I add, in order to give precision to my language in a

---

* *Quatre essais sur l'esprit dans sa condition charnelle,* nouvelle édition revue et augmentée [first edition, 1939], (Paris: Alsatia, 1956), pp. 127–66.

1. Since the time of the first publication of this essay (1938), the studies of Olivier Lacombe and Louis Gardet have made considerable advances in the understanding of the question. (See further on, pp. 99–100)

manner which I believe conformable to reality, but which in any case may be granted me as a convention of speech, that in general I shall understand by the phrase "mystical experience" a *fruitive experience of the absolute.*[2]

I shall now make a few remarks on the manner in which I think it is proper to classify the different types of knowledge through connaturality.

1. I should like in the first instance to single out that type of knowledge by means of *affective connaturality* which in the most general and common fashion concerns human life, because it is in the practical and ethical order. It is the knowledge through affective or tendential connaturality *with the ends of human action,* which is at the heart of *prudential* knowledge. For the moral virtues being conjoint with one another and the prudent man being prudent only if he is also temperate, just, etc., it is necessary that he judge of the things of temperance and justice not only by mode of cognition, after the fashion of the moral philosopher, but also by mode of instinct or inclination, and by consulting his own interior bent, those very habitus of temperance or justice which are present in him and which are himself or something of himself. This knowledge of the things of human life by mode of instinct or inclination covers an immense domain. By the very fact that it is in the practical and ethical order and specifically concerns action, it does not belong to the world of contemplation. And if it can be integrated with the mystical life properly so-called (according as human action itself, in those who have entered into the mystical state, depends on the gifts of the Holy Spirit, especially the gift of Counsel), nevertheless this prudential knowledge by means of connaturality remains as such on an altogether different level from that of mystical experience, understood as a fruitive—and hence contemplative—experience of the absolute. But it is the *basic* type, the type most proportioned to the human, of knowledge through affective or tendential connaturality; and you will recall that Saint Thomas, in order to explain how the mystic "suffers divine things rather

---

2. The word "absolute" is purposely written without a capital "A" here. As we shall see later on, not every mystical experience is an experience *of God.*

than learns them," refers to the case of the chaste man who knows the things of chastity, not by mode of cognition, but by mode of inclination.*

2. In contrast to this fundamental type of knowledge through affective connaturality, and to all knowledge of this sort, I must now call attention to the knowledge through connaturality—not affective, but intellectual—which is due to the *habitus* proper to the speculative man as such, philosopher or scientist. Every *habitus* creates a proportion to the object, and a connaturality; but it is the intelligence of the mathematician or of the metaphysician which is thus connaturalized with the things of mathematics or metaphysics, and this intellectual connaturality tends but to perfect and facilitate the play of knowledge by mode of cognition, by concepts and notions. We have here a knowledge through *intellectual* connaturality with reality as *possible of conceptualization* and made proportionate in act to the human intellect. It goes hand in hand with the development of the *habitus* of the intelligence, and it is to it that belongs the intellectual intuition—abstractive and eidetic, and expressible in a mental word—of the philosopher or scientist, of him who knows by mode of cognition.

Is it possible that by following this way the metaphysician can come to a *natural contemplation* of divine things? Yes, I think so. Is this natural contemplation of divine things a *mystical experience* in the natural order? No, I think not.

Certain thinkers, who somewhat dramatize and push to the extreme, in my opinion, Aristotelian tendencies and the *nihil est in intellectu quod non prius fuerit in sensu*, would seemingly like to say, with Father Thomas Philippe,[3] that metaphysical effort, far from preparing us in some manner for union with God, would rather make us despair of such a union, and throw us back to earth, broken rather than unified, after having caused us to cast ourselves against the barrier of the steely sky which cuts off divine transcendence from every mode of human knowing. The

---

* See *Sum. theol.*, II–II, 45, 2 [Editors].

3. Cf. R. P. Thomas Philippe, "Spéculation métaphysique et contemplation chrétienne," *Angelicum* (Strena Garrigou-Lagrange), Vol. XIV (1937), fasc. 1–2.

philosopher as such cannot contemplate divine things; he is, as it were, an Icarus of contemplation, and the movement proper to him hopelessly imprisons him in the sphere of the multiple and the created. Others, on the contrary, following instead Platonic tendencies, even if they do not go so far as to admit that there is in the soul a door other than the senses whereby the soul naturally opens onto the real by an immediate existential contact, are drawn to think with Father Rousselot and his school or with Father Festugière (author of a recent and much praised study on Plato*) that metaphysical effort can lead (exceeding itself, but moving always in the same direction—which is that of intelligible being to be conquered—and by virtue of the same initial eros) either to a mystical experience in the natural order, to a natural mystical union with that One or that Good which Plato placed above being, or at least to a contemplation which, by its specific dynamism and in order to satisfy its constituent desire, asks to cross the threshold of supernatural realities and to become, by means of the gifts of grace, supernatural mystical union, conceived above all as an intellectual intuition of absolute Being.

If we turn to Saint Thomas, we find that he is less pessimistic with regard to philosophy than is Father Thomas Phillippe. And indeed how could ananoetic intellection, set in motion by the natural movement of metaphysical thought toward the cause of being, and well aware, although riveted to the mode of human knowing, that the divine reality infinitely exceeds our mode of knowing and is not circumscribed by any of our concepts—how could this intellection not seek to stabilize itself in a more and more simplified and in a better and better savoured meditation of that prime reality? Have we not here a normal effect of the intensive increase of the *habitus* of natural wisdom, especially if, as to its conditions of exercise, it dwells in the climate of grace's comfortings? Doubtless such a contemplation is more speculation than contemplation, and its immobility remains very imperfect with respect to the superior immobility of supernatural contem-

---

* A. J. Festugière, *Contemplation et vie contemplative selon Platon* (Paris: J. Vrin, 1936) [Editors].

plation. "It soars and does not stay at rest," whereas of mystical contemplation one must say: *Et volabo et requiescam.* Yet it does merit in its own right the name of contemplation, albeit in an analogical manner. Saint Thomas admits the existence of such a philosophical contemplation, and he admits that it has God for its object. "For, according to the Philosopher in the Tenth Book of the *Ethics,* this contemplation consists in the act of the highest power there is in us, namely, intellect, and in the noblest *habitus,* namely, wisdom, and also in the most worthy object, which is God. This is why the philosophers used to set aside the last days of their lives for the contemplation of divine things, employing their earlier days in the other sciences, in order to become thereby more capable of considering that which is divine."[4]

On the other hand, this natural contemplation of God is not a mystical experience, even in the natural order. It is not a fruitive experience; it occurs at the summit of the intellect's powers of abstractive ideation; it knows God by means of things, at a distance and in an enigmatic manner. Doubtless an eidetic intuitivity can develop there by means of the habit of meditation, of recollection, and of metaphysical serenity, and receive from the natural love of God an affective and experimental coloring, and in some sort mimic a true experience thanks to a high intellectual taste and to a certain simplification. This intuitivity remains, however, far removed either from an intellectual intuition of the *esse divinum,* which is possible only by means of the illumination of the light of glory, or from the unitive experience of the depths of God, which is possible only by means of the gifts of grace. Of itself the philosopher's contemplation stops short at a feeling of presence which, however exalted, however powerful, however illuminating it may be, still only concerns God the Cause of things—God attained in the mirror of things and as present to them—and not the hidden God attained in his incommunicable life by the experience of union. Knowledge through intellective connaturality with reality as capable of conceptualization, knowledge *per modum cognitionis,* this contemplation remains such even when it makes use—dialectically and notion-

4. *In III Sent.,* disp. 35, q. 1, a. 2, sol. 3.

ally— of the *via negationis*.[5] In short, there is no natural intuition, as Plato would have wished, of the supersubstantial One. And the philosophical contemplation of divine things doubtless corresponds—albeit in an extremely imperfect and deficient manner, which only makes one's thirst the greater—to that natural desire to see the First Cause which, although conditional and inefficacious, is at the deepest depth of spiritual creatures.[6] But this desire itself is essentially distinct from the natural tendency of the created intelligence to its proper and specifying object, which is being *in communi,* not the Cause of being. The natural desire to see the Cause of being *derives* from the natural desire to know being; it is a corollary thereof; it is in no way identified with it. Whence it follows that every great metaphysic is indeed traversed by a mystical aspiration, but is not constituted by it; and that by a normal effect, at least theoretically, the philosophical contemplation of God indeed hollows out in the soul a need which mystical union alone will satisfy, and aspires in this sense to such a union, as the lower aspires to the higher, but does not ask to pass over to mystical union in virtue of its specific dynamism and of its own constitutive desire.

That there can exist in the proper sense of the word a natural mystical experience, which prolongs and consummates a metaphysical élan—it is this I shall try to show in the second part of this essay. But—and in my opinion this is the point that the school of Father Rousselot does not sufficiently stress—this philosophical overstepping of philosophy, this *meta-philosophical* contemplation, does not continue in the same direction the natural movement of philosophy, which, according to Aristotle and according to the truth of our nature, is a movement toward things and toward reality to be grasped by eidetic intuition. On the contrary, it inevitably presumes a kind of turning back, a turning back against the grain of nature; and hence the irruption of a desire which is most certainly not the constitutive desire of phi-

5. J. Maritain, *Les Degrés du Savoir* (Paris: Desclée De Brouwer, 1946), p. 470, n. 1; *The Degrees of Knowledge* (New York: Charles Scribner's Sons, 1959), p. 237, n. 3.
6. Cf. J. Maritain, *Approches de Dieu* (Paris: Alsatia, 1953), Chapter V; *Approaches to God* (New York: Harper and Brothers, 1954).

losophy itself, the intellectual desire to know being, but rather a more profound desire, a desire suddenly liberated in the soul and properly religious, and which is no longer that intellectual desire to see the First Cause, which we were speaking of a moment ago and which is consequent upon the intellectual desire to see being. The desire of which I am speaking now is a more radical desire than the natural desire of the intelligence for being and its natural desire for the Cause of being, because it is the natural desire, not of a special faculty, but of the whole man, body and soul. It is, I believe, the desire essential to every creature to rejoin again *its* sources and the principle of *its* singular being, in other words, that natural desire of the part for its Whole, for the divine and separate Whole, which Saint Thomas[7] recognizes in every creature—in the stone, the rose, the bird, as well as in the intellectual creature—and which implants in the heart of all things, tending toward their principle and toward the good of the whole more even than toward their own action and their own good, a sort of hyper-finality.

3. A third category of knowledge through connaturality is that of poetic knowledge, or knowledge by mode of creation. It consists, in my opinion, in a knowledge through affective connaturality with reality as *non-conceptualizable* because awakening to themselves the *creative depths of the subject;* in other words, it is a knowledge through connaturality with reality according as the latter is inviscerated in subjectivity itself insofar as intellectually productive existence, and according as reality is attained in its concrete and existential consonance with the subject *as subject*.

Raïssa Maritain and I have tried in a little book[8] to characterize this sort of knowledge and its relationship to mystical knowledge; therefore I can here treat the matter very briefly. Let it suffice to note that poetic knowledge is indeed, and pre-emi-

---

7. Cf. *Sum. theol.*, I, 60, 5.
8. Jacques and Raïssa Maritain, *Situation de la Poésie* (Paris: Desclée De Brouwer, 1938); new edition, 1947; *The Situation of Poetry* (New York: Philosophical Library, 1955). See also J. Maritain, *Creative Intuition in Art and Poetry*, published by the Bollingen Foundation (New York: Pantheon Books, 1953).

nently, an experience, and is more experience than it is knowledge. But on the one hand be it noted that, standing, as does knowledge through prudential connaturality, in the line of the practical (not in the line of the *agibile,* but in that of the *factibile*), poetic knowledge doubtless disposes to contemplation, and it is full of contemplative flashes, but it is not properly contemplative or fruitive; it is situated at the minimum of knowledge and the maximum of germinative virtuality; it does not have its goal and its fruit in itself; it does not tend toward silence; it tends to the uttering of a word *ad extra;* it has its goal and its fruit in an external work in which it objectifies itself and which it produces. On the other hand, the typical *thing grasped or seized* in this experience is not the absolute, but rather the intercommunion of things with themselves and with the subjectivity which they reveal to itself, in the spiritual flux from which existence derives. Thus poetic knowledge is indeed experience, but it is not mystical experience; it is not fruitive experience of the absolute, even though we are justified in recognizing "the proximity, in the same divine source, of the experience of the poet and the experience of the mystic."[9]

4. I come now to the fourth kind of knowledge through connaturality, and it is this kind which interests us here. It takes place by means of connaturality with reality as *non-conceptualizable* (and in this it is in the same case as poetic experience), but, and here is the distinguishing feature, this reality grasped according as it is *non-conceptualizable* is at the same time grasped as *ultimate term of the act of knowing in its perfect immanence,* term interiorized in which knowledge has its achievement, its fruit, and its living repose. In other words, it is a knowledge by means of connaturality with reality as *non-objectifiable in notions* and yet *as term of objective union.* Here we have the mode of knowledge which to my mind characterizes mystical experience in general: knowledge of contemplation in the strongest sense of the word contemplation (the philosophical contemplation to which we referred earlier in this chapter being the

9. Raïssa Maritain, "Magie, Poésie et Mystique," *Situation de la Poésie,* p. 67.

inferior analogue of contemplation, and mystical contemplation, under present discussion, the superior analogue, itself hierarchically diversified). Knowledge not by mode of practical inclination, like prudential experience; not by mode of cognition, like the natural contemplation of the philosophers; but by mode of nescience, of fruitive not-knowing.

This kind of knowledge is in turn divided, I believe, into two essentially distinct types, according as the connaturality which it involves is itself either *affective* or *intellectual*.

In the first instance—affective connaturality—we have to do (because, as I have tried to explain elsewhere, supernatural charity is alone capable of connaturalizing the soul with deity) with supernatural mystical experience, with a supernatural contemplation attaining as object—through the union of love ("amor transit in conditionem objecti") and through a resonance in the subject itself become a means of knowing—the divine reality inexpressible of itself in any created word. The problems relating to this supernatural contemplation are not germane to the theme I am now discussing. The brief formulas I have just employed in their regard indicate sufficiently that while I have a high regard for the researches of Father Maréchal,[10] researches which supply us with so much precious data on comparative mysticism, I think that the truest theology of supernatural contemplation is to be found less in a theory of the intuition of God than in the substantially converging views of Saint John of the Cross and John of Saint Thomas on divine experience through union of love.

In the second case—intellectual connaturality—we have to do (I come to it at last!) with a natural contemplation attaining by a supra- or para-conceptual intellection a transcendent reality, inexpressible of itself in a human mental word. Here we have the mode of knowing which is typical of natural mystical experience.

Before concerning myself more closely with this natural mystical experience, I must make two further remarks.

In the first place, I should like to make myself clear concern-

10. J. Maréchal, *Etudes sur la Psychologie des Mystiques*, 2 vols. (Paris: Desclée De Brouwer, 1937).

ing the terms *object, objective union,* which I have employed
apropos knowledge of contemplation and mystical experience in
general. These words have the disadvantage of bothering *a priori*
a certain number of philosophers, be they idealists or existentialists (ex-idealist existentialists), and they would be rejected, I
believe, by Hindu thinkers, whose testimony is particularly important in the present discussion. Why? Because in the eyes of
an idealist the object is a product of the mind which separates
being from the subject, and it in any case signifies duality of
known and knower, whereas in mystical experience there is sovereign unity: "two natures in a single spirit and love," says Saint
John of the Cross with perfect precision; "Identity pure and simple," the teachers of the Vedanta like to say, in a language which
is doubtless monist only because of their inability to conceptual-
ize better the experience in question. Well, what I simply wish
to point out is that I am here employing the words "object" and
"objective union" in a strictly Aristotelian and Thomistic sense,
and that under these conditions the difficulties and anxieties to
which I refer lose their reason for existence: for the object is then
only reality itself as present in act to the soul and so far abolishing
all separation with respect to it that the soul *is* intentionally the
reality known, and that in being specified by the object it indeed
itself specifies itself; and objective union is the very consumma-
tion of the unity between the knower and the known, according
as the latter is the terminus in which the knower culminates in
its own actuality and rests in it. For Thomists the intentional
identification of the sense and its object is so strong that pure
sensation is in itself—so much does it absorb the sentient in the
sensed—an unconscious process; and the notion of object so little
implies duality that God, subsisting Simplicity (but transcendent
and infinitely rich Simplicity), is to Himself His own object, in
an intuition which is His very being and the triumph of the most
perfect unity.

My second remark concerns the existence of a vast zone of the
natural *premystical,* of both the intellectual and the affective
order, which is not to be confused with natural or supernatural
mystical experience and which is made up of the intuitions, warn-
ings, forebodings, premonitions, and divinations which bear on

the individual and the concrete and whereof the noetic world of practical affectivity supplies us with so many examples; of certain metaphysical intuitions vouchsafed after the fashion of natural illuminations or revelations,[11] and certain exalted states of philosophical contemplation; of other states of contemplation which have a strongly affective hue and which, without being poetic experience itself, are very frequent in poets (I am thinking of Keats, Shelley, and many others) and which poetic experience induces or presumes; and of the multiple cases of "religious experience" of which William James has collected so many examples, as well as of the luxuriance of "religious phenomena," often more or less aberrant, in which the Orient seems even richer than the Occident. Moreover, all such are not typical and specific forms, but rather accidental emergences or general and inchoate dispositions of natural spirituality.

II THE POSSIBILITY OF AN INTELLECTUAL EXPERIENCE (NEGATIVE) OF THE SUBSTANTIAL "ESSE" OF THE SOUL

I have just said that the problems relating to supernatural contemplation are foreign to the theme of this study. It is nevertheless necessary that I refer briefly to some of these problems in order to find a more ready introduction to the ideas which I should like to propose.

Supernatural mystical experience, or experience through affective connaturality with deity, does not merely find a natural analogy in the prudential experience of the things of human action, in the knowledge by mode of inclination which the chaste man, for example, has of all that which concerns chastity. It has many other natural analogues, in particular, poetic experience. But what I should like to point out is that, being at once knowledge of contemplation and knowledge through love, its typical value as contemplative knowledge will prove deficient the best natural analogues one can find of it in the world of the inclinations and

11. Cf. *Les Degrés du Savoir*, p. 552; *The Degrees of Knowledge* (1959), p. 279.

of affectivity; whereas, inversely, the essential role which love plays in it will prove deficient the best natural analogues one can find of it in the world of contemplative knowledges.

The love of the creature for the creature is thus a most evident natural analogue of supernatural mystical experience. Bergson, in his lectures at the Collège de France, liked to cite the sentence: "I have suffered enough from my friend to know him"; and he also liked to invoke the intimate experience which a mother has of her child. If the child, he said, stirs in its cradle, the mother wakes up, whereas a cannon blast would perhaps not awaken her. The experience of profane love is of the same sort; we have only to recall that the *Canticle of Canticles* is the supreme image, consecrated by Scripture—and also largely exploited by the annoying rhetoric of mystical commonplaces—of the trials and progress of supernatural mystical experience. But whatever incidences the love of the creature for the creature may involve as regards knowledge, its own proper constitutive element is not contemplation and contemplative fruition; its specifying element is not a reality to be contemplated.

In the world of contemplative knowledges there is another natural analogue, of eminent value, which Father Gardeil has admirably expounded in his great book, *La Structure de l'âme et l'Expérience mystique.** It is the knowledge of the soul through itself, the intimate and obscure experience of myself through myself. But if this analogy makes us perceive better than any other the value of unitive contemplation and obscure intellective transparency that is characteristic of supernatural mystical experience, it does not by itself tell us anything about the role of formal means of knowing which accrues to love in the experience in question. For, to tell the truth, this analogy enlightens us in the last analysis by an *as if* rather than by a fact, and presents us with only a virtual image of supernatural mystical experience; the example to which it refers—the even partial actualization of the radical auto-intellection of the soul by itself in reflection on itself —cannot, in fact, be realized in the present life.

John of Saint Thomas, in precious texts of which Father Gar-

---

* Paris: Gabalda, 1929 [Editors].

deil has made use,[12] tells us indeed that the soul insofar as spirit has a habitual, or radical, knowledge of itself—because the intellect, in emanating from the substance of the soul, is intelligibly informed by the latter as by a *species intelligibilis*: here is the permanent privilege of spirituality which the human soul has in common with other spirits. But John of Saint Thomas immediately adds that the actualization of this radical auto-intellection is impeded and prevented by the state of union with the body. Besides, it could not be actualized except as an intuitive vision of the essence of the soul, which vision it is clear we are lacking in this world.

These objections are opposed to certain elements of the conceptualization proposed by Father Gardeil, but not to the substance of his thought and of his views. For, as concerns both the structure of the soul *ut mens* and its radical intellection of itself through itself, the recognition of the obstacle which the state of union with the body offers for their intuitive actualization is not enough to warrant our considering them as of slight account and no longer being concerned with them. These data, on the contrary, are fundamental, and it is impossible that so important an

12. John of Saint Thomas, *Curs. phil.*, t. III, q. 9, a. 1; *Curs. theol.*, t. IV, disp. 21, a. 2, n. 13.

The human intelligence, in emanating from the substance of the soul, is in a radical manner objectively informed by the soul, for the intelligence radically considered is but one indeed with the very soul, as the properties radically considered are but one with the essence. If, in the state of union with the body, this radical informing of the intelligence by the very substance of the soul cannot expand into act, it is clearly not because the substance of the soul would find itself "materialized" and obscured by the fact that it informs matter. It is rather that with respect to the functioning and the activity of the power, it is connatural to the soul united to the body to be turned outwards in order to accomplish the work of intellection, in other words to accomplish the work of intellection by means of the senses and sense-images—which makes of the intelligence a *tabula rasa* so long as the *intellectus agens* does not inform it thanks to abstraction.

This *diversion* or *progression* outwards is required by the human intelligence because of its specific imperfection and weakness; for it is placed at the lowest rung of the ladder of intellectuality, and its intensive power *(vis intellectiva)* is naturally so weak that it needs, in order for it to know in a manner sufficiently distinct and illuminating, that *multiplicity* of concepts and of representative fragments which abstraction alone, starting from the sensible, can procure for it. The human intelligence needs ideas incomparably

ontological privilege should not have a primordial significance for human psychology, especially for everything which touches upon natural spirituality. We have here, more particularly, the metaphysical condition and the first foundation of the faculty of perfect reflection upon its acts which the soul enjoys by title of its spirituality, and which is the proximate reason of the experience which the soul has of itself through reflection on its acts. For in this reflection we have a true experience, attaining in its singular existentiality the principle of my singular operations.

In accordance with the most natural exercise of our faculties and the most natural propensity of the activities of the soul and of the "conversations of common life," there is a universal, a daily experience of the soul through itself, thanks to reflection on its acts. "Such an experimental apprehension of the soul, not through its essence but through its acts, can be termed 'immediate,' in this sense that the reality which it attains is not known through any other intermediary than its own actuation."[13] Here indeed is for each man a true experience of the singular existence of his soul, through and in its operations.

more divided and detailed than those required by the least of the angels; so much so that if the knowledge of which it is capable when it is separated from the body were merely the intuitive knowledge of the substance of the soul, which is natural to the state of separation, that knowledge would be too indeterminate to instruct the intellect about the world and about God.

Hence it can be seen that it is *ad melius animae*, for the good of the soul, and in order that its work of knowing and of intellection may be suitably accomplished, that the human soul is united to the body. One can also understand that if the soul's manner of knowing in the state of separation is "natural" with regard to that which is generally suited to *spirit* as such, it is "preternatural" with regard to the *human intelligence* taken at its own proper degree of intellectuality. Moreover, in the souls of the blessed, the vision of the divine essence and the light of glory supernaturally compensate for the natural imperfection which the state of separation involves, and which will disappear only with the resurrection of the body.

13. *Les Degrés du Savoir*, p. 861. "The object of direct knowledge is present only as the necessary condition of the mind's return upon itself; and its *species*, which, as Father Roland-Gosselin correctly observes, does not prevent it from being immediately known, likewise does not prevent the soul—become, thanks to the species, intelligible in act—from being immediately known precisely insofar as it knows. We have thus a true *experience* of the singular existence of our soul, and the concept we form of ourselves is an *experimental* concept."

But of *what* our soul is, of its essence or its quiddity, this experience tells us nothing. The existence which it grasps is indeed the existence of something, but of a something which is revealed only through the glimmering of the phenomena which emanate therefrom; it is the existence of the principle, unknown in itself, of the operations and states grouped together in the conscious synthesis. In short, the experience of myself has, in the order of *suchness* or of *essentiality,* no other content than my operations themselves, the reflexively grasped flux of more or less profound phenomena. It is of absolutely central importance to understand that my experimental knowledge of my soul (or rather of my substance, which is soul and body, but which is grasped by means of a spiritual activity, an activity of the soul alone) thus remains of an order *purely existential* and implies no other *quid* offered to the mind than my operations reflexively grasped in their emanation from their principle. My soul or my substance cannot be experienced by me in its essence; a *quidditative* experience of the soul is possible only for the separated soul, in which, from the very fact of separation, the radical auto-intellection to which I referred above passes into act. And doubtless, the more my attention will come to bear on the existential *experience* of my soul, the more I shall tend to neglect the diversity of objects and of acts the reflexive grasp of which is nevertheless the very condition of such an experience. The fact remains, however, that we go in the direction of nature: the experimental folding back of which I speak, however powerful it may be in certain "interior" souls, leaves the soul prisoner of mobility and multiplicity, of the fugitive luxuriance of phenomena and of operations which emerge in us from the night of the unconscious—prisoner of the apparent *ego,* if we agree thus to term the phenomenal content which occupies the stage and which is indeed all that a qualitative grasp in the existential experience of ourselves offers. Moreover, concern with the external world is a natural condition of mental equilibrium, and it happens in many cases that the more a man observes himself (observes himself psychologically, which is altogether different from descending into oneself metaphysically or mystically in a disciplined and purified movement), the more he runs the risk of dispersion or of *acedia,* if he does not indeed become a victim of schizophrenia and of the illusions of some pathological introversion.

Well, then, let us suppose now that one forcibly constrains the soul to give precedence—decidedly and absolutely—to reflexivity, but this time by an appropriate ascesis and technique of radical stripping of oneself, and by going deliberately against the grain of nature; supposing this, will not one have a chance—even though running all sorts of risks—of passing from the common experience of the existence of the soul (of which I have just been speaking) to an exceptional and privileged experience, an experience opening onto the abyss of subjectivity? Would not one be able to escape the apparent ego and to attain the absolute self? Modified as we have sought to modify it, reworked and developed, Father Gardeil's schema could thus explain what I here take as the typical case of natural mystical experience, namely, Yoga mysticism, such at least as the best Hindu witnesses have lived and expounded it. This mysticism, reduced to its essential kernel, would be above all a metaphilosophic experience of the substantial *esse* of the soul by means of negative, or rather annihilating, intellectual connaturality. I remember having discussed this question with Father Gardeil a few months before his death. He had not thought of such an application of his views. I, for my part, think that this application is possible and required by the real, and that Father Gardeil has opened up here an extremely valuable line of thought. For it would be an inestimable gain, at least as regards a pre-eminent case, to give of mystical experience, and especially of that of India, an interpretation which respects its authenticity and its truth and which circumscribes with precision its proper domain.

That the various recipes of Yoga can lead to all sorts of illusions and psychological extrapolations, I willingly grant. But counterfeits, however swarming, are counterfeits only of something authentic. Moreover, it does not seem to my mind possible to reduce to a psychological aberration—however respectfully one does it— the age-old and manifold testimony, the testimony in the last analysis concordant, and very intelligent, of men who for a certain kind of deliverance have sacrificed everything else, and

whom we have no reasons, moreover, to consider sick or unbal-
anced. There must be here, at least in certain eminent personalities (whatever may be the case with their followers and their
repetitious verbalism, or even trickery), a real, not a misleading,
experience. I know very well that it is good method to economize
causes, but only on condition that with the explanatory material
one possesses one does not disregard in any respect the data of
experience. And it is also a principle of good method not to reject
the integrality of testimonies such as those of which we are
speaking, unless one is constrained and forced to do so.

It would be singularly unreasonable for us to refuse to non-
Christian mystics the rules of objectivity which we rightly insist
upon for the study of Christian mystics. Now, what do the men
we are speaking of say? They say that they have experience of
the absolute. And what name do they give to this absolute? They
call it *atman,* that is to say, the Self.

I do not mean to say, of course, that these Hindu ascetics succeed in realizing what I just now declared metaphysically impossible—an actualization, however imperfect, however partial, of
the radical auto-intellection of the soul through itself. That
remains excluded for the reasons I have stated.

What I am inclined to believe is, on the contrary, that these
ascetics so thoroughly strip themselves of every image, of every
particular representation, and of every distinct operation that
they themselves in some fashion reduce—by an act still, but a
negative one and one of supreme silence—their soul and their
intellect to this radical, not-actualized auto-intellection. In short,
the idea I am advancing is that they attain, not at all the *essence*
of their soul, but the *existence* of it, the substantial *esse* itself.
And how do they do this? They do it by drastically purifying and
pushing to the extreme limit that ordinary experience of the existence of myself to which I have referred, and which, taking place
by means of operations and acts, remained immersed in their
phenomenal multiplicity and veiled by this multiplicity. Now the
soul, risking everything for everything and assiduously reversing
the ordinary course of mental activity, empties itself absolutely
of every particular operation and of all multiplicity, and knows
negatively, by means of the void and the annihilation of every act

and of every object of thought come from the outside—negatively, but naked and without veils—that metaphysical marvel, that absolute, that perfection of every act and of every perfection, which is *to exist*, its own substantial existence.

But, thus to empty oneself of every representation, is this not rather to open onto nothingness pure and simple? Doubtless this is often the case, whenever the operation involved misfires, and then calls upon some illusion or other to substitute for the missing authentic result. But of itself such an operation, by the very fact that it starts from the normal activity and the immensity, in some sort infinite, of the universe of psychic multiplicity in order actively to reduce and concentrate all this immensity (exalting to an extraordinary degree, through this very death, the vitality of the soul and of the intellect), must, it seems to me, open onto something altogether different from pure and simple nothing, and onto a negation, a void, and an annihilation which are in no way nothingness.

We are here, then, in the face of a negative and apophatic experience—I do not say of a dialectical and conceptual *via negationis*, as in the case of philosophers, but rather of a lived *via negationis*, aneidetic and para- or supra-conceptual—which no more attains (for if it did it would not be negative) the intuitive vision of the essence of the soul than does supernatural contemplation the beatific vision, but which makes use of the void and of abolition in order to know as unknown the substantial existence of the soul (which is the existence of the subject as a whole, for man exists through the existence of his soul), just as supernatural mystical contemplation makes use of the connaturality of love in order to know as unknown the Godhead—*in finem nostrae cognitationis Deum tamquam ignotum cognoscimus.* It is important to observe, as I just now indicated in passing, that in saying void, abolition, negation, laying bare, one in reality designates an act still, and an intensely vital act, the ultimate actuation through which and in which the void, abolition, negation, laying bare, and isolation are consummated and silence is made perfect. Coming at the end of a very long ascetic process in which the intellect more and more connaturalizes itself with silence and negation, it can happen that in certain instances this actuation finally surges up in such a spontaneous manner that it seems altogether given and passively received, and that it loses from the psychological point of view every active and voluntary appearance. Nevertheless, it in reality has its source in an ascending movement which is fundamentally active[14] and in a supreme tension of the forces of the soul; even from the psychological point of view the active and voluntary aspect must therefore remain predominant;[15] and, moreover, there is here ontologically, and of itself, an act, a ἐνέργεια, vital and sovereignly immanent act; so that the principle that the soul knows itself through its acts is still saved here —paradoxically, since the act in question is the act of abolition of all act. It is properly this act of abolition and of annihilation which is, I believe, the formal means of the experience of which we are speaking. And it is in this sense that the void is the term to which this experience tends, and not only its condition, but its proper medium, thanks to which the deep, fathomless "to exist" of the subjectivity is brought—negatively—to the state of object, not certainly of object expressible in a concept and appearing before the mind, but of object entirely inexpressible and engulfed in the night wherein the mind engulfs itself in order to join it.

Instead of saying: *amor transit in conditionem objecti,* we should rather say here: *vacuitas, abolitio, denudatio transit in conditionem objecti.* Here is the most purely existential experience possible, and it is an experience by way of not-knowing.[16] In the supernatural mystical experience, the void is a *condition* of contemplation (a condition actively prepared by the soul and,

14. Cf. *Science et Sagesse* (Paris: Labergerie, 1935), pp. 24–27; *Science and Wisdom* (London and New York; 1940), pp. 7–10.

15. As Marcel de Corte points out (*Etudes Carmélitaines,* October, 1938), the Plotinian void is "entirely active." "Obtaining the vision of God is the proper work of whoever has desired to obtain it" (*Enneads,* VI, 9; 4 and 7). Such also, I believe, is the common teaching of the Hindu samnyasin, except for the school of bhakti.

16. Neither in conceptual and abstractive knowledge nor in any experience of a positive sort (as, for example, poetic experience) is it possible to isolate existence in "prescinding" perfectly from the essence. But the experience here under discussion being negative and by way of not-knowing, it can attain—as unknown—existence alone, without knowing anything besides, precisely because it attains existence by means of the act of abolition of everything else.

much more, passively received from the divine influence), but its *formal means* is sovereignly positive: it is the union of love under the inspiration of the Holy Spirit. Here the void is not only a condition but also the formal means of the experience.

I should like to indicate three other characteristics among the ontological notes of this experience.

In the first place, and as I have already hinted, this experience goes directly—hence the host of techniques—against the grain of nature: it asks the soul to renounce all movement toward things, which amounts to quitting the world. Whereas in poetic recollection the world is drawn into the subjectivity and awakens it to itself, here, on the contrary, the subjectivity separates itself from the world, in order to seek within itself alone a sleep more intense than all awakenings. Then again it may be pointed out that the mystical experience of the Self requires the soul to quit the world in a manner altogether different from that required by Christian ascesis and contemplation. In both cases it is necessary to "cross the threshold," as Father Lallemant used to say; but in the natural effort against the grain of nature it is to satisfy the demands of an ascesis entirely ordered to gnosis[17]—demands at once more negative and less profound than those of evangelic perfection. Demands more negative: for that which is required of the Christian is the utter detachment from a world in which he exists more than ever, which he continues to know and to love, and for the salvation of which he suffers; but that which is required of the soul in the other case is that it purely and simply suppress the world, that it no longer exist in the world, at least until the state of deliverance and "realization" has been obtained. Demands less profound: for a detachment which attains only the roots of intelligence is less profound than a detachment which attains the roots of freedom itself and which causes one not only to quit the world but also to quit oneself (I do not mean merely egoism, the passions, etc.; I mean the supreme governance of self); and a void and a dispossession which take place through the Holy Spirit and

17. That love for the supreme Lord or for one of the lesser lords should be joined in the Yogi to this intellectual contemplation is normal; but it is not the formal means of his experience, and the latter remains essentially gnosis.

through grace should create supplenesses and abandonments and a pliability toward that Spirit which breathes where it will, and a real passivity with regard to God, and a liberty, which are altogether different from the burning immobility, the unbending confidence in the techniques of heroism, the victory over the attractions of multiplicity which result from the most tenacious active tension, concentration, and liberation of which nature is capable at its own highest point.

In the second place, it is indeed a question here of a metaphysical exprience in the strongest sense of the term; and the effort of the Oriental contemplatives seems indeed from this point of view to be an effort to follow the proper line of philosophic intellection beyond philosophy itself: but by means of that turning back of which I spoke at the outset and of the intervention of a natural desire, deeper and more total than that of the philosophic intelligence, for the intellectual conquest of being. The proof of this is that many Yogis—such as Ramana Maharshi, of whom Olivier Lacombe wrote a remarkable study[18]—did not begin with philosophy, but with a first experience of a metaphilosophical character. The metaphysical effort against the grain of nature which is thus required is a slow labor of death, which Plato also knew, but in which India particularly excels, an art of entering while living into death, into a death which is not evangelic death, intended to give place to the life of Another, but a metaphysical death, intended to winnow spiritual activities away from the body.

In the third place and finally—and this is a point of capital importance, but one difficult to express in a few words—from the very fact that the experience we are discussing is a (negative) purely existential experience, and from the fact that existence is transcendent and polyvalent, and is limited only by the essence which receives it, and of which precisely in this case one knows nothing, it is comprehensible that this negative experience, in attaining the existential *esse* of the soul, should at one and the same time attain this proper existence of the soul, existence in

18. Cf. *Etudes Carmélitaines*, "Illuminations et Sécheresses," October 1937, pp. 173 ff.

its metaphysical amplitude, and the sources of existence, according as the existence of the soul, taken concretely and to the extent that it is the exercise of effectuation *extra nihil,* is something emanating from and suffused by an influx wherefrom it attains its all. This influx is not experienced in itself, of course, but rather the effect which it produces is experienced in itself, and the influx in and through this effect. This is why the experience in question answers indeed in a certain fashion—and to the extent that this is possible in the natural order—to the desire of every thing to rejoin its sources and the principle of its being. It is the sources of being in his soul that man thus attains, thanks to the techniques through which nature reascends toward the spirit against the grain of nature and in a certain way disjoints its own proper metaphysical texture. The Hindu experience does appear therefore, to be a mystical experience in the natural order, a fruitive experience of the absolute, of that absolute which is the substantial *esse* of the soul and, in it and through it, of the divine absolute.[19] And how could this experience, being purely negative, distinguish the one of these absolutes from the other? Inasmuch as it is a purely negative experience, it neither confuses nor dis-

19. In terms of our own philosophic vocabulary and in accordance with distinctions which Hindu thought does not know, let us indicate more precisely that it is a question here of the divine absolute as the cause of being, not as giving Himself as an object of fruition. In the experience here analyzed, the divine absolute is not, Himself, properly speaking an object of fruition. It is the substantial *esse* of the soul which is the object of (negative) possession; and by this negative experience of the self God is attained at the same time, without any duality of act, though attained indirectly. God not being known then "through His works," that is to say, through His effects as through things known beforehand and which make us pass discursively to the knowledge of their cause, but being known (1) through and in the substantial *esse,* itself attained immediately and negatively through the *formal medium* of the void; (2) in the negative experience itself of that substantial *esse* (just as the eye, by one and the same act of knowing, sees the image, and in the image the signified)—all this being the case, I think it is permissible in such an instance to speak of a "contact" with the absolute, and of an improperly "immediate" experience (that is to say, one enveloped in the very act of immediate experience of the self) of God creator and author of nature. To explain this we must fall back on considerations *analogous,* on an essentially different plane, to those considerations which make it possible in the supernatural order—and without falling back on a partial or transitory *intuition* of the divine essence—to speak of a truly

tinguishes them. And since no content of the "essential" order, no *quid*, is then attained, it is comprehensible that philosophic thought reflecting upon such an experience inevitably runs the danger of identifying in some measure the one and the other absolute, that absolute which is the mirror and that one which is perceived in the mirror. The same word "atman" will designate the human Self and the supreme Self.

In this attempt at analysis of the intellectual experience of the substantial *esse* of the soul by mode of not-knowing, as in the classification of the different kinds of knowledge through connaturality which I proposed at the outset, it is pure types that I have tried to disengage. In fact, as regards mystical experience, I think that the purest cases of natural mystical experience must be sought in India (the Buddhist Nirvana doubtless corresponding to the same fundamental experience as the Brahmanic *mukti* or deliverance, but translated in a deficient manner, and more easily lending itself to impurities, by reason of the phenomenist philosophy of Buddhism); whereas the purest cases of supernatural mystical experience must be sought in the Christian contem-

---

"immediate" experience this time, an experience by union of love, of God author of grace and dwelling in the soul as in His temple. (Cf. *Les Degrés du Savoir*, pp. 509–12 and p. 652, n. 2; *The Degrees of Knowledge* (1959), pp. 257–59 and p. 328, n. 5.)

In this natural mystical experience we do not have an experience of *the deep things of God*, an experience of Deity, and in this sense I still maintain all that I wrote in the above cited work (pp. 532–34) against the possibility of an authentic mystical experience in the natural order. But here we have an experience of God *inquantum infundens et profundens esse in rebus,* indirectly attained in the mirror of the substantial *esse* of the soul; and in this sense the case of the negative experience of this *esse*, obtained by means of the void and against the grain of nature (and wherein God, without being Himself an object of fruition, is attained by this same act of experience of the self), brings a complement and correction to the pages in question, for it seems to me to constitute an authentic mystical experience in the natural order. I did not take this case into acccount in Chapter VI of the *Les Degrés du Savoir*, for I had in mind there only the mystical experience of the *deep things of God*, and I was taking the word "mystical" only in this major meaning.

I now believe that a sufficiently careful reflection upon Hindu contemplation requires us to recognize the possibility, under the conditions here analyzed, of a negative mystical experience of the *presence of immensity*

platives, particularly in those of the spiritual family of Saint Theresa and of Marie de l'Incarnation (Ursuline), of Saint John of
the Cross, of Tauler, of Father Lallemant. To the extent that
supernatural mysticism requires human preparations, involves
structures and disciplines, one should find therein—transposed
for a specifically different finality, and therefore specifically different in themselves—structures analogically similar to those of
natural mysticism.

It is scarcely necessary to add that the contingencies of history
and of the concrete present us at every level with all sorts of mixtures and minglings of natural and supernatural contemplation
(not to mention parasitic phenomena, mimetic aberrations, or
simple neuropathic interferences, which are not here under discussion), as also with all sorts of mixtures of the various types of
knowledge through connaturality which we have distinguished.
But I believe that one of the advantages of the distinctions
which I propose here is precisely that they permit a more exact
analysis of complex cases. In Plato and Plotinus one finds, in my
opinion, a combination of philosophic contemplation, of poetic
experience, and of natural mystical experience, the role of this
latter, although more or less masked, being much greater in Plo-

---

itself. A positive experience of the presence of immensity would presuppose
an experience of Deity itself and is by nature impossible. "In the degree to
which the natural mystic thinks that he attains experimentally the divine
presence, he cannot in reality grasp it except in its effect, in its created
term. But the fact remains that the intention of infinity and of the absolute
which has commanded all the steps preparatory to the experience colors
the latter as it were from within and confers on it a kind of super-interiority,
of immoble tendency to that which, without being apprehended as distinct
from the soul itself, is nonetheless the ever actual and intimately present
cause without which it would not be." Olivier Lacombe, "La mystique
naturelle de l'Inde," *Revue Thomiste*, 1951, no. 1, p. 147. Cf. the same
author's "Sur le Yoga indien," *Etudes Carmélitaines*, October 1937; "Un
exemple de mystique naturelle, l'Inde," *ibid.*, 1938.
Let us note here the distinction made by Ramanoudja—which affords,
it seems to me, a remarkable confirmation of the views proposed in these
pages—between salvation by knowledge alone (the way of immanence,
and of indifferentiation from the universal Brahman—it's natural mystical
experience such as I have attempted to characterize it), and salvation by
grace (the way of friendship, and of access to the very Personality of Brahman). See Olivier Lacombe's fundamental work, *L'Absolu selon le Védânta*
(Paris: Guethner, 1937), p. 372.

tinus than in Plato.[20] In many Soufis it could be asked if faith in the divine transcendence joined to the natural mystical experience (which of itself would lead rather to a monist conceptualization) does not explain certain traits of Moslem mysticism —poetic experience with its own proper affectivity complicating things still further in the Persians. Among Christian contemplatives Saint Augustine is a great example of the meeting of philosophic or theological contemplation and supernatural mystical experience; and in Christian mystics of a Platonic cast—even in a Ruysbroeck, but much more so in a Boehme—could there not be found a singularly exalting (but sometimes muddy) combination of supernatural mystical experience with poetic experience and with natural mystical experience? The orchestration resulting from these mixtures makes the charm, and also the danger, of all these great spirits.[21]

I should like also to point out that in authentically contemplative souls, poetic experience—drawn outside of its proper sphere and carried away by contemplation—can, it seems to me, exist with supernatural mystical experience in extremely complex relationships of mutual concurrence, powerfully helping the soul to enter into the experience of union and also masking somewhat the real extent of this union. For not only poetic *expression*, but poetic *experience* itself can, by its discoveries and its intuitions, precede mystical experience. And thanks to it, precious illuminations and spiritual lessons can be dispensed by contemplatives whose behavior towards their neighbor—which is the great criterion—still reveals hardnesses of nature and ignorances of self which the grace of supernatural contemplation, at that level, should have reduced.

20. On the affinities between the spirituality of Plotinus and that of the Upanishads, see Olivier Lacombe, "Note sur Plotin et la pensée indienne," Ecole Pratique des Hautes Etudes, Section des Sciences Religienses, *Annuaire 1950–1951*, pp. 1–17.

21. Cf. Louis Gardet, "Recherches sur la mystique naturelle," *Revue Thomiste*, 1948; "Mystique naturelle et mystique surnaturelle en Islam," *Rech. de sc. relig.*, 1950; *La Pensée religieuse d'Avicenne* (Paris: Vrin, 1951); "La mention du nom divin dans la mystique musulmane," *Revue Thomiste*, 1952; *Expériences mystiques en terres nonchrétiennes* (Paris: Alsatia, 1953).

III A FEW CONCLUSIONS AFTER THE FASHION OF HYPOTHESIS FOR RESEARCH

It remains for me only to propose a few of the consequences which seem to me to spring from the preceding analyses, and which above all I present as hypotheses for research.

1. What relationship is it suitable to establish between the *void* of natural mystical experience and the supernatural night of the spirit? It seems to me first of all that the distinction made by Saint John of the Cross beween the night of the senses and the night of the spirit has not only a theological value but also, and first, a philosophical value—I mean, founded on the nature of the human being, and on the double disproportion, on the one hand of sense (imagination, sense affectivity, discursus immersed in signs) with spirit (in the purely metaphysical sense of this word), on the other hand of spirit with things divine (even leaving to one side the supernatural).

But there is no correspondence or parallelism between the two nights of Saint John of the Cross, which relate to certain painful phases of the perfecting and transfiguration of nature by grace, and the void of natural mystical experience, which relates to the essential requirements of a movement against the grain of nature. This void, whatever suffering and terror it may entail, does not go so far as the night of the spirit, inasmuch as the latter dries up, disorganizes, and in some way destroys the spirit (not doubtless physically, but in all its operative measures and proportions and in its natural vital urge) in order to proportion it to Diety. For the void of natural mystical experience does not proportion to the supernatural, to God in His intimate life; moreover, it is accomplished by means of the spirit itself, by means of the effort of the spirit, and it remains altogether intellectual, whereas the night of the spirit is brought about by means of *gratia operans* and by means of love, both of which know how to be impossibly difficult. And this void is not, like the night of the spirit, a passing phase on the road toward a better state (transforming union), but the very goal to which one tends, since it is the formal means of the experience of the Self, and of deliverance.

At the same time this void goes a great deal further than the

night of the senses, inasmuch as the latter "destroys" the senses
in order to proportion them to the spirit. The void of natural mystical experience proportions the spirit to itself. It is like an excess
and a paroxysm of a night of the senses on the natural level,
ordered toward passing beyond the purification of the senses, and
toward a metaphysical death.

Nor is there any correspondence or parallelism between the
nights which correspond in the natural order to the nights
of Saint John of the Cross and the void of natural mystical
experience.

Finally, I have already indicated what a fundamental difference separates in my opinion the void—metaphysical, and by
mode of suppression and concentration—proper to natural mystical experience, and the void or stripping bare—evangelic, and
by mode of gift and of dispossession, for the sake of Another
better loved—which constitutes, not the formal means, but the
condition (itself attributable to cooperating or operating grace)
of supernatural mystical experience. In order to avoid all misunderstanding may I point out that this dispossession of oneself,
this void, or this evangelic stripping bare is linked in an altogether general fashion, according to diverse modalities and degrees, with all the states of supernatural contemplation. It is
something quite other than the night of the spirit and than the
particular void that it involves, which are an altogether special
and, so to speak, violent form of dispossession—torturing and
wholly passive—and produced, as an effect, by the implacable
light of contemplation itself and of the wisdom of love.

2. The distinction between the intellectual union and the union
of love must be held as fundamental.

An altogether intellectual union does not—even when it goes
against the grain of nature—go beyond the order of nature, in
the sense that Christian philosophy and theology give to this
word.

With love, one has to do either with pre-mystical experiences
and modes of contemplation, or else with incidences of poetic
experience, or with a supernatural mystical experience.

Whenever there really exists a mystical experience through
union of love, this experience is supernatural (typical or a-typical,

and perhaps more or less masked[22] or even more or less reduced, deformed, or "crushed" by the effect of environmental conditions, and in the absence of a proportionate mental regime).

The case of bhakti, once more to take our examples from India, is one of those which here pose for us the greatest number of problems; for such of the Hindu contemplatives as thus place piety in the position of first importance attribute a major role to love. To the extent that we have here authentic experiences— those very ones, in particular, which doubtless were at the origin of the doctrine of bhakti—the testimony is such that one must admit (such is Olivier Lacombe's opinion) that these experiences involve, at least participatively, a union of love with the Supreme, whose grace the soul awaits. Here is something which goes beyond the experience of the Self. Since we believe that sanctifying grace is offered to all men, and that souls which do not belong visibly to the Church can effectively receive this grace and with it the organism of the virtues and gifts which are linked to it; since, moreover, it is not believable that God should refuse Himself to souls of good faith who, even if the idea of grace is with them only a natural product of the interpretation of psychological phases of aridity and fullness, invoke nevertheless, with this fabricated idea of grace, grace itself which has not been revealed to them—in view of all this, I do not see why one should deny that mystical experience such as it presents itself in the school of bhakti can depend upon a sort of *composition* of the upward movement of Yoga and the disciplines of the natural contemplation of the Self combined with supernatural touches, and with charity. Explicit knowledge of the mysteries of the redemptive Incarnation and of the gifts of supernatural life creates the mental and moral regime proportioned to the normal development of supernatural mystical experience. In a regime, on the contrary, where supernatural mystical experience can gain admittance only as a stranger and by disguising itself, it is possible to believe that many substitutes are produced, and notably that graces of attraction from afar come to impart to natural mystical experience a

22. See our study "Action et Contemplation" in *Questions de Conscience;* and J. and R. Maritain, *De la vie d'oraison,* second edition, pp. 74 ff.

higher value and a participation in the supernatural union of charity. We are here confronted with the unexplored realm of questions concerning the state of the gifts of grace in non-Christian climates.[23]

3. In order to endure the supernatural night of the spirit, which is a death and a despair of *everything* (even of God)—a lived, not a voluntarily suffered despair—at the heart of which grace alone maintains a secret hope—in order to endure such a night, I repeat, a divine force is necessary.

In the natural order there are nights of the spirit which are also death and despair, and, in the sense defined a few lines back, "destruction" of the spirit even unto its natural desire and its consubstantial taste for its own operative ends—a radical horror as regards its own life. This kind of frightful and suicidal disjunction, between the unalterable ontological structure of the spirit, with which is identified its natural appetite, and this same natural appetite in so far as it is seized and assumed by the movement of the whole of elicited appetivity and of the will, in any case bears witness, in the sphere of the abnormal, as does reflexivity in the sphere of the normal, to the freedom of the spirit with regard to itself and to what one could call the fourth dimension of the things of spirituality. Are these nights the result of some great abuse, making one pass into accursed regions? In

---

23. "Does natural mysticism, supposing it purified of all dross, constitute a valuable preparation for the perfect Christian life here on earth? Prudentially speaking, and in the present stage of works in this area, the answer must be at least a cautious one. But from a historical point of view, from the point of view of the history of religions and of the approaches of the human soul in quest of salvation and beatitude outside the frontiers of explicit revelation, it seems possible—distinguishing moreover a multitude of irreducible cases—to form a more positive judgment. We do not see any reason why an upright soul—one, consequently, inhabited and moved by a hidden grace—could not live a particularly adapted discipline of Yoga as a vicarious exercise of authentic spiritual life. Progress in fidelity to grace would then find expression in a going beyond the proper ends of natural mysticism, and in an entering, doubtless imperceptible and *psychologically* inexpressible, into the ways of an implicit but lively faith, although its source-in-Christ remains masked." Olivier Lacombe, *Revue Thomiste*, 1951, no. 1, p. 148. Cf. L. Gardet, "Vraie et fausse mystique," *Revue Thomiste*, 1954, p. 309.

any case they are, in their own particular order, like unto a hell.[24]

Of these nights of the spirit in the natural order one could cite many examples. May I point out that they can be found in the realm of pure intellectual knowledge, be it metaphysical or moral (it is the case with Faust, *drum hab' ich mich der Magie erge-ben*), in the realm of poetic experience (I think of Rimbaud), in a mixture of these two realms (I think of Nietzsche, and of those words which are so astonishing coming from his pen: *Crux mea lux, lux mea crux*). And I think that it should also be possible to find such nights in the realm of natural mystical experience (I wonder whether tantrism has not some relationship with such a night?), it being understood that the night in question is an altogether different thing from the void which constitutes the formal means of natural mystical experience, and of which this night would tend to induce despair.

For such nights there is no recourse. For here despair reaches, as in the supernatural night, the very junction of soul and spirit. But being in the natural order and hence not involving in their depths the secret power of a superhuman help, these nights of themselves issue in a catastrophe of the spirit (an annihilation in the sensual; magic; insanity; moral or physical suicide). The supernatural night of the spirit is the only night from which the spirit can emerge alive.

The trials and torments of profane love are a natural analogate or an image of this supernatural night; but this love, as I have indicated above, is not a contemplative experience, and these nights are not natural nights of the spirit.

4. Is it possible to set forth the differential ontological characteristics of the supernatural night of the spirit? This question goes beyond the limits of the present study. Yet I may be permitted to indicate that in my opinion three features, when they are all present at once, and are joined to the anguish and shadows which strike at the root of the higher faculties, would seem

24. One could recall here the remarks of John of Saint Thomas concerning the state of lived contradiction wherein the spirit of the fallen angel finds itself, and concerning the kind of radical asthenia with which that spirit is stricken; *Curs. theol.*, t. IV, disp. 24, a. 2 and 3.

to be characteristic of this supernatural night:

   (i) mystical experience through union of love;

   (ii) transcendence with regard to all technique;

   (iii) evangelical behavior, or detachment from perfection in perfection.

I am referring here to the fact that evangelic perfection is not some perfection of spiritual athleticism wherein a man would make himself faultless, nay impeccable, but rather the perfection of love, of love toward Another whom the soul loves more than itself, and whom it is above all important for the soul to love even more and to join, even though the soul in the process carries with it imperfections and weaknesses, deficiencies of the body and spirit, even sins which it detests and which it also gives Him, together with all that He undertakes to take from one. This detachment from perfection in perfection is, it seems to me, the secret of souls who have passed over the threshold of union; and this invisible behavior is reflected, as in a visible mirror, in a certain typical behavior toward one's neighbor.

5

About CHRISTIAN PHILOSOPHY *

Given the presence of religious faith in human minds, especially the presence of a religious faith founded, like Christianity, on the Word of God supernaturally revealed, what is the result of the impact of that religious faith on the structure and development of philosophy? In other terms, is there such a thing as Christian philosophy? What are the meaning and the value of the concept of Christian philosophy?

The problem of Christian philosophy has two implications. The first implication refers to Christian philosophy taken in a *material* sense, that is to say, a philosophy whose features are determined in some way or another by the fact that it has developed in a Christian historical climate, even if this philosophy is far from being in tune with Christian faith. The second implication refers to Christian philosophy taken in a *formal* sense, that is to say, a philosophy which is intrinsically consonant with Christian faith and has been helped and quickened by it in its own philosophical work.

From the first point of view we have to maintain that, to tell the truth, Western philosophy has never shaken free of the Judaeo-Christian fact: there where the latter has not helped philosophy to build itself, it has stood as a stumbling block. In this sense Nicolas Berdyaev said that all the great modern philosophies—and even, very certainly that of Feuerbach and that of Marx—are "Judaeo-Christian" philosophies—philosophies which would not be what they are without the Judaeo-Christian tradition.

* In *The Human Person and the World of Values:* A Tribute to Dietrich von Hildebrand by His Friends in Philosophy, edited by Balduin V. Schwarz (New York: Fordham University Press, 1980), pp. 1–10.

Let us not forget that, to have the Christian movement of thought in its fullness, one must not merely consider *philosophy* (even a Christian one) but also, and indivisibly, *theology,* and the superior, experiential *wisdom of the contemplatives.* As a result of the dissociation of the Christian synthesis, philosophy has inherited all sorts of tasks, preoccupations, and anxieties which formerly, in medieval Christendom, depended on theological wisdom and mystical wisdom. Such was the case, for instance, with the theological notion of the Kingdom of God, which has become the Leibnizian commonweal of the spirits, and finally humanity, in the sense that Herder or Auguste Comte understood it. As philosophy grew intrinsically less Christian, it swelled with Christian remnants. One may thus understand the paradox that the philosophy of Descartes, or even that of Hegel, seems more colored with Christianity and less merely philosophical than the basically Aristotelian philosophy of Saint Thomas Aquinas.

Generally speaking, the effects of what can be called the dissociated Christian regime were manifested by a disastrous break between the proportions normally required between the *object* and the *inspiration.*

One of two phenomena took place: On the one hand, a thought which turned away from superior lights remained cluttered up with Christian *objects* going to ruin—since they were no longer *lived* by intellection according to their total truth, and since they were henceforth deteriorated, decomposed by the inspiration of a reason more and more weighed down. Thus one may discover, at each decisive step of modern rationalism, a process of *petrification* of truths and notions of Christian origin: say, the notion of *natural law* with the geometrically conceived Natural Law of Grotius and his successors, the notion of the *soul* with Cartesian angelism, the notion of *divine omniscience* with Leibnizian logicism (every predicate is inherent in the concept of the subject), and the notion of the *triumph of good over evil by the cross of Christ* with Leibnizian naturalistic optimism, the notion of *divine Ideas* and of the glory of God with Malebranche's theophilosophism, the notion of *divine causality as permeating everything* with Spinoza's monism, the notion of *supernatural infused knowledge* with Berkeley's metaphysical idealism, the notion of *person* and of *divine moral law* (the Decalogue) with Kant's ethical purism, the notion of *human salvation* and of *progress toward final transformation* with Hegelian evolutionism, the notion of the *City of God* with Auguste Comte's humanitarianism, the notion of the *last judgment* and the *New Jerusalem* with Marxian revolutionism.

On the other hand, this may have happened: Deprived of the objective regulations and foods which its very being calls for, a Christian *inspiration*, in a certain sense gone mad, was to lay waste, all the deeper as it remained grander, the field of rational speculation. In varying ways and degrees, thinkers like Böhme, Jacobi, Schelling perhaps, Nietzsche, and Chestov—even that great "knight of faith" Sören Kierkegaard—would have to be named here. I am fully aware that their work is highly stimulating and bears highly significant testimony; yet truth obliges one to say that it represents a corruption of philosophy as such. From that very fact comes its strong taste.

Yet it is the problem of Christian philosophy formally taken that I should like especially to discuss.

Let me say right away what is for me the principle of the solution; it is the classic distinction between the *order of specification* and the *order of exercise*, or else again—and it is these last terms that we will retain—between *nature* and *state*. I say that one must distinguish the *nature* of philosophy, or what it is in itself, from the *state* wherein it finds itself in fact, historically, in the human subject, and which is bound to its conditions of existence and exercise in the concrete life.

This distinction between *nature* and *state* does not matter much regarding sciences which are in the strictest sense of the word science—I mean insofar as "science" is distinguished from "wisdom." For indeed, when it comes to science, human thought is not bound to states that are basically different, unless it be the state of unculturedness and the state of culturedness, and the diversity of historical conditions affects only extrinsically and accidentally the work of science. Speak as one may of "Greek mathematics" or "Hindu logics," these denominations connote a psychological conditioning which remains external to science.

The situation is different as concerns the order of wisdom and we believe that philosophy is a wisdom. For with regard to wisdom—which constitutes, so says Aristotle, a knowledge more divine than human, which we can possess but precariously because of the weakness of our nature, "servile in so many respects" —with regard to wisdom the various spiritual or religious states in which the human subject is existentially placed have an intrinsic and decisive significance.

Thus we have to look first at the *nature,* second at the *existential state* of philosophy.

Considering the *nature* of philosophy, we have to insist that philosophy is specified, or is possessed of its own particular essence, solely in relation to the object; it is the object toward which it moves (and in no way the subject it resides in) which determines its *nature.*

There is in extramental reality (in created and uncreated reality) a whole order of objects which are of themselves *accessible* to the natural powers of the human mind. Were it not so, the distinction between the natural and the supernatural or the order of nature and the order of grace would be meaningless.

Whatever be the conception one has of philosophy, if one does not hold the philosophical domain to be accessible by itself to the natural powers of the human mind, one does not define philosophy, one negates it.

The affirmation of this essential *naturalness* or *rationality* of philosophy was basic with Saint Thomas. One may say that philosophy has taken on with him, from the fact that he was a Christian, a new value and import in relation to the concepts of an Aristotle, who did not have the idea of an order of revelation. That affirmation of the essential naturalness or rationality of philosophy, as it grew precise and explicit with regard to faith and theological knowledge, from which it strictly distinguishes philosophy, must be looked upon as an acquired gain, definitely acquired during the "progress of the Western consciousness."

It follows from these considerations that since the specification of philosophy depends wholly on its formal object, and since this object is of a wholly natural order, philosophy taken in itself— whether it live in a pagan head or a Christian head—depends on the same strictly natural or rational intrinsic criteria; and it follows, too, that the denomination *Christian* applied to a philosophy does not relate to what makes up this last in its *essence of philosophy:* as philosophy, it depends on Christian faith neither in its object, nor in its principles, nor in its methods.

Let us not forget, however, that a pure abstract essence is what we are thus considering.

As soon as one is no longer dealing with philosophy taken in itself, but with the way in which the human subject philosophizes, and with the various philosophies brought to light in the concrete movement of history, the consideration of *essence* no longer suffices and that of the *state* imposes itself.

Considering now the existential state, or the conditions of exercise, it is clear that in order to reach in us its full normal development, philosophy demands from the individual many self-rightings and purifications, an asceticism not only of reason but of the heart, and that one philosophizes with one's whole soul even as one runs with one's heart and lungs.

But here is what, to my mind, constitutes the central point of the debate—over which, moreover, dissension between Christians and non-Christians is unavoidable. One need not be a Christian (even though a Christian knows these things better, knowing that our nature is wounded) to be convinced of the weakness of our nature, and that it is enough for wisdom to be hard to attain for error, in this domain, to be frequent. But the Christian believes that grace alters man's state by raising his nature to the supernatural order, and by making him know things that reason unaided could not attain; he believes also that if reason, to reach with no admixture of error the highest truths which are naturally accessible to it, needs to be helped either from within by internal strengthenings, or from without by having objects proposed to it, such assistance has under the New Law taken in fact an institutional value which creates a new regime for the human intelligence. Hence an unavoidable tension—I do not say conflict—between the supernatural knowledge of faith and the natural knowledge of philosophy; and an unavoidable tension—here I say also conflict—between those philosophies which accept and those philosophies which reject the inner quickening and additional light that reason receives from faith.

What I would wish now is to show briefly what, in my opinion, are the main components of the *Christian state* of philosophy.

First of all there are objects belonging in themselves to the realm of philosophy, but which in fact the philosophers had not recognized explicitly, and which Christian revelation placed in the foreground: for instance, the notion of *creation;* also, to take up again a theme of Gilson's, the notion of God as *Ipsum Esse per se subsistens,* the very act of Existing subsisting through itself, put forward by Moses—"I am that I am"—a notion which has been only glimpsed and suggested by Aristotle,[1] and which the Christian Doctors have extracted from Aristotle thanks to Moses; also, in the moral order, the notion of *sin* in the nakedly ethical sense of the word—that is, in the sense of an offense against God, a notion from which despite much effort Western philosophy has not managed to shake free. Such notions are capital for all philosophy. So far as they are concerned, reason has really received a positive contribution from revelation, and we may say with Gilson: *revelation that generates reason.* But here a few explanations seem necessary.

From the sheer fact that the objects under discussion belong to the rational or philosophic realm, they must have been involved in some way or other—were it in the most virtual manner—in the philosophical treasure of mankind, and one could not say that prior to revelation they were *totally* unknown to philosophers.

The ignorance in question was less a total, absolute night than a darkness more or less deep where thought stopped, or lost its way. Briefly, the question that confronts us here concerns rather —and this remains of an extreme *de facto* importance—differences of lighting, exceedingly strong ones, to tell the truth; things which remained in regions of shadow or of mirage have been put in bright light when philosophy stepped into its Christian state. At the same time, the center of radiation had shifted, the brightest rays issuing now from the regions that were darkest to the natural weakness of human eyes, and as a result all things have taken on a new aspect, all perspectives have been transformed.

1. Did not Aristotle call God "the Principle and the first of all Beings"? *Metaph.* XII, 1073a 23.

Furthermore there are in the revealed deposit data which are not rational objects, but mysteries—mysteries of faith—essentially supernatural, that are by themselves inaccessible to the natural forces of reason. Well, my contention is that those data of revelation are also of consequence—and in an essential manner—for the development and destiny of philosophy.

First of all because philosophy, such as practiced by the human mind in a Christian state of existence, is taken hold of like an instrument by theology for the elucidation of the mysteries in question: how could philosophy fail to learn much from being thus led about paths that are not its own?

It has often been noted that *without* systematic reflection upon the dogmas of the Trinity and the Incarnation, there were very few chances that philosophers would have become aware of the metaphysical problem of the person.

Let us say more. The very experience of the philosopher has been renewed by Christianity. The *datum* which is offered him is a world: work of the Word, where all speaks of the infinite Spirit to finite spirits that know themselves to be spirits; what a beginning! There is a kind of fraternal attitude toward things—I mean insofar as they are things *to be known*—for which speculation is indebted to the Christian Middle Ages, and which seems to have prepared, on the one hand, the blossoming of the experimental sciences of nature, and, on the other hand, the blossoming of the reflexive knowledge upon which our modern times pride themselves.

I have spoken of the *objective contributions* which philosophy in its Christian state receives from faith. Now I should like to mention the *subjective strengthening* which philosophical activity finds in a Christian climate. The superior virtues of the intellect strengthen the inferior ones in the order proper to these latter; the virtue of faith makes it so that the philosopher who knows by merely rational means of God's existence clings rationally with greater strength to this truth. Similarly the habit of contemplation cleanses and pacifies—spiritualizes—the philosophical habitus in its own order. And in the light of theology the metaphysical truths shine forth with such a prompt and decisive vividness that the work of philosophy is made easier and more fruitful; I am convinced that in actual fact metaphysics cannot take on its perfect dimensions in human heads without experiencing the attraction of theology, any more than theology can take on its own dimensions without experiencing the attraction of infused wisdom. This synergia and this vital solidarity, this dynamic continuity of intellectual virtues thus provides philosophical activity with a subjective strengthening and refining of a capital importance.

Thus we may conclude that the expression "Christian philosophy" denotes not merely an essence, but a complexus: an essence considered in a certain state. From this it is inevitable that a certain fuzziness attaches to the term, which yet refers to something very real. Christian philosophy is not a definite doctrine, even though to my mind St. Thomas' doctrine is its most complete and pure expression. Christian philosophy is philosophy itself, insofar as it is placed in the typical conditions of existence and of exercise into which Christianity has introduced the thinking subject, thanks to which certain objects are *seen*, certain assertions are *validly established* by reason—which, under other conditions, more or less escape reason.

This relation is not accidental: it flows forth from the very nature of philosophy, from its natural aspirations to know its own objects as well as possible, and from the very nature of Christian doctrine and life, from the objective and subjective strengthenings these last two bring to reason, and which come down from that which, according to Aristotle's *Ethica Eudemia,* being the principle of reason, is better than reason. The fact remains that what matters to us in a philosophy is not that it be Christian, but that it be true. And yet, in order to be true, it is helped in an irreplaceable manner by Christian faith and inspiration.

As I said in the beginning, there is in Christian philosophy a tension—not a conflict—between *religious faith* and *philosophical reason.* On the one hand philosophical reason is helped and quickened by religious faith; on the other hand it has to maintain its own independence, and the irreducible autonomy of its own ways and its own approach to reality, with regard to the approach and the ways peculiar to those supra-philosophical kinds of knowledge which are faith and theology. As a matter of fact, that tension is not easy to surmount. Now Christian philosophy, which is a servant to theology in the theological field, but which is free in its own philosophical field, only imitates or reflects in its own mirror what theology teaches, or accepts from theology concepts which it fails philosophically and critically to validate (that is the story of textbook scholasticism); now, on the contrary, Christian philosophy happens to mistake its own freedom for an eagerness to get Christian conclusions, like the existence of the soul or the existence of God, at any price whatsoever, and to reach them either through self-imposed arbitrary ways (that was the story of Descartes), or through ways borrowed from any kind of fashionable system (that is the story of contemporary Christian existentialism). The tension which I just described is not easy to overcome; yet it *can* be overcome by dint of intellectual vigor and of attachment both to the light of faith and to the rational requirements of philosophy's very nature.

There is finally another tension between *philosophy which is in a Christian state of existence* and *philosophies which are not.* Nay, more: such a tension will inevitably entail mutual opposition and conflict. I think that nothing causes more damage to the normal progress and development of philosophy than the mutual contempt with which some Christian philosophers regard all secular philosophies as proud foolishness, and some secular philosophers regard all Christian philosophy as subservient dogmatism. Such mutual contempt is based on mutual ignorance. It could and should be overcome; for it is possible for the human intellect to transcend its own system of notions, in order to put itself, for one moment, in the perspective of another human intellect, and to understand the system of notions of the latter. Thus mutual understanding and mutual intellectual justice is possible—but not mutual agreement. In this sense the tension between Christian and non-Christian philosophies can never be overcome. We may be sorry about that, but we should not be *too* sorry; for, in a general way, be they Christian or non-Christian philosophers, the natural condition of any philosopher seems to imply that he can be in agreement only with himself. Even this kind of agreement seems rather difficult, and due to some infrequent piece of luck.

II

Metaphysics

Maritain holds the classical view that the object of metaphysics is being as being, *and he stresses that it is in things themselves that metaphysics finds this object. It is the being of sensible and material things which is metaphysics' immediately accessible field for investigation; it is this which, before seeking its cause, it discerns and scrutinizes—not as sensible and material, but as being.*

Major themes in Maritain's analysis of being *are the essence-existence polarity in* being; *the primacy of esse (the "act-of-existing"); the* analogy of being; *the dynamism and root generosity of* being; *the "transcendentals," or the universal modes of* being—being, *the* true, *the* good, one, "this something," *and the* beautiful; *and the dissymmetry—fundamental, irreducible dissymmetry—between the line of good and the line of evil.*

Maritain has restated the five classical ways of St. Thomas Aquinas to demonstrate the existence of God, divesting them of the examples borrowed from ancient physics and formulating them in a language more appropriate to modern times;

and then he himself proposes a "sixth way." He has also put great emphasis on nonphilosophical or prephilosophical ways of approaching God.

Maritain's major writings in this area are

APPROACHES TO GOD

EXISTENCE AND THE EXISTENT

GOD AND THE PERMISSION OF EVIL

NEUF LEÇONS SUR LES NOTIONS PREMIÈRES DE LA
    PHILOSOPHIE MORALE

A PREFACE TO METAPHYSICS

6

THE INTUITION OF BEING *

I THE INTUITION OF BEING AS BEING

In the preceding lecture** we began to turn our attention to the object of metaphysics, that is to say, being as being, *ens secundum quod est ens*. And in order the better to distinguish this object in its own peculiar characteristics, we found it useful to survey first a certain number of aspects under which being can present itself to our intelligence and which are not the aspect we are seeking. We thus noted in passing four kinds of "being" which are not the proper object of the metaphysician.

We have now to deal with being as being, *ens in quantum ens*. It is the last object the intellect attains to at the summit of its natural knowledge: thus the intellect comes full circle. It sets out from being, but from being as it is immediately apprehended by the intellect at the moment the latter awakens in the world of the senses. That is its starting point. And at the end of its course it still arrives at being, but at being envisaged in itself, disengaged in its own light and according to its own intelligible type. All that we said in the last lecture enables us to understand that it would be an intellectual disaster to confuse this "being" which is the object of the metaphysician with one or the other of the kinds of "being" we then noted. One would thus be led—especially if he

* *Sept leçons sur l'être et les premiers principes de la raison spéculative* (Paris: Téqui, 1934), pp. 51–70.
** *Ibid.*, pp. 23–50 [Editors].

stopped at the being which is the proper object of the logician, or
even at what we have called pseudo-being,* and imagined that
it is on this being or on this pseudo-being that the metaphysician
confers a real value—one would be led to regard being as a resi-
due of language: which would indeed be for the philosopher to
"vanish in his thoughts."

The being that is the object of the metaphysician, being as being, is neither the particularized being of the sciences of nature,
nor the vague being of common sense, nor the de-realized being
of true logic, nor the pseudo-being of pseudo-logic: it is real being
in all the purity and amplitude of its own proper intelligibility or
of its own proper mystery. This being is murmured in things and
in all things; things utter it to the intellect, but not to all intellects
—to those only that can hear, for here also it is true to say: *qui
habet aures audiendi, audiat,* he that hath ears to hear let him
hear. Being appears here according to its own proper characteristics as consistent trans-objectivity, autonomous and essentially
varied, for the intuition of being is at the same time the intuition
of its transcendental character and of its analogical value. It is
not enough to encounter the word "being," to say "being": one
must have the intuition, the intellectual perception of the inexhaustible and incomprehensible reality thus manifested as object.
It is this intuition that makes the metaphysician.

2. There is, as you know, a special intellectual virtue for each
science; there is a *habitus,* or intellectual virtue, of the metaphysician, and this virtue, or *habitus,* corresponds to the being that
is the object of the intuition of which we are speaking. Thus we
must distinguish two "lights" in Scholastic parlance: one on the
side of the object, the other on the side of the *habitus,* or intellectual virtue. The typical mode of intellectual apprehension or
eidetic visualization—the degree of immateriality, of spirituality,
in the manner of seizing the object and of conforming to it, required of itself by the trans-objective real offering itself as object
under this or that intelligible "exponent"—constitutes what the
ancients called the *ratio formalis sub qua,* the objective light

* That is, the object of what Maritain calls (cf. *Sept leçons* . . ., pp. 43–
45) pseudo-logic or degenerate logic—being understood as the supreme
genus and pure form of thought [Editors].

under which things are, at such or such degree of knowledge, knowable to the intellect. At the same time proportionate to this objective light there is a subjective light perfecting the subjective dynamism of the intellect, by which the intellect itself is proportioned to this object, rendered more capable in regard to it. This is why Thomists say that the *habitus* is a *lumen,* a light, not in the objective but in the *effective* order, that is to say, as regards the production or effectuation of the act of knowing.

We may thus say that the metaphysical *habitus* is necessary in order to have the intuition of being as being, *ens in quantum ens,* and that on the other hand it is this intuition that effects, causes, the metaphysical *habitus.* There is reciprocal causation, which simply means that the metaphysical *habitus,* the intellectual virtue of the metaphysician, is born at the same time as its proper and specifying object unveils itself to it. However, there is priority of the object, not in time but in ontological rank. There is priority, in the order of nature, of the intuition of being as being over the internal *habitus* of the metaphysician. It is this perception of being that determines the first moment at which the *habitus* is born, and it is in terms of this same *habitus* thus developed that the being which is the proper object of the metaphysician is more and more clearly perceived.

3. But enough of this digression. We are therefore in the presence here of a genuine intuition, a perception direct and immediate, an intuition not in the technical sense which the ancients gave to the term, but in the sense we may accept from modern philosophy. It is a question of a very simple seeing, superior to any discourse and to any demonstration, since it is at the origin of demonstrations; of a seeing whose richness and virtualities no word uttered externally, no word of human language, can exhaust or adequately express, and in which in a moment of decisive emotion and, as it were, of spiritual fire, the soul is in living, penetrating, and illuminating contact with a reality which it touches and which takes hold of it. Well, what I wish to emphasize is that it is being above all which procures such an intuition.

The characteristics of the intuition such as I have just described them could seem at first glance to fit Bergsonian intuition. Yes, except that this latter presents itself as not being of an intellectual nature. I, on the other hand, hold that that which is preeminently the object of intuition is being, but it is the object of intellectual intuition. We are in reality very far from Bergsonism. Being procures such an intuition, not for that sort of sympathy requiring a twisting of the will back upon itself of which Bergson speaks, but for the intellect—and by means of a concept, an idea. The concept of being, the notion of being corresponds to this intuition. The term "being" is the proper term to express this intuition, though naturally we cannot convey in this poor word, nor in the most ingenious constructions of the art of language, all the riches contained in this intuition. It would take all the metaphysics hitherto elaborated or to be elaborated hereafter in its entire future development to know all the riches implicit in the concept of being. It is in uttering with the real a mental word in its own bosom that the intellect immediately attains being as being, the object of the metaphysician.

There we are then, confronted with things—and as we confront them, as we confront the diverse realities known by our senses or by the different sciences, we have at a certain moment the revelation, as it were, of an intelligible mystery hidden in them. And sometimes this revelation, this sort of intellectual shock occurs in those who are not metaphysicians—it is not reserved to metaphysicians. There is a kind of sudden intuition which a soul can receive of its own existence or of the being inviscerated in all things whatsoever, even the most humble. It may even happen that in the case of a particular soul this intellectual perception may present itself under the guise of a mystical grace. I have quoted elsewhere (*The Degrees of Knowledge* [new translation, 1959], p. 270) a personal experience communicated to me: ". . . it often happened that by a sudden intuition I experienced the reality of my own being, of the deepest, first principle that placed me outside nothingness. It was a powerful intuition and its violence often frightened me; that intuition gave me, for the first time, knowledge of a metaphysical absolute."

A similar intuition is described in the autobiography of Jean-Paul Richter. "One morning, while I was still a child, I was standing on the threshold of my house and looked to the left, towards the woodshed, when suddenly this idea came to me out of the sky like a bolt from the blue: *I am an I* and from that moment it never left me; my ego had seen itself for the first time and for ever."

Thus there are, as it were, kinds of metaphysical intuitions which reveal naturally to a soul, with the decisive, imperious, dominating character of a "substantial word" uttered by the real, that intelligible treasure, that unforgettable trans-objectivity which is either its own consistency, the *I* in it, the *I* that it is, *or* being—its own being or the being discerned in things. It is clear that the intuition of which we are speaking does not necessarily have this appearance of a kind of mystical grace, but it is always, so to speak, a gift made to the intellect, and beyond question it is indispensable in one form or another to every metaphysician. But we must also observe that if it is indispensable to every metaphysician, still it is not given to everyone, nor to all those who philosophize, nor even to all philosophers who desire to be or consider themselves to be metaphysicians: Kant never had it. And why is this so? Because it is difficult, though not in the same way as an operation which would be hard to perform and whose successful performance would require expert skill, for there is nothing simpler (it is precisely because he sought it by technique, and by an intellectual technique of extreme subtlety, that Kant missed it). And it is as true to say that this intuition produces itself within us, through the medium of the vital activity (I mean vitally receptive and contemplative) of our intellect, as to say that we produce it. It is difficult, inasmuch as it is difficult to attain to the degree of intellectual purification at which this act is produced in us, at which we have become sufficiently available, sufficiently empty to *hear* what all things murmur and to *listen* instead of fabricating answers.

It is necessary to attain a certain level of intellectual spirituality, a level where the impact of the intellect against the real, or rather (for this metaphor is much too brutal), where an active and attentive silence of the intellect then causes to surge up, so to speak, from the things received into us through the intermediary of the senses and whose *species impressa* is buried in the depths of the intellect—a level, I say, where this *meeting* of the intellect and the real, this great good fortune causes to surge up from things, in a mental word, another life, a living content which is a world of trans-objective presence and intelligibility. There it is—this other life, this world of trans-objective presence and intelligibility—within us, confronting us, as an object of knowledge, living with the immaterial life and burning translucence of intellectuality in act.

II CONCRETE APPROACHES TO THIS INTUITION

4. It is worth remarking now that there are concrete approaches which prepare for such an intuition and lead up to it. They are different paths which, it is important to observe, are all radically insufficient if one stops with them, but which can be useful to particular individuals if one transcends them, useful on condition that one goes further. I will mention three examples. The first one is the Bergsonian experience of duration. Within limits it is a genuine experience.

Duration appears in such an instance as the lived movement wherein, at a level deeper than that of consciousness, our psychic states fuse in a potential manifold which is, notwithstanding, a unity, and in which we perceive that we are advancing in time, that we are enduring through change indivisibly and yet in a manner that enriches us qualitatively and triumphs over the inertia of matter. We have here a psychological experience which is not yet the metaphysical intuition of being, but which could have led to this intuition, for, enveloped in this psychological duration, implicitly given there, is existence, the irreducible value of *esse;* it is therefore a path, an approach, to the perception of existence. But existence is not yet disengaged apart, in its own intelligible form.

5. Similarly the German philosopher Heidegger assures us that no one can be a metaphysician without first passing through the experience of anguish, this word "anguish" being given a scope not only psychological but as metaphysical as possible. It is the suddenly keen and lacerating feeling of all that there is of the precarious and threatened in our existence, in human existence; and, at the same stroke, this existence divests itself of its banality,

acquires a unique value, *its* unique value—confronts us as something saved from nothingness, snatched from nonentity. Yes, this kind of dramatic experience of nothingness may serve as an introduction to the intuition of being, provided it is taken as no more than an introduction.

6. My third example does not relate to an already fully worked out doctrine, but rather to directions suggested in preliminary sketches or in conversation. Hence I must speak of it with all due reserve and without committing the author to my interpretation. It seems that Gabriel Marcel would seek one of the paths of approach to metaphysical being in the deepening of the sense of certain moral realities such as fidelity. Just as Heidegger attaches himself to a lived experience, to something psychological like anguish, but while taking care to warn us that it is not at all a question of psychology, so the notion of fidelity is here understood in a sense which must or ought to transcend ethics and convey to us a strictly metaphysical value and content. We may observe that all the consistency, *steadfastness,* firmness, and victory over disintegration and oblivion contained in this virtue and suggested by the word "fidelity" are strictly dependent upon a certain *steadfastness* in reality itself in virtue of which I dominate the flux of my own life and possess my metaphysical consistence. So that, in the direction of thought pursued by Gabriel Marcel, we would arrive, if I understand him correctly, at the view that a philosophy of life in which the *I* would be confused with the flux of my life would be incompatible with the experience of fidelity; the experience, the irreducible reality of what I experience and know as fidelity would be pregnant with an ontological realism.

These Approaches Are Useful only if We Take the Decisive Step

7. You see by these three examples that we have to do in them with so many concrete approaches to being. The first of these experiences, that of duration, is more of the speculative order, at once psychological and biological. The two others are more of the practical and moral order, the psychological factor being invested

in the ethical. Well, if we stop here, we have not, I maintain, as yet crossed the threshold of metaphysics. Philosophical approaches of this kind are certainly not to be despised or refused. They can be of immense service in directing towards being many minds immobilized by idealist prejudices or repelled by a text-book pseudo-Scholasticism. They can prepare these minds to recover the sense of being. But they can do this only if one travels further—only if one crosses the threshold, takes the decisive step. Otherwise, whatever one does, one shall remain in the psychological and the ethical, which he will then work up, distend, enlarge, or attenuate to make them mimic metaphysics. One will then have, not genuine metaphysics, but a substitute which may certainly possess a very considerable philosophic interest, yet which is never anything but a substitute just the same. The most that one can obtain along these lines are solutions by an indirect route or by extrinsic delimitations, not the proper solutions demanded by a science worthy of the name, by philosophic knowledge. Even if the psychological and the ethical enrich their own speech with metaphysical echoes or undertones, these will be but echoes.

And what is especially dangerous in all these ways of approaching being is that one runs the risk of remaining imprisoned in one or the other of the concrete analogues of being, the one that he will have chosen as path of approach. The experience in question gives information only of itself. This is indeed the drawback of pure experience in philosophy and the stumbling block of every metaphysics which wishes to be experimental. The experience, though valid for the particular domain in which the intuition in question has arisen, cannot be extended to a vaster intelligible domain and cannot take on an explanatory value, except in an arbitrary manner.

On the other hand, as I have just said, such experiences have the advantage of bringing us to the threshold in question; it is then up to us to cross this threshold, to take the decisive step. We must let fall the veils—too heavy with matter and too opaque—of the psychological and moral concrete, so as to discover in their purity the properly metaphysical values which such experiences concealed. And then we have but one word at our disposal to

express that which reveals itself to us, namely, the word "being."
Let us have the courage to require our intellect, acting as intellect, to look in the face the reality designated by this term. It is a
question here of something primordial, at once very simple and
very rich and, if you will, ineffable, in the sense that it is that
whose perception is the most difficult to describe because it is
what is most immediate. We are here at the very root, at last laid
bare, of the whole intellectual life. You may say, if you please,
for I am here attempting to employ a purely descriptive termi-
nology anterior to the formation of a philosophic vocabulary, that
what I then perceive is, as it were, a pure activity, a consistency,
but a consistency superior to the whole order of the imaginable,
a living tenacity, at once precarious—it is nothing for me to crush
a fly—and indomitable—within and around me there is growth
without ceasing. By this consistency, this tenacity, things come
up against me, overcome possible disaster, endure and possess
in themselves whatever is requisite for this. These are metaphors,
lamentably inadequate, which attempt to express not so much
what my intellect sees, which is supra-empirical, as my experience of this vision, and which do not themselves enter the domain
of metaphysics, but which may perhaps make us aware that to
the word "being," when it expresses a genuine metaphysical
intuition, there must correspond a primary and original datum,
by nature above the scope of observation.

So true is it that the words "being," "existence," are pregnant
with a metaphysical content which transcends observation, that,
in order to free us from it, empiricists consistent with themselves
are led to suggest abandoning the term "existence." It is a bold
though impossible solution, perfectly consistent, as I say, with the
principles of empiricism, inasmuch as they demand the formation
of a philosophic vocabulary completely divested of all ontological
reference. In the *Revue de Métaphysique et de Morale*, April-
June, 1931, I read an article by Madame Christine Ladd-Franklin, entitled *La Non-Existence de l'Existence*, which proposes, in
order to meet the demands of a scientific method devoid of any
ontology (in reality, of a purely empiricist metaphysics), to replace the word "existence" by the phrase "*occurrence* in such
and such a province of thought."

And this metaphysical content of which we are speaking covers the whole domain of intelligibility and reality. It is a question of a gift bestowed upon the intellect in an intuition which infinitely exceeds, I do not say in the intensity of the experience but in intelligible value, the experiences which may have led up to it.

III CONFIRMATORY RATIONAL ANALYSIS

8. I have spoken briefly of the intuition of being and of the paths which can lead up to its threshold. I must add that it is both possible and necessary to show analytically that one has to come to this point. Quite another thing now from the concrete approaches to being of which we have spoken! It is a question now of a rational analysis establishing the necessity of being as being, *ens in quantum ens*, as the supreme object of our knowledge. What such a demonstrative analysis presupposes, either as naturally admitted or as confirmed scientifically by the critique of knowledge, is in a general way what one can call the objective, or, rather, transobjective value of the intellect and of knowledge: to wit, a non-idealist position. It is then easy in the first place to show that it is only in appearance that we can dispense, as Madame Ladd-Franklin would have us do, with the concepts of being and existence, even when one says "occurrence" and attempts to show that it is necessary to replace the word "existence" by this more select term. The whole chain of concepts one employs to establish such a conclusion bears witness at each moment to the primacy of the notion of being. It is argued, for example, that philosophers who employ the term existence *are in error*, and that a sound scientific method *requires* that one brush aside ontological notions. But notice, being is still present—not always the word but the object which it signifies. And at every turn one will make use, without realizing, of this intelligible value of being which one claims to be getting rid of. Every attempt to eliminate the notion of being refutes itself.

In the second place it is easy to show, as Saint Thomas does in the first article of his *De Veritate*, that all our notions, all our concepts, are resolved in the notion of being. It is thus the first of all our concepts, of which all the others are determinations. Being is determined by differences which arise within, not outside, itself. It is therefore to being that we inevitably reascend as to the fountainhead. It is being which the intellect perceives first and before anything else. It is being which the metaphysical intellect must consequently disengage and know according to its distinctive mystery. On this point consult also the texts of the *Metaphysics** mentioned in my last lecture.

9. It is, however, important to observe that the intuition of which we were just speaking and the analysis with which we are at present concerned should accompany each other. Were one content with the intuition without the rational analysis, he would risk having an intuition not confirmed in reason, whose rational necessity would not be manifest. Were one content simply with the analysis—as one runs the risk of doing in pedagogical accounts —the analysis would indeed show that one must come to the intuition of being as being as the terminus of a necessary regressive movement, but it would not of itself furnish this intuition. It is the same here with the analysis as it was with the approaches of which we were speaking earlier. These approaches led concretely (*in via inventionis*) to the metaphysical intuition of being, but it still remained to cross the threshold to which they had led us. It is the same with the rational analysis, which leads us to the metaphysical intuition of being by logical necessity (and more *in via judicii*): it still leads us to a threshold which an intuitive perception alone enables us to cross, the perception of being. And then, let the mind once have such an intuition and it has it for ever.

Observe what an unforgettable event in the history of philosophy was Parmenides' discovery, very imperfect though it still was, of being as being. Plato calls him on this account the "father of philosophy" and in criticizing him accuses himself of parricide. Parmenides was, it would seem, the first Western philosopher to have had the perception, still very imperfect as I have said, of being as such. I say imperfect, for he does not seem to have disengaged it in its naked metaphysical value. He appears, as his theory of the sphere indicates, to have blocked the metaphysical

---

* Aristotle, *Met.*, IV, 1003a 21; St. Thomas, *In IV Met.*, ed. Cathala, §§ 530–533 [Editors].

intuition of being with a still physical perception of sensible reality and to have misunderstood or misinterpreted his intuition of being, at the inevitable moment when it was to pass for him into the sphere of philosophic conceptualization, by understanding it univocally—wherefore his monism.

You will also understand why the intuition of the principle of identity—every being is what it is, being is being—can possess such value for the metaphysician, can be the object of his enraptured contemplation. And yet common sense—and the whole world—makes use of this principle without looking it in the eye ("a cat is a cat," says common sense, and that is all there is to it). So that, if the philosopher comes along and enunciates the principle of identity in the presence of common sense, the latter will not *see* it for that, it will simply have the impression of hearing an insignificant banality, a tautology. The philosopher, on the other hand, when he enunciates the principle of identity enunciates it in keeping with the metaphysical intuition of being, and thus he sees in it the first fundamental law of reality itself—an astonishing law, because it proclaims *ex abrupto* the primal mystery of being, at once its consistency and abundance, a law which will manifest itself in things in an infinite number of ways and according to an infinite number of applications. It is in no way by reason of any sort of logistic process that the metaphysician sees and employs the principle of identity, so that it would be necessary according to this principle to reduce everything to pure identity, that is to say, to efface all the diversities and varieties of being. For it is with its mode of analogical realization that he apprehends this principle. At the same time that he apprehends being as being, being according to its pure intelligible type, he apprehends the essentially analogous value of the concept of being, which is implicitly multiple and is realized in different things in such fashion as to admit differences of essence between them, complete and vast differences. The principle of identity preserves the multiplicity and diversity of things. Far from reducing all things to identity, it is, as I was saying elsewhere, the guardian of universal multiplicity, the axiom of being's irreducible diversities. If each being is what it is, it is not what other beings are.

The Intuition of Being as Being Is an Eidetic Intuition

10. It follows that the metaphysical intuition of being is an abstractive intuition. But the word "abstraction" is an antique term rendered suspect to modern ears by the deformations of long use and by errors and misconceptions of every sort. Therefore instead of saying *abstraction* I propose that we say *eidetic* or *ideating visualization.* I maintain then that the metaphysical intuition of being is an *ideating* intuition, and this in a pre-eminent manner. How could it be otherwise for our human intelligence in its pure speculative exercise? This intuition is at the summit of eidetic intellectuality. What does this phrase eidetic visualization (*abstraction*) mean? It means that the intellect—by the very fact that it is spiritual—proportions its objects to itself, elevates them within itself to diverse degrees, increasingly pure, of spirituality and immateriality. It is within itself that the mind attains reality, stripped of its own existence outside the mind and disclosing, uttering in the mind a content, an intimacy, an intelligible sound or voice, which can possess only in the mind its conditions-of-existence one and universal, and intelligible in act. If being were the object of a concrete intuition like that of the external senses or of introspection, of an intuition centered upon a reality taken concretely in its singular existence, philosophy would have to choose, according as it gave this intuition a realist or an idealist value, between a pure ontological monism and a pure phenomenalist pluralism. If, however, being is, as I have said, analogous, and if the principle of identity is the axiom of reality's irreducible diversities, it is because extramental being is perceived in the mind, under the conditions of the eidetic existence which it receives there, and because the imperfect and relative unity that it has in the mind is broken up (as is also the case with the pure and simple unity of univocal objects of concept) when from its existence in the concept one passes to its real existence. The superior "ideativity" of the intuition of being as being is the very condition and guarantee of its correct metaphysical employment.

It is here that a great confusion separates the Scholastics and many modern philosophers of realist tendencies who seek to construct an "existential" philosophy and ontology. For many modern philosophers being is indeed the object of an intuition and of a decisive encounter,[1] but of an empirical intuition and a concrete encounter, which, however profound, mysterious, and secret one may suppose it to be, always remains of the same nature as those which internal psychological or moral experience can procure for us. It is a question in such a case of disclosing a singular reality or presence actually existing and acting—at any rate a reality which is not grasped by the intellect by means of eidetic visualization, in the transparence of an idea or concept—and of disclosing it with the help of a kind of affective and *lived* connaturality. It is so because of the idealist prejudice which prevents these philosophers from making a frank and deliberate use of eidetic intuition. They fail to see that they do employ it all the same and in spite of everything, but at its lowest degree and in mingling it with sensible and emotional factors; they fail to see that they thus seek the object of metaphysics at a level which is that of

1. In the study [*Position et approches du mystère ontologique* (*Le Monde cassé* [Paris, Desclée de Brouwer, 1933])—Editors] to which I referred above (page 8, note 1 [*Sept leçons* . . .]), Gabriel Marcel employs the term *recollection* (*recueillement*) and rejects the term *intuition*. An intuition of being, he writes, would be "incapable of taking its place in a collection, of being catalogued as an experience or *Erlebnis* of any sort, which on the contrary always presents this character of being able to be now integrated, now isolated, and, as it were, exposed to view. Hence any attempt to recall this intuition—to picture it to oneself, shall I say—cannot but be fruitless. In this sense, to speak of the intuition of being is to invite us to play on a muted piano. This intuition cannot be brought into the light of day, for the simple reason that it is not, in fact, possessed."

In my opinion this passage calls for the following comments:

(1) The metaphysical intuition of being cannot take its place in a collection or be catalogued as an experience or *Erlebnis* of any sort because it is more fundamental and•more immediate than all the rest and bears on a *primary* reality already present to our whole intellectual life.

(2) Nevertheless it is an intuition—not "an experience or *Erlebnis* of any sort," for it is supra-empirical—it is an eidetic intuition, an intellectual perception, the intuition *par excellence* of which our human intellect is capable at the summit of its intellectuality. And for that very reason, because of the interiority to oneself which is characteristic of spirituality, the intellect is able to return upon this direct intuition, an immediate return or reapprehension which is altogether different from a recalling or recreation of the past and by which this intuition is "possessed" in its own spiritual light and "exposed to view," brought out into the daylight of conscience, which it fills with its music. In this sense, to reject the metaphysical intuition of being precisely as intuition is indeed to invite us to play on a muted piano the fundamental harmonies of metaphysics.

(3) If a philosopher who has a profound sense of the ontological mystery

physical experience, or of experiences still more invested in the opacity of the senses.

Well, however much the various experiences of which I have been speaking may serve as paths to the metaphysical perception of being, they cannot of themselves constitute it. This perception, this intuition is of the most highly eidetic order, is purely intelligible, not empirical. This is why many think themselves metaphysicians and are in reality psychologists or moralists, and why, though striving to reach metaphysics, they mimic rather than attain the perception of which we are speaking.

Thomism, as I have already noted, merits the appellation of an existential philosophy, and this already in the speculative order, in what concerns the speculative part of philosophy. But if Thomist metaphysics is an existential philosophy, it is so by being and remaining a metaphysics, a wisdom whose procedure is intellectual and in strict accordance with the demands of the intellect and its distinctive intuitiveness.

is nevertheless persuaded that there can be no question here of an intuition as such, it is because idealist prepossessions keep him from addressing himself to intellect as such and from trusting to it to satisfy his search. It is impossible not to see in this attitude the effect of an unresolved prejudice against the objectivity of the intellect (conceived idealistically), by reason of which it is so to speak thanks to a detour making us pass by the proper paths of subjectivity (and therefore in the last analysis by way of the obscure apprehension of love) to the other side of that object we call being, that one will seek to make contact with the ontological mystery. But this object is not a screen, it is being itself. Love does not pass to the other side of it—it enters into it in its own way, as does intellect in its own way. There is only nothingness on the other side.

(4) Aristotle observed that metaphysics is too lofty to be possessed by us otherwise than by a precarious title. It is only in a precarious manner that the metaphysical intuition of being is "possessed" in that *prise de conscience* of which I spoke. For on the one hand, its object is *par excellence* inexhaustible, and presents itself to us as such; on the other hand, we are constantly forgetting ourselves, and this intuition, together with the *prise de conscience* which reduplicates it, far from being always in act becomes habitual. We actualize it when we will, but in a manner usually imperfect and without recapturing the original freshness, though it is also true that we can—and this indefinitely—render it more intense and more profound.

Let me add that the "assurance which underlies the whole development of thought, even discursive" of which Gabriel Marcel rightly speaks, relates, in fact, to the obscure perception of being by common sense, to the perception of what I have termed "vague being." It is only when the metaphysical intuition of being has occurred that this assurance depends on it also. It is then confirmed and strengthened, and rendered conscious of itself.

7

THE PRE-PHILOSOPHICAL
KNOWLEDGE OF GOD *

1. From Plato and Aristotle to St. Anselm and St. Thomas Aquinas, Descartes and Leibniz, philosophers offered proofs or demonstrations of God's existence, or, as Thomas Aquinas more modestly and accurately puts it, *ways* of making God's existence intellectually sure—all of them are highly conceptualized and rationalized, specifically *philosophical* ways of approach. Kant criticized the proof afforded by Descartes, the so-called ontological argument, and wrongly endeavored to reduce all other ways of demonstration to this particular one, so as to envelop them in the same condemnation.[1] This was a great mistake, for the five ways pointed out by Thomas Aquinas are totally independent of the ontological argument; they hold true before any criticism, and are unshakably valid in themselves.

Yet I do not intend to consider now these highly conceptualized and rationalized, specifically *philosophical* ways of approach. When St. Paul asserted: "What is known about God is clear to them [namely, to the Gentiles], for God Himself has made it clear, for since the creation of the world His invisible attributes —His everlasting power and divinity—are to be discerned and contemplated through His works,"[2] he was not only concerned with the scientifically elaborated or specifically philosophical ways of establishing God's existence, but also, and first of all, with the natural knowledge of God's existence to which the

° *Man's Approach to God* (Latrobe, Pennsylvania: The Archabbey Press, 1930), pp. 5–17.

1. Cf. J. Maritain, *The Dream of Descartes* (New York: Philosophical Library, 1944), Chapter IV.

2. Rom. I: 19–20.

vision of created things leads the reason of any man whatsoever, be he a philosopher or not. It is this natural knowledge of God's existence that I shall consider—a knowledge which is natural not only in the sense of rational or non-supernatural, but also in the sense of *naturally* or *pre*-philosophically acquired, or prior to any philosophical, scientifically rationalized elaboration.

In other words I submit that, before the human mind enters the sphere of perfectly formed and articulate knowledge, particularly the sphere of metaphysical knowledge, it is capable of a pre-philosophical knowledge which is *virtually metaphysical*. It is this pre-philosophical knowledge that I shall now try to outline, at least in a tentative way.[3]

2. What must be first of all stressed in this connection is, I think, the fact that, once a man is awakened to the reality of existence, once he has really perceived this tremendous fact, sometimes exhilarating, sometimes disgusting and maddening, namely: *I exist*, he is henceforth taken hold of by the intuition of Being and the implications it involves.

Precisely speaking, this prime intuition is both the intuition of *my* existence and of the existence of things; but first and foremost of the existence of things. When it takes place, I suddenly realize that a given entity, man, mountain, or tree, exists and exercises that sovereign activity *to be* in its own way, totally self-assertive and totally implacable, completely independent from *me*. And at the same time I realize that I also exist but as thrown back into my loneliness and frailty by such affirmation of existence in which I have positively no part, to which I am exactly as naught. So the prime intuition of Being is the intuition of the solidity and inexorability of existence; and, secondly, of the death and nothingness to which *my* existence is liable. And thirdly, in the same flash of intuition, which is but my *becoming aware* of the intelligible value of Being, I realize that the solid and inexorable existence perceived in anything whatsoever implies—I don't know yet in what way, perhaps in things themselves, per-

3. Cf. J. Maritain, "A New Approach to God," in *Our Emergent Civilization,* ed. Ruth Nanda Anshen (New York: Harper & Brothers, 1947); and *Approches de Dieu* (Paris: Alsatia, 1953); *Approaches to God* (New York: Harper & Brothers, 1954).

haps separately from them—some absolute, irrefragable existence, completely free from nothingness and death. These three intellective leaps—to actual existence as asserting itself independently from me; from this sheer objective existence to my own threatened existence; and from my existence spoiled with nothingness to absolute existence—are achieved within that same and unique intuition which philosophers would explain as the intuitive perception of the essentially analogical content of the first concept, the concept of Being.

Then—this is the second step—a quick, spontaneous reasoning, as natural as this intuition (and, as a matter of fact, more or less involved in it) immediately springs forth, as the necessary fruit of such primordial apperception and as enforced by and under its light. I see that my Being, *first*, is liable to death; and, second, that it depends on the totality of nature, on the universal whole whose part I am; and that Being-with-nothingness, as my own being is, implies, in order to be, Being-without-nothingness. It implies that absolute existence which I confusedly perceived as involved in my primordial intuition of existence. Now the universal whole, whose part I am, is Being-with-nothingness from the very fact that I am part of it; consequently it does not exist by itself. And thus, finally, since the universal whole does not exist by itself, there is another, separate, whole, another Being, transcendent and self-sufficient and unknown in itself and activating all beings, which is Being-without-nothingness, that is, Being by itself.

Thus the inner dynamism of the intuition of existence, or of the intelligible value of Being, causes me to see that absolute existence or Being-without-nothingness transcends the totality of nature, and compels me to face the existence of God.

This is not a new approach to God. It is the eternal approach of man's reason to God. What is new is the manner in which the modern mind has become aware of the simplicity and liberating power, the natural and somehow intuitive characteristics of this eternal approach. The science of the ancients was steeped in philosophy. Their scientific imagery was a pseudo-ontological imagery. Consequently there was a kind of continuum between their knowledge of the physical world and their knowledge of God. The latter appeared as the summit of the former, a summit which was to be climbed through the manifold paths of the causal connections at play in the sublunar world and the celestial spheres. The sense of Being that ruled their universal thought was for them a too usual atmosphere to be felt as a surprising gift. At the same time the natural intuition of existence was so strong in them that their proofs of God could take the form of the most conceptualized and rationalized scientific demonstrations, and be offered as an unrolling of logical necessities, without losing the inner energy of that intuition. Such logical machinery was quickened instinctively by the basic intuition of Being.

We are in a quite different position now. In order to solve the enigma of physical reality and to conquer the world of phenomena, our science has become a kind of Maya—a Maya which succeeds and makes us masters of nature. But the sense of Being is absent from it. Thus when we happen to experience the impact of Being upon the mind it appears to us as a kind of intellectual revelation, and we realize clearly both its liberating and its awakening power and the fact that it involves a knowledge which is separated from that sphere of knowledge peculiar to our science. At the same time we realize that the knowledge of God, before being developed into logical and perfectly conceptualized demonstrations, is first and foremost a natural fruit of the intuition of existence, and forces itself upon our mind in the imperative virtue of this intuition.

In other words, we have become aware of the fact that human reason's approach to God, in its primordial vitality, is neither a mere intuition, which would be suprahuman, nor is it that artlike philosophical reasoning by which it is expressed in its achieved form, each step of which is pregnant with involved issues and problems. Human reason's approach to God in its primordial vitality is a *natural* reasoning, that is, intuitive-like or irresistibly vitalized by, and maintained within, the intellectual flash of the intuition of existence. Then the intuition of existence, grasping in some existing reality Being-with-nothingness, makes the mind grasp by the same stroke the necessity of Being-without-nothingness. And nowhere is there any problem involved, because the illumining power of this intuition takes hold of the mind and obliges it to see. Thus it naturally proceeds, in a primary intuitive flash, from imperative certainty to imperative certainty. I believe that from Descartes to Kierkegaard, the effort of modern thought—to the extent that it has not completely repudiated metaphysics, and if it is cleansed of the irrationalism which has gradually corrupted it—tends to such an awareness of the specific *naturality* of man's knowledge of God, definitely deeper than any logical process scientifically developed. It tends to the awareness of man's spontaneous knowledge of God, and of the primordial and simple intuitivity in which it originates.

3. I have just tried to describe the way in which this *natural* pre-philosophical knowledge spontaneously proceeds. It implies a reasoning, but an intuitive-like reasoning, steeped in the primordial intuition of existence. I would say that this natural knowledge is a kind of *innocent* knowledge—I mean pure of any dialectics. Such knowledge involves certitude, cogent certitude, but in an imperfect logical state; it has not crossed the threshold of *scientific* demonstration, the certitude of which is critical and implies the logical overcoming of the difficulties involved; and by the same token such natural knowledge is blissfully ignorant of these difficulties, of all that burden of objections which St. Thomas puts at the beginning of his demonstrations. Because scientific certitude and objections to be met—and the answers to the objections—come into being together.

We see, then, that the philosophical proofs of the existence of God, say, the five ways of Thomas Aquinas, are a development and explication of this natural knowledge on the level of scientific discussion and scientific certitude. And they normally presuppose this natural knowledge, not as regards the logical structure of the demonstration, but as regards the existential condition of the thinking subject. Thus, if all the preceding observations are true, we should always—before offering the philosophical proofs, say, the classical five ways[4]—make sure that those we are addressing are awakened to the primordial intuition of existence and aware of the natural knowledge of God involved in it.

4. Cf. *Sum. theol.* I, q. 2, a. 3; R. Garrigou-Lagrange, *Dieu, son existence et sa nature*, 6e édition (Paris: Beauchesne, 1933); R. Garrigou-Lagrange, *Le Sens Commun, la Philosophie de l'être et les formules dogmatiques*, 4e édition (Paris: Desclée De Brouwer, 1936); and J. Maritain, *Approches de Dieu*.

8

GOD AND SCIENCE *

PRELIMINARY REMARKS

In the realm of culture, science now holds sway over human civilization. But at the same time science has, in the realm of the mind, entered a period of deep and fecund trouble and self-examination. Scientists have to face the problems of over-specialization, and a general condition of permanent crisis which stems from an extraordinarily fast swarming of discoveries and theoretical renewals, and perhaps from the very approach peculiar to modern science. They have, in general, got rid of the idea that it is up to science to organize human life and society and to supersede ethics and religion by providing men with the standards and values on which their destiny depends. Finally—and this is the point with which I am especially concerned in this essay—the cast of mind of scientists regarding religion and philosophy, as it appeared in the majority of them a century ago, has now profoundly changed.

There are, no doubt, atheists among scientists, as there are in any other category of people; but atheism is not regarded by them as required by science. The old notion of a basic opposition between science and religion is progressively passing away. No conflict between them is possible, Robert Millikan declared. In many scientists there is an urge either toward more or less vague religiosity or toward definite religious faith; and there is an urge, too, toward philosophical unification of knowledge. But the latter

---

* *On the Use of Philosophy* (Princeton: Princeton University Press, 1961), pp. 44–71.

urge still remains, more often than not, imbued with a kind of intellectual ambiguity.

No wonder, then, that the subject with which we are dealing— what is the relation of modern science to man's knowledge of God—demands a rather delicate, sometimes complicated analysis. In order to clear the ground, I shall begin with a few observations concerning the characteristic approach and way of knowledge peculiar to science as it has developed since post-Renaissance and post-Cartesian times and become in our day, through an effort of reflection upon its own procedures, more and more explicitly aware of itself.

I do not disregard the differences in nature which separate physics from other sciences, such as biology or anthropology, for instance. Yet physics is the queen of modern sciences, which, even when they cannot be perfectly mathematized, tend to re- semble physics to one degree or another. So it is that for the sake of brevity I shall, while speaking of modern science, have modern physics especially in view.

Modern science has progressively "freed" or separated itself from philosophy (more specifically from the philosophy of nature) thanks to mathematics—that is to say by becoming a particular type of knowledge whose data are facts drawn by our senses or instruments from the world of nature, but whose intelligibility is mathematical intelligibility. As a result, the primary character- istic of the approach to reality peculiar to science may therefore be described in the following way: that which can be observed and measured, and the ways through which observation and measurement are to be achieved, and the more or less unified mathematical reconstruction of such data—these things alone have a meaning for the scientist as such.

The field of knowledge particular to science is therefore limited to experience (as Kant understood the word). And when the basic notions that science uses derive from concepts traditionally used by common sense and philosophy, such as the notions of nature, matter, or causality, these basic notions are recast and restricted by science, so as to apply only to the field of experience and observable phenomena, understood and expressed in a cer- tain set of mathematical signs. Thus it is that physicists may construct the concept of antimatter, for example, which has a meaning for them, but not for the layman or for the philosopher.

The expression "science of phenomena" is currently employed to designate our modern sciences. Such an expression is valid only if we realize, on the one hand, that the phenomena in question are (especially as far as physics is concerned) mathematized phenomena, and, on the other hand, that they are not an object separate from but an aspect of that reality *in se* which is Nature. Let us say that science is a genuine, though oblique, knowledge of nature; it attains reality, but in its phenomenal aspect (in other words, in the aspect of reality which is definable through observation and measurement), and by the instrumentality of entities, especially mathematical entities, which may be "real" and relate to what Aristotelian realism called "quantity" as an accident of material substance, or may be purely ideal entities (*entia rationis*) and mere symbols grounded on data of observation and measurement.

Such ideal entities are the price paid for a tremendous privilege, namely the mathematical reconstruction of the data of experience. I observed a moment ago that modern science has, thanks to mathematics, freed itself from philosophy. At first mathematics were used by the sciences of nature in the framework of sense experience only. It has happened, however, that for more than a century mathematics themselves, starting with non-Euclidian geometries, have been breaking loose, more definitely and more completely than before, from the world of experience, and insisting on the possibility of developing—in the realm of merely logical or ideal being (*ens rationis*)—an infinite multiplicity of demonstrably consistent systems based on freely chosen and utterly opposed "axioms" or postulates. Consequently the science of phenomena (particularly physics) became able to pick out among various possible mathematical languages or conceptualizations, which make sense only to the mathematician, and deal with entities existing only within the mind, the one most appropriate to a given set of phenomena (while other sets of phenomena may be made mathematically intelligible through quite another conceptualization). So it is that from the point of view of common sense everything in the world capsizes in the highest and most comprehensive theories of contemporary physics as in Chagall's pictures. Modern science of phenomena has its feet on earth and uses its hands to gather not only correctly observed and measured facts, but also a great many notions and explanations which offer our minds real entities; yet it has its head in a mathematical heaven, populated with various crowds of signs and merely ideal, even not intuitively thinkable entities.

These ideal entities constructed by the mind are symbols which enable science to manipulate the world, while knowing it as unknown, for then, in those higher regions where creative imagination is more at work than classical induction, science is intent only on translating the multifarious observable aspects of the world into coherent systems of signs.

The fact remains that the prime incentive of the scientist is the urge to know reality. Belief in the existence of the mysterious reality of the universe precedes scientific inquiry in the scientist's mind, and a longing (possibly more or less repressed) to attain this reality in its inner depths is naturally latent in him.

But as a scientist his knowledge is limited to a mathematical (or quasimathematical) understanding and reconstruction of the observable and measurable aspects of nature taken in their inexhaustible detail.

"EXCLUSIVE" SCIENTISTS AND "LIBERAL" SCIENTISTS

A distinction must be made between two categories of scientists, whom I would like to call, on the one hand, exclusive scientists, and, on the other hand, liberal scientists. This distinction has nothing to do with science itself, for in both categories men endowed with the highest scientific capacities can be found; but it is quite important from the point of view of culture.

"Exclusive" scientists are systematically convinced that science is the only kind of genuine rational knowledge of which man is capable. For them nothing can be known to human reason except through the means and intellectual equipment of science. Exclusive scientists may be of positivist persuasion, and consequently reject any religious belief, save perhaps some kind of mythically constructed atheistic religion, like Auguste Comte's religion of humanity, which its high priest conceived of as a "positive regeneration of fetishism," or like Julian Huxley's "religion without revelation," which mistakes itself for a product of the "scientific method." Or they may shun positivist prohibitions, and superadd to scientific knowledge a genuine, even deep religious faith, but which supposedly belongs to the world of feeling and pure irrationality. In no case is it possible, in their eyes, to establish the existence of God with rational certainty.

To tell the truth, the assertion that there is no valid rational knowledge except that of observable and measurable phenomena is self-destructive (it itself is quite another thing than a mere expression of inter-related phenomena). No wonder, consequently, that in contradistinction to exclusive scientists, "liberal" scientists are ready to look for a rational grasping of things which passes beyond phenomena, and even (when they are perfectly liberal scientists—I think for instance of an eminent chemist like Sir Hugh Taylor, or an eminent physicist like Léon Brillouin) to admit the necessity of philosophy and of a properly philosophical equipment in order to make such grasping feasible, and so to complement the knowledge of nature provided by the sciences.

Nothing is more rational than the kind of extension of Niels Bohr's "principle of complementarity" implied by the cast of mind of these scientists. For, thus extended, this principle means simply that in two different fields of knowledge, or at two specifically distinct levels in our approach to reality, two different aspects in existing things (the phenomenal and the ontological aspect) call for two different explanations (for instance "Man's cerebral activity is stimulated by such or such chemical" and "Man has a spiritual soul")—which are moreover perfectly compatible, since they have to do with two essentially diverse objects to be grasped in things (so the medical approach to a person as a patient and the aesthetic approach to the same person as a poet are both distinct and compatible).

Einstein belonged to the category of liberal scientists. For many years his notion of God was akin to that of Spinoza. Yet, as recent studies have shown, he came, with the progress of age and reflection, to consider the existence of that personal God whom he first doubted as required by the way in which nature lends itself to the rationalization of phenomena operated by science. As he said in an interview in 1950, far from being an atheist he "believed on the contrary in a personal God."[1] Such a conviction meant in no way that the existence of God was supposedly a conclusion established by science, or a principle of explanation used by it. It meant that the existence of God is a conclusion philosophically established with regard to the very possibility of science.

Heisenberg[2] and Oppenheimer[3] are also liberal scientists. So was, at least virtually, Max Planck, though it was under the cloak of science that every bit of philosophizing effort in him was concealed.[4] He believed in an "all-powerful intelligence which governs the universe," but not in a personal God, and he thought that we could and should "identify with each other . . . the order of the universe which is implied by the sciences of nature and the God whom religion holds to exist." Such statements definitely transcend the field of experience and measurable data, though they remain inherently ambiguous: for how could an all-powerful reason govern the universe if it were not personal? The God whom religion holds to exist is a transcendent God, who causes the order of the universe but his philosophical "identification" with this order would make him consubstantial with the world, as the God of the Stoics was.

Such intellectual ambiguity is not infrequent. I have already mentioned the fact. Let us consider it now a little more closely. I would say that the ambiguity in question is essential in exclusive scientists, so far as they take a step outside science itself. They emphatically deny the validity of any kind of rational knowledge of reality which is not science itself. As a result, if they are not of positivist persuasion, and do not think that all we can know

1. Cf. Karlheinz Schauder, "Weltbild und Religion bei Albert Einstein," in *Frankfurter Hefte*, June 1959, p. 426.
2. Cf. Werner Heisenberg, *Physics and Philosophy* (New York: Harper & Brothers, 1958).
3. Cf. Robert Oppenheimer, "The Mystery of Matter," in *Adventures of the Mind* (New York: Alfred A. Knopf, 1959).
4. André George, *Autobiographie scientifique de Max Planck* (Paris: Albin Michel, 1960), pp. 14, 122, 215, 217.

is phenomena alone, in other words, if, recognizing that phenomena are but an aspect of a deeper reality, they endeavor to go beyond phenomena, they do so through an extrapolation of scientific notions which, brilliant as it may be, is essentially arbitrary; or, looking for a "noetic integrator," they borrow it from some kind of metaphysics unaware of itself and disguised as science—and there is no worse metaphysics than disguised metaphysics.

As regards liberal scientists the picture is basically different. I would say that the ambiguity we are discussing can still most often be found in them, but as something accidental, not essential to their cast of mind; so that, as a matter of fact, there are good grounds to hope that more and more of them will, in the process of time, free themselves from it—when philosophers will become more intent on meditating on the sciences and learning their languages, and scientists more familiar with the approach and language of philosophy (each one realizing at the same time that the language or languages of the others are valid instruments only for the others' work).

If a liberal scientist undertakes to go beyond the horizons of science and tackle the philosophical aspects of reality, he too is liable to yield to the temptation of making the concepts worked out by science into the very components of his meta-scientific enterprise. The trouble is that one can no more philosophize with non-philosophical instruments than paint with a flute or a piano.

But such a state of affairs is only a side-effect of the fact that scientists, however liberal, are prone, as everyone is, to overvalue the intellectual equipment they have tested in their particular field, and in the handling of which they have full competence. Liberal scientists do not, for all that, systematically deny the validity of another, perhaps more appropriate, intellectual equipment; they are aware, moreover, of the philosophical nature of their own effort of reflection upon science and its procedures; and by the very fact they are, at least implicitly, prepared to recognize the rights of that purely or genuinely philosophical approach in which they still often hesitate to put their own trust. That is why the ambiguity of the way in which many of them go in for philosophy is accidental ambiguity.

Furthermore, being accidental, such ambiguity can be removed; the best proof of this is the fact that in actual existence it has been most explicitly removed in some scientists who, when it comes to philosophical matters, do not mind using the strict philosophical approach. At this point I am thinking in particular of the Epilogue which the distinguished physiologist Andrew Ivy wrote for the book "The Evidence of God," in which he insists that God's existence can be rationally demonstrated with absolute certainty.[5] Though a professional philosopher would probably have added a few considerations on knowledge through analogy and the non-restricted value of the notion of cause, these pages written by a scientist are, as they stand, a remarkable piece of philosophy, which enters with perfect intellectual frankness and with the appropriate intellectual equipment a sphere inaccessible to the instruments of science, and which gives to a truth intuitively known to the intellect like the principle of causality its full ontological bearing, so as to recognize the necessity of a Prime Cause that absolutely transcends the whole field of experience.

The Crucial Question

The crucial question for our age of culture is, thus, whether reality can be approached and known, not only "phenomenally" by science, but also "ontologically" by philosophy.

This question is still more crucial for the common man than for the scientist. For the impact of the habits of thinking prevalent in an industrial civilization, in which manipulation of the world through science and technique plays the chief part, results in a loss of the sense of being in the minds of a large number of people, who are not scientists but grant rational value to facts and figures only. Whereas exclusive scientists know at least what science is and what its limitations are, the people of whom I am speaking have no experience of science, and they believe all the

5. Cf. *The Evidence of God in an Expanding Universe,* edited by J. G. Monsma, by forty American scientists, with an Epilogue by Dr. Andrew Ivy (New York: Putnam, 1958).

more naïvely that science is the only valid rational approach to
reality, nay more, that science has all the rational answers which
human life can need.

Consequently, any rational knowledge of God's existence—
either prephilosophical (by the simple natural use of reason)
or philosophical (by the use of reason trained in philosophical
disciplines)—is a dead letter as far as they are concerned.

Persons whose intellect has shrunk in this way may adhere to
some religious creed and have a religious belief in God—either
as a gift of divine grace, or as a response to irrational needs, or
as a result of their adjustment to a given environment. But
they are atheists as far as reason is concerned. Such a situation is
utterly abnormal. Religious faith is above reason, but normally
presupposes the rational conviction of God's existence.

At this point we must lay stress on the nature of philosophy
as contradistinguished from science, and insist that philosophy
is an autonomous discipline, which has its own instruments; so
that it is not enough to add to scientific knowledge even a most
intelligent philosophical reflection; the proper philosophical
training and proper philosophical equipment are necessary.

Let us say that whereas science, or phenomenal knowledge,
offers us, with wonderful richness paid for by revolutionary
changes, coded maps of what matter and nature are as to the
multifarious observable and measurable interactions which occur
in them, philosophy makes us grasp, with greater stability paid
for by limitation to essentials, what things are in the intrinsic
reality of their being. Though carrying common sense and the
natural language to an essentially higher level, philosophy is in
continuity with them, and is based on the perceptive (not only
constructive) power of the intellect as well as on sense experience. In other words, being is the primary object of philosophy,
as it is of human reason; and all notions worked out by philosophy are intelligible in terms of being, not of observation and
measurement.

As a result, we have to realize that in the very universe of experience philosophy (the philosophy of nature) deals with aspects
and explanations in which science is not interested. Thus matter
(that is, material substances) is composed, in the eyes of old but

still valid Aristotelian hylomorphism, of two elements: pure and indetermined potentiality (*materia prima*), and determinative form or entelechy (which, in man, is spiritual soul); whereas for science matter (or mass, that is, a given set of measurable data expressed in mathematical equations) is composed of certain particles, most of them impermanent, scrutinized by nuclear physics. It is up to philosophy to try to bring into some sort of unity our knowledge of nature, not by making science's explanations parts of its own explanations, but by interpreting them in its own light. In order to do so, it will have, in the first place, to enlighten us about *the procedure of science itself*, which constructs both ideal or symbolical entities *founded on actual measurement*, and complex notions where reality phenomenally grasped mingles inextricably with these merely ideal entities. In the second place, philosophy will have to determine what kind of *ontological foundation* may be assigned to such or such of these notions, or sets of notions, peculiar to science. In the third place, philosophy will have to point out—and to improve and re-adjust, each time this is needed—*the truths of its own* which have some connection with scientific theories, and especially with all the treasure of facts and factual assertions which is mustered and continually increased by science.

Being, furthermore, is not limited to the field of sense experience; it goes beyond. And the basic concepts of reason which deal with being as such, even though they apply first to the realm of experience, can apply too—in an "analogical" manner—to realities which transcend experience. As a result philosophy (this time I do not mean the philosophy of nature, I mean metaphysics) can attain to realities which escape sense experience and sense verification, in other words which belong to the spiritual or "supra-sensible" order.[6]

Let us remember at this point that philosophy is but a superior stage in the natural use of reason, at the level of a knowledge which is not only knowledge but wisdom, and which (in contra-

6. Cf. J. Maritain, *The Degrees of Knowledge*, new translation (New York: Charles Scribner's Sons, 1959); and *Approaches to God* (New York: Harper, 1954).

distinction to common sense) is critically elaborated and completely articulated. Prior to philosophy, the natural use of reason is natural in an additional sense (in the sense of untrained and merely spontaneous); with philosophy it is perfected by reflectivity, fully mature, and capable of explicit demonstration, aware of its own validity.

It is by virtue of the very nature of human reason—either untrained or philosophically perfected—that the concept of cause and the principle of causality can lead us beyond the field of experience. As Dr. Ivy has rightly pointed out,[7] if the child uses the principle of causality in asking why things exist, he does so not by reason of the transitory peculiarities of "childish mentality," but, on the contrary, because he is awakening to genuine intellecual life.

There is, thus, a pre-philosophical, simply natural knowledge of God's existence. It can be described as starting from the primordial intuition of existence, and immediately perceiving that Being-with-nothingness, or things which could possibly not be— my own being, which is liable to death—necessarily presuppose Being-without-nothingness, that is, absolute or self-subsisting Being, which causes and activates all beings. This pre-philosophical knowledge can also be described as a spontaneous application of the principle: no artifact is possible without a maker.

And there is, in the realm of metaphysical wisdom, a philosophical knowledge of God's existence, which is able fully to justify itself and uses ways of arguing that proceed with full rational rigor.

THE PHILOSOPHICAL PROOFS OF GOD'S EXISTENCE

The "five ways" of Thomas Aquinas are the classical example of the philosophical approach to God of which I just spoke. It seems relevant to give at this point some idea of them, at least of the first and the last two.

The first way proceeds from Motion or Change. There is no fact more obvious here below than the fact of change, through

7. Cf. supra, n. 5.

which a thing becomes what it was not. But no thing can give to itself what it does not have, at least in potency, and potency cannot pass to actuation by itself alone. Everywhere where there is motion or change (even if it is self-motion as in living beings), there is something else which is causing the change. Now if the cause in question is itself subject to change, then it is moved or activated by another agent. But it is impossible to regress from agent to agent without end: if there were not a First Agent, the reason for the action of all others would never be posited in existence. So it is necessary to stop at a Prime Cause, itself uncaused, absolutely exempt from any change for it is absolutely perfect.

In the same manner the second way, which proceeds from Efficient Causes at work in the world, and the third way, which proceeds from Contingency and Necessity in things, lead to a Prime Cause without which all other causes would neither be nor act, and which exists with absolute necessity, in the infinite transcendence of the very *esse* subsisting by itself.

The fourth way proceeds from the Degrees which are in things. It is a fact that there are degrees of value or perfection in things. But, on the one hand, wherever there are degrees it is necessary that there exist, somewhere, a supreme degree; and on the other hand one thing is good and another is better, but there can always be another still better, so that there is no supreme degree in the possible degrees of goodness, or beauty, or finally being, of which things are capable. Goodness, beauty, being are not in their fulness in any one of the things we touch and see. The supreme degree of goodness, of beauty, of being, exists *elsewhere*, in a Prime Being which causes all that there is of goodness, beauty, and being in things, a First Cause which does not *have* goodness, beauty, and being, but *is* self-subsisting Being, Goodness, and Beauty.

The fifth way proceeds from the intrinsic Order and purposeful Governance of the world. The very fact that in the material universe things are engaged in a system of stable relations and that a certain order among them exists and endures shows that they do not result from chance. A purpose is at work in that republic of natures which is the world. But such purpose cannot proceed from the things which compose the world of matter, and which are devoid of understanding. This purpose or intention must exist in an intellect on which things depend in their very essence and natural activities. Thus in the last analysis it is necessary to recognize the existence of a transcendent Intelligence, the existing of which is its very intellection, and which is the Prime Cause of all beings.

I have summarized these ways to God in my own language and in the briefest possible fashion, leaving aside all particular examples, accidental to the demonstration, which were part of the imagery provided to Thomas Aquinas by the physics of his time.

The ways in question pertain to the philosophical order. The notion of cause has here its full ontological import, which connotes productivity in being, in contradistinction to the mere relationships between phenomena which science considers and in which a given phenomenon is a dependent variable of another. Furthermore, we are led by rational argumentation to a Prime Cause which is absolutely and infinitely transcendent, and which the very concept of cause, like those of being, of goodness, of intelligence, etc., attains only "by analogy" or in the mirror of things: what all these concepts mean with respect to God is only similar to—but basically different from—what they mean with respect to things accessible to us; we don't grasp it *in itself*. God exists as no other being exists, He is good as no other being is good, He knows and loves as no other being does.

It must be noted that considered in their very substance the "five ways" of Thomas Aquinas stand fast against any criticism. Modern philosophy has been in this connection the victim of a tragic misunderstanding. Descartes believed that from the sole idea of an infinitely perfect being the existence of this being necessarily followed (the so-called "ontological argument"). Kant rightly stated that such "proof" was no proof at all. But he also stated—quite mistakenly—that all other proofs of God's existence implied the validity of the ontological argument and rested on it; as a result, no valid proof was possible. And Kant's successors followed on Kant's heels. Yet it is crystal clear that Thomas Aquinas' five ways do not start from the *idea* of an infinitely perfect being; they proceed in the opposite manner; they start from certain *facts*, quite general and quite undeniable; and from these facts they infer the necessary existence of a First Cause—which is infinitely perfect. Infinite perfection is at the end, not at the beginning of the demonstration.

Finally let us add that there are other ways, too, than the classical five ways. I myself have proposed a "sixth way." As a matter of fact there are for man as many ways of knowing that God exists as there are steps forward for him on the earth or paths to his own heart. For all our perishable treasures of being and beauty are besieged on all sides by the immensity and eternity of the One Who Is.

SCIENCES AS WITNESSING TO GOD'S EXISTENCE

Among all these approaches to God, one particularly significant for the man of our present civilization is provided by science itself. The sciences of phenomena—though they remain enclosed in the field of experience—bear testimony to the existence of God in a double manner. Here, as I previously noted, it is not a question of what science itself tells us, but of the very existence and possibility of science.

In the first place: if nature were not intelligible there would be no science. Nature is not perfectly and absolutely intelligible; and the sciences do not try to come to grips with nature's intelligibility taken in itself (that is the job of philosophy). They rather reach for it in an oblique fashion, dealing with it only insofar as it is steeped in, and masked by, the observable and measurable data of the world of experience, and can be translated into mathematical intelligibility. Yet the intelligibility of nature is the very ground of those relational constancies which are the "laws"— including that category of laws which deal only with probabilities—to which science sees phenomena submitted; and it is the very ground, in particular, of the highest explanatory systems, with all the symbols, ideal entities, and code languages they employ (and with all that in them which is still incomplete, arbitrary, and puzzlingly lacking in harmony) that science constructs on observation and measurement.

Now how would things be intelligible if they did not proceed from an intelligence? In the last analysis a Prime Intelligence must exist, which is itself Intellection and Intelligibility in pure act, and which is the first principle of the intelligibility and essences of things, and causes order to exist in them, as well as an infinitely complex network of regular relationships, whose fundamental mysterious unity our reason dreams of rediscovering in its own way.

Such an approach to God's existence is a variant of Thomas Aquinas' fifth way. Its impact was secretly present in Einstein's famous saying: "God does not play dice," which, no doubt, used the word God in a merely figurative sense, and meant only: "nature does not result from a throw of the dice," yet the very fact implicitly postulated the existence of the divine Intellect.

But science offers us a second philosophical approach, which, this time, relates to man's intellect. The sciences of phenomena, and the manner in which they contrive ways of knowing and mastering nature—ceaselessly inveigling it into more and more precise observations and measurements, and finally catching it in sets of more and more perfectly systematized signs—give evidence, in a particularly striking manner, of the power that human intelligence puts to work in the very universe of sense experience. Now the intelligence of man—imperfect as it is, and obliged to use an irreducible multiplicity of types and perspectives of knowledge—is a spiritual activity which can neither proceed from matter nor be self-subsisting, and therefore limitless and all-knowing. It has a higher source, of which it is a certain participation. In other words, it necessarily requires the existence of a Prime, transcendent, and absolutely perfect Intelligence, which is pure Intellection in act and whose being is its very Intellection.

This second approach is a variant of Thomas Aquinas' fourth way.

To conclude, let us remark that our knowledge of the created world naturally reverberates in the very reverence and awe with which our reason knows the Creator, and on the very notion, deficient as it is and will ever be, that we have of His ways.

By the very fact that science enlarges our horizons with respect to this world, and makes us know better—though in an oblique way—that created reality which is the mirror in which God's perfections are analogically known, science helps our minds to pay tribute to God's grandeur.

A number of the most basic notions and explanatory theories of modern science, especially of modern physics, recoil from being translated into natural language, or from being represented in terms of the imagination. Nevertheless a certain picture of the world emerges from modern science; and this picture (unification of matter and energy, physical indeterminism, a space-time continuum which implies that space and time are not empty preexisting forms but come to existence with things and through things; gravitational fields which by reason of the curvature of space exempt gravitation from requiring any particular force, and outwit ether and attraction; a cosmos of electrons and stars in which the stars are the heavenly laboratories of elements, a universe which is finite but whose limits cannot be attained, and which dynamically evolves toward higher forms of individuation and concentration) constitutes a kind of framework or imagery more suited to many positions of a sound philosophy of nature than that which was provided by Newtonian science.

Furthermore, at the core of this imagery there are a few fundamental concepts which, inherent in modern science and essential to it, have a direct impact on our philosophical view of nature.

In the first place I shall mention all the complex regularities (presupposed by statistical laws themselves), and the mixture of organization and chance, resulting in a kind of elusive, imperfectly knowable, and still more striking order, that matter reveals in the world of microphysics. It makes our idea of the order of nature exceedingly more refined and more astonishing. And it makes us look at the author of this order with still more admiration and natural reverence. In the Book of Job, Behemoth and Leviathan were called to witness to divine omnipotence. One single atom may be called to witness too, as well as the hippopotamus and the crocodile. If the heavens declare the glory of God, so does the world of micro-particles and micro-waves.

In the second place comes the notion of evolution: evolution of the whole universe of matter, and, in particular, evolution of living organisms. Like certain most general tenets of science, evolution is less a demonstrated conclusion than a kind of primary concept which has such power in making phenomena decipherable that once expressed it becomes almost impossible for the scientific mind to do without it. Now if it is true that in opposition to the immobile archetypes and ever-recurrent cycles of pagan antiquity, Christianity taught men to conceive history both as irreversible and as running in a definite direction, then it may be said that by integrating in science the dimension of time and history, the idea of evolution has given to our knowledge of nature a certain affinity with what the Christian view of things is on a quite different plane. In any case, the genesis of elements and the various phases of the history of the heavens, and, in the realm of life, the historical development of an immense diversity of evolutive branches ("phyla"), all this, if it is understood in the proper philosophical perspective, presupposes the transcendent God as the prime cause of evolution—preserving in existence created things and the impetus present in them, moving them from above so that superior forms may emerge from inferior ones, and, when man is to appear at the peak of the series of vertebrates, intervening in a special way and creating *ex nihilo* the spiritual and immortal soul of the first man and of every individual of the new species. Thus evolution correctly understood offers us a spectacle whose greatness and universality make the activating omnipresence of God only more tellingly sensed by our minds.

I do not believe, moreover, that science fosters a particularly optimistic view of nature. Every progress in evolution is dearly paid for: miscarried attempts, merciless struggle everywhere. The more detailed our knowledge of nature becomes, the more we see, together with the element of generosity and progression which radiates from being, the law of degradation, the powers of destruction and death, the implacable voracity which are also inherent in the world of matter. And when it comes to man, surrounded and invaded as he is by a host of warping forces, psychology and anthropology are but an account of the fact that, while being essentially superior to all of them, he is the most unfortunate of animals. So it is that when its vision of the world is enlightened by science, the intellect which religious faith perfects realizes still better that nature, however good in its own order, does not suffice, and that if the deepest hopes of mankind are not destined to turn to mockery, it is because a God-given energy better than nature is at work in us.

9

THE "SIXTH WAY"*

1. The views which I propose here are based neither on a fact observed in the world of sense experience, nor on the principle "One cannot rise to the infinite in the series of causes," nor does the argument proceed with the royal simplicity of the ways of Thomas Aquinas. It may, indeed, appear too subtle, and for a long time I regarded it as belonging to the domain of research hypotheses. I have, however, come to think that it constitutes a genuine proof, a rationally valid way leading to a firmly established certitude.

Here again** it is appropriate to distinguish two levels of approach—a *prephilosophic* level whereon certitude bathes in an intuitive experience, and a *scientific* or philosophical level whereon certitude emanates from a logically elaborated demonstration and from a rationally developed metaphysical justification.

We shall first take our stand on the prephilosophic level. Indeed it is the intuitive process that, in this case more than ever, matters first of all, although the intuition in question is of a much more peculiar sort than the primordial intuition of existing, and supposes experience of the proper life of the intellect. By feeling the impact of this intuitive experience, the mind discovers the approach to God which this experience brings along with it. Later it is led to formulate in logically conceptualized terms that which I call here a "sixth way."

The intuition of which I speak is related to the natural spirituality of intelligence. I shall try to describe it as it is in its primi-

---

* *Approaches to God* (New York: Harper & Brothers, 1954), pp. 72–83.
** See *ibid.*, pp. 1–11 [Editors].

tive and, so to speak, "wild" state, where it first begins to sprout. I am busy thinking. Everything in me is concentrated on a certain truth which has caught me up in its wake. This truth carries me off. All the rest is forgotten. Suddenly I come back to myself; a reflection is awakened in me which seems to me quite incongruous, altogether unreasonable, but whose evidence takes possession of me, in my very perception of my act of thought: *how is it possible that I was born?*

The activity of the mind develops in two quite different orders. It develops on the one hand in the order of the life which Aristotle called "life proportioned to man." Here the activity of the mind, as it happens in our train of ordinary social or occupational pursuits, is made up of a succession of operations immersed in time and which are for the most part operations of sense and imagination sustained and illuminated by the intellect.

On the other hand it develops in the order of the life which Aristotle called "life proportioned to the intellect." Here the activity of the mind, entirely withdrawn in thought, is centered above the sense and imagination, and is concerned with intelligible objects alone. It is when a man is thus engaged in an act of purely intellectual thought (to the extent that this is possible for a rational animal) that it happens that the intuition in question takes place: how is it possible that that which is thus in the process of thinking, in the act of intelligence, which is immersed in the fire of knowing and of intellectual grasp of what is, should once have been a pure nothing, once did not exist? Where I am now in the act of intellection and of consciousness of my thought, was there once *nothing?* That is impossible; it is not possible that at a certain moment what is now thinking was not at all, was a pure nothing. How could this have been born to existence?

I am not here faced with a logical contradiction. I am facing a *lived* contradiction, an incompatibility of fact (known *in actu exercito*). It is as if I were in a room and, without my having left for an instant, someone were to say to me that I just came in—I know that what he says is impossible.

Thus, I who am now in the act of thinking have always existed. This view imposes itself on me and does not seem strange to me unless I draw myself back from it in order to consider it from without. And perhaps I express it in a deficient way; we shall see about that later. For the moment I speak as I can, and I cannot speak otherwise.

Yet I know quite well that I was born. True, I know it by here-say, but I do know it with an absolute certainty, and besides, I remember my childhood. The certitude of having been born, common to all men, represses in us the blossoming forth—when the natural spirituality of intelligence is activated in us—of another certitude, that of the impossibility that our existence as thinking minds ever began or followed upon the nothingness of itself, and it prevents that other certitude from reaching our consciousness.

So here I am, in the grasp of two contrary certitudes. There is only one solution: I, who am thinking, have always existed, but not in myself or within the limits of my own personality—and not by an impersonal existence or life either (for without personality there is no thought, and there must have been thought there, since it is now in me); therefore I have always existed by a supra-personal existence or life. Where then? It must have been in a Being of transcendent personality, in whom all that there is of perfection in my thought and in all thought existed in a super-eminent manner, and who was, in His own infinite Self, before I was, and is, now while I am, more I than I myself, who is eternal, and from whom I, the self which is thinking now, proceeded one day into temporal existence. I had (but without being able to say "I") an eternal existence in God before receiving a temporal existence in my own nature and my own personality.

2. What shall we say now if we transport ourselves onto the level of rational demonstration? Is it possible to justify philo-sophically the intuitive experience which we have just tried to describe?

What is important to consider first is that the intellect is above time, *intellectus supra tempus:* because the intellect is spiritual, and time, the perseverance of movement in being, or the con-tinuity of perpetually vanishing existence proper to movement, is the proper duration of matter.

The operations of the human intellect are in time, and, indeed, subject to time, but in an extrinsic manner and only by reason of the materiality of the senses and the imagination to whose exercise they are bound. In themselves they are not subject to the flux of impermanence. They emerge above time. They exist in a duration which is a deficient imitation of eternity, a succession of fragments of eternity, for it is the perseverance in being of spiritual acts of intellection or of contemplative gaze. Thus this duration is composed of instants superior to time, each of which may correspond to a lapse of time more or less long, but is in itself without flow or movement or succession—a flash of permanent or nonsuccessive existence. Such is the proper duration of thought. Thought as such is not in time. The distinction between the *spiritual* and the *temporal* appears here in its primary sense. That which is spiritual is not subject to time. The proper place of the spiritual is above temporal existence.

We find a noteworthy indication of this in the fact that spiritual events are "metahistorical" events. Insofar as they are occurrences, they take place in history, but their content belongs in a region superior to history. This is why it is normal for history not to mention them. The word "event" itself is therefore ambiguous. "What happens," in the case of spiritual events, comes on the scene for an instant in temporal existence, but comes forever in the existence of souls and of thought.

But actions or operations emanate from a subject or from a person—*actiones sunt suppositorum*. And no operation is more personal than thought. Thought is exercised by a certain subject, a certain *self*, made of flesh and spirit.

This self exists in time and was born in time. But inasmuch as it exercises the spiritual operation of thought, inasmuch as it is the center of spiritual activity and capable of living or existing by the immaterial superexistence of the act of intellection, it is also superior to time, as is thought itself. It escapes the grasp of time.

This self began in time. But nothing begins absolutely. Everything which begins existed before itself in a certain way, to wit, in its causes. Insofar as it is material, the thinking self existed before itself in time, namely, in the ancestral cells, the physico-chemical materials and energies utilized by life all along the line from which the self has sprung. Whatever of it existed before it pre-existed in time.

But as spiritual, as exercising the spiritual operations of thought, as thinking, it could not have existed before itself in time, because mind can come only from a mind, thought can come only from a thought, and therefore from an existence superior to time.

Moreover, since thought is essentially personal, when it arises in time as the operation of such and such a subject born one day into temporal existence, it cannot come from an existence superior to time unless the self which exercises it now pre-existed in a certain way beyond time.

The self is born in time. But insofar as it is thinking it is not born of time. Its birth is supratemporal. It existed before itself in a first existence distinct from every temporal existence. It did not exist there in its proper nature (since it began to exist in its proper nature by being born in time), but everything that there is in it of being and of thought and of personality existed there better than in itself.

This, however, would not be possible unless everything that exists in temporal existence were a participation of the first existence in question. The latter then must contain all things in itself in an eminent mode and be itself—in an absolutely transcendent way—being, thought, and personality. This implies that that first existence is the infinite plenitude of being, separate by essence from all the diversity of existents. This means that it is not the act of existing of a thing which *has* existence, but the very act of existing itself, subsisting through itself. Thus we are necessarily led to the principle which no concept can circumscribe—Being in pure act, from which comes every being; Thought in pure act from which comes every thought; Self in pure act from which comes every self.

It is thus that the "sixth way" leads us to the existence of God. But it would remain incompletely elucidated if, after recognizing the existence of God, we should not ask ourselves how things exist in Him before being caused by Him in their own *esse*.[1]

---

1. Cf. *Sum. theol.*, I, 18, 4, corp. et ad 3.

Things pre-exist in God not in their proper natures but according as they are known to God, and, therefore, by that which renders them present to the divine intellect, that is to say by the divine essence itself, of which they are participations or likenesses, and which is itself the proper object of the divine intellect. In God they are the divine essence as revealing its participability. They live there, but without existing in themselves, by a life infinitely more perfect than the existence which they have in their proper natures. They live, in God who knows them, by the very life of God. They exist in the divine thought by the very existence of God which is His act of intellection.

This is true of thinking subjects, of *selves* endowed with intelligence, as it is of all other creatures. Before existing in themselves they exist eternally in God by the very existence of God, as participations or likenesses of the divine essence eternally known in that Essence. Therefore I can say that I, who am now in the act of thinking, always existed—I always existed in God. Care must be taken, however, to understand this proposition correctly. It does not mean that in God the human self has always exercised the act of thinking, or that in God it collaborates eternally in the act of divine thought. That makes no sense. In God the unique Self who thinks is the divine Self. The statement signifies rather that the creature which is now I, and which thinks, existed before itself eternally in God—not as exercising in Him the act of thinking, but as thought by Him. It bathed there in the light of God; it lived there by a suprapersonal (suprapersonal in relation to every created personality) and divinely personal life, by that life which is the eternal act of intellection of the divine Self itself, thinking itself.

Thinking subjects, *selves* capable of acting beyond time, which thus pre-exist in God, as do all those other participations of the Divine Essence which are created things—infinitely deficient in relation to their principle—are the most elevated of all things in the whole order of nature, because they are either purely spiritual creatures or creatures composed of matter and spirit, which, once they exist in their proper nature, resemble the divine Self in that they think and can be called, because of this, "images of God."

The reflections we have proposed in this chapter, as well as the intuitive experience which they presuppose, are entirely independent of any contact with Indian thought. It seems to us nevertheless that they can help to clarify in some way the meaning and the origin of the Hindu notion of the Self (Atman), and throw into relief at once the metaphysical truths to which this notion is related and the confusion which it has not succeeded in avoiding between the divine Self and the human self.

On the other hand the importance accorded to the expression *non-born* in many Hindu texts[2] seems to us to suggest a quite remarkable affinity with the intuition of which we have treated here, and to indicate that an intuition of the same type plays a characteristic role in the philosophic thought and the natural mysticism of India.

2. Cf. Louis Gardet, *Expériences mystiques en terres non-chrétiennes* (Paris: Alsatia, 1953), pp. 38–39. Let us take up in particular this passage of the *Katha Upanishad*: "The inspired, the Atman, is not born nor dies. It does not come from anywhere, and it does not become anyone. Not-born, permanent, constant, primordial, it is not destroyed when the body is destroyed." And this passage of the *Yoga-sutra*: "When thought is not dissolved and ceases dispersing itself, neither unstable, nor endowed with images, it becomes then the Brahman. Free, calm, having an inexpressible beatitude, a supreme happiness, not-born with an object of knowledge itself not-born, omniscient, behold how one defines it."

See also Olivier Lacombe, "Sur le Yoga Indien (Report of Ramana Maharshi)," *Etudes Carmélitaines*, October 1937, pp. 174–75; *La Doctrine Morale et Métaphysique de Râmânuja* (Paris: Adrien-Maisonneuve, 1938), pp. 63–68.

10

THE APPROACH OF THE PRACTICAL INTELLECT TO GOD *

1. *Poetic Experience and Creation in Beauty.* The diverse ways of which we have so far spoken are ways of the speculative intellect. The practical intellect also has its ways of approach towards God—which are not demonstrations at all but belong to an existential and prephilosophic order. I shall give here some brief indications concerning them.

There is first, in the line of artistic creation, what one might call the analogy of the approach to God in poetic experience, or the poetic knowledge of the mirrors of God.

The artist is held in the grip of a twofold absolute, which is not the Absolute, but which draws the soul toward it. The demands of that beauty which must pass into his work, and the demands of that poetry which incites him to create, claim him so entirely that, in a certain way, they cut him off from the rest of men.

Beauty is a transcendental, a perfection in things which transcends things and attests their kinship with the infinite, because it makes them fit to give joy to the spirit. It is a reflection in things of the Spirit from which they proceed, and it is a divine name: God is subsistent Beauty, and "the being of all things derives from the divine beauty."[1] Knowing this, we realize that it is impossible that the artist, devoted as he is to created beauty which is a mirror of God, should not tend at the same time—but by a more profound and more secret urge than all that he can know of himself—toward the principle of beauty.

---

* *Approaches to God* (New York: Harper & Brothers, 1954), pp. 84–108.
1. St. Thomas Aquinas, *Comm. in De Divinis Nominibus,* Chapter 4, lecture 5.

A celebrated passage of Baudelaire, inspired by Edgar Allan Poe, reveals in this connection its full import, the import of an unimpeachable testimony: ". . . it is this immortal instinct for the beautiful which makes us consider the earth and its various spectacles as a sketch of, as a *correspondence* with, heaven. The insatiable thirst for all that is beyond, and which life reveals, is the most living proof of our immortality. It is at once through poetry and *across* poetry, through and *across* music, that the soul glimpses the splendors situated beyond the grave; and when an exquisite poem brings tears to the eyes, these tears are not proof of an excess of joy, they are rather the testimony of an irritated melancholy, a demand of the nerves, of a nature exiled in the imperfect and desiring to take possession immediately, even on this earth, of a revealed paradise."[2]

Knowledge, not rational and conceptual, but affective and nostalgic, the knowledge through connaturality which the artist has of beauty in his creative experience, is *in itself* (I do not say for him or for his own consciousness) an advance toward God, a spiritual inclination in the direction of God, an obscure and ill-assured beginning of the knowledge of God—vulnerable, indeed, on all sides because it is not disengaged in the light of intelligence and because it remains without rational support.

Poetry is the prime and pure actuation of the free creativity of the spirit. Awakened in the unconscious of the spirit, at the root of all the powers of the soul, it reveals to the poet, in the obscure knowledge which is born of an intuitive emotion, both his own subjectivity and the secret meanings of things. "The poet completes the work of creation, he cooperates in divine balancings, he moves mysteries about."[3] Poetic experience is a brooding repose which "acts as a bath of refreshment, rejuvenation, and purification of the mind," and which, born of a contact with reality that is in itself ineffable, seeks liberation in song. "It is a concentration of all the energies of the soul, but a pacific, tranquil concentration, which involves no tension. The soul enters into its repose, in this place of refreshment and of peace superior to any

2. Baudelaire, "Théophile Gautier," in *L'Art Romantique.*
3. J. Maritain, "Answer to Jean Cocteau," *Art and Faith* (New York: Philosophical Library, 1948), p. 90.

feeling. It dies 'the death of the Angels,' but only to revive in exaltation and enthusiasm, in that state which is wrongly called inspiration—wrongly, for inspiration was nothing else indeed than this very repose, in which it escaped from sight. Now the mind, invigorated and vivified, enters into a happy activity, so easy that everything seems to be given it at once and, as it were, from the outside. In reality, everything was there, kept in the shade, hidden in the spirit and in the blood; all that which will be manifested in operation was already there, but we knew it not. We knew neither how to discover nor how to use it, before having gained new forces in those tranquil depths."[4]

Poetic experience differs in nature from mystical experience. It is concerned with the created world and with the innumerable enigmatic relations of beings with one another, while mystical experience is concerned with the principle of beings in its unity superior to the world. The obscure knowledge through connaturality proper to poetic experience proceeds from an emotion which shakes the recesses of subjectivity, while the more obscure but more decisive and more stable knowledge through connaturality proper to mystical experience proceeds—either, in the natural mystical experience, from a purely intellectual concentration which produces a void in which the Self is ineffably touched or, in the supernatural mystical experience, from charity, which connaturalizes the soul to God and transcends every emotion. Poetic experience is from the beginning orientated toward expression and terminates in an uttered word; mystical experience tends toward silence and terminates in an immanent fruition of the absolute.

Thus it appears that poetic experience, in its approach to created things, is an unknowing correspondence to the mystical approach to God, a lived analogy of that knowledge (not rational and conceptual, but by union of love) which the contemplative has of God. It is in a kind of connivance with this experience which differs from it essentially; it can be touched by and interlaced with it. Of itself it disposes the soul to aspire to it.

---

4. Raïssa Maritain, "Sens et Non-Sens en Poésie," *Situation de la Poésie*, second edition (Paris: Desclée De Brouwer, 1948), pp. 48–49.

Furthermore, because it detects the spiritual in things and perceives in them a something beyond them, because it is a knowledge of the mirrors of God either in the being of things or, by privation, in the hollow of their nothingness, it is an advance toward God and a spiritual inclination in the direction of God, an obscure and vulnerable beginning, not of mystical experience, but of the natural knowledge of God.

But the poet knows nothing of this, nor of the bonds which in actual existence attach poetry and beauty necessarily to God; or if he does, he knows it only in so confused a way that he can either reject, insofar as his own human choices are concerned, the *élan* which traverses his experience, or divert its trend and stop at the mirror by turning aside from the too real Immensity which it enigmatically reflects. Thus, many poets are convinced that all poetry is religious by essence, though they hardly believe in God[5] or confuse Him with nature.

Others, choosing atheism, commit themselves and commit poetry to the spiritual experience of the void or the search for magical powers. The call which poetic experience normally creates in the soul toward the abyss of light of uncreated Being gives way to another call—the call toward the abyss of the interior desert visited only by vultures of illusion and phantoms of miracles.

Then poetry inevitably suffers some invisible wound, but one which can stimulate it. A poet can reject God and be a great poet.

He cannot, however, free himself from every metaphysical anguish or passion. For the nostalgia for God whom he has rejected remains immanent in the poetic experience itself, whether he wills it or not. And so he is divided in his being. True, the atheism of a poet can never be completely relied upon; surprises are always possible. The same Lautréamont who declares: "I did not merit this infamous torment, thou hideous spy of my causality! If I exist I am not another . . . My subjectivity and the Creator,

5. "Robert Desnos does not believe in God, nevertheless he writes: 'Nobody has a more religious mind than I . . .' (*Revue Européene,* mars 1924)." Raïssa Maritain, *Situation de la Poésie,* p. 37.

that is too much for a brain,"[6] will soon affirm: "If one recalls the truth whence all the others flow, the absolute goodness of God and His absolute ignorance of evil, the sophisms will collapse of themselves . . . We have not the right to question the Creator on anything whatever."[7]

Let us acknowledge it: to confuse essences is easy for poets; it is almost normal for them (that is what Plato did not forgive them). "But if the Poet confounds everything, would it not be because in him the formative powers of the world and of the word and the divine attraction toward pacification and illumination of the spirit, toward mystical knowledge and union, are together at work? We must believe, since the poets tell us that they have discovered in their nocturnal navigations or divagations a Kingdom greater than the world, that an angel is pleased sometimes to tip their bark, so that they take a little of 'that water' of which the Gospel speaks, and do not get away without some inquietude, and some great and mysterious desire."[8]

2. *The Choice of the Good in the First Act of Freedom.* The practical intellect does not deal exclusively with artistic creation. It also, and first of all, has to do with the moral life of man. There exists in this order another approach to God, enveloped in moral experience, which one might call the moral knowledge of God.

It is not possible rationally to justify fundamental moral notions such as the notion of unconditional moral obligation, or inalienable right, or the intrinsic dignity of the human person, without rising to the uncreated Reason from which man and the world proceed and which is the subsistent Good itself. Philosophical reflection on moral life and experience has thus its own proofs of the existence of God.

But it is not of this philosophical approach that I should like to speak here. I should like to speak of a quite particular knowledge of God which is implied in the moral experience itself or in the

6. Lautréamont, "Chants de Maldoror," in *Oeuvres Complètes* (Paris: G.L.M., 1938).

7. Lautréamont, *Préface à des Poèmes Futurs* (*ibid.*).

8. Raïssa Maritain, "Magie, Poésie et Mystique," *Situation de la Poésie,* p. 72.

very exercise of moral life, more precisely in the first act of choice accomplished by the will, when this act is right. I may be permitted here to draw upon the more developed study which I devoted to "the immanent dialectic of the first act of *freedom*."[9]

When a human being is awakened to moral life, his first act is to "deliberate about himself." It is a matter of choosing his way. Psychologists speak of the "Oedipus complex"; why should moralists not speak of "Heracles' choice"? The occasion can be futile in itself; it is the motivation that counts. A child one day refrains from telling a lie; he restrains himself from it on that day, not because he risks being punished if the lie is discovered or because this was forbidden him, but simply because *it is bad.* It would not be good to do that. At this moment the moral good with all its mysterious demands, and in the presence of which he is himself and all alone, is confusedly revealed to him in a flash of understanding. And in choosing the good, in deciding to act in such a way because it is good, he has in truth, in a manner proportioned to the capacity of his age, "deliberated about himself" and chosen his way.[10]

And now, "What does such an act imply? What is the immanent dialectic, the secret dynamism of the primal act of freedom? Let us unfold and make explicit, in terms of speculative knowledge and philosophical discourse, what is contained in the indivisible vitality, both volitional and intellectual, of this act.

"The soul, in this first moral choice, turns away from an evil action because it is evil. Thus, the intellect is aware of the distinction between good and evil, and knows that the good ought to be done because it is good. We are confronted, here, with a formal motive which transcends the whole order of empirical conveni-

---

9. J. Maritain, *The Range of Reason* (New York: Charles Scribner's Sons, 1952), Chapter VI.

10. He has chosen his way and decided about the meaning of his life, inasmuch as an act of the human will, posited in time, enlists the future: that is to say, in a fragile fashion. He is not confirmed forever in such a decision; he will be able, all during his existence, to change the decision which bears on the meaning of his life, but it will only be done by an act of freedom and of deliberation about himself just as profound as that first decision.

ence and desire. This is the primary implication of the first act of freedom when it is good.

"But, because the value with which the moral object and the moral act are permeated surpasses anything given in empirical existence and concerns that which *ought to be*, the notion of a good action to be done for the sake of the good necessarily implies that there is an ideal and indefectible order of proper consonance between our activity and our essence, a *law* of human acts transcending all facts. This is the second implication of the first act of human freedom when it is good.

"Let us reflect upon this law. It transcends the whole empirical order; the act that I bring into existence must conform to it, if it is to be a good act; and the first precept of this law demands of me that my act be good. Such a law carries in the world of actual existence the requirements of an order that depends on a reality which is superior to everything and is Goodness itself—good by virtue of its very being, not by virtue of conformity with anything distinct from itself. Such a law manifests the existence of a Separate Good transcending all empirical existence and subsisting *per se*, and subsists primarily in this Separate Good. But how could I, in an act of total commitment, strive to achieve conformity with this transcendent law unless, by the same token and on a still more profound level, I strive toward this Separate Good and direct my life toward it because it is both *the* Good and *my* Good? The initial act which determines the direction of life and which—when it is good—chooses the good for the sake of the good, proceeds from a natural *élan* which is also, undividedly, an *élan* by which this very same act tends all at once, beyond its immediate object, toward God as the Separate Good in which the human person in the process of acting, whether he is aware of it or not, places his happiness and his end. Here we have an ordainment which is actual and formal, not virtual—but in merely lived act (*in actu exercito*), not in signified act—to God as ultimate end of human life. This is the third implication of the act of which I am speaking.

"These implications are not disclosed to the intellect of the child. They are contained in the act by which, at the term of his first deliberation about himself, he brings himself to do a good act for the sake of the moral good, of the *bonum honestum* of which he has an explicit idea, no matter how confused."[11]

It is not at all necessary that in thus performing his first human act he think explicitly of God and of his ultimate end. "He thinks of what is good and of what is evil. But by the same token he knows God, without being aware of it. He knows God because, by virtue of the internal dynamism of his choice of the good for the sake of the good, he wills and loves the Separate Good as ultimate end of his existence. Thus, his intellect has of God a vital and nonconceptual knowledge which is involved both in the practical notion (confusedly and intuitively grasped, but with its full intentional energy) of the moral good as formal motive of his first act of freedom, and in the movement of his will toward this good and, all at once, toward the Good. The intellect may already have the idea of God and it may not yet have it. The nonconceptual knowledge which I am describing takes place independently of any use possibly made or not made of the idea of God, and independently of the actualization of any explicit and conscious knowledge of man's true last End.

"In other words, the will, hiddenly, secretly, obscurely moving (when no extrinsic factor stops or deviates the process) down to the term of the immanent dialectic of the first act of freedom, goes *beyond* the immediate object of conscious and explicit knowledge (the moral good as such), and it carries with itself, down to that *beyond,* the intellect, which at this point no longer enjoys the use of its regular instruments, and, as a result, is only actualized below the threshold of reflective consciousness, in a night without concept and without utterable knowledge. The conformity of the intellect with this transcendent object, the Separate Good (attainable only by means of analogy) is then effected by the will, the rectitude of which is, in the practical order, the measure of the truth of the intellect. God is thus naturally known,

11. J. Maritain, *The Range of Reason,* pp. 68–69. The *bonum honestum* is the "good as right" (contradistinguished from the "good as useful" and the "good as pleasurable"), in other words that good which is possessed of inherent moral worth and causes conscience to be obliged. More simply —and if we are neither Utilitarians nor Epicureans—we may designate the *bonum honestum* by the expression the *moral* or *ethical* good.

without any conscious judgment, in and by the impulse of the will striving toward the Separate Good, whose existence is implicitly involved in the practical value acknowledged to the moral good. No speculative knowledge of God is achieved. This is a purely practical cognition of God, produced in and by the movement of the appetite toward the moral good precisely considered as good. The metaphysical content with which it is pregnant is not grasped as a metaphysical content; it is not released."[12]

The philosophical and theological problems which arise from these considerations have been discussed in the study from which these pages are extracted. Here we wish only to recall the fact that a radically practical, nonconceptual and nonconscious knowledge of the existence of God is present in act in the depth of the soul by virtue of the first choice of its freedom, when this choice is right. (To simplify things I considered this first choice at the moment of the awakening of the child to moral life. It is clear that such a basic choice can take place at any moment of life.) Even if his conscious reason is in complete ignorance of God, a man can thus know God, in an unconscious but real—practical, existential and volitional—way by virtue of a first free act having for its object *bonum honestum*, the ethical good.

We are not here, as in the case of the experience of the artist and of the poet, in the presence of a simple, fragile and vulnerable beginning of the knowledge of God. We are confronted with an actual and formal knowledge, but one which takes place in the unconscious of the spirit, and is not brought to light except by the consideration of the philosopher analyzing it in the experience of others.

It follows from this that, given all the cleavages and the discords, schisms, divisions, and contradictions, unknown by the subject himself, which can be produced between the conscious and the unconscious, it is possible that a man in whom the knowledge of which we speak exists in an unconscious state, may not only be ignorant of God in his conscious reason but may even

12. J. Maritain, *The Range of Reason*, p. 70. This analysis is related solely to the natural order considered apart, abstraction being made from the interventions of another order which have a place in concrete existence. Cf. *ibid.*, pp. 75–81.

take sides in his conscious reason against the existence of God
(because of some conceptual mistake and error of reasoning) and
profess atheism. He believes that he is an atheist. He cannot
be one in reality if he has chosen, and as long as he has chosen,
the way of the good for the sake of the good, in his basic moral
choice. He is a pseudo-atheist. What he denies in his conscious
reason is an *ens rationis*, whose constituent notes appear to him
as incompatible with real existence or as bound to conditions
which revolt him in nature or in humanity, a fiction of the imagination which he calls God but which is not God; he does not deny
in reality the God who is the authentic object of reason and in
whom he believes in the bottom of his heart without knowing it.

If, on the contrary, it is a question of a true atheist, the atheism
which he professes consciously cannot coexist with that unconscious knowledge of God which is linked to the choice of the good
for the sake of the good, because the true atheist denies not something which is not God and which he mistakes for God, but God
Himself, and by that very denial breaks the movement by which
the will, in moving to the good for the sake of the good, passes
beyond its intended object to the Separate Good, carrying the intellect along with it. Moreover, "positive and absolute" atheism
itself has its origin in a *sui generis* moral experience whose characteristic is the rejection of all transcendence, a rejection decided
upon in the first choice itself by which moral life takes form.[13]
Thence the very idea of the moral good (*bonum honestum*) is
intrinsically vitiated or disorganized, stamped with an inner contradiction, for it becomes the idea of the *bonum honestum taken
as excluding God*. An absolute atheist can order his life to the
good for the sake of the good, but it is to a corpse or an idol of
the ethical good that he thus orders his life—to the good inasmuch as it excludes the Good. "He has killed the moral good by
shattering and destroying the relationship with the Separate Good
which it essentially implies. Moral good, duty, virtue inevitably
become demands of his own perfection viewed as an absolute
center, or a desolate rite of his own grandeur—or a total submis-

13. Cf. J. Maritain, "The Meaning of Contemporary Atheism," *The Range
of Reason*, Chapter VIII.

sion of himself to the sweet will of deified Becoming; and thus moral good, duty, virtue lose their true nature."[14]

But let us return to the man we have described as a pseudo-atheist. While denying a God which is not God, this man really believes in God. The fact remains that he is divided against himself, because certain obstacles to belief in God, which have arisen in him at the level of conscious thought and conceptual elaboration, form a barrier that prevents the existential knowledge which exists in the hidden, active workings of the unconscious (of both his intellect and will) from passing, along with their rational repercussions, into the sphere of consciousness. Such a situation is of itself abnormal.

Normally the unconscious and existential knowledge of God, linked to the first act of freedom when it is right, tends to pass into consciousness and it makes its way there. It creates in the soul dispositions and inclinations which assist reason in its conscious exercise to discover the truth which corresponds to them. *He that doeth the truth cometh to the light.* In normal circumstances the man who has chosen the ethical good (*bonum honestum*) is found instinctively and unconsciously disposed to perceive, when the natural and spontaneous play of his reason is exercised on the spectacle of visible things, the existence of that invisible Good, of that Separate Good which he already knew without being aware of it by virtue of the choice of the good which he effected when he deliberated about himself in his first act of freedom. When, on the level of conscious thought—and thanks to the natural approach due to the primordial intuition of existence of which we treated at the beginning of this book; thanks also to the ways of philosophic reason—he perceives in the full light of intellectual evidence the necessity of the existence of the First Cause, he does not simply know God; he knows and *recognizes* Him.

3. *The Testimony of the Friends of God.* It is fitting, finally, to mention, indirect as it may be, a way of approaching God, the value of which is only auxiliary, and which can be related to the

14. J. Maritain, *The Range of Reason*, p. 85.

order of moral experience. This way is based on testimony and example.

Our ordinary moral life is, indeed, precarious. Many elements are mingled in its structure. Some of them come from outside ourselves: from the manners and customs of the social group projected within us, and from the opinions of the world we live in. Some of them arise from the subterranean depths of our own unconscious—masked interventions which we but dimly discern. So loose in structure, so menaced by our own weakness, so complex and obscure is our everyday moral life that we naturally turn for guidance to those who can show us the way. They have found what we so feebly seek. So to them we turn—those men whom Bergson called the "heroes" of the spiritual life and whose "appeal" he saw traversing mankind.

The quest of the superhuman is natural to man; we find it in every climate of philosophic or religious nostalgia of our species. Without speaking of mirages, illusions, or forgeries which are met in such regions, an authentic quest can get involved in impasses or in byways. But that quest may also lead to the fullness of a love superior to nature which expresses itself in a wisdom ever open and a perfect freedom. It was by such signs that Bergson recognized a supreme accomplishment of human life among Christian mystics, who, he thought, alone had crossed the ultimate barriers.[15]

Consequently, according to Bergson, the philosopher may question them and find in their testimony a confirmation, or rather a "reinforcement,"[16] of that which he has himself, by means proper to a philosopher, caught sight of in the prolongation of another "line of facts." And what is the essential indication which he will receive from the mystics, "when he compresses . . . mystical intuition in order to express it in terms of intelligence?"[17] "God is love, and the object of love: herein lies the whole contribution of mysticism. About this twofold love the mystic will never have done

15. Cf. Henri Bergson, *The Two Sources of Morality and Religion* (New York: Henry Holt, 1935), pp. 215–16 ff.

16. Henri Bergson, *Les Deux Sources* . . . (Paris: Alcan, 1933), p. 266 (my own translation).

17. Henri Bergson, *The Two Sources* . . ., p. 241.

talking. His description is interminable, because what he wants to describe is ineffable. But what he does state clearly is that divine love is not a thing of God: it is God himself."[18] "As a matter of fact," Bergson added, "the mystics unanimously bear witness that God needs us, just as we need God. Why should He need us, unless it be to love us? And it is to this very conclusion that the philosopher who holds to the mystical experience must come. Creation will appear to him as God undertaking to create creators, that He may have, besides Himself, beings worthy of His love."[19]

The movement of thought lived by Bergson is significant: the better we know the sanctity of the saints, and the moral life of those who have ventured to give all in order to enter into what they themselves describe as the divine union and the experience of the things of God, the more we feel that the truth alone can give such fruits, and that the certitude which sustains everything in these men cannot lie.

An act of true goodness, the least act of true goodness, is indeed the best proof of the existence of God. But our intellect is too busy cataloguing notions to see it. Therefore, we believe it on the testimony of those in whom true goodness shines in a way that astonishes us.

This is not a proof of the existence of God. It is an argument based only on testimony. Besides, I do not think—and neither did Bergson—that it is capable of winning the assent of the mind except when in other ways the mind—supposing some obstacle hinders it from feeling the full force with which the being of things manifests the existence of their Cause—is at least solicited by beginnings of proof, signs, and tokens whose rational value imposes itself upon the mind. Neither do I think that this argument commands rational or purely natural assent unless there be also mingled with it a belief of another order, based on the invisible testimony, in the depths of the soul, of the God of whom we hear His friends speak.

But in the end, considering it only in the order and on the level

18. *Ibid.*, p. 240.
19. *Ibid.*, p. 243.

of reason, this argument has its proper value and validity; and it is possible that in fact, in concrete existence, this auxiliary way plays, for many, a more important role than pure logicians think. I wanted in any case to mention it here, for the reasons I have just given, and in memory of the great philosopher whom it helped to discover God.

11

Moral Evil and the Eternal Plan *

. . . The leading idea of *Existence and the Existent*** is very simple. It is a question of following through to the end that dissymmetry between the line of good and the line of evil on which I have already insisted so much; and consequently of recognizing all the bearing of this assertion that the first cause or the *inventor* of moral evil *in the existential reality of the world* is the liberty of the creature—I mean, this liberty *in the line of non-being*. All of this implies that at the very first origin of the evil act—and, above all, of the evil election, which takes place in the depths of the heart—there is not only the *fallibility* of the creature, but an *actual failure* of the creature, a created initiative which—since it is not caused by God—can only be an initiative of non-being, of deficiency in being, of lack, what I have called a nihilation.

At bottom the whole affair is contained in a Gospel saying: *Sine me nihil potestis facere,* it is said in Saint John, 15:5.

Well, this text can be read in two ways.

It can be read: *Without Me you can do nothing*—nothing *good*. This is the line of being or of good, where God has the first initiative.

And it can also be read: *Without Me you can do nothingness,* without me you can introduce into being that nothingness or that *non-being of the due good,* that *privation,* which is *evil*. And this even, this initiative of evil, you can have it only without Me (for with Me it is good only that you can do). Here we have the

---

* *God and the Permission of Evil* (Milwaukee: The Bruce Publishing Company, 1966), p. 33; pp. 85–90.
** New York: Pantheon Books, 1948; paper, New York: Doubleday, Image Books, 1957.

line of non-being or of evil, where created liberty has the first
initiative. . . .

All right! It is indeed true that in this view the Creator of the
world does not provide Himself with the absolutely safe spectacle
of a game of marionettes which would but put into execution a
program that He Himself has conceived for evil as well as for
good. It is indeed true that in this view, if God wills that we
engage ourselves headlong in the battle, it is because He Himself has first engaged in it the glory of His name, nay more, because He has engaged Himself in it completely, by sending us
His Son one with Him in nature.

In this view, the creature, each time that it does evil, introduces to this extent nothingness into being, and undoes for a part
the work that God makes. The work of God runs risks, risks that
are real because the drama is not merely portrayed, it is actually
lived. There are abysses which open out, collapses, disasters. The
gods from below that free agents are when they take the initiative
of nothingness, cause evil and perversion to multiply, and invent
forms of horror and of abomination which astonish the angels
(and, if I may say so, be it only to tease a little my neo-Bañezian
friends, astonish the Author himself of the drama, in this sense
that if He knows in His "science of simple intelligence" all *possible* evil, it is not He, it is the creature who invents *existing* evil,
and in such an invention goes beyond all expectation).

But it is in all this, exactly, that the invincible wisdom and the
dazzling power of the eternal purposes manifest themselves. He
whose Name is above every name, the eternally Victorious is
certain to win the game finally; He wins it at each instant, even
when He seems to be losing it. Each time that a free creature
undoes for its part the work that God makes, God remakes to that
extent—for the better—this work and leads it to higher ends. Because of the presence of evil on earth, everything on earth, from
the beginning to the end of time, is in perpetual recasting. However real the risks may be, much more real still is the strength of
the arm which causes them to be surmounted by creation and
repairs the damages incurred by the latter. However deep the
abysses may be, however great the collapses and the disasters,

sublimer are the heights and the goods to which created being will be transferred. And doubtless there will also be, finally, real losses—all too real—but themselves compensated by the manifestation of eternal justice in the creature when, in order to remain to itself its ultimate End, it prefers over love all the pains of Hell. And the more the gods from below cause horror and evil to multiply, the more the saints in their love, accomplishing in their flesh what is lacking to the sufferings of Christ, cause the magnificence of good to superabound (to the point that they themselves —more teasing of my good friends, but after all the Bible is full of metaphorical figures of speech—will provoke the admiration of their Lord; for as a general rule the good themselves, by all their shortcomings, leave unused many of the treasures that God gives them; so that if someone is so faithful that all the talents, or almost all, that he has received bear fruit, he is worthy of the admiration of Heaven). And finally it is by having made good use of his liberty moved and activated from end to end by God, and by having from all eternity contributed for his part as free second cause to the very establishment of the eternal plan, that the creature saved—the one who in the end will not have said *No*—will enter into the glory that God has prepared for those who love Him, and which was His intention in creating the world, this world where evil is permitted.

It seems to me that it is only in such a perspective that one can glimpse *just a little* the *real* dimensions of the mystery of the Cross, and of the folly of the Cross, and of that other mystery before which Saint Paul knelt in adoration: "Oh, the depth of the riches of the wisdom and of the knowledge of God! How incomprehensible are his judgments, and how unsearchable his ways!"[1] "God hath concluded all in unbelief, that he may have mercy on all."[2] "Where the offence has abounded, grace has abounded yet more."[3] When Jesus said to Angela of Foligno: "It is not in order to laugh that I have loved you," He was not suggesting to her that the sinners responsible for His death were only docile performers of antecedent permissive decrees.

1. Rom. XI: 33.
2. Rom. XI: 22.
3. Rom. V: 20.

All that I have just said was a kind of gloss, not only of the texts of Saint Paul which I have just cited, but also of the text of Saint Augustine which I cited in our preceding seminar:* "God would never permit evil if He was not strong enough and good enough to draw good even from evil."

The greater good of which Saint Augustine speaks—it is in the order of the goods of grace that we have considered it, and rightly so. For it is there that is found the greater good *par excellence*—the only one which can give the final answer to our anxieties,—to which are ordained *absolutely speaking, simpliciter,* all the evils that God permits, evil of fault and evil of suffering.

It is clear that this greater good *simpliciter* cannot be merely the good of the universe or of the world of nature; for if it is a question of the sin of a *person* (and even of his suffering), it is not in the perfection of the machine of the world, it is only in the goods of grace and of glory, and the person-to-person love which unites created agents with God and among themselves there where we are fellow-citizens of the saints, that these evils can be compensated by a good incomparably greater in the line of good than they are in the line of evil.

It is the good which has been prepared for the Jerusalem of heaven and the communion of saints, and creation completely transfigured—and for each friend of God in particular, because "to them that love God, *all things work together unto good,*" says Saint Paul[4]—and in particular for the poor and the persecuted, and for the victims of crimes and abominations of which created liberty has been the nihilating first cause and the execution of which God has permitted (and even also, in a sense, for their authors, to whom the grace of repentance will be offered at any moment whatever, be it the last moment of their life).

After this, however, it seems to me that we must also say that in a relative and secondary, or *secundum quid,* manner the law of the permission of evil for a greater good applies also in the domain of temporal history. It is verified in the law of the twofold simultaneous progress of good and evil, of the wheat and

---

* *God and the Permission of Evil,* Chapter 2 [Editors].
4. Rom. VIII: 28.

the cockle—but progress greater in the case of good or of the wheat; for, everything considered, the good is certainly stronger than evil.

It is true that grace and nature not being two closed worlds, but two worlds open one to the other and in mutual communication, it might happen that the *greater progress* (of the wheat over that of the cockle) of which I have just spoken would occur *more* in the order of grace than in that of nature, where in that case it would be masked by the progress of the cockle. This is why we have the *duty* to *hope* for the temporal history of the world, but without any certitude that the progress of evil will not there accompany, with too much power and too much glitter, the progress of good.

Let us hope (and let us do *all* that is humanly possible—in honesty of conscience—to attain this) that from social evils which revolt us, from slavery, from misery, from the power of great monsters which devour the individual person, from the barbarous conditions in which so many of God's creatures live, human history will emerge not only with the cessation of these evils, but with an increase of goods for humanity—so that the spirit may gain ascendancy, that the unification of the human race may come about under the sign of liberty, not of a herd conformism, and that all men may have access *free of charge* to the elementary goods of human life! But let us not forget that moreover all these advances themselves—we are in the history of this world—will be more or less spoiled (not *too* spoiled, may it please God!) by evil which progresses at the same time. And this kind of overlapping of good on evil, and of evil on good, and more still (with all the reservations I have just indicated) of good on evil—well, such is the history of the human race.

III

Ethics

Maritain holds that moral philosophy—however vast, nec-
essary, and fundamental be the part that natural ethics plays
in it—must, if it is to be adequate to its object, namely, the
direction or regulation of human acts, take into account the
data of revelation and theology as to the existential state *of*
man. Human conduct is the conduct of an existent, *not*
simply the conduct of a nature. *Consequently the moral*
philosopher must take into account all data which contribute
to make the existential condition of man genuinely known
to us. He must take into account the data of ethnology,
sociology, and psychology. And he must also take into ac-
count theological data. Maritain recognizes that the moral
philosopher who does take these data into account will not
be a pure *philosopher, but maintains that he will still be able*
to use the method proper to philosophy and advance with
steps, so to speak, of philosophy, not of theology.

For Maritain moral philosophy is an "after-knowledge," a
"second-glance knowledge" of moral values—the first glance
belongs to reason functioning by way of inclination and con-

geniality, to reason functioning in a quasi-vegetative or quasi-biological manner. Thus the genuine concept of natural law is for Maritain the concept of a law which is natural not only in the sense that it is the normality of functioning of the human nature or essence, but also in the sense that it is naturally known, *that is, known through inclination.*

Maritain's manifold themes in ethics may best be found in

 EDUCATION AT THE CROSSROADS
 AN ESSAY ON CHRISTIAN PHILOSOPHY
 FREEDOM IN THE MODERN WORLD
 MORAL PHILOSOPHY
 NEUF LEÇONS SUR LES NOTIONS PREMIÈRES DE LA
  PHILOSOPHIE MORALE
 THE RESPONSIBILITY OF THE ARTIST
 THE RIGHTS OF MAN AND NATURAL LAW
 SCIENCE AND WISDOM

THE IMPACT OF CHRISTIANITY ON MORAL PHILOSOPHY *

I THE ANCIENT WORLD AND THE COMPETITION OF WISDOMS

The Wisdom of India

1. As we remarked in another work,[1] the spectacle offered in a general way by the ancient world, the world before Christ, is what might be called the *competition of wisdoms*.

We find in the first place the wisdom of India—a wisdom of deliverance and salvation.

The metaphysical speculations of India have always remained bound up with a practical science of spiritual perfection and sanctity. But it is through a desperate impetus issuing from the depths of the soul, a kind of tidal wave of the divine energies which are diffused in the universe and concentrated in man, that man strives to attain this wisdom. It is nature itself which, freed from illusion and from the constraints of causality, must transcend itself in order to arrive at a perfection which Hindu philosophy called "supernatural," in a quite different sense from the Christian sense of the word. Wisdom was thus the wisdom of salvation, the wisdom of the "delivered ones," to be achieved through the ascetic and mystical effort of human nature. Thence that natural mysticism in which, through the abolition of any particular thought, through total emptiness voluntarily produced, the soul

---

* *Moral Philosophy* (New York: Charles Scribner's Sons, 1964), pp. 71–91.
1. *Science and Wisdom* (New York: Charles Scribner's Sons, 1940; London: Bles, 1940).

experiences intuitively the existence of the Self.[2]

What is most apparent here is an ascending effort of the energies immanent in our nature, a supreme tension of the energies of our spirit, an *upward motion* by which man is to accede to superhuman conditions, enter into the divine liberty. This effort was capable, in the order of natural mysticism, of leading to the metaphysical experience of the Self of which I just spoke; in certain cases it was supplemented by a grace whose name was not revealed; at the same time that it sought deliverance in a wisdom of salvation it fell short of the goal, struggling ceaselessly to escape monism, never succeeding in conceptualizing itself without being caught by monism, aspiring ceaselessly to join the divine Absolute and only succeeding, after the Buddhist experiment, in giving an expression to nirvana that was closer and closer to pure negation.

Greek Wisdom

2. In the second place we find Greek wisdom. A wisdom of man, a wisdom of reason, it was turned toward created things and the knowledge of the cosmos, not toward salvation, saintliness, eternal deliverance.

We are aware of the fact that Greek wisdom cannot be called a rational wisdom in a very modern sense of that term. Greek paganism had its roots in magical thought, which continued to furnish the subconscious atmosphere of Greek religion. Sacred traditions did not cease to form an undercurrent beneath Hellenic meditation. Ancient reason was a naturally religious reason. It operated in a climate of natural piety haunted by many terrors. Even at the time when it displayed the most intense rationalism, as in the Stoic school, the rationalism in question remained entirely different from our modern rationalism, and veered toward a kind of magical naturalism, conceiving Reason as a divine fire that permeated matter, and favoring all the pagan superstitions. Greek reason recognized good and bad fortune, believed in higher inspirations, in demonic influences; the idea of destiny,

2. Cf. our study on natural mysticism, "The Natural Mystical Experience and the Void," in *Ransoming the Time* (New York: Charles Scribner's Sons, 1941), Chapter X. (*Redeeming the Time* [London: Bles, 1943].)

and of the jealousy of the gods, the superstitious fear of admitting happiness, the belief in omens and in divination, even the adoration of the divine similitudes scattered through nature, were evidence of a religious appreciation of the supra-human energies at work in the world and sustained a kind of sacred awe, or fear.

But it was precisely against that fear that Stoic pantheism and Epicurean free thought reacted. More generally, it must be said that Greek philosophy developed from the beginning as a work of reason separated from religion, even when it underwent the influence of the sects and their mysteries, and as a wisdom of this world. Greek wisdom was not elaborated out of the fund of hieratic and sacerdotal traditions, like the wisdom of the Orient, but outside of them and sometimes in opposition to them. It does not start out with the Supreme, with absolute Being, as the Vedanta did, wondering how it is possible that something exists which is not the Absolute, superior to the world. On the contrary, it starts out with things, with tangible and visible reality, with becoming, with movement, with that multiplicity which exercises the act of being with scandalous energy. It bears witness to the existence of that which is not God, and to the intelligible structure of things. In the moral realm it succeeded in establishing in its proper order, and as distinct from speculative philosophy and metaphysics, a practical rational knowledge of human conduct and human acts, which was to fix thenceforth the boundaries of ethics. But the peculiar beauty of Greek wisdom is like that of a rough sketch drawn by a genius, in which the outlines and the essential points are indicated with incomparable artistry. It nowhere came to fruition. In the field of moral philosophy in particular we have seen that neither Aristotelian eudemonism, nor the asceticism of pleasure, nor the asceticism of virtue came to a successful issue.

The Wisdom of the Old Testament

3. Finally, there is a third wisdom, Hebraic wisdom, the wisdom of the Old Testament. It is not a human wisdom like Greek wisdom. It is a wisdom of salvation and of saintliness, of deliverance and freedom, of eternal life—but for it, unlike Hindu wisdom,

man does not rise by his own efforts: *quis ascendit in caelum,*
who shall go up for us to heaven, and bring it unto us?[3] No effort
of asceticism or of mysticism could *force* that wisdom. It must
give itself, it must come down and break open the gates of
heaven.

The long, the unflagging Jewish impatience beseeches God to
give Himself, a God who wants only to give Himself, but who
hides Himself. The wisdom of the Old Testament is bound up
with the most intransigeant idea of divine transcendence, with
the idea of creation *ex nihilo,* and at the same time with a profound sense of human personality and human freedom. This perishable and corruptible flesh, this flesh itself will rise again: an
idea that Greek wisdom had no inkling of, and which it was to
find scandalous. The history of Israel—and the individual history
of each human being—consists in the last analysis of the dialogue
between the eternal divine personality and our created persons;
it is a love affair between God and man.

Thus we are there in the presence of a supernatural wisdom
that gives itself, and that freely descends from the Principle of
beings. A wisdom of salvation, a wisdom of saintliness, it is not
man who wins it, it is God who gives it; it is not from an upward
movement of the creature, it is from a downward movement of
the creating Spirit that it proceeds. It is in this opposition of the
two movements of ascent and descent that the whole difference
between the wisdom of the Ganges and the wisdom of the Jordan
must be seen. The wisdom of the sapiential books, like the wisdom of the Gospel, issues from the depths of uncreated love to
descend into the most intimate depths of the creature. The New
Law, the message of the Word made flesh, will tear away the veil
with which the Old Law covered the mystery that the prophets
of Israel glimpsed—through the veil—and obscurely foretold.

The Law of the Incarnation

4. The ancient world offers us the spectacle of a competition
among three wisdoms; and more specifically, the competition between Judeo-Christian wisdom and Greek wisdom, finally gone
to seed and seeking in vain in a syncretism without existential

3. Deuteronomy XXX: 12; cf. Baruch III: 29–30; Romans X: 6.

roots, in mystagogy and gnosis, a cure for the great pagan melancholy. This conflict was to signalize the disintegration of the ancient world.

Later, in the course of the Middle Ages, there was an extended effort to link together divine wisdom and human wisdom, to recognize and establish the order and hierarchy of wisdom, an effort that continued throughout the Christian centuries. This work of synthesis was to be completed in terms of actual doctrine by St. Thomas Aquinas; but divided as they were against themselves, the culture and the intelligentsia of the late Middle Ages were hardly able to profit by the synthesis, and its dissolution commenced with the beginning of modern times. The fact remains that medieval Christianity was cognizant of the order of wisdom—the wisdom of contemplative experience through the union of love, theological wisdom, philosophical wisdom. Medieval Christianity was dominated by the law of *descending motion* of supreme wisdom to which we called attention in speaking of the Old Testament, and knew its name—it is the law of the Incarnation. Thomas Aquinas formulated it in a text of limitless significance: "In the mystery of the Incarnation," he says,[4] "the descent of the divine plenitude into human nature is of greater import than the ascent of human nature, taken as pre-existent, toward Divinity." Similarly, in the relations between God and humanity, the movement of descent of the divine plenitude into the depths of human nature is of greater import than the movement of ascent by which human nature is fulfilled and mounts toward God. We rediscover here the teaching of St. Paul concerning the law and grace: it is not by our own effort that we are rendered just; it is by the gift of Him who loved us first, and who descends into us through faith and love, that we are born to eternal life and can bear good fruit in our weakness. "And he said unto me, My grace is sufficient for thee: for my strength is made perfect in weakness. Most gladly therefore will I rather glory in my infirmities, that the power of Christ may rest upon me . . . for when I am weak, then am I strong."[5] The moral heroism to which we are in truth called is attained neither by the athleticism of mystical concentration, after the Hindu manner, which claims to draw

4. *Sum. theol.*, III, 34, 1, ad 1.
5. II Cor. XII: 9–10.

us into inner solitude in the absolute, nor by the athleticism of
virtue, after the manner of the Stoics, which pretends to render
us incapable of sin. It is attained through the force of another
who descends into us and fills us with His plenitude, and by a
love for Him which even in the depths of our weakness removes
all obstacles to His love.

II THE IRRUPTION OF THE JUDEO-CHRISTIAN REVELATION

5. These very general observations have been by way of preface
to the remarks we should like to make concerning the effects produced in the realm of moral philosophy by the irruption in the
world of the Judeo-Christian revelation and the impact of Christianity on the tradition of Greek philosophy.

Whether one believes in this revelation oneself, or considers
it strictly from without and from a historical point of view, one
is obliged to note that in fact the impact in question produced a
kind of transmutation of ethical values—a unique phenomenon
in the history of humanity, as a matter of fact—and that as a consequence it profoundly transformed the perspectives of moral
philosophy.

Such a transfiguration was due to the influence of a religious
factor, exterior to philosophy as such—let us say, to speak in terms
of its rational formulation, a theological factor—upon a philosophical discipline. In our opinion, that influence was manifested
primarily in the way we are now going to try to define—be it
understood that these incursions into the theological and religious
domain are directed by a philosophical interest, and have as
object to mark certain repercussions which occurred in the
domain of moral philosophy itself.

"To-day thou shalt be with me in Paradise"—The Absolute
Ultimate End and the Subjective Ultimate End

Beatitude

6. It came as a strange novelty to learn that the final End of
human life—not only as supreme Value good in itself and for itself,

but as the supreme Object the possession of which constitutes human happiness—is God Himself, the infinite Good, self-subsistent Being. God in His intimate life, the uncreated Glory itself is the end in which our appetite for happiness will be satisfied beyond measure. In this view the transcendence of the final End is affirmed in an incomparably more decisive way than it was by Plato: the infinite transcendence—with which we are called to unite—of a personal God who created the world out of nothing, whom no concept can circumscribe and whom no creature can comprehend, infinite Self, supremely perfect, independent and free, and who is the boundless ocean of being, of intellection, of love and of goodness.

By the same stroke the notion of happiness was transfigured. Happiness is now Beatitude, absolute happiness, absolutely saturating; "Eye hath not seen, nor ear heard, neither have entered into the heart of man, the things which God hath prepared for them that love him."[6]

That it is possible for man to attain absolute happiness is not a datum of reason or of philosophy, but of Christian faith. Reason by itself, if we consider not the infinite power of God, of course, but the human condition, would have ample grounds to make us doubt the possibility. The most unhappy of animals necessarily desires happiness, and that is no doubt why it is so unhappy. We are starving for happiness, we make of the *pursuit of happiness* one of our fundamental rights, we seek happiness in everything that is perishable, in the love of a woman or in the conquest of power, and it is almost impossible for us to believe that we can be perfectly, totally, absolutely happy; our experience of life affords too much evidence to the contrary. There are two things in which our nature has not the strength to believe: death, which we see, and perfect happiness, which we do not see. *Verily I say unto you, to-day shalt thou be with me in paradise.*[7] That is an astonishing announcement. Faith, not reason, is the source of it. Men seek beatitude, without believing in it. Christians believe in it, through faith.

6. I Cor. II: 9.
7. Luke XXIII: 43.

In that beatitude, the object of Christian faith, we find, more-over, a supreme verification of the law mentioned above[8]—namely, that joy or delectation is a kind of savor issuing from the posses-sion of a substantial good, and always remains distinct from that possession, but is the more closely bound up with it the higher the nature of the substantial good in question. The essence of beatitude—the possession of the supreme substantial good—is the vision of God: the supreme joy which derives from it is in itself distinct from that vision, but is so nearly identical with it that we can hardly distinguish the joy from the vision.

Absolute Ultimate End and Subjective Ultimate End in the Natural Order and in the Supernatural Order

7. It would be well to pause a moment here to take note of two things. In the first place, as we just pointed out, for Christian faith man is called to an absolutely saturating happiness, and it is the possession or intuitive vision of God Himself which consti-tutes that happiness; it is the immediate and transforming union with the ultimate End of all creation—to which, unless it is raised by grace, a created nature can only tend or aspire from afar, in fact, from infinitely far—it is the direct union with the absolute ultimate End, good in and for itself, which constitutes the subjec-tive ultimate End of the human being, his final fulfillment, his perfect and eternal happiness.

But in the second place, Christian faith holds at the same time that this beatitude is of a supernatural order; it is a gift of grace, the gift of grace *par excellence;* it does not arise from nature.

If, therefore, man had not been raised to the state of grace, if God had left him in the purely natural order and with only the resources of his own nature, there would be no question for him either of attaining beatitude or of immediately possessing God as object of his perfect happiness. The happiness toward which he would tend, and which would be the subjective ultimate End of human life, or the end relative to the human subject, would be anything one wished, I mean anything philosophy and

8. See above *[Moral Philosophy]*, Chapter IV, pp. 65–66.

theology can more or less plausibly conceive, but it would not be God possessed. God would remain the absolute ultimate End, good in and for itself, to be loved above all else, for man as for every creature; but the possession of God would not be his subjective ultimate End, his ultimate end in the line of the subject. Between the absolute ultimate End, the transcendent Good which must be loved above all things, and the subjective ultimate End or the happiness of the human being, there would be in such a case an infinite distance, an infinite abyss. At this point we see clearly and explicitly that distinction between the Good and Happiness which Aristotle missed.

The astonishing tidings brought by Christianity were that in fact, and by the free and gratuitous superabundance of divine generosity, the separation, the cleavage of which we have just spoken between the absolute ultimate End and the subjective ultimate End does not exist for man. The subjective ultimate End or the beatitude of man consists in an immediate and indissoluble union with the absolute ultimate End (to which, as the theologians will put it, man is rendered proportionate through grace and the *lumen gloriae*). But in this very union, this kind of coincidence, the distinction between the subjective End or beatitude of man and God Himself or the absolute ultimate End obviously continues to exist, the distinction between the supernatural plenitude in which the human subject is fulfilled, with the endless joy that goes with that fulfillment, and the divine Essence, the subsistent Good, the vision of which beatifies the human subject. And it is for love of the subsistent Good, loved more than all things, more than the human subject itself and more than his own happiness, it is for love of the absolute ultimate End that man desires the beatitude in which his own being is divinely perfect.

Because the notion of the Good in itself and for itself is no longer related only to the *bonum honestum* (Good as right) in the moral order—or, in the metaphysical order, to the suprapersonal Idea of the Good, or to the Thought which thinks itself at the summit of the world—but has its supreme archetype in a subsistent Good which is a living Personality—three Persons in a single nature, one of whom has been incarnated, moral reflection now understands definitively and explicitly that the Good is something other than Happiness, and that the first demand and the first condition of moral rectitude is to love the Good more than Happiness.

Absolute Happiness Is Desired for Love of the Good Subsisting of Itself

8. In the perspective of Christian ethics three things are to be distinguished: in the first place, the absolute ultimate End. God in His infinite goodness and lovability is the absolute ultimate End, and it is in the vision of God, or the possession of the absolute ultimate End, that beatitude, or the subjective ultimate End of the human being, consists.

In the second place, the subjective ultimate End, in its essential constituent element: that is to say, the vision of God, through which the human being, supernaturally fulfilled, enters into the divine plenitude in knowing God through His essence.

In the third place, the subjective ultimate end in its flowering, in its supereffluence: that is to say, the perfect satisfaction of all the aspirations of the soul in the love of God possessed, the joy or delectation which is a participation in the joy of God itself—as it is said in Matthew, *intra in gaudium Domini tui*.[9]

These three things are distinct from one another. The desire of the second is inseparable from the love of the first; and the desire of the third is inseparable from the desire of the second. But the desire of the second and the desire of the third are for love of the first. Beatitude is loved, but God is loved more; and beatitude, precisely because it is union with the supreme Good subsisting in itself, can only be really and truly loved if it is loved in and for the love of that subsistent Good, supremely loved for itself. The love which the human being naturally has for himself is not abolished, certainly, but it loses first place, it is chased from the primary and royal seat; the absolutely primary love, the love which is above and beyond all others, can and must be torn away from the self and directed toward the uncreated Personality with whom the human person is in a direct relation over and above all

9. Matthew XXV: 21.

the things of this world. The absolutely primary love can and must be fixed in Him whose good we then wish more than our own good—and that is possible, and even, in one sense, easy, since according to Christian faith He is our friend, in the supernatural order of charity.

Thus the egocentricity in which Aristotelian eudemonism remained in fact enclosed is definitely overcome. At the very moment that beatitude is promised to man, he is offered the possibility of finally being delivered from himself and from the devouring egoism which perverts his love of himself.

My happiness, which I naturally and necessarily desire, which I cannot help desiring, and which finally consists in the vision of God, has now been subordinated to something better, subordinated to God—and this is implied, as we remarked above, in the very essence of that happiness, since it consists in the possession of God, who is infinitely better than my happiness. According to a precious saying of Cajetan, *"volo Deum mihi, non propter me"*;[10] Christian hope makes me wish that God be mine, but it is not *for me* or by reason of myself, it is not for love of myself that I wish God to be mine; it is for God and for love of God, for I love God more than myself and more than my happiness.

Christian morality is a morality of beatitude, but first and foremost it is a morality of the divine Good supremely loved.

9. The theologians are perfectly clear on all this. But popular preaching is often inclined to put the emphasis above all, if not even, exclusively on the joys of the reward and the pains of punishment. These are truths which immediately stir our natural appetite for happiness and our natural fear of suffering. And even if one insists only on them, one can always hope that once the sinner is turned toward the subsistent Good from motives in which love of self holds first place, the living faith will thereafter make him spontaneously subordinate his own interest to God loved first.

After all, one lends only to the rich. And the preachers of the

---

10. Cf. Cajetan, in II–II, q. 17, a. 5, no. 8: "Et cum dicitur *quia non potest amari Deus propter nos*, respondetur quod non potest amari *propter nos*, sed *nobis*." (Cajetan goes on to say that what is *secundum se* loved only *mihi*, can nevertheless *secundum effectum suum* be loved also *propter me*. None the less God in Himself is desired by me *mihi, non propter me*.)

Gospel feel themselves excused in advance if, in the arguments by which they push us toward salvation, they employ without too much scruple a kind of eudemonism, even hedonism, at least ambiguous in character, in the service of the God of love.

It is for the philosophical intelligence—not to speak of the pseudo-philosophical opinions current in popular thought, and sometimes in textbooks of ethics or the history of philosophy—that the final result of this emphasis is dangerous and can be the occasion for serious misconceptions. Even a philosopher like Kant, following a great many others, could imagine that traditional Christian morality (until revised by Pure Reason) was a morality of sublimated egotistic happiness and personal interest, in which it is for love of itself and of eternal pleasure, to which all else is subordinated, that the soul loves the Author of all good and strives to practice his precepts, which in reality is to conceive of Christianity after the model of the idolatrous cults it overthrew.

The Supernatural Order and the Grace of Virtues and Gifts—Divine Charity and Friendship

Theological virtues and moral virtues

10. With Christianity a new order in being is made manifest to the human mind—essentially distinct from the order of nature and at the same time, perfecting that order—the order of grace and of supernatural realities. This word "supernatural" signifies for Christianity a participation in that which is actually divine, in the intimate life itself of God—something, as we have already noted, which is beyond the possibilities of any created nature through its own capacities, and which is not *owed* to nature, but depends on free and gratuitous divine communication.

From this moment the very concept of nature undergoes a change, opens out, so to speak. Nature is not closed in upon itself, impenetrable by a superior order. It blossoms in grace, is "perfected" or fulfilled by grace, which is not simply added to it like an ornamental façade, but which penetrates its most intimate depths, and which, at the same time that it elevates nature to a life and an activity of another order, of which nature is not capable by itself, heightens it in its own order and in the domain of its own proper activities.

Several remarks may be tendered on this subject. The first concerns the three virtues to which Christianity has given absolutely first rank, and which are called the three *theological* virtues. They do not figure in the Aristotelian list of virtues. It was St. Paul who named them, and who, in a singular reversal of values, gave precedence over the powerful cardinal virtues to interior dispositions—adherence of the intellect to an object which is not seen, confidence in one more powerful than oneself, love—which in the purely human order were too humble to constitute virtues, but which in the divine order, and because they are directed toward God Himself, are henceforward recognized to be the virtues *par excellence:* "And now abideth faith, hope and charity, these three: but the greatest of these is charity."[11]

The object of the theological virtues is the transcendent God, the divine Good with which they unite the human soul. They are a gift of grace. In opposition to them, the term "moral" virtues will be reserved for the virtues enumerated by the philosophers, in the sense that the latter have to do with simply human morality or the conduct of life in relation to goods of the human order. Unlike moral virtues, the theological virtues do not consist in a mean between excess and defect; no excess is possible in the exercise of these virtues—one never believes too much in God, one never puts too much hope in Him, one never loves Him too much.[12] For Christian ethics the theological virtues are superior to the moral virtues. The latter are still required, but they are no longer supreme. The supreme virtues are of a supra-moral order, and the highest of them, on which the perfection of human life depends, is charity.

In order to clarify the distinction between the narrow sense ("moral virtues") and the broad sense ("The moral life," "moral science") of the word "moral," we may arrange the notions with which we have just been dealing in the following table:

11. I Cor. XIII: 13.
12. *"Circa Deum non contingit peccare per excessum."* Sum. theol., I–II, 64, 4.

Supra-moral or theological virtues and rules (proportioned to the divine life)	The moral life (or the ways in which man makes use of his freedom)—the object of moral science
Moral virtues and rules (proportioned to human life)	

The theological virtues are not the only supernatural energies the notion of which Christianity introduced into our knowledge of the moral life of man. Divine grace, according to the teaching of the Fathers and the theologians, also produces supernatural or "infused" moral virtues in the soul, which are of a higher order than the natural moral virtues or those acquired through the exercise of the will, and which have to do with the life men lead among themselves as members of the city of God and "fellow-citizens with the saints." And the term "gift" is especially reserved for still other capacities that the soul receives through grace and which are the gifts of the Spirit enumerated by Isaiah:[13] they bring the theological virtues to an experimental stage, so to speak, and, like a keyboard in us, touched by divine inspiration, they permit man while he is still here below to have a foretaste of the eternal Life, in other words, contemplative experience through union of love. (This is especially true of the gift of wisdom, the highest of gifts.) With respect to this contemplative experience of divine things, the moral virtues have only the rank of means for Christian ethics. St. Thomas Aquinas says that the virtue of Prudence "is in the service of Wisdom, introductory to it, and preparing the way for it, like a gatekeeper in the service of the king."[14]

It is thus that Christianity has suspended the moral from the supra-moral in the moral life of man.

Friendship's Love Between God and Man

11. All this shook the foundations of the purely philosophical

13. Isaiah XI: 2.
14. *Sum. theol.*, I-II, 66, 5, ad 1.

theory of the virtues elaborated by the moralists of antiquity, and singularly transformed it. And all this depended—this is our second remark—on a fundamental change in the notion of the relations between man and God. A *friendship* properly so called, and in the strongest, the most extravagant sense of the word, *a love as between friends* is possible, between man and God, and this love between friends—charity, the gift of grace, the highest of the theological virtues—is, over and above the moral virtues, the keystone of the whole edifice of morality. Such a teaching, brought to the ancient world by the evangelic message, was indeed a scandal for philosophy.

How, asked Aristotle, could any kind of friendship worthy of the name exist between Jupiter and man? And in the purely natural order it is quite true that divine transcendence excludes a friendship properly so called between God and man, because all friendship presupposes a certain equality. It is normal for man to love the First Cause. But he loves God in fear and trembling, as his sovereign, not as his friend. If he loved Him as his friend, it would be because God also loved him in the same way, for love between friends is a mutual love. And how (continuing in the perspective of the purely natural order) could God love man as being His friend, or "another Himself"? If man is loved by God, it is in quite a different way, in the sense that God wishes him well, as He does all that exists, but without having any community of life and interest in common with him, and remaining enclosed in His transcendence.

We find a similar position maintained by the orthodox Moslem theologians, who thought that love from person to person being a passion, and among the most extravagant, it cannot exist in God, and who condemned the mystic al Hallaj to be crucified because he believed in such a love between God and man.[15]

And an analogous position is also to be found in Spinoza, in his great arrogant notion of *amor intellectualis Dei*, of the perfect love with which the sage loves the God immanent in the world

---

15. Cf. Louis Massignon, *La Passion d'al Hallaj* (Paris: Geuthner, 1922). Al Hallaj was put to death in Bagdad, March 26, 922.

without any hope or desire of being loved in return.[16]

As far as Aristotle is concerned, "it would be ridiculous," he says, "to reproach God because the love we receive from him in return is not equal to the love we give him, just as it would be ridiculous for the subject to make a similar reproach to his prince. For it is the role of the prince to receive love, not to give it, or at least to love only in a different way."[17] Here it is philosophical wisdom itself which loses its head, for even in the purely natural order, and even in a love which is not between friends but between sovereign and subject, how could we give more than we received, and love God more than He loves us?

For Christianity, in any case, grace, by raising man to the supernatural order, makes him partake of the very life and goods of God, and by the same token produces that community of life and of goods, and that kind of equality, however scandalous in the eyes of pure philosophy, which are the conditions of friendship properly so called. God is no longer enclosed in His transcendence, He communicates it. Between God and man, as between friends, there can be love from person to person, with all its extravagance, love as between father and son, love as between husband and wife, the love of total giving hailed by the Song of Songs, and to which God was the first to surrender Himself, when He was incarnated. And the mystics will be able to say in this sense that God, because He thus wished it, needed our love as the friend needs the love of his friend, who is "another self." The great news, which is identical with that which promises us absolutely flawless happiness, or beatitude, is that God yearns toward us with love, and that He wishes to be loved by us as His friends.

This news was already contained in the Old Testament. "I love

16. Spinoza, *Ethics*, V, 19: "Qui Deum amat, conari non potest, ut Deus ipsum contra amet." Spinoza then tries, in vain (*ibid.*, prop. 36, corollary and scholium), to save nevertheless a certain amount of God's love for man (which is no other than His love for Himself working through the human spirit, in other words the *amor intellectualis Dei* itself).—Cf. *ibid.*, 17: "Deus *proprie loquendo neminem amat* neque odio habet" (our italics); and the *Short Treatise*, 2nd part, Chap. 24.

17. Aristotle, *Eudemian Ethics*, VII, 3, 1238 b 26–29.

those who love me."[18] It was fully manifested in the Gospel. "He who loves me will be loved by my Father, and I will love him."[19] "Henceforth I call you not servants . . . *but* I have called you friends."[20] And St. Thomas was to define the virtue of charity as the friendship created by grace between man and God, therefore involving mutual love from person to person, and founded on God's communication to man of His own life and finally of His own beatitude.[21]

This charity-love goes out to God first and foremost, and by the same token it goes out to all those who are called to be His friends, it goes out to all men. Love of God and fraternal love are one indivisible charity. And it is on this charity that Christianity makes the whole moral life of the human being depend. The whole law is contained in the precept to love God with our whole soul, and in the precept to love all men as our brothers, and these two form one single precept.

The Reversal of Values—the Call of the Ultimate End

12. A corollary to all the preceding remarks is the absolute primacy accorded by Christianity to charity-love in the scale of values relating to human life and conduct.

Without it, wisdom and virtue are empty and without value for eternal life. Our good acts are definitely good only by virtue of the charity which animates them. And if it is there it makes up for all the mistakes resulting from our weakness. As St. John of the Cross was to put it, "in the evening of this life it is on love that we shall be judged."

18. Proverbs VIII: 17. Similarly, we read in Isaiah: "Can a woman forget her suckling child, that she should not have compassion on the son of her womb? Yea, they may forget, yet I will not forget thee. Behold, I have graven thee upon the palms of my hands" (XLIX: 15–16); "Since thou wast precious in my sight, thou hast been honourable, and I have loved thee: therefore will I give men for thee, and people for thy life" (XLIII: 4); "I, even I, am he that blotteth out thy transgressions for mine own sake, and will not remember thy sins" (XLIII: 25). Thus does God declare His love to His people.
19. John XIV: 21.
20. John XV: 15.
21. Cf. *Sum theol.*, I-II, 23, 1.

Thus, in the last analysis, mercy fulfills justice; the mercy of God comes to man's rescue while he is bound to the precepts of the law. God forgives, something the God of the Platonic Republic did not do. And He does not assign to the earthly city the task of forcing men to be good, and irreproachably men; He leaves it to His grace, to His own kingdom, which is universal and above all earthly cities, to work within them to make them His sons and make them good through the very exercise of their most intimate freedom, through the love of charity which animates their acts and which is the form of their virtue, and which also compensates for their weaknesses. As we have already noted,[22] the Christian saint is not a superman formed by human agency, a Hercules of moral virtue like the Stoic sage; he is a friend of God who draws his life from supernatural charity and is formed by the divine hand, and who throws human weakness open to the divine plentitude descending into him. The vainglory of man is dethroned, and humility, wherein lives the force of God, is exalted.

This reversal of values in relation to the perfection of human life, henceforth conceived as the perfection of charity whose working in the soul no obstacle can stop or restrain, is tied up with a similar reversal regarding wisdom and contemplation. Supreme wisdom and supreme contemplation are no longer the summit of human Science and philosophy, but the abyss in man of the gift of the uncreated Spirit which makes him experience in faith and through Charity and the union of love, what no effort of the human intelligence can comprehend, and the things of God known as unknown. The very notion of contemplation changes in meaning, because from now on it designates an experience in which love instructs the intelligence, and a veiled communion with subsistent Truth, Life, and Goodness, a communion which is the work of charity under the very touch of God. Christian contemplation exists not "for the perfection of him who contemplates, and does not terminate in the intellect, like the contemplation of the philosophers. It exists for the love of Him who is contemplated and does not terminate in the intellect, for

22. Cf. above, p. 189.

the sake of knowing, but passes into the heart, for the sake of loving,"[23] because it proceeds itself from love. And for the same reason it does not terminate in a "theoretical" accomplishment but superabounds in action.

And all are called to such contemplation, from near or from afar, because it does not depend on nature, or on the knowledge of man, but on grace and divine gift—just as all are called to perfection. "Be ye therefore perfect, even as your Father in heaven is perfect,"[24] is a precept addressed to all, as indicating the end toward which each one should tend according to his ability and his condition. The great novelty introduced by Christianity is this appeal to all, to free men and slaves, to the ignorant and the cultivated, adolescents and old men, a call to a perfection which no effort of nature can attain but which is given by grace and consists in love, and from which therefore no one is excluded except by his own refusal.

The same thing is true regarding final Beatitude, the possession of the ultimate End through vision. It is promised to all, if only they really wish it. Impossible to attain through the capacities of nature alone, it offers itself as incomparably more attainable than earthly happiness and Aristotelian eudemonia, for which there is no Penitent Thief.

Thus the moral ideal of Christianity, and the ultimate End it proposes, finally possess that effectiveness of appeal to the human being and his thirst for happiness (now transfigured) which was lacking in the rational ethics of Aristotle, and to which Stoic and Epicurean ethics sacrificed everything, but only to be disappointed in the end. This moral ideal of Christianity is not an easy one; and if one considers only the capacities of human nature, and its infirmities, its propensity to evil, it would seem even more impossible to realize than the Stoic or Epicurean ideal. The fact is that Christianity has only raised the level of human civiliza-

---

23. "Contemplatio philosophorum est propter perfectionem contemplantis, et ideo sistit in intellectu, et ita finis eorum in hoc est cognitio intellectus.

"Sed contemplatio sanctorum . . . est propter amorem ipsius, scilicet contemplati Dei: idcirco, non sistit in fine ultimo in intellectu per cognitionem, sed transit ad affectum per amorem." Saint Albert the Great, *De Adherendo Deo*, cap. IX.

24. Matthew V: 48.

tions at the price of bringing about trouble and division in them at the same time, as a result of the yes or no it requires of the heart. It has not put an end to wars. It has activated history—it has not subjugated it (God Himself does not do that). It has evangelized the earth—it has not subdued it. Not only contrary efforts and the rebellions of nature, but the action of humanity's own deficiencies upon the divine leaven itself, when the forces of man have undertaken to serve Christ with their own means, have brought it about that Christianity has increased suffering in our species, at the same time that it brought about all real moral progress and every real increase of goodness. But the evangelic hope has left its mark forever in the depths of humanity. Saintliness has transfigured the heart of man, not only among the saints, but among all the sinners whom a ray of it has touched. And in revealing to us that God is love and makes us His sons through grace, that the ultimate fulfillment toward which our poor life proceeds is to possess Him through vision, Christianity, without giving way to any illusions about the potentialities of nature or underestimating its dignity either, has succeeded in assuring the decisive effectiveness of the appeal to the human soul of the ultimate end which is proposed to it—and this is the crucial concern for ethics.

Philosophy Put to The Test

13. Where the New Law has been received, the various factors of which we have spoken in the preceding pages have been integrated into the common consciousness and the rule of common morality, which form the proper subject of the moralist's reflection. And thereby moral philosophy is placed in an embarrassing position. If the moral philosopher recognizes these factors, he makes a place in his philosophy for things which depend on religious faith, not on philosophy. If he fails to recognize them, he is leaving out things which form an integral part of that human reality which he intends precisely to elucidate on the level of reflection, and so he causes moral philosophy to quit the soil of existence and fly off into the void.

In actual fact, not to speak of certain authors of textbooks of

Christian philosophy who have naively taken the tack, as vain from the point of view of the faith as from that of reason, of making moral philosophy a kind of decalcomania or counterfeit of moral theology, we have seen the philosophers engage first in an attempt at *separation,* seeking with Descartes a more or less Stoic natural morality which Science would establish to ensure happiness in the life here below, while Faith would in addition provide man conceived along the lines of this kind of Christian naturalism with eternal delights for life in the hereafter. Or, like Spinoza, they made of ethics a world apart, reserved for the rationalist sage. Or they followed the theoreticians of natural religion, and reduced all the data issuing from Christian revelation, and even God Himself, to the measure of deist philosophy and its enterprise of rational eviction. Later, with Kant, and particularly with Hegel, in their desire to construct an ethics capable of integrating all values, and the most vital ones, recognized by the common consciousness, the philosophers were to engage in an enterprise of *absorption* and *substitution* of vastly more profound significance, in which philosophy would explicitly assume the whole burden which theology regarded as its own, and finally, in the name of the God of history, would take charge of the destinies and salvation of the human race.

III REVEALED ETHICS

The Tables of Moses and the Gospel—Moral Law Divinely Promulgated

14. There exists for man a natural knowledge of moral rules— natural, though more or less perfect and developed—a knowledge which presents itself in two quite different modes: in the first place, what can be called a *natural-spontaneous* knowledge of moral rules, which is at work, without words, in the conscience of everyone and which expresses itself socially—at a level which is no longer the level of natural law itself—in the customs and taboos of primitive tribes, then in the laws and customs of political societies. In the second place there is what can be called a

natural-reflexive knowledge of moral rules, which is the concern of philosophers (it constitutes the object of our present historical analysis). Religious belief, moreover, has always influenced the social expression of the natural-spontaneous knowledge of moral rules, and in an especially direct way in primitive civilizations and in the great ancient civilizations, in which religion was closely incorporated with the social group as one of the organs proper to it.

When Christianity spread in the ancient world, it brought with it—along with the idea of the distinction between the things that are Caesar's and the things that are God's—what may be called a *revealed knowledge* of moral rules—which did not render the efforts of philosophical reason superfluous in this domain, but relegated them to second place, and, if I may say so, remarkably simplified the task to which the great ethical systems of antiquity had dedicated themselves in their search for the moral ideal to propose to men. This was a change of incalculable significance.

God, the ultimate absolute End, He who Is and whose Name is above all names, God the creator and savior, the personal and infinitely transcendent God of the Judeo-Christian tradition, God Himself speaks and instructs men in His precepts, declares to them what are the right ways in human life.

Through Moses He gave them the Decalogue. Through Christ He gave them the New Law.

The rules of human life are taught from on high. The knowledge of them is brought to us by faith, not by reason. It is a revealed knowledge, even the knowledge of the moral rules which are otherwise naturally knowable by the human intelligence and are, in a more or less obscure, imperfect or warped way, spontaneously perceived by human intelligence (the precepts of the Decalogue are essentially a revealed formulation of the principles of natural law).

Humanity finds itself in the presence of a *revealed ethics,* an essentially religious ethics. It is given to man with the absolute, unquestionable, infallible authority which belongs to the Word of God. Let us recall the thunder and lightning, and the voice of the trumpet, and the flames and the smoking mountain, which made the people tremble and kept them at a distance;[25] and the glory which hindered the children of Israel from fixing their gaze on the face of Moses, because of the brightness of his countenance.[26] Such was the attire in which the Tables of the Law were given to men, and the revealed Ethics enthroned before them.

The moral order in consequence will acquire a fixity, a solidity, a rigor; it will deliver itself in unconditional commandments and in absolute requirements which did not appear in any of the ethical theories elaborated by the reason of the philosophers of classical antiquity. It was under the influence of the Judeo-Christian revelation that these properties of the moral law were inscribed in common consciousness.

The New Law, Thomas Aquinas explains,[27] is less severe than the Old Law, because the Old Law imposed on man a far greater number of external actions and obligations. But the New Law carries its precepts and prohibitions into the very intimacy of the heart, the internal acts and movements of the soul; and in this sense Augustine could say that the New Law is easy for him who loves, but hard for him who does not.[28]

In any case, the Old Law and the New Law have both given a sacred significance, immediately referred to God and the Sanctity of His Justice, to the notion of the precept, as to that of sin and of duty; and this significance was even more profound and more exacting in the New Law.

As a result of the impact of Christianity, the sense of transgression and of obligation were thus to take on a new character, both in common consciousness and in ethical theory.

The sense of transgression and the sense of obligation are both natural to us. They derive from the natural functioning of the practical intellect in each of us (whatever the adventitious part played by the constraints of the group or by social taboos in their development). Yet Greek reason, in its philosophical elucidations, except perhaps in the case of the Stoics, had a rather lowered notion of moral obligation and moral fault, which it considered

25. Exod. XX: 18.
26. II Cor. III: 7.
27. *Sum. theol.*, I-II, 107, 4.
28. *De natura et gratia*, cap. LXII.

on a level close to that of art. The Judeo-Christian revelation, on the contrary, raised them to the supra-rational level of divine injunction obeyed or transgressed, and reinforced and magnified them by giving them a sacred status much more profound and purer (because related to a transcendent God, and disengaged from the particularisms of the human group) than the sacro-social regimes of the primitive and ancient religions had been able to do.

Sin is henceforth an offense to God—and according to the Christian faith it is responsible for the death of the Son of God on the cross.

Duty is henceforth a requirement in us emanating from the Creator whom heaven and earth obey, and from the Father whom we love if we do His will.

As for the notion of moral rule or of moral law, it will continue to bear the mark imprinted on it at Sinai, the character of commandment laid down by the hand of God in the radiance of His glory, even if, with the Gospel, it was to be interiorized. The tables of the Decalogue have had the same importance in the history of moral ideas as the words repeated by Moses, "I Am Who Is," or, according to modern exegesis, "I am who I am,"[29] have had in the history of speculative reason. The rules of human conduct no longer have to be discovered by the gropings of the tribe's collective conscience or by the philosophic reason. They are made manifest by God Himself, in a code of morality fixed from on high.

A Reinforcement Which May Regenerate Moral Philosophy or Endanger It

15. Here again it is well to remark on the fact that God is more interested in the salvation of the human race than in the labor of philosophers. No doubt revealed ethics offers invaluable assist-

---

29. Exod. III: 14. Actually, in both interpretations "He who is" or "He who alone knows his being and his name" asserts himself equally as Being infinitely transcendent *a se*. In any case it is the interpretation which was accepted for many centuries (He who is) which had a decisive effect on speculative reason and on what Etienne Gilson has called the metaphysics of Exodus.

ance to moral philosophy, if the latter knows how to profit from it; in particular, it was no small matter for philosophy to see the unwritten law written and formulated by its Author. But philosophy does not always know how to profit by divine occasions; they put a purely rational discipline in an embarrassing position, concerned as it is on its own account with primary realities and supreme Laws. If it is not tempted to reject that which it has not itself discovered, and which escapes the grasp of pure reason, philosophy is tempted to bring divine revelation down to its own level, use it to increase its own store by denaturing it in order to bring it within the grasp of pure reason.

The historian of culture has no trouble observing that this divine reinforcement, and, if I may put it so, this sacred aggravation of human morality, have been an immensely valuable help to humanity in its forward movement. But he is also aware that in order correctly to understand the contribution made by the Decalogue and revealed ethics to the moral life of humanity, one condition is necessary: namely, that one also understand that such a reinforcement and such an absolutization of the moral rule must be nurtured in the climate of the supernatural reality of grace given to men, and of the redemptive Mercy in which the Justice of the Author of the Law is consummated, and in the climate of the primary precept—the love above all else of Him who is love itself and who wishes to give Himself, to make the human creature partake of His own life.

If we secularize the Tables of the Law, if we transfer the features of the morality of the Ten Commandments to the natural moral law as it derives from reason alone, and is supposed to operate in the order and climate of pure nature, from which all that pertains to the faith and to grace has been eliminated, then we debase and degrade revealed ethics, the morality of the Ten Commandments, and at the same time we deform and harden, perhaps not in its content but in its attitude, the countenance of natural morality—I mean the spontaneous ethics of the conscience which is guided by the inclinations of nature and the reflective ethics of philosophical reason. We arm natural morality with a thunder which properly belongs only to revealed ethics.

Let us think about the natural rule of morality, that rule of which St. Paul spoke apropos of the pagans, whose conscience, with its reproaches and incitements, witnesses that they bear in themselves their own law;[30] one may compare it, in its natural manner and bearing, to a child of man, a young hunter armed with his bow, who trudges along as best he can in the forest. He has a good eye, he aims straight, but his equipment is humble and primitive. He has a long way to go to become an expert hunter in the years to come. And now suppose that we conceive of this natural rule of morality after the model of revealed ethics. Here is our same apprentice hunter transformed into a king seated on his throne, a crown on his head and a scepter in hand— and giving stern looks, because he is, after all, only a child of the woods.

The last three centuries have been rich in examples of social formations in which the inherited rules of revealed ethics were still to be found in force, but in which the context normally furnished by the order of grace had been lost from sight, and in which a kind of natural religion or decorative Christianity, maintained as a moralizing agency, protected and sheltered earthly interests which were very sure of themselves. If people who shared in this way of thinking were not much interested in God, except as a guardian of order, they nevertheless believed firmly in a code of moral austerity filled with commandments all the more unconditional, with prohibitions all the more rigorous, and with condemnations all the more severely applied because the code was primarily concerned with external acts and aimed above all at the conservation of the structures of the social group. This was a case of a deconsecrated and secularized sacred morality. It was not a Christian morality, which is suspended from the theological order and from love, which knows pardon and pity, and which is attuned to contemplation, and to what St. Paul calls "the goodness and love of God our Savior toward man."[31] Nor was it natural morality, which has its source in our essential inclinations and in reason, and which shares the human mood and the seeking attitude of authentic reason, an attitude in which

30. Rom. II: 14–15.
31. Tit. III: 4.

there is indulgence, curiosity, sympathy, always a little hesitation and a little irony, and always a desire to understand and clarify.

But it is in the realm of philosophy, with Kant and Kantian ethics, that we find the most significant example of the way in which the influence of Christianity and of revealed ethics can impair a reason which in other respects repudiates the most essential content of Christianity. It is always dangerous to be half Christian. The impact of Christianity quickens reason (without rendering it infallible) when reason nourishes itself on the substance of Christianity. When reason fattens itself on the leftovers of Christianity, the impact of Christianity warps it. The sacralization of the moral life becomes a dangerous blessing when we cease to understand what that sacralization means. Then what was a supernatural reinforcement and a sacred promulgation of the moral law, becomes a hardening and an arrogance against nature in an ethics which only retains the imprint of the Tables of the Law in order to make of them the Tables of Pure Reason.

Another historical accident, another misconception for which revealed ethics offered an occasion to human reason, and for which certain theologians this time bore primary responsibility, can also be pointed out. I allude here to the line of thinkers (the teachers of Islam above all, but also, on the Christian side, Scotus and Occam in the Middle Ages, Descartes in modern times) who, struck more or less consciously by the grand image of the revelation of the Decalogue amid the lightning and thunder of Omnipotence, believed that the moral law, and finally even the distinction between good and evil, depended not at all on divine Wisdom and Reason, the foundation of eternal necessities, but uniquely and exclusively on the pure Will or the pure All-Powerfulness of God, and on an arbitrary decision of His sovereign Freedom. A kind of divine despotism thus became the source of the moral law, decreed and imposed without reason by the celestial High Command. It seems probable to me that this way of looking at things, which St. Thomas Aquinas considered blasphemy, but which was not without its effect here and there on popular consciousness, or popular ignorance, exercised a serious influence on Kant, and played a double role in his thought. On the one hand, I believe, it made him reject, as subjecting the spirit of man to a despotic heteronomy, any idea of making the authority of the moral law depend on the Creator of nature. On the other hand, it made him transfer this same despotic sovereignty to the pure practical Reason, itself identified with the autonomous Will of Man, taken in its supra-empirical dignity.

13

Natural Law and Moral Law [*]

In this chapter I should like to try to clarify certain basic concepts—basic for the theory of Natural Law—in the perspective of Thomistic philosophy.

Natural Law (Lex Naturalis)

Reason is "the measure of human actions." Thus reason—human reason—is a measuring measure (*mensura mensurans*). Yet reason is also a measured measure (*mensura mensurata*), for human reason is not the supreme rule of good and evil. In order to measure human conduct, practical reason has to be measured by something. What is it by which practical reason is measured? Natural Law (*lex naturalis*. In the expression "natural law" it is appropriate to understand "law" in the sense of *lex*, not of *jus*). Let us summarize as briefly as possible the fundamental characteristics of Natural Law.[1]

Two essential components must be recognized in the notion of Natural Law: the *ontological* and the *gnoseological*.

Considered in its ontological component, Natural Law is the normality of functioning of the human being. Every kind of being existing in nature, a plant, a dog, a horse, has its own "natural law," that is, the proper way in which, by reason of its specific

---

[*] From *Moral Principles of Action: Man's Ethical Imperative,* planned and edited by Ruth Nanda Anshen (New York and London: Harper & Brothers, 1952), pp. 62–76.
1. Cf. J. Maritain, *Man and the State* (Chicago: The University of Chicago Press, 1951).

structure and ends, it "should" achieve fullness of being in its growth or in its behavior. Now this very word "should" begins to have a *moral* sense, that is, to imply moral obligation, when we pass the threshold of the world of free agents. Natural Law—strictly speaking, Natural Law for man—is moral law, because man obeys or disobeys it freely. We might compare natural law in general with an algebraic equation according to which a curve develops in space. But with man the curve must conform freely to the equation.

Let us say, then, that in its ontological aspect Natural Law is an ideal order or a *divide* between the suitable and the unsuitable, the proper and the improper, which depends on human nature and its essential ends. In this first consideration (ontological) Natural Law is co-extensive with the whole field of moral regulations which concern man as man—even if they are grounded on the most subtle and refined considerations—with the whole field of ethical philosophy, as universally valid.

But the second essential component of the notion of Natural Law, the gnoseological component, causes the extent of this notion to be greatly restricted. For Natural Law is natural not only in so far as it is the normality of functioning of human nature, but also in so far as it is *naturally known:* that is to say, known *through inclination,* by way of congeniality or connaturality, not through conceptual knowledge and by way of reasoning. Here we have a crucial point, which in my opinion has been too often disregarded. It deals with the manner in which Natural Law is made manifest to practical reason. Natural Law is made manifest to practical reason in certain judgments, but these very judgments do not proceed from any conceptual, discursive, rational exercise of reason. They proceed from *connaturality* or *congeniality* through which what is consonant with the essential inclinations of human nature is grasped by the intellect as good; what is dissonant, as bad. And they therefore remain always more or less immersed in the vital and experiential, conceptually inexpressible dynamism of inclinations and tendencies. The motive power on which they depend is not reason, demonstration, *logos,* but nature and nature's root inclinations. Thus it is that Natural Law is, in the fullest sense of this word, *unwritten* law. And, by the same token, it appears that Natural Law, considered not in its ontological component alone but also in its gnoseological component, only embraces those requirements of the human being's normality of functioning which are *known through inclination*—in other words, the principles "immediately" known (that is, without conceptual or rational medium) of human morality.

At this point two observations of the utmost importance should be made, which, to my regret, I cannot discuss here as fully as I should like. First, the inclinations to which I have just referred are not the animal instincts, qua animal, but the inclinations—ontological, animal, and rational—of the human being *in so far as they are human,* or in so far as they are vitally rooted in the non-conceptual life of the mind, that is, in reason as "form" or entelechy of our psychological energies (a function of reason which is performed in a pre-conscious manner). Let us say, then, inclinations of nature as refracted through the crystal of reason in its unconscious or pre-conscious life. For what is consonant with reason spontaneously pleases the rational animal.

Second, these natural inclinations rooted in reason presuppose a primary, self-evident principle: "the good is to be done, the evil is to be avoided," of which all men are aware. But as to further determinations, they are dependent upon historical progress which is characteristic of mankind. For man is an animal of culture, an historical animal. As a result, the essential inclinations of which we are speaking either developed or were released in the course of an historical progress which was constantly thwarted, moreover, by any kind of accidental process of regression or perversion. Thus it is that man's knowledge of the content of Natural Law was progressively formed and molded by the inclinations of human nature, starting with the most basic ones. The very history of human conscience distinguishes genuine human inclinations from spurious or perverted ones. The truly authentic inclinations were those which, in the long history of human conscience, led reason to an awareness of the regulations which, recognized more or less indeterminately from the time of the oldest social communities, have remained permanent in the human race, while assuming forms more definite and more clearly determined. At this point nothing appears more valuable to moral philosophy, especially to the theory of Natural Law, than the data of anthropology. An attentive examination of such data shows that what I venture to call the fundamental *dynamic schemes* of Natural Law are susceptible only of indeterminate expression (for example: "no family group exists without some kind of fixed pattern"), but that they are the object of a considerably more universal knowledge—at all times and in all places —than would appear upon superficial inspection.

We can understand, moreover, why there is a large measure of variability in the particular rules, customs, standards of life through which, among all of the earth's people, mankind has conveyed its knowledge of the most fundamental and deep-seated principles of Natural Law. This spontaneous knowledge does not bear upon conceptually discovered and rationally deduced moral regulations but upon regulations known through inclination, and in its ultimate source, upon general frameworks, which are tendential in nature, dynamic schemes of moral regulations still in a primitive state. Within such tendential frameworks or dynamic schemes the content may be considerably varied and more or less deficient, not to mention those warped, perverted, or devious inclinations which may be intermingled with authentic and fundamental inclinations.

ETERNAL LAW

These explanations, although summary, provide a sufficiently clear idea of what Natural Law is. It is necessary, however, to proceed further, for the concept of Natural Law is given its definitive meaning only when that of Eternal Law has been established.

This concept of Eternal Law is not solely theological. It is a philosophical truth as well, one which the philosopher with his means alone can reach and establish. God exists. He is the first cause of being, activating all beings. It is by His intellect and will that He acts: whence the notion of Providence. The entire community of the universe is governed by the divine reason. Hence there is in God, as in One who governs the entirety of created beings, this very reality which is the judgment and command of the practical intellect applied to the governing of a unified community: in other words, this very reality which we call *law*. Eternal Law is one with the eternal wisdom of God and the divine essence itself. Saint Thomas defines this Eternal Law as "nothing other than the exemplar of divine wisdom insofar as this wisdom directs all the actions and movements of things."[2]

It is evidently to this Eternal Law that we must have recourse if we are in search of the first foundation of Natural Law. Because every law is a work of reason, at the source of Natural Law there must be reason: not human reason but Subsistent Reason, the intellect which is one with the First Truth itself. "Law is a measure and a rule," says Saint Thomas, "and hence is found in him who rules, and also in that which is measured and ruled, for a thing is ruled and measured insofar as it participates in the measure and rule existing in the one who rules. Now, since all things are ruled and measured by the Eternal Law, we must conclude that they participate in this Law insofar as they derive from it the inclinations through which they tend naturally toward their proper operations and ends. Now among all creatures, the rational creature is subject to divine providence in a particular and more excellent way, inasmuch as it has a share in providential government, by being provident both for itself and others. Thus the rational creature by its very rationality participates in the eternal reason and because of this participation has a natural inclination to the actions and ends proper to it." (What is meant here are those inclinations "rooted in reason" of which we were just speaking.) "It is this participation in the Eternal Law enjoyed by the rational creature which is called the Natural Law."[3]

What emerges from this doctrine—and this is a fundamental point—is that the Natural Law is known by human reason, but that human reason, in its rational exercise, has no part in its establishment. The divine reason alone is the author of Natural Law. It alone causes that Law to exist, and it alone causes it to be known, insofar as it is the cause of human nature and of its

2. *Sum. theol.*, I–II, 93, 1.
3. *Ibid.*, 91, 2.

essential inclinations. Let us not say merely (as was generally held in the sixteenth and seventeenth centuries) that God guarantees the exercise and value of our reason as though it were our reason which instituted Natural Law, or at least deciphered it in nature and made it known by its own effort and authority. Let us say rather that here the divine reason is *the only reason* to be considered. The law, in effect, is essentially an ordinance of reason (*ordinatio rationis*), so that without an ordering reason there is no law. The notion of law is essentially bound up with that of an ordering reason. Indeed, in the case of Natural Law, human reason has no share in the initiative and authority establishing the Law, either in making it exist or in making it known. How then does it know Natural Law? It knows it through inclination, by connaturality—through the inclinations of nature, which is the work of God, and not by its own rational effort. It knows the Law; it in no way makes it. According as human reason knows Natural Law through inclination, it is in a very precise sense "natural reason," *ratio naturalis,* and the light of this natural reason is "nothing other than a certain impression of the divine light upon us."[4] The author of Natural Law is exclusively the divine reason.

The fact that the divine reason is the only reason which is author of the Law enables us to understand better the meaning of Saint Thomas' expression: Natural Law is a participation in the Eternal Law. It is the divine reason which is involved. If human reason had a hand in it, the Law would, to that extent, have no more than the value of human authority.

The formal medium by which we advance in our knowledge of the regulations of Natural Law is not the conceptual work of reason, but rather those inclinations to which the practical intellect conforms in judging what is good and what is bad. Through the channel of natural inclinations the divine reason imprints its light upon human reason. This is why the notion of knowledge through inclination is basic to the understanding of Natural Law, for it brushes aside any intervention of human reason as a creative factor in Natural Law.

4. *Ibid.*

It is evident, then, how strongly and decisively Natural Law obliges *by virtue* of Eternal Law. It is from the divine reason that it possesses its rational character, and consequently, it is from the divine reason that it possesses its genuine nature as law and its obligatory character.

We can understand at this point in what the error in the conceptions of a thinker like Grotius consisted. While maintaining that Natural Law presupposed in fact God's existence, he wrote the celebrated sentence in which he said that even if, on an absurd supposition, God did not exist, Natural Law would continue to exercise its dominion and its authority over us. The fact is that he was concentrating solely upon the order of nature—as deciphered by human reason—and did not perceive the relationship between the order of nature and the eternal reason.

Two things are to be considered here. Suppose, absurdly, that God does not exist and that nothing is changed in things: then, by hypothesis, nature would continue to exist, and consequently the normality of functioning of human nature; the exigencies of the ideal order based upon the essence of man would likewise continue to exist. But a second question presents itself: is this order rational, is it wise, does it oblige me in conscience? Indeed, the only foundation for its rationality is the Eternal Law, the divine reason, and it is precisely this which Grotius did not perceive. Thus began the process (prepared by Scholastic doctors who came after Saint Thomas and who neglected the essential importance of the component: knowledge through inclination) of a rationalistic deformation of the concept of Natural Law. At that moment a separation took place, a schism, between Eternal Reason and the order of nature. God became merely the guarantor of that order, and Natural Law ceased to be a participation in Eternal Law. It became the order of a nature which was sufficient to herself, an order for which the conceptual and discursive reason provided knowledge. But why should I be obliged in conscience by a purely factual order? In reality, if God does not exist, the Natural Law lacks obligatory power. If the Natural Law does not commit the divine reason, it is not a law, and if it is not a law, it does not oblige.

I would like to remark further, concerning the concept of Eternal Law, that this concept enables us to realize the essentially analogical character of the notion of law. The word "law" in the expression "natural law" admits of the danger of a misunderstanding because the most obvious and the most immediate notion that we have of law is that of written law or positive law: consequently, if we overlook the analogical character of the notion of law, we run the risk of conceiving Natural Law and every species of law after the pattern of the type of law best known to us, written law.

But the very notion of Eternal Law brings this analogical character to light in an undeniable manner. For the definition of law: "A certain ordinance of reason for the common good, promulgated by him who has the care of the community,"[5] has its first realization—in itself, *secundum se,* and not with regard to us and our manner of knowing—in the Eternal Law. But God is not a legislator like the others. The community that He heads is the entire created universe. The Eternal Law is not written upon paper, it is promulgated in the divine intellect and is known in itself solely by God and by those who see Him in His essence. However, Saint Thomas writes that every rational creature knows a certain reflection of it insofar as this creature knows truth. "For all knowledge of truth is a sort of reflection of and participation in the Eternal Law, which is the unchangeable truth."[6] The Eternal Law is as infinitely distant from written or human law as the divine essence is from created being. Between the two there is only an analogical community. Likewise, the notion of law is only analogically common to the concepts of Natural Law and positive law, and so also to the concepts of Natural Law and Eternal Law. This analogicity of the notion of law will be even more readily grasped if we discuss the concept of "right" (*jus*) and compare it with that of "law" (*lex*).[7] What is the relation between law and right?

5. *Ibid.,* 90, 4.
6. *Ibid.,* 93, 2.
7. In current language, these two concepts are expressed in English by the same word, "law." Hence a supplementary difficulty arises. For the sake of clarity, we may be permitted to use the word "right" to signify *jus* (*droit Recht*), and the word "law" to signify solely *lex* (*loi, Gesetz*).

NATURAL RIGHT

When it is a question of positive law (written law), the relation between law and right is very simple—it is a relation of identity. Positive right and positive law are the same thing; they are synonyms, because the notion of right, or of juridical order, signifies a code of laws suited to a certain type of common life which men are not only obliged to obey in conscience, but can be constrained to obey by the coercive power of society. We are confronted, therefore, with the notion of *debitum legale*, of what is legally due or legally just, the neglect of which is punishable by the external sanctions established by law. Given this meaning of the word "right," it is clear that positive right and positive law are the same thing: positive right and positive law emanate from social authority and are sanctioned by the constraints of society. We have here the order of legality or the juridical order which supposes the moral order, but which adds something to it, namely, this possibility of constraint by society.

But let us consider now the domain of Natural Law, which is that of morality, and not of legality. As we have already remarked, although the notion of Natural Law in itself (*secundum se*) is prior to that of positive law, nevertheless, *as far as we ourselves* and our manner of knowing are concerned (*quoad nos*), it is from the idea of the positive law, which is first known, that we proceed to the idea of the Natural Law. Consequently, since we say positive law and positive right with equivalent meaning, it seems natural to say *right* and *law* equivalently when the question is one of Natural Law. Hence the use of the expression "natural right" (*Naturrecht, droit naturel*) in the habitual language of philosophers and jurists.

The application of the notion of right in such a domain, however, involves us in serious difficulties. Natural Law—which is not written, which concerns man as man, and a community which is neither the body politic nor the civilized community but simply the community of the human species, and which obliges us in conscience—Natural Law is promulgated in our reason as knowing (insofar as it knows through inclination), and not as legislating; and it concerns the moral, not the juridical order. What we have here is nothing other than the notion of *debitum morale*, of that which is morally due by virtue of right reason, or by virtue of Natural Law, but not by virtue of a juridical constraint. How, then, under these conditions, can we speak of natural *right?* Is there not a simple contradiction in terms here, and would it not be preferable to rid oneself of such an expression? This is a temptation for the philosopher, for it would be the most convenient thing to do. Nevertheless, I do not believe that we must yield to it. In considering things more closely, we see that, in spite of everything, we do have a solid basis for speaking of natural right, and not only in the sense that this or that precept of Natural Law may become an object of a prescription of the positive law. For in a considerably more profound and universal sense it is necessary to say that each.man bears within himself the *judiciary authority* of humanity. (It is not a question here of the civilized community, as in the case of the law of nations, but of the human species.) This is true in an analogical but nonetheless real sense. Each member of the human species bears within him in a certain manner the judiciary authority of humanity, and consequently, the right of imposing constraint which derives from this authority.

How can we justify philosophically the right of legitimate defense? How can we say that a man has the right of killing another man when he is attacked by the latter, or that I have the right of putting to death a man who before my eyes throws himself upon a child to assassinate it? Is this simply a biological reflex? If so, there could be no question of a right. No, we are faced with a properly *judiciary* act. That is why this act is moral by virtue of a judiciary authority which transcends me and which goes back to the Author of nature and of humanity. Without possessing the function of a judge in society—and outside of the order of constituted tribunals to which punishment normally belongs—but simply as a member of the human species, I exercise in such a case a judiciary authority which is virtually inherent in the species and which may be actualized, in any man whatsoever under such exceptional circumstances. And this is not only the case in the examples I have just given. Each time that we give a counsel, or guide another man, or try to dispose circumstance so as to help him avoid an error in his moral life, we exercise in a certain measure and to a certain degree an authority which is derived in us from the Author of human reason. Each time that States, in the absence of an international judiciary power, have recourse to sanctions such as war or just reprisals against the aggression of another State, or against the barbarous procedures it employs, it is the judiciary authority virtually inherent in the human species which is being exercised. These acts of political power would have neither meaning nor moral justification if it were merely a question of defensive reflexes; they have human meaning and moral value only if the States in question decide upon such acts in the name of the judiciary authority of which they are the organs so long as there does not yet exist a supranational political society capable of putting the judgments of its tribunals into effect.

By reason of the fundamental notion which I have just expressed, we can say, in an analogical but real sense, that there is a natural juridical order contained within the Natural Law and the natural order of morality, but in a simply virtual manner. And in this sense the expression *natural right* is valid, but, once again, in an altogether analogical sense.

We have, then, the notion of a virtual juridical order which always remains virtual, and which never unfolds as a juridical order expressed in positive law and in the judiciary authority of human society, for we cannot conceive of a tribunal which would be charged with enforcing the Natural Law. As soon as a precept of Natural Law is expressed in written law, it becomes a precept of written law and by this token it is part of positive right, of the juridical positive order. But the *natural right* itself, insofar as it is natural *right*, remains *virtual*, enveloped in the Natural Law, and it is actualized in exceptional cases, for example, as we have seen, when a man or a State finds it necessary to exercise the judiciary authority of which the human species as such is depositary and which is derived from its Author, from the Divine Reason and Subsistent Justice.

Thus, natural right does not require, as a fulfillment which it should receive, formulation in positive law and in the juridical order in the full and formal sense of the word. It remains enveloped in the Natural Law.

JUS GENTIUM

With the *jus gentium* (the law of nations),[8] on the contrary, we
enter a domain in which the notion of right (*jus*) no longer takes
on merely a virtual but a formal and actual meaning as well. For
the philosopher or jurist, there is no notion more fraught with
difficulties than that of the law of nations. The different theories
which have been advanced since the sixteenth century have succeeded in obscuring the concept rather than clarifying it. It is
difficult to define the law of nations, because it is intermediary
between the Natural Law and the positive law—although Saint
Thomas does connect it rather with the positive law. Our thought
on the subject would profit greatly if, as a result of the systematic elucidation to which we now proceed, we were able to
determine clearly and exactly in what the law of nations consists.

Let us say, then, that in its most profound meaning, as we are
able to disengage it from the thought of Saint Thomas, the law
of nations (I would prefer to say the common law of civilization)
differs from the Natural Law in the manner in which it is *known,*
or in relation to the second essential component, the gnoseological component of the Natural Law. It is necessary to insist on the
manner in which the law in question is known. The law of nations
is known, not through inclination, but through the conceptual
exercise of reason. This is the specific difference distinguishing
the law of nations from the Natural Law. The Natural Law is
known through inclination, the law of nations is known through
the conceptual exercise of the human reason (considered not in
such and such an individual, but in common civilized humanity).
In this sense, it pertains to the positive law, and for this reason
Saint Thomas relates it to positive law: since wherever human
reason intervenes as author, we are in the general domain of the
positive law. In this case, the human reason does not intervene

8. We use the expression "law of nations" as equivalent to *jus gentium*
(*le droit des gens*), because the term is so well established in the language
of political science and political philosophy, although the term "right of
nations" would perhaps correspond better to our use of "positive right"
and "natural right." (It is true that the *law* of nations is distinguished in
this section from natural and positive *law*.)

as the author of the *existence of the law* (which is the case with positive law in the strict sense), but it does intervene as the author of the *knowledge of the law*. In consequence, with the law of nations, we have already a juridical order, no longer virtual as in the case of natural right but formal, although not necessarily written into a code. As to the manner in which the regulations of the law in question are known, it must be said that they are known through the rational, logical, conceptual exercise of the common reason, starting from more profound and more primary principles which are the principles of Natural Law.

Now it is necessary to make a distinction concerning the *content* of the law of nations. In the first place, the law of nations may include regulations pertaining also to the Natural Law (since the principle of distinction is not the content of the law, but the manner in which the knowledge of the law takes place). Hence, certain regulations which are based upon human nature, and which are connected necessarily with the first principle: "Do good and avoid evil," may be known on the one hand through inclination (in which sense they belong to Natural Law), and on the other hand through the conceptual exercise of reason (in which sense they belong to the law of nations).

Take this example: "We must obey the laws of the social group." This prescription may be a rational conclusion, established through the logical exercise of reason, for the common sense of humanity can deduce it from a more primitive principle: "Men should live in society," in which case we are in the presence of a precept of the law of nations. Now this same regulation: "Obey the laws of the group," is also a norm known not by way of conceptual demonstration, but through inclination, by conformity with the radical tendency which urges men to dwell in society, in which case it is a principle of the Natural Law. Hence the same thing may belong to the Natural Law if it is known through inclination and if the divine reason is the only operative principle causing it to be known as well as to exist, and to the law of nations if it is known by human reason which, intervening between the Divine Reason, the cause of nature, and the knowledge of the precept, acts on its own account and thus introduces an element of positive law.

In the second place, and this is the most general and most interesting case, the content of the law of nations may concern things which, although universally obligatory since they are deduced from a principle of the Natural Law, and although necessarily connected with the first principle: "Do good and avoid evil," go beyond the Natural Law because they are not previously known through inclination but are known *only* as the result of the conceptual exercise of reason, a deduction made not by jurists or philosophers, but by the common reason of humanity. Take this example: "Do not condemn anyone without a hearing." I do not think that this rule is first known through inclination; it is known only as a conclusion logically deduced from what is due in justice to an accused man. In such a case we have a precept of the law of nations which is not a precept of the Natural Law. Similarly, the precept: "Treat prisoners of war humanely," is known only through a logical operation accomplished by the human reason starting from a first principle of the Natural Law.

The law of nations or the common law of civilization has to do with duties which are necessarily bound up with the first principle: "Do good and avoid evil," but in cases like those I have just mentioned, this necessity is seen and established by human reason. And precisely because the regulations dealing with social life are *par excellence* the work of human reason, we have been gradually led to regard the law of nations as pertaining more to the social domain and especially to the international domain. But it is absurd to reduce the law of nations to the laws of international morality. According to what we have seen, every norm of conduct which is universally valid, but which is known to common consciousness because necessarily deduced by human reason, is a part of *jus gentium* or the common law of civilization.

The law of nations belongs at once to the moral order and to the juridical order; it presupposes a *debitum morale,* a moral obligation appealing to conscience, before the legal obligation, *debitum legale.* At the same time the law of nations is a formal juridical order, although not necessarily a written one. Hence it differs at once from natural right because it is not merely virtually contained in the order of natural morality, and from positive right because it is not necessarily promulgated by social authority

and applied by judiciary authority. It may be formulated juridically; in fact, it seeks to be, but is not necessarily so formulated.
Before it is at some future time formulated in the code of a
supranational world society whose tribunals would be required
to enforce it, the law of nations is first of all formulated in the
common conscience by human reason in its legislative role, making the law known through its own conceptual means. In a word,
it is based upon the natural order of morality, but it emanates
necessarily from this order as the first formal juridical order.

Positive Right

We come finally to positive law. The positive law in force in any
particular social group, whether it be a question of customary
right or written right, has to do with the rights and duties which
are bound up in a *contingent,* not a necessary, manner with the
first principle of the practical intellect: "Do good and avoid evil."
And it has as its author not the divine reason but the human
reason.[9]

By virtue of determined rules of conduct, established by the
reason and will of men when they institute the laws or engender
the customs of a particular social group, certain things will be
good and permissible and certain things bad and not permissible,
but it is the human reason which establishes this. Human reason
intervenes here as a creative factor not only in that which concerns the knowledge of the law—as in the case of the law of
nations—but in that which concerns the very existence of the law.
It has the astounding power of laying it down that certain things
will henceforth be good and others bad. Thus, for example, a
police ordinance has decreed that it will henceforth be good for
motorists to stop at the red light and to go when the light is
green. There is no kind of natural structure which requires this;

9. We are speaking here of human positive law and passing over what
concerns the divine positive law (which has God for its author, but those
regulations are contingent with regard to what is required by the nature of
the human being).

it depends uniquely upon the human reason. But once this regulation has been promulgated, it is evil not to stop at the red light. There is thus a moral good and a moral evil which depend upon the human reason because it takes into consideration the particular exigencies of the common good in these given circumstances, in conformity, however, with principles of the Natural Law, as for example: "Do not harm your fellow men." But the Natural Law itself does not prescribe the rules in question, it leaves them to the ultimate determination and initiative of the human reason. The Natural Law itself requires that what it leaves undetermined be ultimately determined by human reason.

Hence, the positive law obliges men in conscience—in other words the *debitum legale* that it institutes is also a *debitum morale*—because it obliges by virtue of Natural Law. By the same token we see that an unjust law is not a law. This follows as a consequence from what I have just said, that is, from the fact that the positive law obliges by virtue of the Natural Law which is a participation in the Eternal Law. It is inconceivable that an unjust law should oblige by virtue of the Natural Law, by virtue of regulations which go back to the Eternal Law and which are in us a participation in that Law. It is essential to a philosophy such as that of Saint Thomas to regard an unjust law as not obligatory. It is the counterpart of this truth that the just law binds in conscience because it binds by virtue of the Natural Law. If we forget the one, we forget the other.

14

THE "NATURAL" KNOWLEDGE
OF MORAL VALUES *

We must distinguish between a *philosophical* knowledge of moral values and a *natural, pre-philosophical* knowledge of these values. We must make this distinction because moral philosophy presupposes moral experience. There is a moral knowledge—that of the ordinary man, or that of common experience—which precedes philosophical knowledge. Men did not wait for philosophy in order to have an ethic.

As far as the *philosophical* knowledge of moral values is concerned, it comes about, as does any philosophical knowledge, by means of concepts and judgments. It presupposes a developed rational knowledge; it entails a scientific justification of values by the demonstrative determination of that which is consonant with reason, and of the proper ends of the human essence and of human society. We are here in the presence of the explaining, justifying, and manifesting function of truth, which belongs to moral philosophy. Moral philosophy is a reflexive knowledge, not, to be sure, in the same sense as logic, but still a "second-glance" knowledge. It presupposes the natural knowledge included in common moral experience, in the moral experience of the man who is not a philosopher, and on the perceptions and judgments of which the philosopher turns his gaze so as to justify and critically elucidate them. In Kantian ethics, one has the impression that the philosopher has received a sort of revelation of pure reason. He is its messenger, he announces the law. No! The law is neither made by

---

* *Neuf leçons sur les notions premières de la philosophie morale* (Paris: Téqui, 1951), pp. 47–59.

the philosopher, nor revealed to the philosopher, whether by Nature, or by Reason. The philosopher discovers the law in the moral experience of humanity, he disengages it, he does not make it; he is not a legislator. He does not announce the law, he reflects on it and explains it.

So that what must interest us above all, and what poses moreover a difficult philosophical problem, is the other knowledge of moral values, the knowledge I call *natural*, the *pre-philosophical* knowledge. In what manner does a man, any man at all, a man who never pursued science or philosophy, who is content with trying to live as best as possible, a simple member of common humanity—in what manner does he know moral values?

It seems to me that it is essential to understand that there is a very vast field where reason or intelligence functions in a manner which is as yet neither conceptual, nor logical, nor discursive —in a so-to-speak biological manner, as "form" of the psychic activities and under an unconscious or preconscious mode. There is not only the Freudian *unconscious* of instincts, images, and animal tendencies; there is another unconscious, which I would rather call preconscious, and which is the unconscious of the spirit in its living springs, the preconscious of the life of intelligence itself and of reason, when it disengages from sensible experience a view, a new intuition, which is not yet formed in a concept, but which aspires to be formed progressively into a concept. There is here a whole life, at once intuitive and unexpressed, of intelligence and reason, which precedes rational explications; it has a particularly manifest importance in the things of art and poetry, but it is also active at the sources of philosophical and even of scientific activity.

Two Categories of Inclinations

In the case of moral values, what seems to me important to point out is that we are in the presence of an implicit and preconscious rational knowledge, proceeding, not by mode of reason or of concepts, but by mode of inclination. Here we must distinguish two sorts of inclinations, two kinds of tendencies or—in the most general sense—of instincts: on the one hand, there are inclinations or instincts rooted in the *animal nature* of man, in the heredity of each one, instincts which are not absolutely predetermined, which are progressively fixed in the course of childhood, and which can be perverted, but which are nevertheless deeply rooted in the biological nature of man, whence they receive a powerful though not absolute fixity and stability. And then there is another category, an altogether different class of inclinations which emanate from *reason*, or from the *rational nature* of man. These inclinations *presuppose* the instinctive inclinations—for example, the animal instinct of procreation tending to the conservation of the species—let us say, more generally, they presuppose the tendencies inscribed in the ontological structure of the human being; but they presuppose also that these instinctive tendencies and inclinations have been seized and transferred into the dynamism of the intellect's apprehensions and the proper sphere of human nature as typically such, that is to say, as endowed and imbued with reason. They are a specifically new recasting, a transmutation or re-creation of these instinctive tendencies and inclinations which has its point of origin in the intellect or reason as "form" of the interior universe of man. Thus we will have, for example, the inclination to the not only physical but also moral begetting of children, and to the unity and stability of family society. We have here inclinations specifically human, even if they concern the animal domain. Nature has passed through the lake of the intellect (functioning unconsciously). The element which stabilizes these inclinations is not an ontological or instinctive structure, a "condition of construction," but rather the object of an (unformulated) insight on the part of the intellect—let us say, certain essential finalities perceived or felt in a non-conceptual and preconscious manner. And these inclinations born of reason or rooted in reason (for example, the inclination not to maltreat one who is held to be a human being)[1] can be in conflict with the purely instinctive inclinations

---

1. I say "who is held to be a human being" because in the most primitive societies (and not only in them) the idea of man remained, in the practical order, very much this side of its proper universality. Only the members of the tribe were held to be men.

(for example, the inclination to murder).

These inclinations rooted in reason are progressively fixed not only in the individual but in humanity in the course of its historical existence. They can be perverted as can the instinctive inclinations. They are stable *in their specific roots,* that is to say in reason, and to the extent that the life of reason prevails, but they have no stability in the specifically animal or biological sphere.

INCLINATIONS ROOTED IN REASON AND JUDGMENTS OF MORAL VALUE

Once we are in possession of the distinction between these two sorts of inclinations, how can we picture to ourselves the psychological process of the natural knowledge of moral values? I recall to mind that we are assuming an intelligence ignorant of any moral science: the intelligence of the child not yet formed to philosophical reflection, or of a primitive man, or of any man at all in whom reflection has not yet awakened, who simply exercises his natural powers, but not in a technical manner.

To understand the process in question, we must start from concrete situations, from facts of experience. The man of whom we are speaking finds himself in the presence of certain concrete facts, of concrete cases which are perceived by the senses, which act on the imagination and concern sense experience. He finds himself in the presence of a man who pays his workers the salary agreed upon; or, if it is a question of an example concerning the primitives, of a tribal chief who is hard and severe but who treats each one according to his acts, without making exception of persons. In the presence of an example like these, there is a certain pleasure of reason. Reason is content, it feels at home. I shall say (this is my first point) that the situation in question is seized in a certain concrete insight or notion of reason which remains engaged, immersed, incarnated in this situation itself, inseparable from it, and preconscious, not expressed in a mental word, but which, if it were translated into abstract terms, would doubtless come to something like this: "Render to each one what is his due." And while remaining implicit, immersed, not disengaged for itself, this concrete notion envelops two things in lived act (*in actu exercito*): (1) the insight that the man in question, in acting as he does, treats others as men (the philosopher will say that to treat men not as things but as persons is one of the essential finalities of human nature); and (2) the insight or the feeling that consequently such conduct is in accord with something true that we carry within us (the philosopher will say: with reason). Nothing of all this is expressed conceptually, all of it remains preconscious. And the notion of reason of which we are speaking —enveloped, immersed, unconscious, incarnated in images, and inseparable from the sense experience—does not operate as the logical beginning of a conceptual development; it operates as a guide for the tendencies.

In fact, and this is my second point, for the affective and tendential dynamism of man this unconscious and *immersed* notion of reason is a point of convergence, a point of determination which sets in motion proportionate inclinations and emotions. For example, complaisance and sympathy in the case of which we are speaking. And this by reason of a principle which might be formulated thus: *what is in tune with reason, pleases the rational animal; what is out of tune with reason, displeases him.* But this principle goes a great deal further. The animal tendencies and inclinations, the instincts predetermined by nature are as a pre-existing matter, whence the attraction of the immersed notions—points of irradiation, "centers of organization"—of which we are speaking will disengage and cause to emerge the inclinations of a specifically different and typically human order of which it was just now a question, and which result from a transmutation of the pre-existing tendencies transferred into a superior sphere, where the psyche receives the form and the irradiations of reason. It is as if the whole substance, the whole universe of tendencies and inclinations of the rational animal split in two, one half remaining the world of pre-existing animal instincts—the instinct of murder, for instance—and the other half constituting the world of properly human inclinations, rooted, as I have said, in reason, and which are progressively disengaged as essential to our nature—for example, the inclination not to maltreat one who is held to be a human being. (In the case that we have chosen, the pre-existing animal inclination would be the inclination to gregarious life, and the typically human inclination which is a transmutation of it would be the inclination to properly social life, and to justice.)

There, then, we have disengaged these essential inclinations rooted in reason as well as in nature, and in some way born of reason, not as conscious reason, proceeding conceptually and acting in an autonomous manner, but as form—in some way vegetative—of the natural dynamism of human tendencies and inclinations, and as center of unconscious or preconscious irradiations. And it is according to these inclinations that conscious reason, reason functioning as reason, will now produce spontaneously its judgments of value. This is my third point. Judgments of value, ethical judgments such as one finds at work in the common conscience of humanity, are not fundamentally and as a general rule judgments "by mode of cognition"; they are primarily and above all judgments *by mode of inclination*. Our intelligence does not judge here in virtue of reasonings and connections of concepts, or of demonstrations and logical constraints; it judges, in a nonconceptual manner, by conformity to the inclinations which are within us, and without being able to express the reasons for its judgment; its judgment has an implicitly rational value which is not disengaged. It is thus that the *natural* knowledge of ethical values proceeds. It is thus that the *common man* we are concerned with will come, in the presence of the cases we have chosen as examples, to say: this master, or this tribal chief, is *just*, and to be just is *good*. But do not ask him why! He knows that this is so, but he cannot explain it. The origin of his judgment has been an inclination, a tendency, which a preconscious and "immersed" notion of reason has caused to spring forth from the instinctive dynamism of nature. Even if he should succeed in formulating the abstract notion: render to each one what is his due—he will find himself embarrassed to justify it, to explain why this conduct is good and required.

The sociologists profit from this embarrassment to say: we are in the presence of simple emotional coefficients of social origin and without any objective content, not in the presence of rational notions. In reality, we are in the presence of judgments deter-

mined by inclinations which are themselves rooted in reason operating in a preconscious manner; there we have the authentic
schema of the natural knowledge of moral values. In the work of
philosophical reflection, in that second-glance knowledge which
is moral philosophy, reason operating in a logical and conscious
manner, the reason of the philosopher will conform itself to reason acting vitally, vegetatively, as a catalytic ferment which
releases, in virtue of a preconscious notion, not disengaged in
concepts, natural inclinations on which moral judgments will be
founded. Afterwards, once these moral judgments have been
consciously produced, they will be the source of secondary inclinations and tendencies; the dynamism of inclinations will progressively enrich itself; new typically moral tendencies will arise,
dependent on explicitly formulated notions of values and which
will be expressed by praise or blame, approbation, indignation,
etc. This process will continue to snowball; inclinations and
judgments of reason working mutually to enrich the natural
knowledge of moral values.

The schema I have just outlined must be completed in two
different ways.

There is a first complication. In the original experience that we
have considered and taken as point of departure, one finds, as we
have seen, a concrete notion of reason—for example: render to
each one what is his due—which is unconsciously present, enveloped, immersed in images, but not expressed. We must now add
that other notions—conscious concepts this time—accompany the
process and are normally engaged in the affair, since it is a question of a human and not an animal experience. And one or
another of them can play a role in emphasizing or highlighting
this or that aspect in the experience in question. Suppose that I
am in a fit of anger because one refuses to me what he accords
to my brother: the notion of justice is implicitly present; and then
suddenly a concept arises in my mind: "It's my *father* with whom
I am angry"; this concept will release a flow of emotions which
will counteract the first tendency to revolt against injustice and
which will perhaps perfect my moral experience, render purer
my notion of justice. Another example: for many centuries prisoners of war were considered as still being enemies in act; it was

fitting to maltreat them, to mutilate them, to make slaves of them; and for common consciousness, in the ages in question, this manner of acting seemed just because what is due to the enemy as such is punishment. Well, suppose that at a given moment in human history a concept or idea arises: "Ah, he's a man!" The sudden appearance of such a concept suffices for the inclination on which the moral judgment depends to find itself changed and for the notion of a purer justice to be by this very fact disengaged, because I will have understood that what I must consider in a prisoner is not the enemy in act, but the man. You see the importance of the repercussion of ideas on natural inclinations in the progress of moral conscience.

The second complication comes from the social milieu, from the role played by education, customs, taboos, the traditions of the group. I am not speaking now of the process of imitation, or of submission, or of external conformity to the judgment of society; nor am I speaking of the effects of social constraint. What I would like to note is that independently of all this the mere fact that we *are told* certain things, that our attention is drawn to them, the mere fact that certain concepts and certain values are thus pointed out to us, stimulates or fortifies the natural development of the tendencies and inclinations rooted in reason. It is the same here as with the conscious concepts, spontaneously arisen in our mind, of which I was just speaking. This time they are uttered by the milieu. The social milieu functions as a beacon projecting light on a given aspect. All this conceptual and rational work is produced on a base which is that of inclinations rooted at once in nature and in reason, which depend on unconscious and "immersed" notions of reason, and on which depend judgments by mode of inclination, not by mode of cognition.

The ancients emphasized very vigorously the natural inclinations toward the moral good; they spoke of them a great deal, perhaps in a somewhat too simple manner, for these inclinations are not always stable and suffer exceptions. Maternal love is a natural inclination, but there are hens which kill their chickens.

This is why there is need, it seems to me, to distinguish in a more precise manner than is usually done the two categories of instincts and inclinations which I have just now mentioned: on the one hand the instincts relating to the *animal nature* of man, the hereditary tendencies, the factors determined by nature; on the other hand the inclinations and tendencies born of reason, because man is by nature a rational being and because, as we remarked above, what is in tune with reason is by nature pleasing to the rational animal.

In the second place, we must recognize that both of these categories of instincts or inclinations can be perverted.

Thirdly, we must recognize that these two categories are often in mutual conflict or, on the contrary, more or less mingled or intertwined, so that the natural tendencies and inclinations born of reason can be vanquished or warped by the other instincts.

Fourthly, we must recognize the fact that the natural tendencies or inclinations born of reason are relatively fragile and are not immutably determined in themselves. In their development they depend on the *notional state* of the intellect, and depend also on social customs. But, not only can these two factors be aberrant, but their evolution is slow; thus we must not be surprised that there is a progressive enlightenment of the moral domain and a progressive *prise de conscience,* in the course of history, of moral values. All this relates to the natural knowledge of moral values, not to the philosophical knowledge.

Conclusions

What consequences can we draw from these remarks?

First of all, the natural tendencies and inclinations do not furnish philosophy with good instruments of argumentation. They provide valuable experimental data, but the reasonings and demonstrations of moral philosophy must proceed by the conceptual determination and scientific elucidation of that which is in conformity or not in conformity with reason and with the ends of human nature; philosophy has to give us the theory of the natural inclinations, to explain their existence and their role, not to invoke them as proof. But, on the other hand, these same natural tendencies or inclinations are the normal way, the natural way, and the *only way,* of the natural knowledge—not philosophical, but pre-philosophical—of moral values. All of which implies that it belongs to philosophy and to the disciplines of moral science to decide in the last analysis and to discriminate the authentic values and the apocryphal values. It is not the natural knowledge of moral values which is capable of this definitive discrimination, because it does not proceed in a scientific way, but by way of inclination (centered in the preconscious play of reason as form of the human psyche).

We see at the same stroke that there is no moral *intuition* in the manner of a sixth sense, and no moral *sentiment* in the manner of a revelation of nature, as certain English moralists held; and that on the other hand it is nonsense to claim, with the positivist or sociologist school, to reduce values to subjective sentiments deriving from the social milieu, and deprived of any intelligible content and of any possibility of being true or false.

It is very true that the natural moral knowledge is not rational in its mode, at least as regards its basic process. It is not rational in its mode, but the positivist-sociologist philosophers have been led astray because they have misunderstood the extent of the domain of reason. From the moment that they were not in the presence of a knowledge of scientific type, they concluded that there was here no knowledge at all, that judgments of value are purely and simply irrational, outside the sphere of reason, that it is a question simply of an emotional orchestration whose cause is society. In reality, as we have seen, the natural knowledge of ethical values, though of a non-rational mode, is rational in its root; it is a knowledge by inclination, but the inclinations in question are those of nature as *grafted with reason.* And, assuredly, with the development of culture, the natural knowledge of moral values also implies an increasing number of conceptual elements, of judgments by mode of cognition, of reasonings. In fact, therefore, there is something of the rational even in its mode; but essentially, primitively, it is of a non-rational mode.

As to the philosophical knowledge of ethical values, it is rational in its very mode, in its manner of proceeding and developing; it is demonstrative and scientific.

IV

Esthetics

From his earliest years Maritain has been the friend and con-fidant of numberless artists, writers, poets, and musicians. He is considered by many as having the finest esthetic sensi-bility among the major figures of modern philosophy. His long reflection—beginning with Art et Scolastique *in 1920— on almost every facet of the artistic process culminated in 1953 with the publication of his monumental* Creative Intui-tion in Art and Poetry.

Maritain likes to say with Dante that human art is, as it were, the grandchild of God—it continues in its own way the labor of divine creation. But he keeps reminding the modern artist that human art cannot create out of nothing; it must first nourish itself on things, which it transforms in order to make a form grasped in them shine on a bit of matter. For Maritain, human art is in the last analysis doomed to sterility and failure if it cuts itself off from the existential world of nature and the universe of man.

The deepest concern of Maritain has been with the nature of poetic knowledge *and* poetic intuition—*that is, with the nature of the knowledge immanent in and* consubstantial *with* poetry, *poetry as distinct from art and quickening all the arts. Other major themes of his are the* prise de conscience *(growth in self-awareness) of art and poetry in modern times; art as a virtue of the practical intellect; art and beauty, and the relationship between transcendental beauty and esthetic beauty; art as "imitation"; and the relationship between art and morality.*

Maritain's works in esthetics are

ART AND FAITH

ART AND POETRY

ART AND SCHOLASTICISM AND THE FRONTIERS OF POETRY

CREATIVE INTUITION IN ART AND POETRY

THE RESPONSIBILITY OF THE ARTIST

THE SITUATION OF POETRY *(in collaboration with Raïssa Maritain)*

15

CREATIVE INTUITION AND
POETIC KNOWLEDGE *

AT THE SINGLE ROOT OF THE SOUL'S POWERS

1. In the last chapter** I gave a few indications, general in
nature, about the existence in us of a spiritual unconscious or preconscious, specifically distinct from the automatic or Freudian
unconscious, though in vital intercommunication and interaction
with it. I also suggested that it is in this translucid spiritual night
that poetry and poetic inspiration have their primal scource. And
I referred to the views of Thomas Aquinas on the structure of
the intellect and the preconscious intellectual activity on which
the birth of ideas depends.

It is once again with some philosophical considerations borrowed from Thomas Aquinas that I shall preface our discussion
of creative or poetic intuition. These considerations deal with the
manner in which the powers of the soul, through which the various operations of life—biological, sensitive, intellective life—are
performed, emanate from the soul. As soon as the human soul
exists, the powers with which it is naturally endowed also exist,
of course, though with regard to their exercise, the nutritive
powers come first (they alone are in activity in the embryo); and
then the sensitive powers, and then the intellective powers. But
at the very instant of the creation of the soul, there is an order—
with respect not to time but to nature—in the way in which they

---

* *Creative Intuition in Art and Poetry* (New York: Pantheon Books,
1953), pp. 106–145.
** *Ibid.,* Chapter III [Editors].

flow or emanate from the essence of the soul.[1] At this point St. Thomas states that with respect to this order of natural priorities, the more perfect powers emanate before the others, and he goes on to say (here is the point in which I am interested) that in this ontological procession one power or faculty proceeds from the essence of the soul *through the medium or instrumentality of another*—which emanates beforehand.[2] For the more perfect powers are the principle or *raison d'être* of others, both as being their end and as being their "active principle," or the efficacious source of their existence. Intelligence does not exist for the senses, but the senses, which are, as he puts it, "a certain defective participation in intelligence," exist for intelligence. Hence it is that in the order of natural origin the senses exist, as it were, from the intellect, in other words, proceed from the essence of the soul through the intellect.

Consequently, we must say that imagination proceeds or flows from the essence of the soul through the intellect, and that the external senses proceed from the essence of the soul through imagination. For they exist in man to serve imagination, and through imagination, intelligence.

2. I am fond of diagrams. I hope that the one I am offering here and which represents this order of emanation, will help me to clarify the matter, poor as it may be from the point of view of abstract drawing.

The point at the summit of the diagram represents the essence of the soul. The first—so to speak—cone represents the Intellect, or Reason, emanating first from the soul. The second, which emerges from the first, represents the Imagination, emanating from the soul through the Intellect. The third, which emerges from the second, represents the External Senses, emanating from the soul through the Imagination.

The first circle represents the world of Concepts and Ideas in a state of explicit formation, say, the conceptualized externals of Reason: the world of the working of conceptual, logical, discursive Reason.

---

1. *Sum. theol.*, I, 77, 4 and 6.
2. *Ibid.*, a. 7.

The second circle represents the world of the Images in a state of explicit and definite formation, say, the organized externals of Imagination. This is the world of the achievements of Imagination as stirred by, and centered upon, the actual exercise of External Senses and held in unity by it: in other words, as engaged in the process of sense perception and used for practical purposes in the current activities of man in the waking state.

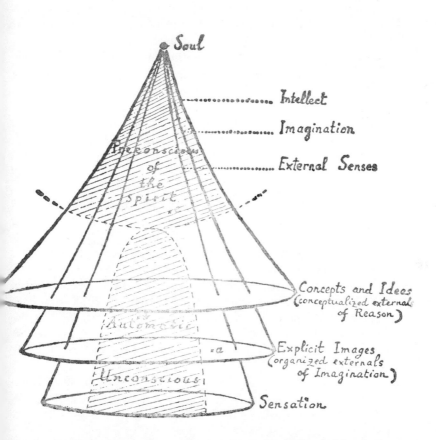

The third circle represents the intuitive data afforded by external Sensation (which is, of itself, almost unconscious, and becomes sense perception when it is interpreted and structured through the instrumentality of memory, imagination, and the other "internal senses").

Now our three cones are not empty; each one should be imagined as filled with the life and activity of the power it symbolizes. The life and activity of the Intellect or Reason are not to be viewed only in the circle of the conceptualized externals of Reason. They are an immense dynamism emanating from the very center of the Soul and terminating in this circle of externals.

The life and activity of Imagination are not to be viewed only in the circle of the organized externals of Imagination. They are an immense dynamism working upwards and downwards along the depths of the Soul and terminating in this circle of externals.

As to the life and activity of the External Senses, it takes place, no doubt, at the level of the intuitive data afforded by Sensation— there where the mind is in contact with the external world. But it radiates upwards into the depths of the Soul; and all that it receives from the external world, all things seized upon by sense perception, all treasures of that sapid and sonorous and colorful Egypt, enter and make their way up to the central regions of the soul.[3]

Finally, we can delimit by a dotted line the region of what I have called the Spiritual Unconscious or Preconscious. Another dotted line can indicate the area of the Animal or Automatic Unconscious. So the fact is represented that concepts and ideas as well as images and sense perceptions can be contained in these two obscure areas. And as for images, they can be considered in three different states. They can belong in the field of consciousness (say, at a place like *a*, for instance), or in the field of the Automatic Unconscious (*b*), or in the field of the Spiritual Preconscious (*c*). This is a point which can be remembered for some further discussions.

3. So much for the diagram. What matters to us is the fact that there exists a common root of all the powers of the soul, which is hidden in the spiritual unconscious, and that there is in this

---

3. Edgar Allan Poe defined art as "the reproduction of what the senses perceive in nature through the veil of the soul." *Marginalia*, LXXXVI, in *Complete Works* (New York: The Lamb Publishing Co., 1902), Vol. IX.

spiritual unconscious a root activity in which the intellect and the imagination, as well as the powers of desire, love, and emotion, are engaged in common. The powers of the soul envelop one another, the universe of sense perception is in the universe of imagination, which is in the universe of intelligence. And they are all, within the intellect, stirred and activated by the light of the Illuminating Intellect. And, according to the order of the ends and demands of nature, the first two universes move under the attraction and for the higher good of the universe of the intellect, and, to the extent to which they are not cut off from the intellect by the animal or automatic unconscious, in which they lead a wild life of their own, the imagination and the senses are raised in man to a state genuinely human where they somehow participate in intelligence, and their exercise is, as it were, permeated with intelligence.

But in the spiritual unconscious the life of the intellect is not entirely engrossed by the preparation and engendering of its instruments of rational knowledge and by the process of production of concepts and ideas, which we analyzed at the end of the preceding chapter* and which winds up at the level of the conceptualized externals of reason. There is still for the intellect another kind of life, which makes use of other resources and another reserve of vitality, and which is free, I mean free from the engendering of abstract concepts and ideas, free from the workings of rational knowledge and the disciplines of logical thought, free from the human actions to regulate and the human life to guide, and free from the laws of objective reality as to be known and acknowledged by science and discursive reason. But, as it appears, at least in certain privileged or ill-fated people, this freedom is not freedom at random, this free life of the intellect is also cognitive and productive, it obeys an inner law of expansion and generosity, which carries it along toward the manifestation of the creativity of the spirit; and it is shaped and quickened by creative intuition. Here it is, in this free life of the intellect which involves a free life of the imagination, at the single root

---

* *Creative Intuition in Art and Poetry,* Chapter III [Editors].

of the soul's powers, and in the unconscious of the spirit, that poetry, I think, has its source.[4]

Poetry's freedom resembles, thus, as Plato pointed out, the freedom of the child, and the freedom of play, and the freedom of dreams. It is none of these. It is the freedom of the creative spirit.

And because poetry is born in this root life where the powers of the soul are active in common, poetry implies an essential requirement of totality or integrity. Poetry is the fruit neither of the intellect alone, nor of imagination alone. Nay more, it proceeds from the totality of man, sense, imagination, intellect, love, desire, instinct, blood, and spirit together. And the first obligation imposed on the poet is to consent to be brought back to the hidden place, near the center of the soul, where this totality exists in a creative source.[5]

POETIC INTUITION

4. Thus, when it comes to poetry, we must admit that in the spiritual unconscious of the intellect, at the single root of the soul's powers, there is, apart from the process which tends to knowledge by means of concepts and abstract ideas, something which is preconceptual or nonconceptual and nevertheless in a

---

4. We may observe at this point, in regard to Coleridge's celebrated distinction between imagination and fancy, that what Coleridge called fancy relates to the "externals of imagination" (the second circle in our diagram) inasmuch as the streams and associations of images are released from the actual service of sense perception and man's practical life ("Equally with the ordinary memory the Fancy must receive all its materials ready-made from the law of association." *Biographia Literaria,* Chapter XIII).

What he called imagination relates to the imagination and the intuitive intellect *together* as vitally united in the preconscious life of the spirit.

In forging—or rather borrowing from Schelling, as Huntington Cairns observes (*Invitation to Learning* [New York: Random House, 1941], p. 244)—the expression *esemplastic Imagination* (εἰς ἕν πλάττειν, "to shape into one"), Coleridge had in view the implied tendency toward creation and the unifying power involved.

5. Cf. Raïssa Maritain, "Sens et Non-sens en poésie," in *Situation de la Poésie* (Paris: Desclée De Brouwer, 1938), pp. 21–22 (new ed.: 1947, pp. 22–23).

state of definite intellectual actuation: not, therefore, a mere way to the concept, as was the "impressed pattern" I spoke of in the preceding chapter,* but another kind of germ, which does not tend toward a concept to be formed, and which is already an intellective form or act fully determined though enveloped in the night of the spiritual unconscious. In other words, such a thing is knowledge in act, but nonconceptual knowledge.

The problem, then, that I should like to discuss now deals with that kind of knowledge which is involved in poetic activity.

Clearly, what we are considering at this point is not the previous (theoretical) knowledge, in any field whatever of human experience and culture, that is *presupposed* by art and poetry, and which provides them with external materials to be integrated in, and transformed by, the fire of creative virtues.

What we are considering is the kind of inherent knowledge that is immanent in and *consubstantial* with poetry, one with its very essence.

Here our first signpost is, I think—the notion, which I have previously pointed out, of the free creativity of the spirit. In the craftsman the creativity of the spirit is, as it were, bound or tied up to a particular aim, which is the satisfying of a particular need. In the poet it is free creativity, for it only tends to engender in beauty, which is a transcendental, and involves an infinity of possible realizations and possible choices. In this respect the poet is like a god. And in order to discover the first essentials of poetry there is nothing better for us to do than to look to the First Poet.

God's creative Idea, from the very fact that it is creative, does not receive anything from things, since they do not yet exist. It is in no way *formed* by its creatable object, it is only and purely *formative* and *forming*. And that which will be expressed or manifested in the things made is nothing else than their Creator Himself, whose transcendent Essence is enigmatically signified in a diffused, dispersed, or parceled-out manner, by works which are deficient likenesses of and created participations in it. And God's Intellect is determined or specified by nothing else than His own essence. It is by knowing Himself, in an act of intellection

---

* *Creative Intuition in Art and Poetry,* Chapter III, pp. 97–98 [Editors].

which is His very Essence and His very Existence, that He knows His works, which exist in time and have begun in time, but which He eternally is in the free act of creating.

Such is the supreme analogate of poetry. Poetry is engaged in the free creativity of the spirit. And thus it implies an intellective act which is not formed by things but is, by its own essence, formative and forming. Well, it is too clear that the poet is a poor god. He does not know himself. And his creative insight miserably depends on the external world, and on the infinite heap of forms and beauties already made by men, and on the mass of things that generations have learned, and on the code of signs which is used by his fellow men and which he receives from a language he has not made. Yet, for all that he is condemned both to subdue to his own purpose all these extraneous elements and to manifest his own substance in his creation.

At this point we see how essential to poetry is the subjectivity of the poet. I do not mean the inexhaustible flux of superficial feelings in which the sentimental reader recognizes his own cheap longings, and with which the songs to the Darling and Faithless One of generations of poets have desperately fed us. I mean subjectivity in its deepest ontologic sense, that is, the substantial totality of the human person, a universe unto itself, which the spirituality of the soul makes capable of containing itself through its own immanent acts, and which, at the center of all the subjects that it knows as objects, grasps only itself as subject. In a way similar to that in which divine creation presupposes the knowledge God has of His own essence, poetic creation presupposes, as a primary requirement, a grasping, by the poet, of his own subjectivity, in order to create. The poet's aim is not to know himself. He is not a guru. To attain, through the void, an intuitive experience of the existence of the Self, of the Atman, in its pure and full actuality, is the specific aim of natural mysticism. It is not the aim of poetry. The essential need of the poet is to create; but he cannot do so without passing through the door of the knowing, as obscure as it may be, of his own subjectivity. For poetry means first of all an intellective act which by its essence is creative, and forms something into being instead of being formed by things: and what can such an intellective act possibly express and manifest in producing the work if not the very being and substance of the one who creates? Thus it is that works of painting or sculpture or music or poetry the closer they come to the sources of poetry the more they reveal, one way or another, the subjectivity of their author.

5. But the substance of man is obscure to himself. He knows not his soul, except in the fluid multiplicity of passing phenomena which emerge from it and are more or less clearly attained by reflective consciousness, but only increase the enigma, and leave him more ignorant of the essence of his Self. He knows not his own subjectivity. Or, if he knows it, it is formlessly, by feeling it as a kind of propitious and enveloping night. Melville, I think, was aware of that when he observed that "no man can ever feel his own identity aright except his eyes be closed; as if darkness were indeed the proper element of our essences."[6] Subjectivity *as subjectivity* is inconceptualizable; it is an unknowable abyss. How, then, can it be revealed to the poet?

The poet does not know himself in the light of his own essence. Since man perceives himself only through a repercussion of his knowledge of the world of things, and remains empty to himself if he does not fill himself with the universe, the poet knows himself only on the condition that things resound in him, and that in him, at a single wakening, they and he come forth together out of sleep.[7] In other words, the primary requirement of poetry, which is the obscure knowing, by the poet, of his own subjectivity, is inseparable from, is one with another requirement—the grasping, by the poet, of the objective reality of the outer and inner world; not by means of concepts and conceptual knowledge, but by means of an obscure knowledge which I shall describe in a moment as knowledge through affective union.

Hence the perplexities of the poet's condition. If he hears the passwords and the secrets that are stammering in things, if he perceives realities, correspondences, ciphered writings that are at the core of actual existence, if he captures those more things

6. Herman Melville, *Moby Dick* (New York: Random House, The Modern Library, 1926), p. 53.

7. Cf. J. Maritain, *Art and Poetry* (New York: Philosophical Library, 1943), p. 89.

which are in heaven and earth than are dreamt of in our philosophy, he does not do so by knowing all this in the ordinary sense
of the word "to know," but by receiving all this into the obscure
recesses of his passion.[8] All that he discerns and divines in things,
he discerns and divines not as something *other* than himself,
according to the law of speculative knowledge, but, on the contrary, as inseparable from himself and from his emotion, and in
truth as identified with himself.

His intuition, the creative intuition, is an obscure grasping of
his own Self and of things in a knowledge through union or
through connaturality which is born in the spiritual unconscious,
and which fructifies only in the work. So the germ of which I
spoke some pages back, and which is contained in the spiritual
night of the free life of the intellect, tends from the very start to
a kind of revelation—not to the revelation of the *Übermensch*
or of the omnipotency of man, as the Surrealists believe, but to
the humble revelation, virtually contained in a small, lucid cloud
of inescapable intuition, both of the Self of the poet and of some
particular flash of reality in the God-made universe; a particular
flash of reality bursting forth in its unforgettable individuality,
but infinite in its meanings and echoing capacity—

> To see a World in a Grain of Sand,
> And a Heaven in a Wild Flower.

Such is the answer of philosophical analysis to the problem
which had imposed itself on our consideration at the end of the
merely descriptive or inductive inquiry conducted in the first
chapter of this book.* At that moment we observed that Oriental
art, only intent on Things, nevertheless reveals obscurely, together with Things (and to the very extent to which it truly succeeds in revealing Things), the creative subjectivity of the artist;
and that, on the other hand, Occidental art, more and more intent

---

8. "This thing which is in me *but* which no efforts of mine can slay!
"Wherefore time and again I stroke my empty bosom in pity for myself:
so ignorant am I of what causes the opening and the barring of the door."
Lu Chi, *Wen Fu*, II, (o), 6–7, in *The Art of Letters: Lu Chi's "Wen Fu,"*
A.D. 302, trans. and ed. E. R. Hughes, Bollingen Series XXIX (New York:
Pantheon Books, 1951), p. 108.

* *Creative Intuition in Art and Poetry*, Chapter I [Editors].

on the artist's Self, nevertheless reveals obscurely, together with this Self (and to the very extent to which it succeeds in revealing it), the transapparent reality and secret significance of Things. And we concluded that at the root of the creative act there must be a quite particular intellectual process, a kind of experience or knowledge without parallel in logical reason, through which Things and the Self are obscurely grasped together.

Now, availing ourselves of the self-awareness which the progress of reflexivity has developed in modern art and poetry, and which causes poets to say with Pierre Reverdy that "the value of a work is proportional to the poignant contact of the poet with his own destiny,"[9] we come to perceive in philosophical terms how and why the process in question takes place. A direct inquiry into the inner functioning of the intellect in its preconceptual life makes us realize that poetic intuition and poetic knowledge are both one of the basic manifestations of man's spiritual nature, and a primary requirement of the creativity of the spirit steeped in imagination and emotion.[10]

NATURE OF POETIC KNOWLEDGE

6. I used a moment ago the expression "knowledge through connaturality." It refers to a basic distinction made by Thomas Aquinas,[11] when he explains that there are two different ways to judge of things pertaining to a moral virtue, say fortitude. On the one hand we can possess in our mind moral science, the concep-

9. "La valeur d'une oeuvre est en raison du contact poignant du poète avec sa destinée." *Le Gant de crin* (Paris: Plon, 1926), pp. 48–49.—"To the modern poet," Allen Tate wrote, "poetry is one of the ways that we have of knowing the world." *On the Limits of Poetry* (New York: The Swallow Press and William Morrow, 1948), p. 117.

10. "Poetry, I think, must be much more 'creative' than science is, or at least much more spiritedly, incessantly so. It is such an eager cognitive impulse that it overreaches its object. That is its glory, and one of the causes of its delightfulness perhaps, and certainly the source of its bad reputation. It goes where science hardly cares to set foot." John Crowe Ransom, *The World's Body* (New York: Charles Scribner's Sons, 1938), p. 165.

11. *Sum. theol.*, II–II, 45, 2. Cf. J. Maritain, *The Range of Reason* (New York: Charles Scribner's Sons, 1952), Chapter III.

tual and rational knowledge of virtues, which produces in us a merely intellectual conformity with the truths involved. Then, if we are asked a question about fortitude, we will give the right answer by merely looking at and consulting the intelligible objects contained in our concepts. A moral philosopher may possibly not be a virtuous man and know everything about virtues.

On the other hand, we can possess the virtue in question in our own powers of will and desire, have it embodied in ourselves, and thus be in accordance with it or connatured with it in our very being. Then, if we are asked a question about fortitude, we will give the right answer, no longer through science, but through inclination, by looking at and consulting what we are and the inner bents or propensities of our own being. A virtuous man may possibly be utterly ignorant in moral philosophy, and know as well (probably better) everything about virtues—through connaturality.

In this knowledge through union or inclination, connaturality or congeniality, the intellect is at play not alone, but together with affective inclinations and the dispositions of the will, and as guided and shaped by them. It is not rational knowledge, knowledge through the conceptual, logical, and discursive exercise of reason. But it is really and genuinely knowledge, though obscure and perhaps incapable of giving account of itself.

St. Thomas explains in this way the difference between the knowledge of divine reality acquired by theology and the knowledge of divine reality provided by mystical experience. For the spiritual man, he says,[12] knows divine things through inclination or connaturality: not only because he has learned them, but because he suffers them, as the Pseudo-Dionysius put it.

Knowledge through connaturality plays an immense part in human life. Modern philosophers have thrown it into oblivion, but the ancient Doctors paid careful attention to it and established upon it all their theory of God-given contemplation. I think that we have to restore it, and to recognize its basic role and importance in such domains as moral practical knowledge and natural or supernatural mystical experience—and in the domain

12. *Sum. theol.*, I, 1, 6, ad 3.

of art and poetry. Poetic knowledge, as I see it, is a specific kind of knowledge through inclination or connaturality—let us say a knowledge through affective connaturality which essentially relates to the creativity of the spirit and tends to express itself in a work. So that in such a knowledge it is the object created, the poem, the painting, the symphony, in its own existence as a world of its own, which plays the part played in ordinary knowledge by the concepts and judgments produced within the mind.

Hence it follows that poetic knowledge is fully expressed only in the work. In the mind of the poet, poetic knowledge arises in an unconscious or preconscious manner, and emerges into consciousness in a sometimes almost imperceptible though imperative and irrefragable way, through an impact both emotional and intellectual or through an unpredictable experiential insight, which gives notice of its existence, but does not express it.

7. This particular kind of knowledge through connaturality comes about, I think, by means of emotion. That is why, at first glance, one believes, and often the poet himself believes, that he is like the Ahab of *Moby Dick:* "Here's food for thought, had Ahab time to think; but Ahab never thinks; he only feels, feels, feels; *that's* tingling enough for mortal man! to think's audacity. God only has that right and privilege."[13] Well, in this people are mistaken. The poet also thinks. And poetic knowledge proceeds from the intellect in its most genuine and essential capacity as intellect, though through the indispensable instrumentality of feeling, feeling, feeling.[14] At this point I would wish to insist that

13. Herman Melville, *op. cit.,* p. 554.
14. Must I quote at this point the testimony of painters? "Be guided by feeling alone," Corot said. "We are only simple mortals, subject to error; so listen to the advice of others, but follow only what you understand and can unite in your own feeling. . . . While I strive for a conscientious imitation, I yet never for an instant lose the emotion that has taken hold of me."
Similarly van Gogh: "Is it not emotion, the sincerity of one's feeling for nature, that draws us, and if the emotions are sometimes so strong that one works without knowing one works, when sometimes the strokes come with a sequence and a coherence like words in a speech or a letter, then one must remember that it has not always been so, and that in the time to come there will again be heavy days, empty of inspiration."
And Braque: "Emotion . . . is the seed, the work is the flower."
And Hopper: "I believe that the great painters, with their intellect as master, have attempted to force this unwilling medium of paint and canvas into

it is in no way a merely emotional or a sentimentalist theory of poetry that I am suggesting. First, I am speaking of a certain kind of knowledge, and emotion does not know: the intellect knows, in this kind of knowledge as in any other. Second, the emotion of which I am speaking is in no way that "brute or merely subjective emotion" to which I alluded in the first chapter, and which is extraneous to art.[15] It is not an emotion expressed or depicted by the poet, an emotion as *thing* which serves as a kind of matter or material in the making of the work, nor is it a thrill in the poet which the poem will "send down the spine" of the reader. It is an emotion as *form*, which, being one with the creative intuition, gives form to the poem, and which is *intentional*, as an idea is, or carries within itself infinitely more than itself. (I use the word "intentional" in the Thomistic sense,[16] reintroduced by Brentano and Husserl into modern philosophy, which refers to the purely tendential existence through which a thing

a record of their emotions. I find any digression from this large aim leads me to boredom."

And Matisse: "I am unable to distinguish between the feeling I have for life and my way of expressing it."

All from *Artists on Art* (New York: Pantheon Books, 1945), pp. 241, 381, 423, 472, 410 respectively.

15. See supra [*Creative Intuition in Art and Poetry*], pp. 6–7 and 8. As I put it in *Art and Scholasticism* (New York: Charles Scribner's Sons, 1930): "I will willingly suffer the domination of the *object* which the artist has conceived and which he puts before my eyes; I will then yield myself unreservedly to the emotion roused in him and me by one same beauty, one same transcendental in which we communicate. But I refuse to suffer the domination of an art which deliberately contrives means of suggestion to seduce my subconscious. I resist an emotion which the will of a man claims to impose upon me" (p. 66).

See also E. I. Watkin, *A Philosophy of Form*, revised edition (London and New York: Sheed & Ward, 1951), Chapter II, section IV. In his remarkable analysis of aesthetic contemplation, Mr. Watkin rightly points out both the intellectuality and objectivity of artistic intuition, and its essential difference from the emotion or vital pleasure which normally accompanies it. These pages afford us the most correct philosophical approach I have read on the matter—except for the lack of the key notion of intentional emotion, as contradistinguished to ordinary or "vital" emotion.

16. On the notion of intentionality, which is absolutely basic in the theory of knowledge, see J. Maritain, *Réflexions sur l'Intelligence* (Paris: Desclée De Brouwer, 1924), pp. 59–68, and *Les Degrés du Savoir* (Paris: Desclée De Brouwer, 1932), pp. 221–24 [*The Degrees of Knowledge*, new translation (New York: Charles Scribner's Sons, 1959), pp. 114–17. Editors].

—for instance, the object known—is present, in an immaterial or suprasubjective manner, in an "instrument"—an idea for instance, which, in so far as it determines the act of knowing, is a mere immaterial tendency or *intentio* toward the object.)[17]

How can emotion be thus raised to the level of the intellect and, as it were, take the place of the concept in becoming for the intellect a determining means or instrumental vehicle through which reality is grasped?

That's a difficult question, as are all similar questions dealing with the application of the general concept of knowledge through connaturality to the various particular fields in which this kind of knowledge is at play. I think that in all these cases, where the soul "suffers things more than it learns them," and experiences them through resonance in subjectivity, we have to find out a certain specific way in which the great notion developed by John of St. Thomas apropos of mystical knowledge—*amor transit in*

17. The distinction made in this paragraph is basically important, and it is relevant to discuss in this connection certain views expressed by T. S. Eliot in *The Sacred Wood* (London: Methuen, 1920). Eliot, in his essays on "The Perfect Critic" and on "Tradition and the Individual Talent," points to valuable truths but at the price of serious equivocation, because he overlooks this distinction. He makes his point with regard to brute or merely subjective emotion (emotion as a simple psychological state), but glosses over what matters most: intentional or creative emotion (emotion as the proper medium of poetic knowledge).

It is quite true that, as he puts it in "The Perfect Critic," one who reads poets should not mistake for the poetry "an emotional state aroused in himself by the poetry, a state which may be merely an indulgence of his own emotions." (This deals with brute or merely subjective emotion.) It is quite true that "the end of the enjoyment of poetry is a pure contemplation from which all the accidents of personal emotion are removed"—that is, all the accidents of brute or merely subjective emotion. But this pure contemplation itself is steeped in the *creative emotion* or poetic intuition conveyed by the poem.

The emotions and feelings of which Eliot speaks in "Tradition and the Individual Talent" are, too, only brute or merely subjective emotions and feelings. Such affective states are indeed merely matter or material, as I have said, which poetry must "digest" and "transmute." "It is not the 'greatness,' the intensity, of the emotions, the components, but the intensity of the artistic process, the pressure, so to speak, under which the fusion takes place, that counts." That is perfectly right, but it is through the creative, or intentional emotion that the fusion takes place. The pressure of the artistic process would be of no avail to poetry if it did not proceed from poetic intuition or creative emotion. "It is not in his personal emotions, the emotions provoked

conditionem objecti, love passes on to the sphere of the intentional means of objective grasping—has to be used analogically. Here I would say that in poetic knowledge emotion carries the reality which the soul suffers—a world in a grain of sand—into the depth of subjectivity, and of the spiritual unconscious of the intellect, because in the poet, contrary to other men (especially those involved in the business of civilized life), the soul remains, as it were, more available to itself, and keeps a reserve of spirituality which is not absorbed by its activity toward the outside and by the toil of its powers. And this deep unemployed reserve of the spirit, being unemployed, is like a sleep of the soul; but, being spiritual, is in a state of virtual vigilance and vital tension, owing to the virtual reversion of the spirit on itself and on everything in itself. The soul sleeps, but her heart is awake; allow her to sleep. . .

Well, let us suppose that in the density of such a secretly alert

by particular events in his life, that the poet is in any way remarkable or interesting. His particular emotions may be simple, or crude, or flat. The emotion in his poetry will be a very complex thing, but not with the complexity of the emotions of people who have very complex or unusual emotions in life. One error, in fact, of eccentricity in poetry is to seek for new human emotions to express: and in this search for novelty in the wrong places it discovers the perverse. The business of the poet is not to find new emotions, but to use the ordinary ones and, in working them up into poetry, to express feelings which are not in actual fact emotions at all." All this deals with emotion as material, with brute or merely subjective emotion. It would mislead us if we forgot the essential, necessary part played by that emotion which *causes to express,* emotion as formative, emotion as intentional vehicle of reality known through inclination and as proper medium of poetic intuition. This creative emotion, moreover, distinct as it is from the merely subjective emotions or feelings of the poet as a man, lives on them, so that, while being bound to transmute them, he cannot "escape from them" as simply as Eliot seems to suggest. It would be misunderstanding Eliot in a most unfortunate manner to believe that self-restraint is enough for this, and finally to mistake poetic discipline for artistic skill *plus* dessication of the heart. The escape of which he speaks cannot come about except through poetic knowledge and creative emotion, and in the very act of creating. And this is what he means.

"Poetry is not a turning loose of emotion, but an escape from emotion." An escape from brute or merely subjective emotion, yes! But, as I just said, through and in creative emotion!

One single sentence in this essay touches the core of the matter. "Very few," Eliot writes, "know when there is expression of *significant* emotion, emotion which has its life in the poem and not in the history of the poet." At last! At last we are told of the *significant* emotion, the intentional and

sleep and such a spiritual tension, emotion intervenes (whatever this emotion may be; what matters is where it is received). On the one hand it spreads into the entire soul, it imbues its very being, and thus certain particular aspects in things become connatural to the soul affected in this way. On the other hand, emotion, falling into the living springs, is received in the vitality of intelligence, I mean intelligence permeated by the diffuse light of the Illuminating Intellect and virtually turned toward all the harvests of experience and memory preserved in the soul, all the universe of fluid images, recollections, associations, feelings, and desires latent, under pressure, in the subjectivity, and now stirred. And it suffices for emotion disposing or inclining, as I have said, the entire soul in a certain determinate manner to be thus received in the undetermined vitality and productivity of the

creative emotion, without which there is no poetry. It deserved better than to be only alluded to in passing.

It seems also relevant to add at this point a few remarks about the indictment of Western art that Lionel de Fonseka offers us in the name of Eastern wisdom. The author has the merit of frankness in stating the issue in extreme terms. But he irremediably mistakes intentional emotion for brute emotion and the creative Self for the self-centered ego. In binding, moreover, art to utility, and making the artist an artisan at the service of human life, he simply disregards both the transcendental nature of beauty and the spiritual value of poetic knowledge and creative emotion.

"An obscene work to us [Orientals]," he writes, "is one wherein the artist lays bare his soul, and many of your modern artists we should consider spiritual prostitutes." *On the Truth of Decorative Art, A Dialogue between an Oriental and an Occidental* (London: Greening and Co., 1912), p. 56. This sentence typifies the philosophy of those *enemies of poetry* who hold forth on art without recognizing its deepest life force, and who ignore the law of generosity proper to the spirit. For them, in the last analysis, any gift of oneself is prostitution. It is but natural that they regard as prostitution (which means no real gift but only making oneself into an instrument of pleasure) the gift of himself through which the artist discloses in his work his soul and the world, so as to become a free *creator* (through the work) of joy and delectation—of the spiritual delectation by which men are liberated from their material ego and raised to experimental knowledge and love of what is better than human life.

When Baudelaire spoke in his own way of art as prostitution (*Fusées*, I, in *Journaux intimes*, ed. van Bever [Paris: Crès, 1919], p. 4), he made just the reverse error, in the opposite direction, and used a perverse image to humiliate what he revered and express the supreme law of the laying bare and giving of oneself which commands poetic creation.

spirit, where it is permeated by the light of the Illuminating Intellect: then, while remaining emotion, it is made—with respect to the aspects in things which are connatural to, or like, the soul it imbues—into an instrument of intelligence judging through connaturality, and plays, in the process of this knowledge through *likeness* between reality and subjectivity, the part of a nonconceptual intrinsic determination of intelligence in its preconscious activity. By this very fact it is transferred into the state of objective intentionality; it is spiritualized, it becomes intentional, that is to say, conveying, in a state of immateriality, things other than itself.[18] It becomes for the intellect a determining means or instrumental vehicle through which the things which have impressed this emotion on the soul, and the deeper, invisible things that are contained in them or connected with them, and which have ineffable correspondence or coaptation with the soul thus affected, and which resound in it, are grasped and known obscurely.

It is by means of such a spiritualized emotion that poetic intuition, which in itself is an intellective flash, is born in the unconscious of the spirit. In one sense it is, as I said a moment ago, a privilege of those souls in which the margin of dreaming activity and introverted natural spirituality, unemployed for the business of human life, is particularly large. In another sense, because it emanates from a most natural capacity of the human mind, we must say that every human being is potentially capable of it: among those who do not know it, many, in point of fact, have repressed it or murdered it within themselves. Hence their

18. In the case of mystical contemplation, love of charity (which is much more than an emotion) becomes a means of experiential knowledge for the virtue of faith which already tends toward and knows (though not experientially) the reality with which to be united. And a special inspiration of the divine Spirit is necessary, because a supernatural object is then to be experienced in a supernatural manner.

In the case of poetic knowledge, on the contrary, no previous virtue of the intellect is already in the act of knowing when emotion brings the enigmatic reality which moves the soul, the world which resounds in it and which it suffers, to the bosom of subjectivity and of the creativity of the spirit. And the entire process needs no inspiration whatever from the outside—no more than the knowledge a mother has of her child through affection or connaturality—because the object as well as the mode of experience are simply natural.

instinctive resentment against the poet.

Of itself poetic intuition proceeds from the natural and supremely spontaneous movement of the soul which seeks itself by communicating with things in its capacity as a spirit endowed with senses and passions. And sometimes it is in mature age, when the spirit has been fed with experience and suffering, and turns back toward itself, that it best experiences the sapid sleep in which poetic intuition awakes—and which also exists, in another fashion, and with the acrid taste of greenness, in the child and the primitive. Poetic knowledge is as natural to the spirit of man as the return of the bird to his nest; and it is the universe which, together with the spirit, makes its way back to the mysterious nest of the soul. For the content of poetic intuition is both the reality of the things of the world and the subjectivity of the poet, both obscurely conveyed through an intentional or spiritualized emotion. The soul is known in the experience of the world and the world is known in the experience of the soul, through a knowledge which does not know itself. For such knowledge knows, not in order to know, but in order to produce. It is toward creation that it tends.

"Je est un autre," Rimbaud said: "I is another." In poetic intuition objective reality and subjectivity, the world and the whole of the soul, coexist inseparably. At that moment sense and sensation are brought back to the heart, blood to the spirit, passion to intuition. And through the vital though nonconceptual actuation of the intellect all the powers of the soul are also actuated in their roots.[19]

Among the pages which have been inserted in the volume as a kind of literary illustration, the ones* pertaining to this chapter

19. Thus it is through the notion and reality of poetic knowledge that the sentence of Novalis quoted in the preceding chapter [*Creative Intuition in Art and Poetry*, pp. 84–85] takes on philosophical sense, and appears not as a pure élan of lyricism, but as a justifiable statement: "The poet is literally out of his senses—in exchange, all comes about *within him.* He is, to the letter, subject and object at the same time, soul and universe."

Rimbaud's saying "Je est un autre" is found in his letter of May 15, 1871, to Paul Demeny ("Lettre du Voyant"), first published by Paterne Berrichon in *La Nouvelle Revue Française,* October, 1912.

* *Creative Intuition in Art and Poetry*, pp. 146–59 [Editors].

contain texts which seem to be significant for my present purpose. I think that by reading those collected under heading II we can see better than through any philosophical arguments how the subjectivity of the poet is revealed (but together with things) in his poem; and by reading the texts collected under heading III, how the *Another,* the things of the world and of the intellect, and their meanings, are also (but together with the Self) revealed in the poem; and how, in this single *and* double revelation, everything derives from a primal creative intuition, born in the soul of the poet, under the impact of a definite emotion.

The direct, intuitive contact with any genuine work of painting, sculpture or architecture, or music, which has spiritual depth and conveys a message of its own, affords us the same evidence.

POETIC INTUITION AS COGNITIVE

8. I should like to add a few remarks in an effort to bring out the main aspects or implications involved in the notion of poetic intuition.

It seems to me that the first distinction to be made in this regard deals with the fact that poetic intuition, which is both creative and cognitive, can be considered especially either as creative, and therefore, with respect to the engendering of the work, or as cognitive, and therefore with respect to *what is grasped* by it.

Let us, then, consider first poetic intuition as cognitive. It is cognitive, as we have seen, both of the reality of things and of the subjectivity of the poet. Now is it possible to try to make more precise that "reality of things" of which I just spoke? In other words, what is the *object* of poetic intuition? But the word "object" is equivocal here, for things are objectivized in a concept, and there is no concept, therefore no objectivization, in poetic intuition. Let us say, then, What is the *thing grasped* by poetic intuition?

Our previous consideration of poetic knowledge already contained the answer: poetic intuition is not directed toward essences, for essences are disengaged from concrete reality in a concept, a universal idea, and scrutinized by means of reasoning; they are an object for speculative knowledge, they are not the thing grasped by poetic intuition. Poetic intuition is directed toward concrete existence as connatural to the soul pierced by a given emotion: that is to say, each time toward some singular existent, toward some complex of concrete and individual reality, seized in the violence of its sudden self-assertion and in the total unicity of its passage in time. This transient motion of a beloved hand —it exists an instant, and will disappear forever, and only in the memory of angels will it be preserved, above time. Poetic intuition catches it in passing, in a faint attempt to immortalize it in time. But poetic intuition does not stop at this given existent; it goes beyond, and infinitely beyond. Precisely because it has no conceptualized object, it tends and extends to the infinite, it tends toward all the reality, the infinite reality which is engaged in any singular existing thing, either the secret properties of being involved in its identity and in its existential relations with other things, or the other realities, all the other aspects or fructifications of being, scattered in the entire world, which have in themselves the wherewithal to found some ideal relation with this singular existing thing, and which it conveys to the mind, by the very fact that it is grasped through its union with, and resonance in, subjectivity spiritually awakened.

Such is, I think, the thing grasped by poetic intuition: the singular existent which resounds in the subjectivity of the poet, together with all the other realities which echo in this existent, and which it conveys in the manner of a sign.

So it is true that poetry, as Aristotle said, is more philosophic than history.[20] Not, surely, with respect to its mode or manner of knowing, for this mode is altogether existential, and the thing grasped is grasped as nonconceptualizable. But with respect to the very thing grasped, which is not a contingent thing in the mere fact of its existence, but in its infinite openness to the riches of being, and as a sign of it. For poetic intuition makes things which it grasps diaphanous and alive, and populated with infi-

20. *Poetics,* Chapter 9, 1451 b 6.

nite horizons. As grasped by poetic knowledge, things abound in significance, and swarm with meaning.

Things are not only what they are. They ceaselessly pass beyond themselves, and give more than they have, because from all sides they are permeated by the activating influx of the Prime Cause. They are better and worse than themselves, because being superabounds, and because nothingness attracts what comes from nothingness. Thus it is that they communicate with each other in an infinity of fashions and through an infinity of actions and contacts, sympathies and ruptures. I would think that this mutual communication in existence and in the spiritual flux from which existence proceeds, which is in things, as it were, the secret of creative sources, is perhaps in the last analysis what the poet receives and suffers, and grasps in the night of his own Self, or knows as unknown.[21]

9. Coming now to the other cognitive function of poetic intuition, I mean poetic intuition as obscurely revealing the subjectivity of the poet, I need not dwell long on this subject. It is clear that poetic intuition is filled with the subjectivity of the poet as well as with the thing grasped, since the thing grasped and the subjectivity are known together in the same obscure experience, and since the thing grasped is grasped only through its affective resonance in and union with the subjectivity. Nay more, as we have seen, it is in order to express the subjectivity of the poet in the work which proceeds from the creativity of the spirit that the grasping of things comes about, together with the awakening of subjectivity to itself. As a result, we may say, it seems to me, that in the attainments of poetic intuition what is *most immediate* is the experience of the things of the world, because it is natural to the human soul to know things before knowing itself; but what is *most principal* is the experience of the Self—because it is in the awakening of subjectivity to itself that emotion received in the translucid night of the free life of the intellect is made inten-

21. "En poésie c'est seulement à partir de la communication et de la libre-disposition de la totalité des choses entre elles à travers nous que nous nous trouvons engagés et définis, à même d'obtenir notre forme originale et nos propriétés probatoires." René Char, *Seuls demeurent* (Paris: Gallimard, 1945), p. 75.

tional and intuitive, or the determining means of a knowledge through congeniality.

10. As concerns finally the work, it also will be, in indissoluble unity—as the poetic intuition from which it proceeds—both a revelation of the subjectivity of the poet and of the reality that poetic knowledge has caused him to perceive.

Be it a painting or a poem, this work is a made object—in it alone does poetic intuition come to objectivization. And it must always preserve its own consistence and value as an *object*. But at the same time it is a sign—both a *direct sign* of the secrets perceived in things, of some irrecusable truth of nature or adventure caught in the great universe, and a *reversed sign* of the subjective universe of the poet, of his substantial Self obscurely revealed. Just as things grasped by poetic intuition abound in significance, just as being swarms with signs, so the work also will swarm with meanings, and will say more than it is, and will deliver to the mind, at one stroke, the universe in a human countenance.

> Il fallait bien qu'un visage
> Réponde à tous les noms du monde.[22]

The work will make present to our eyes, together with itself, something else, and still something else, and still something else indefinitely, in the infinite mirrors of analogy. Through a kind of poetic ampliation, Beatrice, while remaining the woman whom Dante loved, is also, through the power of the sign, the light which illuminates him. Sophie von Kühn, while remaining the dead fiancée of Novalis, is also the call of God that seduces him.

Thus it is that poetry captures the secret senses of things, and the all-embracing sense, still more secret, of subjectivity obscurely revealed: in order to throw both into a matter to be formed. And both, the senses perceived in things and the deeper and more vital, unifying sense of the avowal of creative subjectivity, compose together one single complete and complex sense, through which the work *exists*, and which is what we called in a previous chapter the poetic sense of the work.

22. Paul Eluard, *L'Amour la Poésie* (Paris: N.R.F., 1929).

11. Are there some particular observations to be made regarding poetic intuition in the painter, as contradistinguished to poetic intuition in the poet? I would say that in both of them poetic intuition has the same fundamental characteristics, but with further differences which seem to me to have essential significance. The reason for this is the fact that the reality with which the poet is confronted is the very object of intelligence, that is, the ocean of Being, in its absolute universality; whereas the reality with which the painter is confronted is the universe of visible matter, of Corporeal Being, through which alone the ocean of Being in its infinity comes to show through for him. The world of the painter is the world of the eye before being and while being the world of the intellect.

As a result, in order to describe the painter's poetic intuition, we must first remember that he is a captive of Nature, he is bound to her, he cannot escape her—"one cannot go against nature," as Picasso himself put it: and all painters feel the same way. But, as I pointed out in previous remarks[23] (that I should like to resume in giving them now full philosophical bearing), the painter does not look at nature as at a separate thing-in-itself, to be copied or imitated in its external appearances. He looks at nature as at a creative mystery which he tries to imitate in its secret workings and inner ways of operation, and which, by means of poetic intuition, comes through his eyes to the recesses of his own creative subjectivity as a germ or a key[24] of that object which is the work to be produced into existence. What the intellect of the painter grasps in the dark of Things and his own Self together, is an aspect of the infinite depths of Visible Corporeal Being in so far as constructible or feasible in colors and lines, an aspect or element of the mystery of the universe of visible matter or corporeal existence in so far as this aspect or element is meant to fructify into a work—which itself is an object for the eye before being and while being an object for the intellect.[25]

But this very process cannot come about without going at the

23. See Chapter I [*Creative Intuition in Art and Poetry*], pp. 29–30.
24. See [*ibid.*], p. 29, n. 23.
25. See Chapter II [*ibid.*], p. 49, n. 4.

same time beyond the universe of visible corporeal existence and attaining enigmatically the infinity of the universe of Being and existence. Since in poetic intuition subjectivity is the very vehicle to penetrate into the objective world, what is looked for by the painter in visible things must possess the same kind of inner depth and inexhaustible reserves for possible revelation as his own Self. While grasping some aspect of visible corporeal exist-ence as a reality, he grasps it also as a sign, through which are brought to him, in a kind of indeterminable fluidity, the same secret meanings, correspondences, echoes, and intercommunica-tions which the poet obscurely catches in the universe of Being and the human universe. Yet the painter catches them still more obscurely, and only in the manner of resonances or overtones. The painter's poetic intuition conveys to him—as a "seminal prin-ciple" or key to operation—some of the inexhaustible inside aspects of visible matter, and, by the same stroke, some of the more inexhaustible meanings which make the invisible universe of Being show through—and all this is caught by way of knowl-edge through connaturality, according to any direction whatever in which an act of spiritual communication with the things of the world can be brought about, and all this can be expressed only by recasting these things into a new visible fabric.

Thus it is that genuine painting, while remaining strictly painting, attains—especially after the "liberation" accomplished in modern times—to a kind of metaphysical vastness and a degree of intellectuality which resemble those peculiar to poetry. It does so through its obscure grasping, by means of creative intuition, both of the workable secrets of the world of visible matter and the implied or suggested inner realities of the world of Being.

Modern painting longs, like modern poetry, for a superior degree of intellectuality, and is intent on the impact of Things on intuitive reason—to the very extent to which it is true to poetic knowledge. But at the same time modern painting (like modern poetry) is tempted to go in the opposite direction, and runs the risk of dispersing in mere sensationalism or in a merely taste-guided and superficial release of imagination, to the very extent to which it mistakes the nonlogical character of poetic knowl-edge, or the liberation from conceptual reason, for a total break with and liberation from reason itself and the intellect itself, thus losing any spiritual or emotional gravity, and neglecting those "mysterious centers of thought" of which Gauguin spoke. This ambivalence of modern painting seems to me singularly striking, and singularly instructive for the philosopher.

I should like to observe, in addition, that it is not surprising—precisely because of the particular conditions I just tried to point out—that the utterances of painters about the peculiar poetic intuition of their own are poorer than those of the poets. They confess themselves in their canvas, not in their words. And they use as a rule, in point of introspection, a humble vocabulary, in which they choose quite modest (sometimes all the more moving) words that convey in reality a deeper meaning for which they have no expression. They speak in this way of their "little sensation,"[26] as Cézanne put it, of their "impressions,"[27] their "feelings,"[28] their "interior promptings,"[29] their "vision"[30]—this word "vision" is probably for them a very close equivalent of what in a philosophical perspective we call poetic intuition.

Yet some more significant evidences are not lacking, not to speak of the great testimony of Chinese painters. It is in the full force of the sense with which they are laden that we must understand the words of a painter or a sculptor when he tells us that for him "everything he sees has an inexhaustible fullness and value,"[31] that he has put "as far as possible . . . the logic of the visible at the service of the invisible,"[32] or that "the artist . . .

26. "J'ai une petite sensation, mais je n'arrive pas à m'exprimer, je suis comme qui posséderait une pièce d'or sans pouvoir s'en servir." Ambroise Vollard, *Paul Cézanne* (Paris: Crès, 1924), p. 102.

27. "My aim in painting has always been the most exact transcription possible of my most intimate impressions of nature." Edward Hopper in *Artists on Art,* p. 471.

28. See supra [*Creative Intuition in Art and Poetry*], p. 119, note 13.

29. Georges Rouault in *Artists on Art,* p. 415.

30. "It is the first vision that counts. The artist has only to remain true to his dream and it will possess his work in such a manner that it will resemble the work of no other man—for no two visions are alike." Albert Pinkham Ryder, *ibid.,* p. 356. "Time and reflection, moreover, little by little modify our vision, and at last comprehension comes to us." Cézanne, *ibid.,* p. 366.

31. Hans von Marées, *ibid.,* p. 388.

32. Odilon Redon, *ibid.,* p. 361.

sees; that is to say, his eye, grafted on his heart, reads deeply into the bosom of nature";[33] or that to express the "big forms" in which all the richness of nature is concealed "you have to love these, to be a part of these in sympathy";[34] or the words of van Gogh, when he writes: "Instead of trying to reproduce exactly what I have before my eyes, I use color more arbitrarily so as to express myself forcibly,"[35] "I want to paint men and women with that something of the eternal which the halo used to symbolize, and which we seek to give by the actual radiance and vibration of our colorings";[36] and the words of Poussin when he says that "painting is nothing but an image of incorporeal things despite the fact that it exhibits bodies," and that there are, in the components of the work, "parts" which "are of the painter himself and cannot be learned. That is the golden bough of Vergil, which no one can find nor gather if he is not led by destiny."[37]

33. Rodin, *ibid.*, p. 325.

34. "Seems to me the true artist must perforce go from time to time to the elemental big forms—Sky, Sea, Mountain, Plain—and those things pertaining thereto, to sort of re-true himself up, to recharge the battery. For these big forms have everything. But to express these, you have to love these, to be a part of these in sympathy." John Marin, *ibid.*, p. 468.

Did not the Chinese poet quoted by Mr. Rowley similarly say: "The mountain and I never grow tired of one another"? Chou Mushih slept in a boat so that "his dreams might mingle with those of the lotus." George Rowley, *Principles of Chinese Painting* (Princeton: Princeton University Press, 1947), pp. 21–22.

35. He goes on to say: "I should like to paint the portrait of an artist friend, a man who dreams great dreams, who works as the nightingale sings, because it is his nature. He'll be a fair man. I want to put into the picture my appreciation, the love I have for him. So I paint him as he is, as faithfully as I can, to begin with. But the picture is not finished yet. To finish it I am now going to be the arbitrary colorist. I exaggerate the fairness of the hair, I come even to orange tones, chromes, and pale lemon yellow. Beyond the head, instead of painting the ordinary wall of the mean room, I paint infinity, a plain background of the richest, intensest blue that I can contrive, and by this simple combination of the bright head against the rich blue background, I get a mysterious effect, like a star in the depths of an azure sky." From a letter to his brother Theo, 1888, in *Artists on Art*, p. 383.

36. To Theo, 1888, *ibid.*

37. "Ces dernières parties sont du peintre et ne se peuvent apprendre. C'est le rameau d'or de Virgile, que nul ne peut trouver ni cueillir s'il n'est conduit par la fatalité." From a letter to M. de Chambray, 1665.

On the other hand, if the observations I have submitted are true, we may realize that friendship and community of effort and theories between painters and poets, as developed especially since the time of German Romanticism and of Baudelaire and Delacroix, are of course a blessing, but that they can also be detrimental to both sides. The groups in which they exchange ideas, claims, mutual admiration, and mutual jealousy, serve to stimulate and enlarge the creative instinct in an invaluable manner.[38] But they also may result in having either painters or poets disregard what is most specific in their own particular approach to the work. Poets instructed by painters may see in the poem a mere construction of images. Painters instructed by poets may try to get clear of that concentration on the world of visible corporeal existence which a Cézanne went in for with such heroic tenacity,[39] and thus forget the primary requirement of painting's peculiar poetic intuition. Then, in quest of a direct attainment of the world of Being in its absolute universality, they will endeavor to go out of painting—only to slip into some kind or other of expressionist literature; or else, disappointed and discouraged, they will fall back on any new sort of academicism, covered by a pretense of freedom and a display of ideological tenets.

38. ". . . Chacun des maîtres d'aujourd'hui avait son poète avant la guerre de 14: Picasso, Max Jacob; Braque, Pierre Reverdy; Juan Gris, Ricciotto Canudo; Léger, Chagall, Roger de La Fresnaye, Modigliani, je m'excuse, Blaise Cendrars; et toute l'Ecole de Paris, cubistes et orphistes, Guillaume Apollinaire; ce ne sont ni les marchands de tableaux ni les critiques d'art ni les collectionneurs mais les poètes modernes qui ont fait ces peintres célèbres, on l'oublie un peu trop, et l'oublient un peu trop tous ces peintres aujourd'hui millionnaires qui restent nos débiteurs, à nous, pauvres poètes!" Blaise Cendrars, *Le Lotissement du Ciel* (Paris: Denoël, 1949), p. 226.

39. ". . . treat nature by the cylinder, the sphere, the cone, everything in proper perspective so that each side of an object or a plane is directed toward a central point. Lines parallel to the horizon give breadth—that is, a section of nature or, if you prefer, of the spectacle that the Pater Omnipotens Aeterne Deus spreads out before our eyes. Lines perpendicular to this horizon give depth. But nature for us men is more depth than surface, whence the need of introducing into our light vibrations, represented by reds and yellows, a sufficient amount of blue to give the impression of air." April 15, 1904, in *Artists on Art*, p. 363.

POETIC INTUITION AS CREATIVE

12. My last remarks will deal with the second of the two aspects that can be distinguished in poetic intuition, namely poetic intuition as creative.

From the very start poetic intuition is turned toward operation. As soon as it exists, the instant it awakens the substance of the poet to itself and to an echoing secret of the reality, it is, in the depth of the nonconceptual life of the intellect, an incitation to create. This incitation can remain virtual. The poet, because poetic intuition is his ordinary frame of mind, is constantly open to such hidden incitations,

> Tu lis les prospectus, les catalogues, les affiches
> qui chantent tout haut,
> Voilà la poésie ce matin. . . .[40]

and not all of them can pass to the act. Nay more, a poetic intuition can be kept in the soul a long time, latent (though never forgotten), till some day it will come out of sleep, and compel to creation. But at that moment there is no need of any additional element, it is only a question of application to actual exercise. Everything was already there, contained in poetic intuition, everything was given, all the vitality, all the insight, all the strength of creativity which is now in act, like a dart empowered with a power of intellectual direction; and in a certain sense (intensively— whatever part adventitious chance may have in the development) the totality of the work to be engendered was already present in advance, whether this totality is now virtually given in the first line of a poem, as a gift from the preconscious life of the soul, or virtually concentrated in the spiritual germ of a novel or a drama.

With respect to the work made, it might be said, it seems to me, that that element in beauty which is *integrity* has principally to do with poetic intuition as objectivizing itself into the action or the theme,[41] whereas that element which is *radiance* has principally to do with poetic intuition in its native and origi-

---

40. Apollinaire, "Zone," *Alcools.*
41. See Chapter IX [*Creative Intuition in Art and Poetry*], pp. 369–70.

nal state. Hence it is that poetic intuition may happen to appear with striking radiance even in a poem lacking in integrity; and such splintered fragments, transparent to the rays of being, may be enough to reveal the pure essence of poetry. For nothing is more precious than a capture on the high seas of poetry, be it offered in a single line—

L'espoir luit comme un brin de paille dans l'étable. . . .[42]

O Thou steeled Cognizance whose leap commits
The agile precincts of the larks' return. . . .[43]

Odour of blood when Christ was slain
Made all Platonic tolerance vain.[44]

And I shall always prefer a haikai, if it has this kind of transparency, to a big noisy machine deafening me with ideas. Yet the fact remains that from the very start poetic intuition virtually contains and encompasses the poem as a whole, and demands to pass through it as a whole; when it does not succeed in appearing save in a fragmentary way, it is because it has been betrayed by the art of the poet.

13. Now a further issue must be examined. If we turn to the useful arts we observe that poetic knowledge or intuitive emotion is not in them the spiritual germ of the work to be made. Poetic intuition can play a part in them—then a concern for beauty will creep into them; but poetic intuition is not the determinative focus of their creativity. This determinative focus is what the Schoolmen called the *idea factiva*, say the "creative idea." They took care, moreover, to warn us that the craftsman's creative idea is in no way a *concept*, for it is neither cognitive nor representative, it is only generative; it does not tend to make our mind conformed to things, but to make a thing conformed to our mind. They never even used the word "idea" in the sense of "concept," as we have done since the time of Descartes. And so, if we may continue to speak of the craftsman's creative idea, it is on the

42. Verlaine, in "L'espoir luit," *Sagesse.*
43. Crane, in "Atlantis," *The Bridge.*
44. Yeats, in "Two Songs from a Play," *The Tower.*

condition that we be aware of the fact that this word "idea" is merely analogous when applied to that creative idea and to what we usually call ideas. The craftsman's creative idea is an intellectual form, or a spiritual matrix, containing implicitly, in its complex unity, the thing which, perhaps for the first time, will be brought into actual existence. And this creative idea pertains to the virtue of art, is involved in the virtue of art, is the initial determinative focus in the exercise of this virtue.

Well, by a most unfortunate occurrence, it happened that this same expression, "creative idea," was transferred from the realm of the useful arts to the realm of the fine arts, better to say, of those arts which depend on the Platonic *mousikè*, or on poetry. As a result, the worst confusions came about. Theoreticians of art, mistaking this "idea" for a concept, fancied that the so-called creative idea was an ideal model sitting for the artist in his own brain, the work supposedly being a *copy* or portrait of it. This would make of art a cemetery of imitations. The work is an original, not a copy, and never has such a thing as this idea as model existed except in the mind of some estheticians imbued with spurious Platonism, or some philosophers misreading the theological notion of the divine Ideas.

At the same time the expression "creative idea," which makes sense only as the craftsman's creative idea, was used to designate the poetic intuition itself in its creative aspect, the poetic intuition born in emotion, in the primeval sources of the preconscious life of the intellect. And poor Eckermann was to ask his wonderful Goethe what was the *idea* he had endeavored to embody in *Faust*. "As if I knew," Goethe answered, "as if I myself could tell! *From Heaven, through Earth, down to Hell*, there's an explanation, if you want one: but that is not the idea, that's the development of the action. . . ."

That was not the idea, for there was no idea, but only poetic intuition, which is in no way an idea. In reality—this is a point I shall emphasize again in the next chapter*—poetic intuition transcends the virtue of art. And poetic intuition involves and contains within itself, in a superior state and eminent manner, *for-*

---

* *Creative Intuition in Art and Poetry*, Chapter V [Editors].

maliter-eminenter, as a scholastic would say, all that exists—and infinitely more (for it is both cognitive and creative)—in the craftsman's creative idea. It is enough for poetic intuition to pass to actual operative exercise; by the same stroke it will enter the sphere and dynamism of the virtue of art, whose more or less adequate means it will bring into play.[45]

14. Such is the case, indeed, with every genuine poet. Now not all artists and poets are genuine poets. What I mean is that, at the initial moment of the operative exercise, another process can take place. Then, the poetic intuition becomes a craftsman's creative idea, losing its inherent transcendence and descending, as it were, into the mechanical noise and the merely intellectual concerns for manufacturing with which the craftsman's creative idea is pregnant; and to the extent to which it becomes a craftsman's creative idea, the poetic intuition leaves behind many of its essentials, especially the creative power inherent in the superior unity of the grasping effected by poetic knowledge and intuitive emotion.[46] This phenomenon comes about, it seems to me, when man, in a hurry to display his own energy and to produce something great, or because poetic intuition is weak in him, goes *beyond* poetic intuition, and, instead of listening to it, endeavors to supplement it in his own way—not to speak of those in whom poetic intuition is simply lacking.[47] Thus it is that we meet in bookstores, concerts, and exhibitions so many works which have nothing or little to say; and that in so many dramas there is plot but no action, and that in so many novels the characters are either creatures deprived of freedom which only execute the pre-established plan of a watchmaker god, or creatures wandering

45. Let us not be deceived by the language of painters. What they sometimes call the "original idea" is but the sketch itself in which poetic intuition first takes visible form. "The original idea, the sketch, which is so to speak the egg or embryo of the idea, is usually far from being complete. . . ." Delacroix, *Journal,* 1854, in *Artists on Art,* p. 234.

46. "It is not enough for a painter to be a clever craftsman; he must love to 'caress' his canvas too," Renoir said to Ambroise Vollard; *Artists on Art,* p. 322.

47. "The so-called conscientiousness of the majority of painters is only perfection applied to the *art of boring.*" Delacroix, *Journal,* 1850, in *Artists on Art,* p. 230.

on the loose which ceaselessly escape the weak purpose of an impotent god. Only, I think, an exceptionally powerful poetic intuition can cause the relationship between the novelist and his characters to be what it must be—an image, I mean, of the relationship between the transcendent creative eternity of God and the free creatures who are both acting in liberty and firmly embraced by His purpose.

The remarks I just put forward give account, I believe, of a distinction which, like all essential distinctions, can be difficult of application in particular cases, but of which literary and art criticism has always been basically aware: on the one hand, the sons of *Mousikè*, the poets and creators (who can also be perfect craftsmen), and on the other hand the sons of *Technè*, the men of letters, or the professionals (who can also be bad craftsmen).

15. We may observe, in closing, that the craftsman's creative idea, which is part of the virtue of art, improves from the very fact that this virtue itself improves, both by exercise and by discipline.

On the other hand, poetic intuition can neither be learned nor improved by exercise and discipline, for it depends on a certain natural freedom of the soul and the imaginative faculties and on the natural strength of the intellect. It cannot be improved in itself, it demands only to be listened to. But the poet can make himself better prepared for or available to it by removing obstacles and noise. He can guard and protect it, and thus foster the spontaneous progress of its strength and purity in him. He can educate himself to it, by never betraying it (this is a serious school in discipline) and by making everything second to it (this a serious school in sacrifice).

As to the operative exercise of poetic intuition, moreover, it can be improved by a certain humility, I don't mean with regard to men, but with regard to this intuition itself—and also by the work of intelligence and of the virtue of art dealing with the ways and means of execution. For poetic intuition, as concerns its operative exercise, perfects itself in the course of the artistic process. I do not mean that at the beginning poetic intuition is something either formless or fragmentary, as Claudel says—too harshly—of the results of inspiration[48] (because he thinks only of what emerges as conceptually seizable into the field of consciousness); I mean that poetic intuition, though full and complete from the very start, involves, at the beginning, a great part of virtuality. It is with the steady labor of intelligence intent on the elaboration of the form that this virtuality contained in poetic intuition actualizes and unfolds itself all along the process of production. And then the very exercise of artistic science and intellectual perspicacity, choosing, judging, cutting out all the nonsignificant, the fat, the superfluous, causes—precisely because it is always listening to creative emotion and appealing to it—new partial flashes of poetic intuition to be released at each step of the work. Without this steady labor poetic intuition would not, as a rule, disclose its entire virtue.

But let us return to the intrinsic quality of poetic intuition itself in the poet, and to the question of its higher or lesser degree. What matters most in this connection is inner experience and its deepening into further and further recesses of subjectivity. Since poetic intuition is born in these recesses, where the intellect, the imagination, all the powers of the soul suffer in unity some reality of existence brought to them by intentional emotion, it involves first of all a certain alert receptivity. As the mystic suffers divine things, the poet is here to suffer the things of this world, and to suffer them so much that he is enabled to speak them and himself out. And when he is most engaged in the act of spiritual communication, it is because then he still suffers attentively an inexorable hand stronger than he, that passes and does not return. The degree of creative strength of poetic intuition is proportional to the degree of depth of such attentive passivity.

I should like to repeat at this point what I have tried to say in another essay.[49] "In order that there should grow unceasingly, conforming to its law, the life of the creative spirit, it is necessary that the center of subjectivity where this creative spirit awakens

48. See infra [Creative Intuition in Art and Poetry], texts without comment for Chapter VII, no. 8.
49. J. Maritain, "The Freedom of Song," in Art and Poetry, pp. 90–91.

to itself in suffering the things of the world and those of the soul should unceasingly be deepened. In following this line of reflection one would probably be led to ask oneself whether, beyond a certain degree of depth, this progress in spirituality can continue unless, under one form or another, a religious experience properly so called helps the soul of the poet to quit the surface levels. Continuing at any price, refusing heroically to renounce the growth of the creative spirit, when one has nevertheless made impossible such an experience postulated by the whole being, wasn't this perhaps the secret of Nietzsche's disaster? In any case, what I want to keep in mind here, is that creation takes form at different levels within the spiritual fabric of the soul—everyone by this very fact confesses what he is. The more the poet grows, the deeper the level of creative intuition descends into the density of his soul.[50] Where formerly he could be moved to song, he can do nothing now, he must dig down deeper. One would say that the shock of suffering and vision breaks down, one after another, the living, sensitive partitions behind which his identity is hiding. He is harassed, he is tracked down, he is destroyed. Woe to him if in retiring into himself he finds a heaven devastated, inaccessible; he can do nothing then but sink into his hell. But if at the end of the ends the poet turns silent, it is not that the growth of which I speak may ever come to an end, it is not that of itself the song does not still ask to be more deeply born in him, less distant from the creative uncreated spirituality, archetype of all creative life: it is that the last partition of the heart has been attained, and the human substance consumed."

These lines, which deal with poetic intuition in general, were written in relation to music, and to Arthur Lourié, who to my mind provides us with the greatest example, in contemporary music, of that depth in creative inspiration of which I spoke.[51]

50. "Le poète . . . doit se lover sans de nouvelles larmes et pousser plus avant dans son ordre." René Char, *Feuillets d'Hypnos* (Paris: Gallimard, 1946), p. 20.
51. In his book *The Perfect Conductor* (New York: Pellegrini and Cudahy, 1951, pp. 101–102), Frederick Goldbeck stresses the direct line which relates the "unprecedented" symphonic works of Lourié to Monteverde—"a sort of al fresco polyphony of unrelated colors, as are piano, choir, brass, and double bass in his admirable *Concerto spirituale*."

The composer offers indeed a privileged experience to the speculations of the philosopher. Less bound to the universe of human
ideas and human values than he who creates with the vocables
of the language of men, less bound than the painter or the sculptor to the forms and images of things, less bound than the archi-
tect to the conditions for the use of the thing created, it is in the
composer that are verified in the most limpid fashion the metaphysical exigencies of poetry. It is in him, when he falls short of
them, that the gap is most apparent. None other than a maker of
operas could instruct a Nietzsche by so perfectly decisive a
disappointment.

THE CREATIVE SELF AND THE SELF-CENTERED EGO

16. All the preceding considerations on poetic knowledge help us
to understand the essential disinterestedness of poetic activity.
They also oblige us to realize that a crucial distinction must be
made between the creative Self and the self-centered ego.

   This distinction has something to do with the metaphysical distinction between the human person *as person* and the human
person *as individual*. Matter (in the Aristotelian sense of *materia
prima*) is the primary root of individuality, and matter both longs
for being (as a pure potency which has no determination of itself)
and narrows being (which it limits to its own capacity or receptivity under given conditions). In each of us, individuality, being
that which excludes from ourselves that which other men are,
might be described as the narrowness of the ego, always threatened and always eager to grasp for itself. Personality, on the
other hand, is rooted in the spirit inasmuch as the spirit holds
itself in existence and superabounds in existence. It is the subsistence of the spiritual soul communicated to the whole fabric
of the human being and holding it in unity, and it testifies to
the generosity or expansiveness in being which pertains to its
spiritual principle. Personality means interiority to oneself and
requires at the same time the communications of knowledge and
love. By the very fact that each of us is a person and has spiritual
inwardness, each of us requires communication with *other* and

the others in the order of knowledge and love; and the supreme act of the person as such is that giving of oneself which is one with love.[52] The new and eternal name, inscribed on the white stone, which will be given us one day, and "which no one knoweth but he that receiveth it,"[53] reveals our personality. The name by which men know us, and which is inscribed on our passports, is but one of the designations of our individuality. "Thou art thyself though," Juliet said, "not a Montague. . . . Romeo, doff thy name; And for that name, which is no part of thee, Take all myself."[54]

The creative Self of the artist is his person as *person*, in the act of spiritual communication, not his person as material individual or as self-centered ego.

Lionel de Fonseka asserts that "vulgarity always says *I*."[55] Let us add that vulgarity says *one* also, and this is the same thing, for vulgarity's *I* is nothing but the self-centered ego, a neuter subject of predicates and phenomena, a subject as *matter*, marked with the opacity and voracity of matter, like the I of the egoist.

But in an entirely different manner poetry likewise always says *I*. "*My* heart hath uttered a good word," David sang, "Vivify *me* and I will keep Thy commandments." Poetry's *I* is the substantial depth of living and loving subjectivity, it is the creative Self, a subject as *act*, marked with the diaphaneity and expansiveness proper to the operations of the spirit. Poetry's *I* resembles in this respect the *I* of the saint, and likewise, although to quite other ends, it is a subject which gives.[56]

52. Cf. J. Maritain, *The Person and the Common Good* (New York: Charles Scribner's Sons, 1947), Chapter III.
53. Apocalypse II:17.
54. *Romeo and Juliet*, II, ii.
55. Lionel de Fonseka, *On the Truth of Decorative Art, a Dialogue between an Oriental and an Occidental*. (French translation: "La vulgarité dit toujours *je*" [Paris: Chitra, 1930]).
56. I am afraid that T. S. Eliot, in his essay "Tradition and the Individual Talent" in *The Sacred Wood* (London: Methuen, 1920, pp. 47–53), missed the distinction between creative Self and self-centered ego, just as that between creative emotion and brute or merely subjective emotion (see p. 255, note 17). That is probably why, rightly stressing that poetry is not "expression of personality" in the sense of *individuality* or *self-centered ego*,

Thus, by necessity of nature, poetic activity is, of itself, disinterested. It engages the human Self in its deepest recesses, but in no way for the sake of the ego. The very engagement of the artist's Self in poetic activity, and the very revelation of the artist's Self in his work, together with the revelation of some particular meaning he has obscurely grasped in things, are for the sake of the work. The creative Self is both revealing itself and sacrificing itself, because it is *given;* it is drawn out of itself in that sort of ecstasy which is creation, it dies to itself in order to live in the work (how humbly and defenselessly).

The artist as a man can be busy only with his craving for creation. He can say, like Baudelaire: "I don't give a damn for the human race," he can be concerned only with his work, like Proust, he can be an out-and-out egoist, as Goethe was: in his process of creation, inasmuch as he is an artist, he is not an egoist, he is disinterested in his ego.

But the artist as a man can have his craving for creation involved in the movement of expansion and generosity of a soul whose passions and ambitions are not those of an egoist. And

but disregarding the fact that the poet is not only an individual, a material ego, but also (and, as a poet, much more essentially) a person, a creative Self, he uses the word "personality" where *individuality* is concerned, and conceives the poet as a mere "catalyst" and "only a medium, not a personality."

"The more perfect the artist, the more completely separate in him will be the man who suffers and the mind which creates." In reality the man who suffers *is in* the mind which creates—as creative subjectivity and to be given in the work—separated from the self-centered ego by the operation of poetic knowledge and creative emotion. In this sense only it is true that "the emotion of art is impersonal"—that is to say detached from the self-centered ego and one with poetic intuition, the most personal act of the creative Self.

"The progress of an artist is a continual self-sacrifice, a continual extinction of personality"—that is to say of individuality, of the self-centered ego with its natural claims and its deep natural, too natural entanglement with the activity of art. But at the same time the progress of an artist is an evermore significant assertion of personality, that is to say of the creative subjectivity—revealed in the work together with things.

In *Man and Superman*, Bernard Shaw condemned Shakespeare on the ground that his philosophy was "only his wounded humanity." Well, I do not complain of being taught by the *wounded humanity of a Shakespeare* about man and human existence, and many things which matter to me in the reality of this world.

such internal abundance and magnanimity is the normal and con-natural climate of the virtue of art. Narrowness and avarice in human desires make it live in cold and sleet. After all Shelley was right in writing that the "state of mind" naturally linked with poetic inspiration "is at war with every base desire."[57]

17. It is, I think, an effect of the essential disinterestedness of the poet in the very act of poetry, and an effect of his natural orientation toward creation, that the poets and artists of the past gave us such poor indications of their own inner creative experience. They spoke in the most conventional and shallow rhetoric and the most commonplace stock phrases—*nascuntur poetae,* the Muses, the Caelestial Patroness, the Genius, the Poetic Faculty, the divine spark, later on the goddess Imagination—of this experience, which at least the greatest among them lived in fact, to be sure, but which their conscious intellect did not seek to grasp. They were not interested in reflexive self-awareness. The *reflex age,* the age of *prise de conscience,* which roughly speaking began for mysticism at the time of St. Teresa of Avila and St. John of the Cross, came later for poetry. When it began for it, at the time of Romanticism, it brought to completion the slow process of "revelation of the Self" which had developed in the course of modern centuries.[58]

This revelation of the Self is a blessing inasmuch as it takes place in the genuine line of poetry. It becomes a curse when it shifts from the line of poetry, and of the creative Self in the fire of spiritual communication, to the line of man's material individuality, and of the self-centered ego, busy with self-interest and power. Then the egoism of man enters the sphere of the poetic act, and feeds on this very act. And being there in an unnatural state, it grows boundlessly. The poetic act itself, on the other hand, is insidiously wounded, even in great poets, as some points taken up in the next chapter* will permit us to see.

The shift in question came about, in fact, simultaneously with the incomparable progress that poetry owes to the definitive

---

57. P. Shelley, *A Defence of Poetry.*
58. See Chapter I [*Creative Intuition in Art and Poetry*], pp. 21–34.
* *Creative Intuition in Art and Poetry,* Chapter V [Editors].

revelation of the creative Self. That is one of the usual predicaments of human history. And nevertheless the essential disinterestedness of the poetic act is so ineradicable that the final result of this invasion by the human ego in the universe of art could not possibly be to make the artist into a *creative usurer* (that is a contradiction in terms); it was—I shall return to this point*— to make him into a hero, a priest, or a savior, offering himself in sacrifice no longer to his work but both to the world and to his own glory.

* *Ibid.*, p. 191 ff.

V

Politics

Much of Maritain's effort has been directed to working out
the character of authentically Christian politics. For a time
he had been somewhat naively attracted to Charles Maurras'
largely nationalist and monarchical L'Action Française party.
He was never a member of the party, and indeed at that
particular time of his life he was almost entirely occupied
with questions of metaphysics and esthetics. But when
Maurras' party was condemned in 1926 by Pius XI, Maritain
quickly awakened to a keen and abiding concern for political philosophy. As he wrote in his diary many years ago:
"There began for me then a period of reflection devoted to
moral and political philosophy in which I tried to work out
the character of authentically Christian politics and to establish, in the light of a philosophy of history and of culture,
the true significance of democratic inspiration and the nature of the new humanism for which we are waiting."

Major themes in Maritain's political philosophy are the
distinction between man as an individual and man as a person; man's being a social being because of his abundance and

root generosity as well as because of his indigence; modern man's awakening to the conquest of freedom and the realization of human dignity, and this in social and political life itself; pluralistic co-operation among men of different spiritual convictions in the pursuit of the common good of political life; and democracy's need of the quickening ferment of Gospel inspiration if it is to realize its goals.

Maritain's political philosophy is expressed in many works, chief among which are

> CHRISTIANITY AND DEMOCRACY
> TRUE HUMANISM
> MAN AND THE STATE
> THE PERSON AND THE COMMON GOOD
> THE RANGE OF REASON
> SCHOLASTICISM AND POLITICS

16

THE HUMAN PERSON AND SOCIETY *

The subject treated in this chapter is, truly speaking, the fundamental subject of all social and political philosophy. But, at the same time, I must admit that it is an extremely difficult subject, and one which, in the beginning at least, is unavoidably arid.

Whence this aridity? It is due to the fact that it is impossible to discuss such matters without first embarking upon rather abstract philosophical considerations concerning *individuality* and *personality*—two notions which are usually confused and whose distinction I consider to be highly important.

After attempting to explain how man is as a whole an *individual* and also as a whole a *person*, and how at the same time the focus of *individuality* is quite different from that of *personality*, I will consider the applications of this distinction, especially in *social* matters. Lastly, I shall conclude by saying, that *humanism of the individual* and *democracy of the individual*, in which the nineteenth century had placed its hopes, must be replaced today—if we want to save civilization—by *humanism of the person* and by *democracy of the person*.

I INDIVIDUALITY AND PERSONALITY

The person, is it not the I, the *ego?* Is not *my* person *myself?* Let us immediately observe the peculiar contradictions to which this word and this notion of *ego* give rise.

Pascal tells us that "the ego is hateful." It is a commonplace

* *Scholasticism and Politics* (New York: Macmillan, 1940), pp. 56–88.

expression of Pascalian literature. And in the current language, when it is said of someone that he has very "personal character," this usually means a character shut up in itself, imperious, domineering, barely capable of friendship. A great contemporary artist once said: "I don't like others." Such an affirmation reveals a terribly "personal" character. And, considered from this angle, one might think that personality consists in realizing itself at the expense of others, and that it always implies a certain impermeability, or a certain selfishness, due to the fact that, in a man *occupied* with himself and with his own affairs, there is no room for anyone or anything else.

On the other hand, it sounds like a bitter reproach to say of someone: "He 'is a man without personality." And do not the saints and heroes appear to us as the very highest achievement of personality and at the same time of generosity? Nothing great is accomplished in the world without a heroic fidelity to a truth which a man who says "I" beholds, and to which he bears witness; a fidelity to a mission, which he, a human person, must perform—of which perhaps he alone is conscious, and to which he sacrifices his life. One need only open the Gospel to see that no personality is more magnificently affirmed than that of Christ. The theologians tell us that it is the personality of the Uncreated Word itself.

And so, as a counterpart to the words of Pascal which I have just quoted, "the *ego* is hateful," we must remember the words of St. Thomas: "The person is that which is noblest in the whole of nature."

Pascal says that "the *ego* is hateful." But St. Thomas teaches that the man who loves God must also love himself for God's sake; he must love his soul and his body in a spirit of charity.

To be wrapped in oneself—a state which contemporary psychologists call introversion—can cause much havoc. And, I believe, many people brought up in a spirit of strict puritanism complain of the suffering and a sort of inner paralysis created by *self-consciousness*. But, on the other hand, the philosophers, and particularly Hegel, tell us that the faculty of becoming conscious of oneself is a privilege of the spirit and that the chief progress of humanity consists perhaps in this growing consciousness of self.

Concerning art, Mr. Lionel de Fonseca, an esthetician of the East, declares that "vulgarity always says I." But one might answer that vulgarity says "everybody" also, and that it is the same thing. In quite a different way, poetry also, and always, says "*I.*" Here again, if the selfish ego is hateful, the creative self is that which is noblest and most generous of all.

What do these contradictions mean? They mean that the human being is held between two poles: a material pole, which in reality does not concern authentic personality, but rather the material condition and the *shadow*, as it were, of personality; and a spiritual pole, which concerns personality itself.

It is this material pole, and the *individual* becoming the centre of all things, that the words of Pascal aim at. And it is on the contrary with the spiritual pole, and with the *person*, source of freedom and of goodness, that the words of St. Thomas are concerned.

Herein we face the distinction, which I mentioned at the beginning, between *individuality* and *personality*.

There is nothing new in this distinction; it is indeed a classical distinction, belonging to the intellectual heritage of humanity. And the distinction between the "ego" and the "self" in Hindoo philosophy is—with other metaphysical connotations—its equivalent. This distinction is fundamental in the doctrine of St. Thomas. The sociological problems of our day, as well as our spiritual problems, have bestowed upon it a fresh actuality. It is invoked by very different schools, by the Thomists, by certain disciples of Proudhon, by Nicholas Berdyaev, and by the so-called "existential" philosophers. Dr. Salazar declares himself attached to it. I remember that a few years ago, when I was in Lisbon with François Mauriac and Georges Duhamel, we were received by the Portuguese ruler. And Duhamel, who is a confirmed "individualist," asked him how could a dictatorship—even of a non-totalitarian type—be combined with the free development of individual beings, which alone makes human life tolerable. "Ah," answered Dr. Salazar, "in order to explain this to you, I would have to speak of the distinction between the individual and the person." Mauriac fully enjoyed this philosophical answer, addressed by a dictator to a novelist.

Does this distinction find its best application in dictatorship? I greatly doubt it. As for dictators other than Dr. Salazar, who do not possess his culture, I would say that instead of distinguishing personality and individuality, they precisely confuse these two terms. I recollect that one of them, whom a member of the French Academy visited a long time ago, praised that which he believed was saintliness in the following manner. "What moral strength," he exclaimed, "what prodigious energy, must develop in a man who, as he gets up each morning, says to himself: *act well, and you will be canonized!*" To install one's ego on the altar is hardly the ideal of these heroic personalities whom one calls saints.

It is therefore extremely important to distinguish the person from the individual, and it is also extremely important to grasp the exact significance of this distinction.

Let us first speak briefly of individuality. Suffice it to recall that, according to St. Thomas Aquinas, the *individuality* of inanimate and animate things is rooted in *matter,* as far as matter has uniquely distinct determinations with respect to location in space. The word "matter" designates here, not a concept used in physics, but in philosophy: that of the *materia prima,* pure potentiality, able neither to *be* nor to *be thought* by itself, and from which all corporeal beings are made. Prime matter or 'matter absolute' is a kind of non-being, a simple power of receptivity and of substantial mutability, an avidity for being. And, in every being made of matter, this avidity bears the imprint of a metaphysical energy—"form" or "soul"—which constitutes with matter a substantial unity, and which determines the latter to be that which it is, and which, by the simple fact that it is ordained to inform matter, is particularized to such and such a being, sharing with other beings, equally immersed in space, the same specific nature.

According to this doctrine, the human soul constitutes, with the matter which it informs, a unique substance, both spiritual and fleshly. It is not as Descartes believed: the soul is not *one thing* —thought—existing as a complete being; and the body *another thing*—extension—existing in its own way as a complete being. But soul and matter are two substantial coprinciples of one and the same being, of a single and unique reality whose name is man. It is because each soul is made to animate a particular body (which derives its matter from the germinative cells from which it springs with all their load of heredity); it is because each soul has a substantial relation, or rather *is* a substantial relation with a particular body; it is for these reasons that it has in its very substance individual characteristics which differentiate it from every other human soul. For man, as for all other corporeal beings—as for the atom, the molecule, the plant, the animal—individuality has its primary ontological root in matter. Such is the doctrine of St. Thomas concerning individuality.[1]

I said that matter is an avidity for being, without determination, an avidity which receives its determination from form. One might say that in each of us, *individuality*, being in one that which excludes from one all that other men are, is the narrowness in being, and the 'grasping for oneself,' which, in a body animated by a spirit, derives from matter.

Man, in so far as he is a material individuality, has but a precarious unity, which wishes only to slip back into multiplicity; for matter as such tends to decompose itself. In so far as we are individuals, each of us is a fragment of a species, a part of this universe, a single dot in the immense network of forces and influences, cosmic, ethnic, historic, whose laws we obey. We are subject to the determinism of the physical world. But each man is also a person and, in so far as he is a person, he is not subject to the stars and atoms; for he subsists entirely with the very subsistence of his spiritual soul, and the latter is in him a principle of creative unity, of independence and of freedom.

---

1. With spiritual beings, as Angels, it is not the same; their individuality is rooted not in matter (they have no matter) but in their form itself, that is to say their essence (which is pure form); each Angel being his own specific nature and differing from another Angel as the lion differs from man and from the oak. They are individuals, they are not individualized. God is at the summit of individuality, but He is not individualized. In Him, individuality and personality are one and the same, as all his perfections. In Angels as in man, the proper root of personality is not the essence itself, but a metaphysical achievement of the essence, thanks to which the essence is sealed in itself, and facing existence as a whole able to possess itself and give itself. In this essay, we consider only the individuality of corporeal beings (inanimate and animate), that is to say, individuality in so far as it involves individualization (*individuatio*).

I have spoken briefly of *individuality*. Now *personality* is an even deeper mystery, whose profound significance it is still more difficult to discover. In order to embark upon the philosophical discovery of personality, the best way is to consider the relation between personality and love.

Pascal said: "On n'aime jamais personne, mais seulement des qualités. One never loves anybody, one only loves qualities." This is a false assertion. It reveals in Pascal himself the traces of that very rationalism which he fought against. Love does not aim at qualities, one does not love qualities. What I love is the deepest reality, the most substantial, hidden, *existing* reality in the beloved—a metaphysical center, deeper than all qualities and essences which I can discover and enumerate in the beloved. That is why such enumerations pour endlessly from the lover's mouth.

Love aims at this center, without separating it from the qualities—in fact, merging into one with them. This center is in some way inexhaustibly a source of existence, of goodness and of action, capable of giving and of *giving itself*—and capable of receiving not only this or that gift from another, but another self as gift and giver.

Thus, through considering the very law of love, we are introduced to the metaphysical problem of the person. Love does not aim at qualities, or at natures, or at essences, but at persons.

"Thou art *thyself* though," says Juliet to Romeo, "not a Montague. . . . Romeo, doff thy name; and for that name, which is no part of thee, take all myself."

In order to be able to *give* oneself, one must first exist, and not only as the sound which passes in the air, or this idea which crosses my mind, but as a thing which subsists and which by itself exercises existence. And one must not only exist as other things, one must exist in an eminent way, by possessing oneself, by holding oneself in hand and by disposing of oneself; that is, one must exist through a spiritual existence, capable of enveloping itself by intelligence and freedom, and of *super-existing* in knowledge and free love. That is why the Western metaphysical tradition defines the person by independence: the person is a reality, which, subsisting spiritually, constitutes a universe by itself and an independent whole (relatively independent), in the great whole of the universe and facing the transcendent Whole, which is God. And that is why this philosophical tradition sees in God the sovereign personality, since God's existence consists itself in a pure and absolute super-existence of intellection and love. The notion of personality does not refer to matter, as does the notion of individuality applied to corporeal things. It refers to the highest and deepest dimensions of being; personality is rooted in the spirit, in so far as the latter stands by itself in existence and super-abounds in it. Metaphysically considered, personality, being in one's substance a signature or a seal enabling one freely to perfect and freely to give this substance, evidences in each of us that expansiveness of being which, in a corporeal-spiritual being, is linked to the spirit, and which constitutes, in the secret depths of our ontological structure, a source of dynamic unity and of inner unification.

Thus, personality means interiority to oneself. But precisely because it is the spirit which—in a manner unknown to the plant and animal—makes man cross the threshold of independence, properly speaking, and of interiority to oneself, consequently the subjectivity of the person has nothing in common with the unity without doors and windows of the Leibnitzian monad; it demands the communications of intelligence and love. Because of the very fact that I am a person and that I express myself to myself, I seek to communicate with *that which is other* and with *others*, in the order of knowledge and love. It is essential to personality to ask for a dialogue, and for a dialogue wherein I really give myself, and wherein I am really received. Is such a dialogue actually possible? That is why personality seems to be linked in man to the experience of suffering even more deeply than to that of creative conflict. The entire person is relative to the absolute, in which alone it can find its fulfillment. Its spiritual fatherland is the whole order of goods having an absolute value, and which serve as an introduction to the absolute Whole, which transcends the world. Finally, the human person not only bears to God the common resemblance borne by other creatures; it resembles Him in a proper and peculiar fashion. It is the image of God. For God is spirit, and the person proceeds from Him, having as its principle of life a spiritual soul, a spirit capable of knowing and loving, and of being elevated by grace to participate in the very life of God, so as to finally love Him and know Him even as He knows and loves Himself.

Such are, if I have succeeded in describing them correctly, the two metaphysical aspects of the human being: individuality and personality, each with its own ontological physiognomy. Let us note that we do not represent two separate things. There is not in me one reality called my individuality and another called my personality. It is the same entire being which, in one sense, is an individual and, in another sense, a person. I am wholly an individual, by reason of what I receive from matter, and I am wholly a person, by reason of what I receive from spirit: just as a painting is in its entirety a physico-chemical complex, by reason of the coloring materials out of which it is made, and a work of beauty, by reason of the painter's art.

Let us note, moreover, that material individuality is not something bad in itself. No, it is something good, since it is the very condition of our existence. But it is precisely in relation to personality that individuality is good; what is bad, is to let this aspect of our being predominate in our actions. No doubt, each of my acts is an act of myself-the-individual, and an act of myself-the-person. But even as it is free and engages my whole self, each of my acts is drawn *either* into the movement which tends to the supreme center toward which personality strives, *or* into the movement which tends towards dispersion, to which, if left to itself, material individuality is bound to fall back.

Now it is important to observe that man must complete, through his own will, what is sketched in his nature. According to a commonplace expression, which is a very profound one, man must become what he is. In the moral order, he must win, by himself, his freedom and his personality. In other words, his action can follow either the slope of personality or the slope of individuality. If the development of the human being follows the direction of *material individuality*, he will be carried in the direction of the "hateful ego," whose law is to *snatch*, to absorb for oneself. In this case, personality as such will tend to adulterate, to dissolve. If, on the contrary, the development follows the direction of *spiritual personality*, then it will be in the direction of the

generous self of saints and heroes that man will be carried. Man
will really be a person, in so far as the life of spirit and of freedom will dominate in him that of passion and of the senses.

Here we stand before the crucial problem of the education of
the human being. Certain educators confuse person and individual; in order to grant personality the development and the freedom of expansion to which it aspires, they refuse all asceticism,
they want man to yield fruit without being pruned. They think
that the happiness of man consists in that joyous smile which is
seen, in the advertisements, on the faces of boys and girls relish-
ing a good cigarette or a glass of Coca-Cola. Instead of fulfilling
himself, man disperses and disassociates himself. The heart
atrophies itself and the senses are exasperated. Or, in other cases,
what is most human in man falls back into a kind of vacuity,
which is covered by frivolity.

And there are other educators and rulers who misunderstand
the distinction of person and individual. They mistake it for a
separation. They think that we bear in ourselves two separate
beings, that of the individual and that of the person. And, according to these educators: *Death to the individual! Long live the person!* Unfortunately, when one kills the individual, one also kills
the person. The *despotic* conception of the progress of the human
being is no better than the *anarchic* one. The ideal of this despotic conception is first to take out our heart, with anaesthetics
if possible, and next to replace it by the heart of an angel. The
second operation is more difficult than the first one, and is but
rarely successful. Instead of the authentic person, imprinted with
the mysterious face of the Creator, there appears a mask, the
austere mask of the Pharisee.

In reality, what is especially important for the education and
the progress of the human being, in the moral and spiritual order
(as well as in the order of organic growth), is the interior principle, that is to say, nature and grace. The right educational
means are but auxiliaries; the art, a co-operating art, at the service of this interior principle. And the entire art consists in cutting
off and in pruning—both in the case of the person, and of the
individual—so that, in the intimacy of our being, the weight of

individuality should diminish, and that of real personality and of its generosity, should increase. And this, indeed, is far from easy.

II APPLICATIONS TO SOCIAL MATTERS

Before undertaking the second part of this essay, I wanted to say these few words concerning the moral development of the person. Let us now approach the problems which concern society and its relation to the person.

We have noted, in discussing the typical character of the person, that it is essential for personality to tend towards communion. We must insist on this point which is often forgotten: the person, by virtue of his dignity, as well as of his needs, requires to be a member of a society. Animal societies are improperly called societies or cities. Society, properly speaking—human society—is a society of persons. In so far as a city deserves this name, it is a city of human persons.

And why does the person demand for himself life in society? He demands this, first, by virtue of the very *perfections* which are inherent in him, and because of the fact of his being open to the communications of knowledge and of love, of which I have spoken, and which require an entrance into relations with other persons.

Taken in the aspect of its radical generosity, the human person tends to super-abound in social communications, according to the law of super-abundance which is inscribed in the very depths of being, of life, of intelligence, of love.

And, secondly, it is because of his *needs* that the human person demands this life in society. Taken in the aspect of his indigences, he demands to be integrated to a body of social communications, without which it is impossible for him to attain to his full life and achievement.

Society thus appears as furnishing the person with the conditions of existence and development which he definitely needs. The human person cannot achieve his fullness alone, but only through receiving certain goods essential to him from society. I do not mean only material needs, of bread, of clothes and lodging, for all of which man depends upon the aid of his fellows; but also, and first of all, the need of their aid in acting according to reason and virtue, which corresponds to the specific character of the human being. In order to attain to a certain degree of elevation in knowledge and perfection of moral life, man needs the education and the aid granted by his fellows. It is in this sense that one must give a very strict meaning to the words of Aristotle that man is naturally a political animal. He is a political animal because he is a reasonable animal, because his reason seeks to develop with the help of education, through the teaching and the co-operation of other men, and because society is thus required to accomplish human dignity.

Yet we must not say that the aim of society is the individual good (or the mere collection of individual goods) of each person who constitutes it! This formula would dissolve society *as such* for the benefit of its parts, and would lead to the "anarchy of atoms." It would mean either a frankly anarchic conception or the old disguised anarchic conception of individualistic liberalism—according to which the entire duty of society consists in seeing that the freedom of each should be respected, though this permit the strong freely to oppress the feeble.

The end of society is its *common good,* the good of the body politic. But if one fails to grasp the fact that the good of the body politic is a common good of *human persons*—as the social body itself is a whole made up of human persons—this formula may lead in its turn to other errors of the collectivist or totalitarian type. The common good of society is neither a simple collection of private goods, nor a good belonging to a whole which (as in the case of the species in relation to its individual members) draws the parts to itself, as if they were pure means to serve itself alone. The common good is the good *human* life of the multitude, of a multitude of *persons;* it is their communion in the good life; it is therefore common *to the whole and to the parts,* on whom it flows back and who must all benefit from it. Under pain of being itself denatured, such a good implies and demands the recognition of the fundamental rights of the person (and of the rights of the family, in which the persons are engaged in a more primitive mode of communal living than in political society). It involves, as its chief value, the highest possible accession (an accession compatible with the good of the whole) of persons to their life as persons, and to their freedom of expansion, as well as to the communications of goodness which in turn proceed from it.

The end of the state is the common good, which is not only a collection of advantages and utilities, but also rectitude of life, an end good in itself, which the old philosophers called *bonum honestum*, the intrinsically worthy good. For, on one hand, it is a thing good in itself to insure the existence of the multitude. And, on the other hand, it is the just and morally good existence of the community which may thus be insured. It is only on this condition, of being in accordance with justice and with moral good, that the common good is what it is: the good of a people, the good of a city, and not the "good" of an association of gangsters or of murderers. That is why perfidy, the contempt of treaties and of sworn faith, political murder or unjust war—all these can be *useful* to a government, and procure, if only for a time, *advantages* to the peoples who have recourse to them; but they debase and destroy, as far as in them lies, the *common good* of these peoples.

The common good is a thing ethically good. And this common good itself includes, as an essential element, the greatest possible development of human persons, of those persons who form the multitude, united, in order to constitute a community, according to relations not only of power, but also of justice. Historical conditions, and the present inferior state of humanity's development, make it difficult for social life fully to attain its end. But the end toward which it tends, as is shown in another chapter,[2] is to procure to the multitude the common good in such a fashion that the concrete person gains a real independence regarding nature, which is insured through the economic guaranties of labor and of property, through political rights, the civil virtues, and culture of the mind.

2. Chapter V [*Scholasticism and Politics*], "The Thomist Idea of Freedom."

I have insisted upon the sociability of the person and on the properly human nature of the common good, which is a good according to justice, which must flow back to the persons, and whose chief value is the accession of persons to their freedom of expansion.

But I have not yet entered into what one might call the typical paradox of social life. Here we shall find once more the distinction between individual and person. For this paradox is linked to the fact that each of us is altogether an individual and altogether a person.

The person, as such, is a whole—a whole open and generous. Truly speaking, if human society were a society of *pure persons*, the good of society and the good of each person would be one and the same good. But man is very far from being a pure person. The human person is an unfortunate material individual, an animal who is born in an infinitely more depraved state than all the other animals. If the person, as such, is an independent whole, and that which is noblest in all of nature, yet the human person is placed at the lowest degree of personality. He is destitute and miserable—an indigent person, full of needs. Because of these profound indigences— deriving from the matter of which man is made and from material individuality—and because of the limitations of his perfection itself, which also, in another way, derive from material individuality, it so happens that, when such a person enters into the society of his fellows, he becomes a *part* of a whole, a whole which is larger and better than its parts, in so far as they are parts. According, not to his entire self, but to all the complements which he receives from society, and without which he would remain, so to speak, in a state of latent life, the human person is part of a larger whole, a whole which surpasses the person in so far as the latter is a *part*, and in so far as the common good is other than the good of each (and than the sum of the good of each). And yet, it is by reason of personality, as such, and of the perfections which it involves as an independent and open *whole*, that man must enter into society; so that it is necessary for the good of the social whole, as I have said, to flow back in a way to the person of each of its members. It is the *human person* which enters into society. And in so far as he is a *material individuality*, he enters into society as a part whose good is inferior to the good of the whole; nevertheless, this good itself of the whole, in order to be what it is—that is to say, superior to the private good—must necessarily profit individual persons and be redistributed to them, in respect of their rights and their dignity. Because, finally speaking, society, being a whole of persons, is a *whole of wholes*.

On the other hand, by reason of his destination to the absolute, and because he is called upon to fulfill a destiny superior to time —in other words, according to the highest exigencies of personality as such—the human person, as spiritual totality, referring to the transcendent Whole, *surpasses* all temporal societies and is superior to them. And from this point of view—in other words, as regards the things *that are not Caesar's*—it is to the perfect achievement of the person and of its supra-temporal aspirations, that society itself and its common good are subordinated, as to the end of *another* order, which transcends them.

A single human soul is of more worth than the whole universe of bodies and material goods. There is nothing above the human soul—except God. In regard to the eternal destiny of the soul, and its supra-temporal goods, society exists for each person and is subordinated to it.

It is thus in the nature of things that man sacrifices his temporal goods, and if necessary his life itself, for the sake of the community, and that social life imposes upon the life of the person, taken as part of the whole, many a constraint and many a sacrifice. But even as these sacrifices and constraints are demanded and accepted by justice and by friendship, even so they raise the spiritual level of the person. When man gives his life for the community's sake, he accomplishes, through an act of such great virtue, the moral perfection by which the person asserts his supreme independence as regards the world. By losing himself temporally for the city's sake, the person sacrifices himself in the truest and most complete fashion, and yet does not lose the stakes; the city serves him even then, for the soul of man is not mortal, and there is an eternal life.

In brief, while the person as such is a *totality*, the individual as such is a *part;* while the person, as person or as totality, demands that the common good of temporal society should flow back to him, and while through his ordination to the transcendent whole, he even surpasses the temporal society, the same person, as an individual or as part, is inferior to the social whole, and must serve the common cause as a member of the whole.

We thus perceive the state of tension and of conflict, which human society inevitably involves. Social life is naturally ordained —in the measure in which I have tried to define—to the good and to the freedom of the person. And yet there is in this very social life, a natural tendency to enslave the person and to diminish him, in so far as this person is considered by society as a simple part and as a simple material individual. "Every time I have been amongst men," said Seneca, "I have returned a diminished man."

The person—so far as a person—wishes to serve the common good freely, by tending at the same time towards its own plenitude, by surpassing himself and by surpassing the community, in his proper movement towards the transcendent Whole. And, in so far as he is a material individuality, the person is obliged to serve the community and the common good by necessity, and even by constraint, being surpassed by them, as the part by the whole.

This paradox, this tension and conflict, are something natural and inevitable. Their solution is not static, it is dynamic, *in motu.* For thus is provoked a double motion, surely a deeper one than the dialectic motion of the Marxists. The first of these motions is a movement of progression of temporal societies, which operates above all through the energies of spirit and of freedom, and which is continuously thwarted by forces of inertia and degradation: this movement tends to bring the law of personality to prevail over the law of individuality in social life. In other words, it tends toward the realization of man's aspiration to be treated, in social life itself, as a whole and not as a part. Such a formula offers to us a very abstract but correct definition of the supreme ideal towards which modern democracies are aspiring, and which has been betrayed by a false philosophy of life. This ideal is to be completely achieved only at the end of human history; it requires the climate of a heroic conception of life, fixed on the absolute and upon spiritual values. It can be progressively realized only by means of the development of a sacred feeling, as it were, for justice and honor, and by the development of law and of civic friendship. For justice and law, by ruling man as a moral agent, and appealing to reason and free will, concern personality as such, and transform into a relation between two wholes—the individual and the social—what must otherwise be a mere subordination of the part to the whole. And love, by assuming voluntarily that which would have been servitude, transfigures it into freedom and into free gift.

The second motion is a motion which one might call vertical, the motion of the life of persons themselves inside social life. It is due to the difference of level between the plane on which the person has the center of its life as person, and the low-water mark, where it constitutes itself as a part of a social community. By reason of this difference of level, the person always claims society and yet tends to surpass it.

But let us return to the complex relations of structure which we have tried to characterize. One could, it seems, apply the following formulas.

The human person is a *part* of the political community and is inferior to the latter, according to the things which compensate in him the needs of material individuality: that is to say, according to the things which, in him and of him, depend as to their very essence on the political community, and can be called upon to serve as means for the temporal good of this community. Thus, for instance, a mathematician has learned mathematics thanks to the educational institutions which social life alone has made possible; this progressive formation, received from others, and attesting the needs of the individual, depends on the community. And the community is entitled to ask the mathematician to serve the social group by *teaching* mathematics.

And, on the other hand, the human person, as a superior *whole*, dominates the political community according to the things which belong to the ordination of personality as such to the absolute: that is to say, according to the things which, in him and of him, depend as to their very essence on something higher than political community, and properly concern the supra-temporal achievement of person as person. Thus, for instance, mathematical truths do not depend on social community, and concern the order of absolute goods of the person as such. And the community will never have the right to ask a mathematician to *hold as true* one mathematical system in preference to another one, and to teach such mathematics as may be considered more suitable to the law of the social group; for example, and to speak madly, *Aryan* mathematics or *Marxist-Leninist* mathematics.

Man is constituted as person, made for God and for eternal life, before being constituted part of a human community; and he is constituted part of familial society before being constituted part of political society. Hence, there are primordial rights, which the latter must respect, and which it dare not wrong when it demands for itself the aid of its members because they are its parts.

To sum up: on one hand, it is the person itself, which enters into society; and, on the other hand, it is finally by reason of its material individuality that the person is in society as a part, whose good is inferior to the good of the whole. If this is the case, we understand that society cannot live without the perpetual gift and the perpetual surplus which derive from persons, each *irreplaceable* and incommunicable; and that, at the same time, what in social use is retained from the persons is transmuted into something communicable and *replaceable*, into something ever individualized and yet depersonalized.

We could also say that society—its life, its peace—cannot exist without the efficient causality of love, which is essentially personal, and yet the formal structure of society is constituted by justice, which is essentially measured according to things, and merits, without respect for persons.

III DEMOCRACY OF THE INDIVIDUAL, AND DEMOCRACY
    OF THE PERSON

Now let us briefly turn our attention to the materialist philosophies, the materialist conceptions of the world and of life. And let us ask ourselves what happens to the person according to these views. We must not forget, however, that when one deals with a philosophy, there are three things which should be distinguished regarding it. First, the values of sentiment, which exercise a seduction over the minds of its followers, and the simple human aspirations which the latter actually obey, perhaps even without knowing it. Second, what this philosophy *says*. Third, what it *does,* and the results to which it leads.

We shall then observe that the materialist philosophies of man and of society, are subject *in spite of themselves*—I mean because of the actual aspirations of their followers who are men—to the attraction of the proper values and the proper goods of personality, which they desire obscurely even when they ignore them. Hence, in practice, these doctrines can act upon men, only through invoking justice, liberty, the goods of the person.

But what do they perceive, what are they capable of perceiving and of saying, in so far as they are doctrines? Recognizing only that which belongs to the world of matter, blind to the realities of spirit, they perceive in man only the shadow of real personality—the material individuality. And of man they can only tell us this much. Thus, what they do, the result to which in fact they lead, is to deteriorate, to vilify, and to enslave the person, either by dissolving it in anarchy, or, as inevitably happens under the natural necessities of political life, by submitting it entirely to the social body as Number, as Economic Community, or as State.

I can only indicate briefly the criticisms to which we should submit the materialist philosophy of society, considered under its three chief forms: bourgeois individualism, communist anti-individualism and the combined anti-individualism and anti-communism of the dictatorial or totalitarian type.

These three doctrines equally ignore the *human person,* and are reduced to considering instead the *material individual* alone.

As one has often observed, bourgeois liberalism, whose pretension it is to base everything on the individual considered as a little god, and on his caprice, on the absolute liberty of property, of commerce, and of the pleasures of life—this liberalism inevitably ends in *étatisme,* the hypertrophy and absolute primacy of the State.

The rule of numbers produces the omnipotence of the State—a State of the ruminant or plutocratic type. If, in fact, one wants to build up a city, with individuals free *in this sense* that their first duty is *to obey only themselves*—it will be possible only upon condition that each one relinquishes his own will to the General Will. Man, considered in his material individuality, being only a part and not a whole, the individual will finally find himself entirely subjected to the social whole by the mechanical connections which insure his junction with it. No doubt, his freedom will remain full and complete, but in an illusory mode and in the world of dreams. Or else he will anarchically refuse the conditions of social life, and there will be the insurrection of the parts against the whole, mentioned by Auguste Comte.

Communism can be regarded as a reaction against this individualism. Its pretension is to aim at the absolute liberation of man, who will become the god of history. But, in reality, this liberation, supposing it were achieved, would be the liberation of collective man, and not of the human person. And even supposing that the *political* State were finally abolished, Society, as an *economic* community, would in turn subjugate the entire life of the person. Why? Because the reality of the person as such has been ignored from the very beginning and, with it, the very function of civil society—to procure a common good essentially human, whose chief value is the freedom of expansion of persons, with all the guaranties this entails. Under the pretext of replacing the government of men by the administration of things one transforms this administration of things—that is, economic functions of production and distribution—into the *chief* work of civil society. But, according to the nature of things, the work of civil society mobilizes for itself the human life of persons, and therefore this life, being no longer mobilized for a common work whose chief aim is the freedom of expansion of persons—but only for the economic output—will find itself inevitably referred in its entirety to this output and to the society which procures it.

As to the anti-communist and anti-individualist reactions of the totalitarian or dictatorial type, it is not in the name of the social community and of the freedom of collective man, but rather in the name of the sovereign dignity of the State, or in the name of the spirit of a people, the *Volksgeist*, or in the name of race and of blood, that they seek to annex the entire man to a social whole, composed of a multitude of material individualities, and not of genuine persons. And it is in the person of a master—the only person in political life who remains facing a regimented world of material individualities—and, as it were, absorbed in the unique person of this master, that the multitude will become conscious of itself and will realize its almightiness.

In all three cases, we behold the conflict of the whole with the parts, of social life with man, considered as material individuality. That which is inherent in the human person as person, and that which is inherent in society as a community of persons, have equally disappeared.

Let me add that we seem to witness to-day a sort of tragedy of these three opposite forms of social and political materialism. The tragedy of bourgeois individualism appears but too clearly in the crisis of morality of our Western civilization and in the disastrous spasms of liberal and capitalist economy.

The tragedy of communism is above all manifest in the interior failure to which its first realizations have led of themselves in Russia, and in the inner conflicts which it cannot help engendering. The successive waves of terrorism in the Soviet Republics have, from this point of view, an extraordinary significance for the philosopher: communism, which is a sort of economic theocracy, requires an extremely rigorous and tense discipline. But it can only seek this discipline through *external methods* of pedagogy and constraint. Now, without some sort of *interior* ethics, implying and respecting the aspirations of the soul and of the person, without a vivid faith which communicates its fervor to the minds of people, no strong social discipline is really possible. And thus is inevitable the internal conflict between an anarchy of passions, ambitions, individual energies, employing no matter what means—an anarchy continually reborn—and an "order" which ignores the very principle of order.

Finally, the tragedy of totalitarian States seems to us especially manifest in the fact that, requiring for themselves the total devotion of the person, yet having no respect for the person and its inner reserves, they fatally seek a principle of human exaltation in the myths of external greatness; in an effort toward prestige and external power, never to be achieved. And this inevitably leads to war and to the self-destruction of the civilized community.

Thus, materialistic conceptions of life and of the world—philosophies which do not recognize in man the eternal, the spiritual element—are incapable of guiding man in the building up of a society, because these philosophies are incapable of respecting the exigencies of the person, and this means that they cannot understand the nature of society.

If this spiritual, this eternal element, is recognized, then one also recognizes the aspiration immanent in the person to surpass, by reason of what is highest in it, both the life and the conditions of temporal societies. But then, and at the same time, temporal society can be built up according to the proper order of its being. Its nature as a society of persons is understood, and the natural tendency of the person towards society, and the fact of its belonging morally and legally to the society of which it is part, are equally understood.

This means, definitely speaking, that the relation of the individual to society must not be conceived according to the atomistic and mechanistic type of bourgeois individualism, which suppresses the social organic totality; neither must it be conceived according to the biological and animal type, characteristic of the communist and totalitarian doctrines, which engulf the person, as an histological element of Behemoth or of Leviathan, in the body of the social community or of the State, and which enslave it to the work of this totality. The relation of the individual to society must be conceived according to a type irreducibly human and specifically ethico-social—that is, both personalist and communal—and this will then mean an *organization of freedoms*. Now this is strictly inconceivable without those *moral* realities which are called *justice* and *civic friendship*, the latter being a natural and temporal correspondence of that which, in the spiritual and supernatural plane, the Gospel calls brotherly love.

It thus appears that the most excellent common work toward which, as toward a heroic ideal, the city of our desires must tend is the arduous instauration of this friendship between brothers in labor and hope of the earthly community, which is not granted ready-made by nature, but which can be achieved by virtue.

Here we find once more the considerations which we have expressed earlier concerning the way in which (through a movement of progression which will never find its term on earth) is solved what we have called the paradox of social life. There is a common work to be accomplished by the social whole as such, by that whole of which human persons are parts, and which is not "neutral," which is itself engaged, held by a temporal calling. And thus the persons are *subordinated to this common work*. And yet, not only in the temporal order itself, is it essential for the common good to flow back to the persons; but in addition, with regard to an altogether different order, concerning what is deepest in the person, his eternal calling, with the goods attached to this calling—there is in each human person a transcendent end, to which *society itself and its common work is subordinated*.

Do not forget that society's common work itself has its chief value in the freedom of personal expansion, with the guarantees it involves and with the diffusion of goodness which proceeds from it. Because the temporal common good is a common good of human persons, it happens, by the grace of justice and friendship, that through subordinating himself to the common work, each one still subordinates himself to the good of persons—that is, to the accomplishment of the personal life of *others*—and at the same time to the interior dignity of his own person. But this solution can acquire a practical value only if the real nature of common work is recognized, and if at the same time there is recognized, as Aristotle taught, the political value and importance of the virtue of *friendship*.

It is difficult not to think that the temporal advent of such a city of persons would come as a consequence and an earthly effectuation of this consciousness of the dignity of the human person and his eternal calling in every man whomsoever, which has forever penetrated, through the Gospel, into the heart of humanity.

Democracy inspired by Rousseau, which is now threatened in the world, suffers from a philosophy of life which attempted an illusory naturalization or secularization of evangelical truths.

Rather, is not human history laboring to achieve another sort of democracy, which would be an *evangelization of nature?*

In his book *The Two Sources of Morality and Religion,* Bergson emphasized the originally religious character of the democratic ideal; in a formula charged with sense (and even with opposite senses), he wrote that one must perceive "in the democratic state of mind a great effort whose direction is inverse to that of nature."

This can mean that it is an effort finally *contrary to nature;* which, to my mind, exactly qualifies *false democracy,* such as bourgeois individualism originating from Jean-Jacques Rousseau's conceptions, and which bases everything on the native goodness and native freedom of the *individual*—a fictitious individual, shut up in himself. But it can also mean a properly human effort to *redress* nature, an effort which is linked to the developments of reason and of justice, and which is to be achieved in humanity under the influence of the Christian leaven; an effort demanding that human nature should be super-elevated in its proper order, in the order of the movement of civilization, through the action of this Christian ferment. And I think this is true of *genuine democracy,* of organic democracy, ordained to the human expansion of concrete and open persons. It is such a democracy, to the preparation for which a well-founded philosophy of history and of society invites us to labor.

Democracy of the individual and humanism of the individual arise from an anthropocentric inspiration. Materialism, atheism, dictatorship, are their fatalities. By saying to men, you are gods by your own essence and will, they have debased men. Practically they have left to men no other internal weight than flat egoism and longing for material possessions.

Democracy of the person and humanism of the person spring forth from a theocentric inspiration. Conquest of freedom in the social and political, as well as the spiritual order, is their aim—I mean freedom of expansion, exultation, and autonomy, so far as it conforms to the image of God. They say to men: you are gods by the gift and the calling of God, gods in becoming and in suffering and in hope; gods by means of humanity, virtue, and grace. Their weight in men is the weight of love. They dignify the creature really—in God and as made by God and for God; not illusively—as a god itself. They know the grandeur of man, and they know his misery. They respect human dignity, not as something abstract, timeless and non-existent, ignoring historic conditions and historic diversities and devouring men pitilessly. They respect human dignity in each concrete and existing person, in its flesh and blood and in its historical context of life.

It is to the democracy of the person that one must apply, I think, and not without certain comments, the thought of Bergson when he writes that at the extreme limit one might say, "democracy is evangelic in its essence, and that its motive power is love."

I do not mean, in quoting this formula of Bergson, to link religion and the Gospel to any form of government whatsoever. The Christian religion is not enslaved to any temporal regime. It is compatible with all forms of legitimate government. It is not its business to determine which one of them must be adopted by men *hic et nunc*. It imposes none of them upon their preference. Neither does it impose—so long as certain superior principles are safeguarded—a particular political philosophy. In contrast with individualist democracy, inspired by Rousseau, certain implications of which (as, for instance, the idea that law holds its force from the Number and not from justice) cannot be reconciled with Christian principles, I am convinced that there is nothing in personalist democracy which is not in accordance with the common doctrine of the Catholic Church. Both Rousseauan and personalist conceptions are very general conceptions of political life, reconcilable to a monarchic as well as to a strictly democratic form of government; but, contrary to the conception of Rousseau, the personalist conception of democracy is first of all determined by the idea of man as God's image, and by the idea of the common good, of human rights and of concrete liberty; and it is based on Christian humanism. I do not pretend at all, however, that personalist democracy may ever impose itself in the name of the Christian creed, no more than, in the speculative order, Thomist metaphysics can impose itself in the name of this creed.

But the relation which was noticed—I believe justly—by Bergson, between the Gospel and democracy, is not a relation of *right*, which would oblige us, in the name of Christian doctrine and of the Kingdom of God, to recognize a certain temporal conception and a certain social and political philosophy. It is a relation of *fact*, which concerns only—as in the question of slavery—the germinations naturally produced in the depths of profane and temporal conscience itself under the influence of the Christian leaven. It is from the historical and cultural point of view, from the point of view of the philosophy of history and culture, that things are here considered. Even under mixed and aberrant forms, and even in the Rousseauan tendency to naturize (and denaturize) the Gospel, is it not the Christian leaven that is still seen fermenting in the bosom of human history, while the unhappy adventure of the individualist democracy is unfolding itself? Under purer forms, and tending this time, as I have said before, to evangelize nature, is it not always, and more truly, the Christian leaven that is at work in history, preparing in it a personalist democracy?

In brief, the question is to know whether, in fact, in the historic development of humanity, a slow work is not being performed, a slow and spontaneous activation of the human mass and of profane conscience, tending to bring the temporal regime of men closer to an order, of which democracy of the individual was but a counterfeit, and which I call here a democracy of the person. And the question is also to know whether this democracy of the person is not inconceivable without the super-elevation which nature and temporal civilizations receive, in their proper order, from the energies of Christian life.

These reflections induce me to think that the drama of modern democracies is to have sought, without knowing it, something good: the democracy of the person, disguised in an error, viz. the democracy of the individual, which leads by itself to serious failures. If democracies are still able to escape grave dangers, it is by turning themselves decisively in the direction of an essentially different type—the democracy of the person, discovered in its real significance. And this presupposes, truly speaking, something quite different from a simple weakening or a simple extenuation of the errors of the democracy of the individual; it means an internal transformation, a complete turn about toward spirit.

Is not the tragedy of our age to be found in the fact that modern democracies have lost all confidence in themselves? Their vital principle is justice, and they do not want to run the risk of justice. They do not want, it seems, to run any risk whatsoever. They invoke justice, but they pursue purely utilitarian politics, and they pursue them inefficiently and clumsily.[3]

During the same period, totalitarian dictatorships, which put Machiavellian policies much better into practice, have the fullest confidence in their principle, which is barbaric force, and they risk everything thereon.

Modern democracies suffer from a philosophy of life which undermines and annihilates their vital principle from within. If they must refind the sense of justice, and of risk, and of heroism, it is under condition of rejecting their materialist philosophy, and of viewing in full light a personalist conception of life and of society.

To the inhuman humanism of the individual would thus succeed a new humanism—the integral humanism of the person, open to that which surpasses it and leads it to achievement, and open to the common service of justice and friendship.

3. This was written before the second European war. In the face of catastrophe, the Western Democracies have been compelled by the force of things to choose finally, and courageously, to struggle for justice, at the risk of unheard of sacrifices.

17

CHURCH AND STATE*

PRELIMINARY REMARKS

Before embarking on the problems of Church and State, I should like to make two preliminary remarks: First, my own faith is the Roman Catholic one; hence the concept of the Church which I shall rely upon in my discussion is the Catholic concept of the Church. As far as the relation of other Churches or religious institutions with the State is concerned, my line of argumentation therefore will apply only in an indirect and qualified manner. Second, I shall try to discuss my subject in the perspective of adequate practical philosophy: that is to say, as a philosopher, not as a theologian, but as a Christian philosopher, who takes into account the theological data fit to provide a genuine grasp of the concrete realities he is talking about.

I shall divide my discussion into three main parts: First, the general immutable principles; second, the analogical way in which, by virtue of their very transcendence, they are to be applied; third, some practical conclusions relating to our time. The issue is a highly controversial one. At the beginning of the seventeenth century Cardinal Bellarmine's positions were strongly attacked, before he became one of the greatest authorities on the question. Today a conflict of opinion exists on the matter among men who belong to the same faith, but whose historical outlooks

---

* *Man and the State* (Chicago: The University of Chicago Press, Phoenix Books edition, n.d.), pp. 147–87 [a clothbound edition was published by the same Press in 1951; for this paperback edition Professor Maritain made a few minor additions and alterations, especially in this particular essay. Editors].

can be traced back either to St. Louis or to Philip the Second. I shall express my own opinion with the candor and humility of a layman firmly attached to his faith and seeking a right solution—which, after all, should not be so difficult of attainment if one is attentive both to eternal truths and to human history.

I have meditated and written on these problems for twenty-five years or so. I have a bit of a hope, nevertheless, that I shall not get entangled too much in the labyrinthine ways of the issue, and that I shall be able to discuss it in less than twenty-five "disputations."

I THE GENERAL IMMUTABLE PRINCIPLES

1. *The Human Person and the Body Politic*

From a philosophical point of view, the first thing, it seems to me, that we have to stress is the relationship between the human person and the body politic, namely the fact that the human person is both part of the body politic and superior to it through what is supra-temporal, or eternal, in him, in his spiritual interests and his final destination.

That very superiority of what is eternal in man over the political society can already be seen in the merely natural realm. We know that the whole man is engaged in the common good of civil society. But we also know that in respect to things *which are not Caesar's,* both society itself and its common good are indirectly subordinated to the perfect accomplishment of the person and his supra-temporal aspirations as to an end of another order—an end which transcends the body politic.

I say that this subordination exists already in the natural order, with regard to supra-temporal natural goods, which of themselves are related to the common good of what might be called civilization as a whole or the spiritual community of minds; for instance the sense of justice for all men and love for all men; the life of the spirit and all that which, in us, is a natural beginning of contemplation; the intangible dignity of truth, in all domains and all degrees, however humble they may be, of knowledge, and the intangible dignity of beauty: both of which—truth and beauty—

are nobler than the social ingredients of life and, if curbed by the latter, never fail to avenge themselves. In the measure that human society attempts to free itself from this subordination and to proclaim itself the supreme good, in the very same measure it perverts its own nature and that of the political common good. The common good of civil life is an ultimate end, but an ultimate end in a relative sense and in a certain order, not the absolute ultimate end. This common good is lost if it is closed within itself, for, of its very nature, it is intended to foster the higher ends of the human person. The human person's vocation to goods which transcend the political common good is embodied in the essence of the political common good. To ignore these truths is to sin simultaneously against both the human person and the political common good. Thus, even in the natural order, the common good of the body politic implies an intrinsic though indirect ordination to something which transcends it.[1]

Now the Christian knows that there is a supernatural order, and that the ultimate end—the absolute ultimate end—of the human person is God causing His own personal life and eternal bliss to be participated in by man. The direct ordination of the human person to God transcends every created common good— both the common good of the political society and the intrinsic common good of the universe. Here is the rock of the dignity of the human person as well as of the unshakeable requirements of the Christian message. Thus the indirect subordination of the body politic—not as a mere means, but as an end worthy in itself yet of lesser dignity—to the supra-temporal values to which human life is appendent, refers first and foremost, as a matter of fact, to the supernatural end to which the human person is directly ordained. To sum up all this in one single expression, let us say that the law we are faced with here is the law of the *primacy of the spiritual*.[2]

1. Cf. J. Maritain, *The Person and the Common Good* (New York: Charles Scribner's Sons, 1947), Chapter IV; paper: Notre Dame: University of Notre Dame Press, 1966.
2. Cf. J. Maritain, *Primauté du spirituel* (Paris: Plon, 1927); (English translation: *The Things That Are Not Caesar's* [New York: Charles Scribner's Sons, 1930]).

2. *The Freedom of the Church*

Let us now go one step further, and consider the Church in her own realm or order. What is the Church? To begin with, what is the Church *for the unbeliever?* In the eyes of the unbeliever, the Church, is, or the Churches are, organized bodies or associations especially concerned with the religious needs and creeds of a number of his fellow-men, that is, with spiritual values to which they have committed themselves, and to which their moral standards are appendent. These spiritual values are part—in actual fact the most important part, as history shows it—of those supra-temporal goods with respect to which, even in the natural order, the human person transcends, as we have seen, political society, and which constitute the moral heritage of mankind, the spiritual common good of civilization or of the community of minds. Even though the unbeliever does not believe in these particular spiritual values, he has to respect them. In his eyes the Church, or the Churches, are in the social community particular bodies which must enjoy that *right to freedom* which is but one, not only with the right to free association naturally belonging to the human person, but with the right freely to believe the truth recognized by one's conscience, that is, with the most basic and inalienable of all human rights. Thus, the unbeliever, from his own point of view—I mean, of course, the unbeliever who, at least, is not an unbeliever in reason, and, furthermore, who is a democratically-minded unbeliever—acknowledges as a normal and necessary thing the freedom of the Church, or of the Churches.

But what is the Church *for the believer?*[3] For the believer the Church is a supernatural society, both divine and human—the very type of perfect or achieved-in-itself, self-sufficient, and independent society—which unites in itself men as co-citizens of the Kingdom of God and leads them to eternal life, already begun

3. Cf. Humbert Clérissac, O.P., *Le Mystère de l'Église* (Paris: Crès, 1918; ed. du Cerf, 1934); (English translation: *The Mystery of the Church* [New York: Sheed & Ward, 1937]); and, first and foremost, the admirable treatise by Msgr. Charles Journet, *L'Église du Verbe Incarné* (Paris: Desclée De Brouwer, 1941); with the additional essays published by him in the review *Nova et Vetera* (Fribourg, Switzerland), and in *Revue Thomiste* (particularly nos. 1–2 [1949], "Nature du corps de l'Eglise").

here below; which teaches them the revealed truth received in trust from the Incarnate Word Himself; and which is the very body of which the head is Christ, a body *visible*, by reason of its essence, in its professed creed, its worship, its discipline, and sacraments, and in the refraction of its supernatural personality through its human structure and activity,[4] *invisible* in the mystery of the divine grace and charity vivifying human souls, even those which belong to that body without knowing it and only through the inner movement of their hearts, because they live outside the sphere of explicit faith but seek for God in truth. For the believer the Church is the body of Christ supernaturally made up of the human race, or, as Bossuet put it, *le Christ répandu et communiqué*, Christ Himself diffused and communicated.

In such a perspective, not only is the freedom of the Church to be recognized as required by freedom of association and freedom of religious belief without interference from the State, but that freedom of the Church appears as grounded on the very rights of God and as identical with His own freedom in the face of any human institution. The freedom of the Church does express the very independence of the Incarnate Word. As a result, the first general principle to be stated, with respect to the problem we are examining, is *the freedom of the Church to teach and preach and worship, the freedom of the Gospel, the freedom of the word of God.*

3. *The Church and the Body Politic*

We come now to a further point, namely the relation between the Church and the body politic. It is clear, on the one hand, that the freedom and independence of which I just spoke, since they belong to a true and genuine society, imply for the Church the freedom of developing her own institutions and governing herself without interference by the body politic. Here we are confronted with the basic distinction, stated by Christ himself, between the

4. Cf. Charles Journet, "L'Église mystérieuse et visible," *Nova et Vetera*, July–September, 1940.

things which are God's and the things which are Caesar's. From the advent of Christianity on, religion has been taken out of the hands of the State; the terrestrial and national frameworks in which the spiritual was confined have been shattered; its universality together with its freedom have been manifested in full bloom. Nay more, how could that universality of the Church be manifested except as a token of her superiority?

From the point of view of the political common good, the activities of the citizens as members of the Church have an impact on that common good; they and the institutions supported by them are part of the political society and the national community; under this aspect and in this manner it can be said that the Church is *in* the body politic. But this very point of view remains partial and inadequate. While being *in* the body politic—in every body politic—through a given number of members and her institutions, the Church as such, the Church in her essence, is not a part but a whole; she is an absolutely universal realm stretching all over the world—*above* the body politic and every body politic.

There is no distinction without an order of values. If the things that are God's are distinct from the things that are Caesar's, that means that they are better. The said distinction, developing its virtualities in the course of human history, has resulted in the notion of the intrinsically *lay* or *secular* nature of the body politic. I do not say that the body politic is by nature irreligious or indifferent to religion ("lay" and "laicized," "secular" and "secularized" are two quite different things); I say that by nature the body politic, which belongs strictly to the natural order, is only concerned with the temporal life of men and their temporal common good. In that temporal realm the body politic, as Pope Leo XIII has insisted, is fully autonomous;[5] the State, the modern State, is under the command of no superior authority in its own order. But the order of eternal life is superior in itself to the order of temporal life.[6]

---

5. Cf. encyclicals *Immortale Dei* ("utraque potestas est, in suo genere, maxima") and *Sapientiae Christianae.*
6. Cf. Charles Journet, *Exigences chrétiennes en politique* (Paris: Egloff, 1944), Chapter II.

The Kingdom of God is essentially spiritual, and by the very fact that its own order is not of this world, it in no way threatens the kingdoms and republics of the earth. *Non eripit mortalia, qui regna dat caelestia.*[7] But precisely because it is spiritual, the Kingdom of God is of a better and higher nature than the kingdoms and republics of the earth. Let us remove from the word "superiority" any accidental connotation of domination and hegemony; let us understand this word in its pure sense; it means a higher place in the scale of values, a higher dignity. The second general principle to be stated, with respect to the problems we are examining, is *the superiority of the Church—that is, of the spiritual— over the body politic or the State.*

On the other hand it is clear that, as sharply distinct as they may be, the Church and the body politic cannot live and develop in sheer isolation from and ignorance of one another. This would be simply anti-natural. From the very fact that the same human person is simultaneously a member of that society which is the Church and a member of that society which is the body politic, an absolute division between those two societies would mean that the human person must be cut in two. The third general principle to be stated with respect to the problems we are examining is the *necessary cooperation between the Church and the body politic or the State.*

II THE APPLICATION OF THE IMMUTABLE PRINCIPLES IN ACTUAL HISTORICAL EXISTENCE

1. *Thesis and Hypothesis. Historical Climates and Concrete Historical Ideals*

And now what is the form, or what are the forms, that the principle of the spiritual superiority of the Church will take in practical application? What is the form, or what are the forms, which the principle of the necessary cooperation between Church and State will take in practical application? With those questions we are

7. Cf. Pope Pius XI, encyclical *Quas primas.*

tackling our second issue—the way in which the general immutable principles that sway the issue are to be applied amidst the adventures and the vicissitudes of the terrestrial powers.

At this point we meet with a distinction often used by theologians, the distinction between what they call (in their own vocabulary, quite different from the vernacular) the *thesis* and the *hypothesis:*[8] the "thesis" expressing the way in which the general principles at stake should be applied; the "hypothesis" meaning the field of practical possibilities and impediments offered by actual circumstances.

That distinction between the thesis and the hypothesis is quite respectable and can of course be used in a valid manner. Yet I do not believe that it has very deep traditional roots. And, what matters more, it is often incorrectly construed, namely, understood in a *univocal* sense. Then the thesis is regarded *as the ideal* —the absolute ideal, the ideal in itself—as to the way of applying principles; and it is only because we are prevented by circumstances stronger than our wills that we renounce enforcing—or enforce only indifferently—that unique ideal way of applying principles.

Such a univocal conception does not take into account the intrinsic reality as well as the intelligible meaning of time. On the one hand the very notion of an absolute ideal, an ideal in itself, a supra-temporal ideal as to the way of *applying* or *realizing* principles, is self-contradictory, since any application or realization is existential and takes place in time, therefore is relative to some given set of historical conditions. On the other hand the corresponding conception of the hypothesis deals with conditions and circumstances considered in a merely empirical manner and from the point of view of mere expediency, as if time were but a refuse-bin in which we would have to pick up more or less profitable opportunities; whereas in actual fact time has a meaning and a direction, human history is made up of periods each one of which is possessed of a particular intelligible structure and

8. Cf. Maritain, *Du régime temporel et de la liberté* (Paris: Desclée De Brouwer, 1933); (English translation: *Freedom in the Modern World* [New York: Charles Scribner's Sons, 1936]), Chapter II.

therefore of basic particular requirements, a fact that no political brain should ignore.

Furthermore the univocal conception of the thesis and the hypothesis entails for us a risk of mistaking either for the so-called absolute ideal as to the way of applying principles, or even for the immutable principles themselves, the particular way in which the general principles at stake were applied in a more or less idealized past; then we shall disregard the relativity of the existential forms of the past, and a contingent example offered to our imagination will be raised to an absolute. Finally the *hypothesis*, which is incompatible with that image of the past—owing of course to the wickedness of our contemporaries!—will mean a forced abandonment of the principles, and we shall yield to such abandonment with a conscience all the more untroubled as we fiercely claim a *thesis* which we have no means of realizing—except when we get a chance to enforce our image of the past by violence, which is another way of betraying the immutable principles, by putting a ghost in their place.

We shall have an intellectual equipment more fit to deal with the problem if we understand the genuine value of the philosophical notion of *analogy*, which plays so great a part in Thomas Aquinas' metaphysics, and if we place ourselves in the perspective of analogy, in contradistinction to the perspective of univocity. I do not mean, assuredly, that the *meaning* of the general principles which hold sway over the issue is analogical, in such a manner that they would acquire in the course of time I know not what new meanings, having driven out the former ones; the meaning of statements like: "the full freedom of the Church is both a God-given right belonging to her and a requirement of the common good of political society," or "the spiritual order is superior to the temporal one," or "Church and State must cooperate"—the meaning of such statements is immutable. What I mean is that the *application* of the principles is analogical—the more transcendent the principles are, the more analogical is the application—and that this application takes various typical forms in reference to the *historical climates* or *historical constellations* through which the development of mankind is passing; in such a manner that the same immutable principles are to be applied or realized in the course of time according to typically different patterns.

For there are in human history typical climates or constellations of existential conditions, which express given intelligible structures, both as concerns the social, political, and juridical dominant characteristics and the moral and ideological dominant characteristics in the temporal life of the human community, and which constitute frames of reference for the ways of applying in human existence the immutable principles that hold sway over the latter. And it is according to these historical climates, as are recognized by a sound philosophy of history, which is here indispensable, that we have to conceive the *concrete historical ideals* or prospective images of what is to be hoped for in our age: ideals which are neither absolute nor bound to an unrealizable past, but which are *relative*—relative to a given time—and which moreover can be claimed and asserted as *realizable*.[9]

Thus the *principles* are absolute and immutable and supratemporal. And the particular, concrete applications through which they are to be analogically realized, and which are called for by the various typical climates that replace each other in human history, change, according to the specific patterns of civilization, the intelligible features of which it is imperative to recognize as peculiar to every given historical age.

2. The Historical Climate of Modern Civilization

I would therefore say, summing up quite briefly what would require a long historical analysis:[10] there was a *sacral* age, the age of medieval Christendom, mainly characterized on the one hand by the fact that the unity of faith was a prerequisite for political unity, and that the basic frame of reference was the unity of that social body, religio-political in nature, which was the *respublica*

9. Cf. *ibid.* and *Humanisme intégral* (Paris: Aubier, 1936); (English translation: *True Humanism* [New York: Charles Scribner's Sons, 1938]), Chapter IV.
10. Cf. J. Maritain, *Humanisme intégral (True Humanism)*, Chapters IV and V.

Christiana,[11] on the other hand by the dominant dynamic idea of strength or fortitude at the service of justice. In that sacral era, the principles that we are considering were therefore applied principally in terms of the social power of the Church—the superior dignity of the Church (that is, the principle) found its ways of realization in her superior power over the prince (that is, the application)—and as a result the political power of the Holy Empire and the kings was an instrument for the spiritual aims of the Church. In this way the Church was to assert the freedom of the spirit in the face of the ruthlessness of the temporal power, and to impose on it such restraints as the truce of God. Let us not forget, moreover, that in the Middle Ages not only the differentiation of the body politic as such was not completely achieved, but the Church had, as a matter of fact, to make up for a number of deficiencies in the civil order, and to take upon herself, because she was shaping civilization in her own womb, many functions and responsibilities pertaining of themselves to political society.[12] In post-medieval centuries—a period which can be called the baroque age—sacral civilization disintegrated, while in the political order the notion and reality of the State was gradually arising, yet the tenets of sacral civilization were more or less pre-

---

11. Cf. John Courtney Murray, *Governmental Repression of Heresy*, reprinted from the *Proceedings of the Catholic Theological Society of America*, 1949, pp. 56–57.

12. On the distinction between the "sacral" and the "secular" age of civilization see Charles Journet, *L'Église du Verbe Incarné*, p. 243. The régime of "sacral Christendom," peculiar to the Middle Ages, is thoroughly analyzed in this book (pp. 253–96). Let us quote p. 254: "Il serait inexact [the author says] de définir l'époque médiévale comme une époque de confusion du spirituel et du temporel. Depuis la parole décisive du Christ sur les choses de Dieu et les choses de César, les deux pouvoirs, même quand ils seront réunis dans un même sujet, resteront pour les chrétiens formellement distincts. Mais leurs rapports seront caractérisés par le fait que, dans la cité médiévale, le spirituel ne se bornait pas à agir sur le temporel comme un élément régulateur des valeurs politiques, sociales, culturelles. Il tendait en outre, en vertu d'un processus qui s'explique historiquement, à associer une portion de lui-même au temporel, à devenir, uni au temporel, un élément *composant* de la cité. La notion de chrétien tendait à entrer dans la notion de citoyen, et la notion de christianisme dans la définition de la cité, non pas seulement comme une cause extrinsèque et une *puissance inspiratrice*, mais encore comme une cause intrinsèque et une *partie intégrante*. Il fallait être, en effet, chrétien, membre visible de l'Église, pour être citoyen; la cité, en vertu

served—in forms which were hardening, since they became more legal than vital—so that the notion of State-religion,[13] for instance, then came to the fore.

The modern age is not a sacral, but a secular age. The order of terrestrial civilization and of temporal society has gained complete differentiation and full autonomy,[14] which is something normal in itself, required by the Gospel's very distinction between God's and Caesar's domains. But that normal process was accompanied—and spoiled—by a most aggressive and stupid process of insulation from, and finally rejection of, God and the Gospel in the sphere of social and political life. The fruit of this we can contemplate today in the theocratic atheism of the Communist State.

Well, those Christians who are turned toward the future and who hope—be it a long range hope—for a new Christendom, a new Christianly inspired civilization, know that "the world has done with neutrality. Willingly or unwillingly, States will be obliged to make a choice for or against the Gospel. They will be shaped either by the totalitarian spirit or by the Christian spirit."[15]

---

de son principe constitutionnel, n'était faite que de chrétiens. Ceux qui n'appartenaient pas visiblement à l'Église étaient d'emblée rejetés hors de la cité: les Gentils aux frontières, les Juifs dans les ghettos; pour ceux qui, d'abord chrétiens, brisaient ensuite avec l'Église, comme les hérétiques et les schismatiques, ils étaient un danger bien pire; ils ébranlaient les assises de la nouvelle cité et apparaissaient comme des ennemis du salut public."

Further (pp. 298–300), the author explains in what sense this "sacral" régime was not a "theocratic" régime, as some historians put it in an oversimplified manner.

13. Without embarking on a discussion on the *Syllabus* and the degree of authority of its various articles, as excerpts taken from other papal documents, I would like only to observe that, at the time (1855) when proposition 77 (about State-religion) was set forth, Concordats previously agreed upon were being brutally violated in the name of Liberalism, whose struggle against the Church was in full swing, so that, by virtue of this factual context, the vicious manner in which a false ideology often spoils a historical process in the making was then especially conspicuous. At such moments no one is prepared to discard weapons that are at his command in actual fact.

14. I mean, in its own sphere and domain. See supra, pp. 313–15.

15. Cf. J. Maritain, *The Rights of Man and Natural Law* (New York: Charles Scribner's Sons, 1943), p. 23.

They know that a new Christianly inspired civilization, if and when it evolves in history, will by no means be a return to the Middle Ages, but a typically different attempt to make the leaven of the Gospel quicken the depths of temporal existence. They feel that such a new age will aim at rehabilitating man in God and through God, not apart from God, and will be an age of sanctification of secular life. But along what lines can this be imagined? This means that the Christians of whom I am speaking have to establish and develop a sound philosophy of modern history, as well as to separate from the genuine growth of time, from the genuine progress of human consciousness and civilization, the deadly errors which have preyed upon them, and the tares which are also growing among the wheat and which foster the wickedness of the time. In order to conceive our own concrete historical image of what is to be hoped for in our age, we have to determine and take into account, as an existential frame of reference, the basic typical features which characterize the structure of our age, in other words the *historical climate* or the *historical constellation* by which the existence and activity of the human community is conditioned today.

As I just put it, the historical climate of modern civilization, in contradistinction to medieval civilization, is characterized by the fact that it is a "lay" or "secular," not a "sacral" civilization. On the one hand the dominant dynamic idea is not the idea of strength or fortitude at the service of justice, but rather that of the conquest of freedom and the realization of human dignity. On the other hand the root requirement for a sound mutual cooperation between the Church and the body politic is not the unity of a religio-political body, as the *respublica Christiana* of the Middle Ages was, but the very unity of the human person, simultaneously a member of the body politic and of the Church, if he freely adheres to her. The unity of religion is not a prerequisite for political unity, and men subscribing to diverse religious or non-religious creeds have to share in and work for the same political or temporal common good. Whereas "medieval man," as Father Courtney Murray puts it,[16] "entered the State (what State

---

16. Murray, *op. cit.*, p. 57.

there was) to become a 'citizen,' through the Church and his membership in the Church, modern man is a citizen with full civic rights whether he is a member of the Church or not."

Hence many consequences derive. First, the political power is not the secular arm[17] of the spiritual power, the body politic is autonomous and independent within its own sphere. Second, the equality of all members of the body politic has been recognized as a basic tenet. Third, the importance of the inner forces at work in the human person, in contradistinction to the external forces of coercion; the freedom of individual conscience with regard to the State; the axiom—always taught by the Catholic Church, but disregarded as a rule by the princes and kings of old—that faith cannot be imposed by constraint[18]—all these assertions have become, more explicitly than before, crucial assets to civilization, and are to be especially emphasized if we are to escape the worst dangers of perversion of the social body and of state totalitarianism. Fourth, a reasoned-out awareness has developed, at least in those parts of the civilized world where love for freedom is still treasured—and is growing all the keener as freedom is more threatened—with regard to the fact that nothing more imperils both the common good of the earthly city and the supra-temporal interests of truth in human minds than a weakening and breaking down of the internal springs of conscience. Common consciousness has also become aware of the fact that freedom of inquiry, even at the risk of error, is the normal condition for men to get access to truth, so that freedom to search for God in their own way, for those who have been brought up in ignorance or semi-ignorance of Him, is the normal condition in

17. On the question of the "secular arm" see *ibid.*, pp. 62 ff.; Journet, *L'Église du Verbe Incarné*, pp. 249, 317–26. Be it noted in passing that the stock phrase "recourse to the secular arm," that is, to civil law, to enforce, in certain circumstances dealing with the public order and the temporal domain, a canonic regulation concerning the members of the Church, means something quite different from the concept of the political power as being the secular arm or instrument of the Church. In a pluralistic society it is but normal that the particular regulations of an autonomous body may be sanctioned by civil law, from the civil society's own viewpoint, when the interests of the common good are concerned.
18. See Journet, *L'Église du Verbe Incarné*, pp. 261–64.

which to listen to the message of the Gospel, and the teachings of the Church, when grace will illumine their hearts.[19]

Given such an existential frame of reference, what can be the ways of applying and realizing, in our historical age, the supreme principles that hold sway over the relationship between Church and State? Let us say that in a new Christianly inspired civilization, as far as we are able to see it,[20] those principles would in general be applied less in terms of the social power than in terms of the vivifying inspiration of the Church. The very modality of her action upon the body politic has been spiritualized, the emphasis having shifted from power and legal constraints (which the Church exercises, now as ever, in her own spiritual sphere over her own subjects, but not over the State) to moral influence and authority; in other words, to a fashion or "style," in the external relations of the Church, more appropriate to the Church herself, and more detached from the modalities that had inevitably been introduced by the Christian Empire of Constantine. Thus the superior dignity of the Church is to find its ways of realization in the full exercise of her *superior strength of all-pervading inspiration.*

3. *The Principle of the Superiority of the Church*

The supreme, immutable principle of the superiority of the Kingdom of God over the earthly kingdoms can apply in other ways than in making the civil government the secular arm of the church, in asking kings to expel heretics, or in using the rights of the spiritual sword to seize upon temporal affairs for the sake of some spiritual necessity (for instance in releasing the subjects of an apostate prince from their oath of allegiance). These things we can admire in the Middle Ages; they are a dead letter in our age. The supreme, immutable principle of the primacy of the spiritual and the superiority of the Church can apply otherwise—

---

19. Cf. infra, pp. 341–42 (and nn. 33 and 34).
20. On the notion, and possible advent, of a "Chrétienté profane" (lay or secular Christendom, in contradistinction to the sacral Christendom of the Middle Ages) see Journet, *L'Église du verbe incarné*, pp. 243–52.

but not less truly, and even more purely[21]—when, from the very
fact that the State has become secular, the supreme functions of
moral enlightenment and moral guidance of men, even as concerns the standards and principles which deal with the social
and political order, are exercised by the Church in a completely
free and autonomous manner, and when the moral authority of
the Church freely moves human consciences in every particular

21. Commenting upon the Concordat concluded in 1940 between the
Holy See and the Portuguese State (according to which the Portuguese
State, while ensuring full freedom to the Catholic Church, does not support
any official Church, and the clergy, except for the assistance given some
overseas mission works, do not receive any subsistence from the State),
Cardinal Cerejeira, patriarch of Lisbon, said in a remarkable address delivered on November 18, 1941:

"Another aspect of the agreement instituted by the Concordat is the reciprocal autonomy of the Church and the State. Each one is independent
and free in its respective sphere of competence. Neither does the State keep
the Church under its tutelage, nor does the Church interfere with matters
pertaining to the State.

"The advocates of the supremacy of the State would like to add: enslave-
ment of the Church, and by the same token, of Catholic conscience. But
we say: according to the very doctrine of the Church, the State has full
authority, but only in its own field.

"It was Christianity which introduced into the world that separation between the temporal and the spiritual, upon which rests the foundation of
all Christian civilization. Here is the fountainhead of liberty of conscience. . . .

"The Portuguese State recognizes the Church as she is, and ensures her
freedom; but it does not support or protect her as a State established religion. . . .

"What the Church loses in official protection, she regains in virginal
freedom of action. Free from any liability toward the political power, her
voice gains greater authority upon consciences. She leaves Caesar a completely clear field, in order for herself better to attend to the things that
are God's. She is the pure crystal from which the treasure of the Christian
revelation is streaming forth."

Cardinal Cerejeira gave another important address on the same subject,
November 18, 1946.

On the Portuguese Concordat see our book *Raison et raisons* (Paris: Luf,
1947), Chapter XIII; *Commonweal*, February 5, 1943 (in that issue excerpts from the 1941 address are unfortunately often translated in a defective manner); the London *Tablet*, October 2, 1948; Yves de la Brière, "Le
Concordat du Portugal," *Construire*, 1941 (*Construire* was the wartime substitute for the Jesuit periodical, *Études*); Murray, *op. cit.*, pp. 71–72 n.

case in which some major spiritual interest is at stake.[22] Then the superior dignity and authority of the Church asserts itself, not by virtue of a coercion exercised on the civil power, but by virtue of the spiritual enlightenment conveyed to the souls of the citizens, who must freely bear judgment, according to their own personal conscience, on every matter pertaining to the political common good. This way of carrying into effect the primacy of the spiritual can be thwarted or checked by the opposite course of action chosen by other citizens (no infallible way has ever existed). But, other things being equal, it seems to be surer in the long run than the ways conceived of in terms of State power, and it manifests in a clearer manner the freedom and purity of the spiritual, because the latter is under no obligation to a secular arm always eager to take the upper hand, and has not to extricate itself more or less painfully from the too mighty embrace of the State, which never serves unless with a view to be served.

Let us not forget what constitutes the essential sign and property of superiority. A superior agent is not confined or shut up within itself. It radiates. It stimulates the inner forces and energies of other agents—even autonomous in their own peculiar spheres —whose place is less high in the scale of being. Superiority implies a penetrating and vivifying influence. The very token of the superiority of the Church is the moral power with which she vitally influences, penetrates, and quickens, as a spiritual leaven, temporal existence and the inner energies of nature, so as to carry them to a higher and more perfect level in their own order[23]—in that very order of the world and of the life of civilization, within which the body politic is supremely autonomous, and yet inferior with regard to the spiritual order and the things that are of the eternal life. This is exactly what the absolutist or the totalitarian States (as well as, in the intellectual realm, rationalist philosophy) most stubbornly refuse to admit, even when they

22. "Through the free citizen, who freely consents to her doctrine and law, and who likewise by his free consent directs the processes of the City, the Church indirectly touches the life of the City. Through him too the processes of the City are so directed that they indirectly aid the supernatural mission of the Church." (Murray, *op. cit.*, p. 43).
23. See Journet, *L'Église du Verbe Incarné*, pp. 229–42.

claim to respect freedom of religion (by shutting up religion in its own heavenly sphere, and forbidding it any influence on earthly life, as if it were possible to forbid heaven to send rain on the earth or shine upon it). But this—the vivifying influence of the Church and the Gospel on the things of the world—is, on the contrary, what is actually and genuinely ensured in a type of Christian civilization and a "style" of Church-State relations such as those we are now discussing.

At this point I should like to observe that the stock phrase, "the problem of Church and State," is to some extent ambiguous, for what is the meaning of this word *State?* There was an age in which the Church had to do with the kings of Christendom and the Germanic Emperors. There was an age in which she had to do with absolute kings, then with modern absolute States claiming to be personal or supra-personal entities ruling the body politic from above. Today she has to do either with totalitarian States bound by nature to persecute her, or with democratic States still entangled in the remnants of the past, which do not know exactly how to deal with her because they have not yet realized that not they but the body politic in the whole range of its institutional organization, is henceforth the *dramatis persona* with whom the Church is confronted. If the democratic principle is to develop fully in the world, there will be an age in which the Church will have to do with the peoples; I mean with political societies in which the State will cease pretending to be a person and will only play its true part as central agency of the body politic. The problem of Church and State has not the same significance in these various instances.

Let us consider especially the obligations that the human being, not only in his individual life but also in his social life, bears toward truth. Everyone is obliged to truth to the extent that he knows it. The kings of old—or the absolutist States, heirs of the kings, and conceived in a kind of Hegelian manner—had an obligation to the truth to which *they themselves,* as distinct from the people and ruling over the body politic, adhered in conscience. But the body politic as such has an obligation to the truth to which *the people themselves,* the citizens—who constitute the body politic—adhere in conscience. The body politic does not know another truth than that which the people know.

As a result, the supreme principle that the political society bears obligations toward truth, and that its common good implies the recognition, not in words only, but in actual fact, of the existence of God, was implemented in the past by the duty incumbent on the kings—or on the absolutist States, heirs of the kings—of leading the body politic or the people to what those kings, or (supposing they had a soul of their own) those absolutist States held to be the true religion. But in our historical climate (once the genuine notion of the State and its merely instrumental function in a democratic society has been recognized) the same supreme principle is to be implemented by the duty incumbent on the people, and enforced by their own consciences, of giving expression to, and adopting as the enlightening and inspiring moral standard in their own social and political life, what the people themselves, or the citizens, hold to be the true religion. Thus everything will depend, in practice, on what the people freely believe in conscience—and on the full freedom of teaching and preaching the word of God, which is the fundamental right of the Church and which is also needed by the people in their search for the truth—and on the degree of efficacy with which the members of the Church, laity as well as clergy, give testimony, in actual existence, to their living faith and to the Spirit of God.

If a new civilization is to be Christianly inspired, if the body politic is to be quickened by the leaven of the Gospel in temporal existence itself, it will be because Christians will have been able, as free men speaking to free men, to revive in the people the often unconscious Christian feelings and moral structures embodied in the history of the nations born out of old Christendom, and to persuade the people, or the majority of the people, of the truth of Christian faith, or at least of the validity of Christian social and political philosophy.

Such a body politic Christianly inspired, such a political society really and vitally Christian, by virtue of the very spirit that would animate it and give shape to its structure—let us say, a political society evangelically Christian—would have its own social and

political morality, its own conception of justice and civic friendship, temporal common good and common task, human progress
and civilization, vitally rooted in Christian awareness. Considering now a new and particularly difficult issue, which deals with
the temporal society itself in its proper order and life, and with
its legislation, we may ask ourselves what kind of notions this
legislation would call into play when it comes to matters of conscience or questions directly concerned with personal creeds
and standards as well as with civil law. At this point we have to
maintain that the legislation of the Christian society in question
could and should never *endorse* or *approve* any way of conduct
contrary to Natural Law. But we have also to realize that this
legislation could and should *permit* or *give allowance to* certain
ways of conduct which depart in some measure from Natural
Law, if the prohibition by civil law of these ways of conduct
were to impair the common good, either because such prohibition
would be at variance with the ethical code of communities of
citizens whose loyalty to the nation and faithfulness to their own
moral creed, however imperfect it may be, essentially matter to
the common good, or even because it would result in a worse
conduct, disturbing or disintegrating the social body, for a great
many people whose moral strength is not on a level with the
enforcement of this prohibition.[24]

24. Thomas Aquinas states the principles of the matter in a basically
significant article: "Law," he says, "is established as a certain rule and
measure of human acts. Now every measure must be homogeneous with
the thing measured. . . . Hence it is necessary that even laws be imposed
on men according to the condition of them: for, as Isidore puts it (*Etym.*,
Bk. V, c. 21) law must be *possible, both with regard to nature and to
fatherland's custom.*

"Now the power or ability to act proceeds from the inner disposition or
habitus of the subject: for the same thing is not possible to the one who does
not possess virtue, and to the virtuous man; just as to the child and to the
perfect man (the grownup). As a result, we do not have the same law laid
down for children and for adults; and many things are permitted to children
which for adults are punished by the law or held to be shameful. Similarly,
many things must be permitted to men who are not perfected by virtue,
which could not be tolerated in virtuous men.

"Now human law is laid down for the multitude, the major part of which
is composed of men not perfected by virtue. Consequently, all and every
vice, from which virtuous men abstain, is not prohibited by human law,

I would say, therefore, that in the matters we are considering, civil legislation should adapt itself to the variety of moral creeds of the diverse spiritual lineages which essentially bear on the common good of the social body—not by endorsing them or approving of them, but rather by giving allowance to them. In other words, civil law would only lay down the regulations concerned with the allowance of the actions sanctioned by those various moral codes, or grant such actions the juridical effects requested by their nature; and consequently the State would not take upon itself the responsibility for them, or make them valid by its own pronouncement, but only register (when the matter is of a nature to require a decision of civil authorities) the validity acknowledged to them by the moral codes in question.

Thus, in the sense which I just defined, a sound application of the pluralist principle[25] and the principle of the lesser evil would require from the State a juridical recognition of the moral codes peculiar to those minorities comprised in the body politic whose rules of morality, though defective in some regard with respect to perfect Christian morality, would prove to be a real asset in the heritage of the nation and its common trend toward good human life. Such recognition would not be grounded on a right, I know not what, of which any moral way of life whatsoever would be possessed with regard to civil law, but on the require-

---

but only the gravest vicious actions, from which it is possible for the major part of the multitude to abstain, and mainly those—like homicide, theft, etc.—which are harmful to others, and without the prohibition of which human society could not be preserved." (*Sum. theol.*, I-II, 96, 2).

And he goes on to say: "Human law aims at leading men to virtue, not at one sweep, but gradually. As a result, it does not immediately impose on the multitude of the imperfect those things which are required from already virtuous men, so that they would be obliged by the law to abstain from every kind of evil. Otherwise imperfect people, being unable to bear such obligations, would plunge into worse evils, as is said in Prov. XXX:33: *the wringing of the nose bringeth forth blood,* and in Matt. IX:17: *if they put new wine*—that is, the precepts of perfect life—*into old wine-skins*—that is, into imperfect men—*the skins burst, and the wine is spilled*—that is, the precepts are contemned, and from such contempt men plunge into worse evils." (*Ibid., ad* 2).

25. Let us not understand "that because all human opinions of whatsoever kind have a right to be taught and propagated the commonweal should be obliged to recognize as juridically valid for each spiritual group the law

ments of the political common good, which in a democratic society demands on the one hand a particular respect for the inner forces and conscience of the human subject, and, on the other hand, a particular care not to impose by force of law rules of morality too heavy for the moral capacity of large groups of the population. It would be up to the political wisdom of the lawmaker, furthermore, to determine what communities of citizens could enjoy the pluralistic legal status which I have described.

As a result, I would see, in some conceivable future society, the laws of the body politic recognizing in such matters—not by virtue of a right belonging to any moral way of life whatever, but by virtue of the free decisions of political wisdom—the moral codes to which the consciences of the main spiritual stocks or lineages that make up the national community and its complex moral heritage are attached; of course on the condition that the body politic, while granting such freedoms to its own parts, were heedful of the moral interests of the whole, and made as restricted

worked out by this group according to its own priniciples. This is not my meaning. To me this principle signifies that, in order to avoid greater evils (that is, the ruin of the society's peace and either the petrification or the disintegration of consciences), the commonweal could and should tolerate (to tolerate is not to approve) ways of worship more or less distant from the true one: *the rites of the unfaithful must be tolerated,* St. Thomas Aquinas taught (*Sum. theol.,* II–II, 10, 11); ways of worship, and then also ways of conceiving the meaning of life and modes of behavior; and that in consequence the various spiritual groups which live within the body politic should be granted a particular juridical status which the legislative power *of the commonweal itself in its political wisdom* would adapt on the one hand to their condition and, on the other, to the general line of legislation leading toward virtuous life, and to the prescriptions of the moral law, to the full realization of which it should endeavor to direct as far as possible this diversity of forms" (*Humanisme intégral,* pp. 172–73; *True Humanism,* pp. 160–61; I made some amendments to the English translation). Cf. also *Du régime temporel et de la liberté (Freedom in the Modern World),* Chapter I, n. 12. In such a pluralist conception, as I noted (p. 80, French ed.; p. 66, English ed.), "civil legislation might coincide or concur with Canon Law for the Catholics," while for other spiritual lineages it might be different, yet always *oriented* in the direction of the true moral principles. It can be observed in this connection that art. 24 of the Portuguese Concordat forbids divorce only to those who have contracted a Catholic marriage. "This provision," Father John Courtney Murray comments, "illustrates what I meant by saying that the State organizes what is 'there' in society (*op. cit.,* p. 72 n.).

as possible, in actual existence, the derogations to the highest requirements of Natural Law which the legislators would allow as a lesser evil for the sake of the common good. The final objective of law is to make men morally good. Civil law would adapt itself, with a view to the maximum good of which the multitude is capable, to various ways of life sanctioned by various moral creeds, but it should resist changes which were requested through sheer relaxation of morality and decaying mores. And it should always maintain a general orientation toward virtuous life, and make the common behavior *tend*, at each level, to the full accomplishment of moral law.

4. *The Principle of Cooperation*

But let us now turn back to the relationship between Church and State, and consider our second immutable principle, the principle of cooperation. The things that are Caesar's are not only distinct from the things that are God's; but they must cooperate with them. What, then, in the particular type of Christian political society which I am discussing, would be the appropriate means through which the principle of the *necessary cooperation* between the Church and the body politic would apply?

The question, it seems to me, has three implications: the first, which concerns both the body politic and the State, deals with the most general and indirect form of mutual assistance between them and the Church; the second, which concerns especially the State or the civil authority, deals with the public acknowledgment of God; the third, which concerns in one case especially the State, in another case especially the body politic, deals with the specific forms of mutual help between the Church and the political society.

The most general and indirect form of cooperation

As regards the first point (the most general and indirect form of mutual assistance), I would say with Father John Courtney Murray, in his paper to the American Society of Theology, that "the major assistance, aid, and favor" that the body politic and the State "owe to the Church (one might better say, to the human

person with respect to his eternal destiny)" consists in the entire
fulfillment of their own duties with respect to their own ends, in
their own attention to a Natural Law, and in the full accomplishment of their political duty of creating "those conditions in
society—political, social, economic, cultural—which will favor
the ends of human personality, the peaceful enjoyment of all its
rights, the unobstructed performance of all its duties, the full
development of all its powers. There is here a material task, the
promotion of prosperity, the equitable distribution of the material
things that are the support of human dignity. There is also a moral
task, the effective guarantee of the juridical order. This organization of society according to the demands of justice" is "the first,
most proper and necessary contribution" of the body politic and
the State to the spiritual interests of the Church—"an indirect
contribution, but one apart from which the end of the Church is
impossible, or too difficult, of attainment."[26]

The public acknowledgement of the existence of God

As concerns the second point (the public acknowledgment of the
existence of God), I have already observed that a political society
really and vitally Christian would be conscious of the doctrine
and morality which enlighten for it—that is, for the majority of
the people—the tenets of the democratic charter, and which guide
it in putting those tenets into force. It would be conscious of the
faith that inspired it, and it would express this faith publicly.
Obviously, indeed, for any given people such public expression
of common faith would by preference assume the forms of that
Christian confession to which the history and traditions of this
people were most vitally linked. But the other religious confes-
sions institutionally recognized would also take part in this public
expression—just as it happens now in this country—and they

26. Murray, *op. cit.*, p. 48. "Nothing is clearer than the Pope's insistence
that the conscientious exercise by the State of its direct power over temporal
life is the essential exercise of its indirect power and duty to favor and assist
the ends of the Church. . . . The spiritual problem of our times is in fact
centered in the temporal order. And the modern 'welfare-state,' simply by
serving human welfare, would serve the Church better than Justinian or
Charlemagne ever did." (*ibid.*, p. 49).

would also be represented in the councils of the nation, in order that they might defend their own rights and liberties and help in the common task. As for the citizens who were unbelievers, they would have only to realize that the body politic as a whole was just as free with regard to the public expression of its own faith as they, as individuals, were free with regard to the private expression of their own non-religious convictions.

The specific forms of mutual cooperation

With respect to the third point—the specific forms of mutual help between the body politic and the Church—I should like first to make clear some preliminary remarks. It is obvious that it is the spiritual mission of the Church which is to be helped, not the political power or the temporal advantages to which certain of her members might lay claim in her name. In the stage of development and self-awareness which modern societies have reached, a social or political discrimination in favor of the Church, or the granting of juridical privileges to her ministers or to her faithful, would be precisely of a nature to jeopardize, rather than to help, this spiritual mission.

I just spoke of the ministers of the Church. Regarding their particular position, it is appropriate to enter into some more detailed elucidations.

The exemption from military obligations granted to the clergy in many countries is not a *social privilege*. To be exempted from having to shed blood is for a man a high moral privilege, but it is, at the same time, from the temporal and terrestrial point of view—because in the modern regime of "a nation in arms" it involves an exception to a common rule and to common dangers —a socially humiliating condition (not to speak of the resentment it may sometimes engender) imposed on men consecrated to God by the recognition of their essentially peaceful mission in the human community.

On the other hand, a distinction must be made between *simple adjustment of law and custom* to various functions or states of life which matter to the common good of the social body, and *juridical privilege* favoring a particular category with certain temporal advantages by virtue of an infraction of the principle of the equality of all before the law. The rights enumerated in the Code of Canon Law, in the chapter *de privilegiis clericorum,* through which the Church sanctions from her own point of view certain requirements of the priestly condition, should be recognized by a civil society of a pluralistic type as pertaining to the first case: adjustment of law and custom to various functions or states of life.

Instances of the same case are obviously to be found in certain advantages sometimes granted to the clergy, which it would never occur to the Church, for her own part, and at her own level as an autonomous society, to inscribe in her Code, and which she does not regard as rights required by the priestly condition. Thus it is that in certain countries, the United States for instance, the railroad companies offer clergymen reduced fares. Similar advantages might conceivably be granted to persons exercising other functions, the medical function, for instance. The fact remains that in any case the use of such advantages supposes in those who profit by them a general behavior that is modest enough to prevent these minor inequalities from seeming offensive, or even scandalous, as the equestrian array of Benedictine Abbots did in the thirteenth century (St. Thomas Aquinas rode a donkey, as was suitable for a member of a mendicant Order).[27]

But let us leave this digression and return to our purpose, namely, to the discussion of the specific forms of mutual cooperation between the body politic and the Church in our historical

27. Let us note, finally, in order to avoid any misinterpretation, that, from the point of view of what is usually called the "thesis," and on the condition that one be aware of the real bearing of words, there is no opposition between all that is said in this chapter and the fate of considering a privileged juridical situation for the Catholic Church the ideal situation to be sought, by virtue of the rights she possesses as a messenger of divine truth. For, given the factual circumstances created by the advent of modern societies and democratic regimes, the conditions of realization (what is called the "hypothesis") for such an ideal situation suppose a people in whom division in religious matters has disappeared, and in whom the Catholic faith is accepted by all. (And let us not forget that, by reason of the intercommunication between all nations of the world, no religious unanimity is possible in a given people if such unanimity does not actually extend to mankind as a whole.)

Then the Catholic Church would obviously be alone in enjoying in actual

age. The care that the State must take not to encroach upon matters of religion does not imply that as soon as it comes to the moral and religious realm the State should stand aloof and be reduced to sheer impotency. The State has no authority to impose any faith whatsoever upon, or expel any faith whatsoever from, the inner domain of conscience. But the State, as we have seen in a preceding chapter,* has to foster in its own way general morality, by the exercise of justice and the enforcement of law, and by supervising the development of sound conditions and means in the body politic for good human life, both material and rational. And as to religious matters, the State has to deal with them on a certain level, which is the level of civil peace and welfare, and from its own point of view, which is the point of view of the temporal common good; for instance, as we just said, the civil power has, as representing the people, to request the prayers of the religious communities historically rooted in the life of the people. And it is but normal that in applying the laws concerned with the exercise of the right of association, it should grant institutional recognition to those religious communities—as well as to all associations, religious or secular, educational, scientific, or devoted to social service, whose activity is of major importance for the common welfare—in contradistinction to other religious groups or secular associations which enjoy freedom but not institutional recognition. Moreover, assuming the formation of some religious sect aimed at the destruction of the bases of common

fact the right and liberties granted *de jure* to the various religious bodies institutionally recognized in a Christian society of the type we are describing: consequently the ideal envisaged in the thesis would be fulfilled in a situation which was actually privileged, but which implied neither temporal advantages granted to a category of citizens as opposed to others, nor any departure from the principle or equality of all before the law, nor, with greater reason, any pressure exercized by the State in matters of conscience, nor any instrumental role played by the State as secular arm of the Church.

And, to tell the truth, the ideal situation in question would correspond to the rights of the Church—the first of which is to convey divine truth— as well as to the dearest aspirations of the Christian heart, first and foremost through that which it presupposes, namely, the general disappearance of religious division in the world, and the general adherence to the true faith.

* *Man and the State*, Chapter III [Editors].

life, say, prescribing collective suicide or racial annihilation, it would be up to the State to dissolve such a religious sect, as well as any other association either criminal or destructive of national security. All this deals with the administration of justice, and implies the equality of rights of all citizens, whatever their race, their social standing, or their religious denomination may be.

It should be pointed out in this connection, first, that the subjects of rights are not abstract entities like "truth" or "error," but human persons, individually or collectively taken; second, that the equality of rights of all citizens is the basic tenet of modern democratic societies. Therefore the very fact (on which I have so often laid stress in this chapter) that the temporal society, become secular or strictly temporal, unites in its common task and common good men belonging to different religious lineages, has as its consequence that the principle of equality of rights is to be applied—not to "doctrines" or "creeds," this would have no meaning—but to the *citizens* who belong in these different religious lineages, which the body politic, from its own point of view, regards as parts of its own common moral heritage. Is it not, as I have previously remarked, through the citizens who are members of the Church that the Church, who is above the body politic, enters the sphere of the body politic and of its temporal common good? As a result it is from the point of view of the rights of the citizens who compose the body politic that the State will define its own positions with regard to the juridical status of the Church within the temporal sphere and in relation to the temporal common good.

Thus the Christian political society which I am discussing—supposing that the faith to which the majority of the people belonged were the Catholic faith—would know perfectly well that the Church herself was no part of it, but above it. And in this connection it would recognize the juridical personality of the Church as well as her spiritual authority in ruling her members in her spiritual realm, and it would deal with her as a perfect and perfectly independent society, with which it would conclude agreements and with the supreme authority of which it would maintain diplomatic relations. Yet, for all that, this Christian political society would have to hold that, in its own temporal sphere, and with regard to the rights they possess, Christian citizens (with the collective activities they and their multifarious institutions freely display in the national community) are no more legally privileged than any other citizens.

In other terms, this Christian political society would realize that there is only one temporal common good, that of the body politic, as there is only one supernatural common good, that of the Kingdom of God, which is supra-political. Once the political society had been fully differentiated in its secular type, the fact of inserting into the body politic a particular or partial common good, the temporal common good of the faithful of one religion (even though it were the true religion), and of claiming for them, accordingly, a privileged juridical position in the body politic, would be inserting into the latter a divisive principle and, to that extent, interfering with the temporal common good.[28]

After these preliminary remarks, I come to the point under discussion, namely the specific forms of mutual help between the Church and the political society.

As I have observed in the first part of this chapter, man is a member both of the body politic and, if he adheres to the Church, of that supra-temporal society which is the Church. He would be cut in two if his temporal membership were cut off from his spiritual membership. They must be in actual contact and connection. And an actual contact and connection, if it is not a contact and connection of mutual antagonism, is a contact and connection of mutual help. Moreover the common good itself of the temporal society implies that human persons are indirectly assisted by the latter in their movement toward supra-temporal achievement, which is an essential part of the pursuit of happiness. Finally (not to speak even of the fact, defined by theology, that human nature in its existential condition needs divine grace in order to achieve its highest human ends, social as well as individual), the Christian political society which we are discussing would be aware of the fact that Christian truths and incentives and the inspiration

---

28. Cf. J. Maritain, *The Rights of Man and Natural Law*, pp. 26–27. See also Heinrich Rommen, "Church and State," *Review of Politics*, July 1950.

of the Gospel, awakening common consciousness and passing into the sphere of temporal existence, are the very soul, inner strength, and spiritual stronghold of democracy. Just as democracy must, under penalty of disintegration, foster and defend the democratic charter; so a Christian democracy, that is, a democracy fully aware of its own sources, must, under penalty of disintegration, keep alive in itself the Christian sense of human dignity and human equality, of justice and freedom. For the political society really and vitally Christian which we are contemplating, the suppression of any actual contact and connection, that is, of any mutual help, between the Church and the body politic would simply spell suicide.

What are then, the specific forms of mutual assistance to which I am alluding?

The most basic of them is the recognition and guarantee by the State of the full freedom of the Church. For the fact of insuring the freedom of somebody is surely an actual, and most actual, though negative, form of cooperation with him and assistance to him. It has been an illusion of modern times to believe that mutual freedom means mutual ignorance. Can I be ignorant of the one whose freedom I insure? The theory of mutual ignorance between State and Church is self-deluding: either it veers in actual fact (as was the case in France in the nineteenth century) to having the State encroach upon spiritual matters and oppose the Church in order to define and enforce in its own way a so-called freedom of the Church, or it veers in actual fact to having the State know the Church (without confessing it) in order really to insure, somehow or other, the freedom of the Church.

Insuring to the Church her full liberty and the free exercise of her spiritual mission is fundamentally required by the God-given rights of the Church as well as by the basic rights of the body politic. For it is the condition for that spreading of the leaven of the Gospel throughout the whole social body which the temporal common good needs in its own sphere. The State acts simply in its own way, as providing the common good of the body politic, in guaranteeing the full freedom of the Church in her spiritual mission. And, as we have seen, it can insure that guarantee—in our historical age it ensures it in the best way—without granting any juridical privilege to the citizens who are members of the Church.

Finally there is a second specific form of mutal assistance which is also required. I mean not only a negative assistance, as is the insurance of freedom, but a positive one. This time I am not speaking of the State, but of the body politic with its free agencies and institutions. In the Christian political society which we are discussing this positive form of assistance would in no way infringe upon the basic rule of equal laws and equal rights for all citizens. The State would not assist the Church by granting her favored juridical treatment, and by seeking to gain her adherence through temporal advantages paid for at the price of her liberty. It is rather by *asking the assistance* of the Church for its own temporal common good that the body politic would assist her in her spiritual mission. For the concept of help is not a one-way concept; help is a two-way traffic. And after all, is it not more normal to have what is superior, or of greater worth in itself, aiding what is of lesser dignity, than to have what is terrestrial aiding what is spiritual? For the latter, moreover, giving more help amounts to being better assisted in its proper task.

Thus the body politic, its free agencies and institutions, using their own freedom of existential activity within the framework of laws, would ask more of the Church. They would ask, on the basis of freedom and equality of rights for all citizens, her cooperation in the field of all the activities which aim at enlightening human minds and life. They would positively facilitate the religious, social, and educational work by means of which she—as well as the other spiritual or cultural groups whose helpfulness for the common good would be recognized by them—freely cooperates in the common welfare. By removing obstacles and opening the doors, the body politic, its free agencies and institutions, would positively facilitate the effort of the apostles of the Gospel to go to the masses and share their life, to assist the social and moral work of the nation, to provide people with leisure worthy of human dignity, and to develop within them the sense of liberty and fraternity.[29]

29. Cf. J. Maritain, *Humanisme intégral*, pp. 184–85 (*True Humanism*, pp. 172–73); *The Rights of Man and Natural Law*, pp. 28–29.

Such would be, as I see it, the positive cooperation between the body politic and the Church. And because of the fecundity of truth, we may have confidence that among all the religious or cultural institutions thus freely cooperating with the body politic, the Church which holds in trust the true faith—in contradistinction to religious creeds whose message is more or less faltering, and with greater reason to more or less erroneous human philosophies—would, as a matter of fact, turn to better account the opportunities offered to all by freedom.

III SOME PRACTICAL CONCLUSIONS

The present is but a limit, a line of demarcation between the past and the future. So we can understand the present only in terms of the past or in terms of the future. That is why I think it would be advisable for Christians to dedicate in their own way a bit of meditation to the future.

As concerns my attempt to outline a future type of Christian political society, whatever one may think of its particular features, what matters essentially to me is the fact that the supreme general principles are immutable, and that the ways of applying or realizing them are analogical, and change according to the variety of historical climates. So the principles which were applied in a given way by the sacral civilization of the Middle Ages always hold true, but they are to be applied in another way in modern secular civilization.[30]

These things being understood, we see that many problems which embarrass contemporary consciousness are solved by the same token.

30. To express the same point otherwise, we might make use of the distinction which I stressed in a previous chapter [*Man and the State*, Chapter IV. Editors], between the possession of a right and its exercise. I can possess a right, for instance, to personal freedom, and be prevented in justice from claiming its actual exercise if my country is waging a just war and assigns me to be drafted.

The Church does not lose any of the essential rights she has claimed or exercised in the past. Nevertheless, she can renounce the exercise of certain of them, not because she is forced to do so, but voluntarily and by virtue of the consideration of the common good, the historical context having

On the one hand we see that the condemnation of theological liberalism by the Catholic Church will never be amended. This is because theological liberalism implied the false philosophy of the absolute metaphysical autonomy of human reason and will. It made the so-called "modern liberties" absolute and limitless to such an extent that man's obligations either toward truth or toward the common good simply vanished away. And it insisted that the very principles which had been applied in the Middle Ages or in the baroque age in a way inapplicable today were perishable principles, which have been dismissed by the evolution of ideas and societies. Such positions are intrinsically erroneous. Yet that does not mean that the "modern liberties" soundly understood are to be denied. And that does not prevent the Church from putting forward today such freedoms as freedom of conscience, freedom of teaching, etc.[31]

On the other hand we see that statements like Cardinal Manning's famous reply to Gladstone are unquestionably true. "If Catholics were in power tomorrow in England," Cardinal Manning wrote, "not a penal law would be proposed, not the shadow of a constraint put upon the faith of any man. We would that all men fully believed the truth; but a forced faith is a hypocrisy hateful to God and man. . . . If the Catholics were tomorrow the 'Imperial race' in these kingdoms they would not use political power to molest the divided and hereditary religious state of the people. We would not shut one of their Churches, or Colleges, or Schools. They would have the same liberties we enjoy as a minority."[32] Such a statement is valid, not only for England, but for every freedom-loving country. It does not refer to the requirements of an hypothesis reluctantly accepted, but to the require-

---

changed. She exercised in the past the right of making null and void a civil law which severely impaired the spiritual welfare of the people. She always possesses this right in its roots. If she made it emerge in actual exercise in the historical climate of today, this very exercise would harm the common good both of the Church and of civil society. So by reason of justice (justice toward the common good both of civilization and of the Kingdom of God) does the Church give up the exercise of such right.

31. Cf. J. Maritain, *Raison et raisons*, pp. 289–83.

32. Henry Edward Manning, *The Vatican Decrees in Their Bearing on Civil Allegiance* (London, 1875), pp. 93–96.

ments of the very principles soundly applied in the existential framework of the modern historical climate. Even if one single citizen dissented from the religious faith of all the people, his right to dissent could by no means be infringed upon by the State in a Christianly inspired modern democratic society. Even if, by the grace of God, religious unity were to return, no return to the sacral regime in which the civil power was the instrument or secular arm of the spiritual power could be conceivable in a Christianly inspired modern democratic society. The Catholics who are ready to give their lives for freedom do not cling to these assertions as a matter of expediency, but as a matter of moral obligation, or of justice. Yet that does not mean that they disregard in any respect, it means that they assert and maintain more than ever, the principle of the superiority of the spiritual order over the temporal order and the principle of the necessary cooperation between the Church and the body politic.

I know that there are people who would like, for the sake of religious truth, to set forth the concept of civil intolerance.[33] Well, they should frankly propose their own solution to the world, require that the State make all non-Christians and non-orthodox second-rate citizens, and they should be ready to contemplate the consequences that such a claim would entail, not only for themselves but for the very work of the Church in the world, as well as for the peace and common good of the civil society.[34]

I also know that, from the opposite side, there are people who would like, for the sake of civic tolerance, to make the Church and the body politic live in total and absolute isolation. Well, let me say, as the testimony of one who loves this country, that a European who comes to America is struck by the fact that the

33. Cf. the remarks made by Father Max Pribilla, "Dogmatische Intoleranz und bürgerliche Toleranz," *Stimmen der Zeit*, April 1949, and by Father Robert Rouquette, S.J., "Chronique de la vie religieuse," *Études*, September 1949.

34. In the theological vocabulary the notion of "civil tolerance" (imposing on the State respect for conscience) has been coined in contradistinction to that, obviously erroneous, of "dogmatic tolerance," which means that in the very sphere of the conscience and with regard to divine revelation man has a right to freedom *from* truth, or that the human mind has no obligation toward truth.

expression "separation between Church and State," which is in itself a misleading expression, does not have the same meaning here and in Europe. In Europe it means, or it meant, that complete isolation which derives from century-old misunderstandings and struggles, and which has produced most unfortunate results. Here it means, as a matter of fact, together with a refusal to grant any privilege to one religious denomination in preference to others and to have a State established religion, a distinction between the State and the Churches which is compatible with good feeling and mutual cooperation. Sharp distinction *and* actual cooperation, that's an historical treasure, the value of which a European is perhaps more prepared to appreciate, because of his own bitter experiences. Please to God that you keep it carefully, and do not let your concept of separation veer round to the European one.

Far beyond the influences received either from Locke or the eighteenth century Enlightenment, the Constitution of this country is deep rooted in the age old heritage of Christian thought and civilization.[35] Paradoxically enough, and by virtue of the serious religious feelings of the Founding Fathers, it appeared, at a moment of unstable equilibrium (as all moments in time are) in the history of ideas, as a lay—even, to some extent, rationalist—fruit of the perennial Christian life-force, which despite three centuries of tragic vicissitudes and spiritual division was able to produce this momentous temporal achievement at the dawn of the American nation: as if the losses suffered by human history in the supreme domain of the integrity and unity of faith, and in the interest in theological truth, had been the price paid, with respect to human weakness and entanglements, for the release at that given moment of humbler, temporal Christian energies

---

35. As I put it in *Scholasticism and Politics* (New York: Macmillan Co., 1940), p. 91, "its structure owes little to Rousseau, if I am to believe some Dominican friends of mine that this Constitution has rather some relation to ideas which presided in the Middle Ages at the constitution of St. Dominic's Order."—On the history and meaning of the American attitude toward the problem of Church and State, see Anson Phelps Stokes, *Church and State in the United States* (New York: Harper & Bros., 1950); Wilfrid Parsons, S.J., *The First Freedom* (New York: The Declan X. McMullen Co., Inc., 1948).

that must at any cost penetrate the historical existence of mankind. Peerless is the significance, for political philosophy, of the establishment of the American Constitution at the end of the eighteenth century. This Constitution can be described as an outstanding lay Christian document tinged with the philosophy of the day. The spirit and inspiration of this great political Christian document is basically repugnant to the idea of making human society stand aloof from God and from any religious faith. Thanksgiving and public prayer, the invocation of the name of God at the occasion of any major official gathering, are, in the practical behavior of the nation, a token of this very same spirit and inspiration.

The Catholic Church is sometimes reproached with being an "authoritarian Church," as if the authority—that is, the right to be listened to—that she exercises on her faithful in seeing to the preservation of revealed truth and Christian morality were to result in fostering authoritarian trends in the sphere of civil life and activities.[36] May I be allowed to say that those who make such reproaches lack both in theological and historical insight.

They lack in historical insight, because they do not grasp the significance of the diversity of historical climates which in past times made the authority of the Church over the State—and now make the mutual freedom of the State and the Church—requisites of the common good of civilization.

They lack in theological insight, for they do not see that the authority of the Church in her own spiritual sphere is nothing else than her bondage to God and to her mission. This authority concerns her own organization precisely as contrasted in essence with the organization of civil society. As Pope Pius XII has put it in an address delivered on October 2, 1945, the foundation of the

36. I am alluding to serious-minded authors, not to Mr. Paul Blanshard. His handling of the question (*American Freedom and Catholic Power* [Boston: Beacon Press, 1949], Chapter III) is not worth discussion because it is simply unfair, like the rest of his book, whose criticisms, instead of clarifying matters, are constantly vitiated by biased and devious interpretation, and which confuses all issues in a slandering manner, up to ascribing to the Catholic Church "a full-blown system of fetishism and sorcery" (p. 215).

Church as a society was accomplished from above downwards, but political society originates from below upwards.[37] In other words, authority in the Church comes down from above, but authority in political society rises from below; and whereas the Pope in the Church is the Vicar of Christ, the rulers in political society are the vicars of the people. As a result, it is a particular emphasis on political freedom which corresponds, in the sphere of civil society, to the particular emphasis on teaching authority in the sphere of the Church.

Be it noted, furthermore, that, as a matter of fact, no government is less authoritarian than the government of the Catholic Church. It governs without police force and physical coercion the immense people for whose spiritual common good it is responsible. Here we have a society the order of which primarily depends on the non-material influence on human souls of teaching, preaching, worshipping, and the sacramental life, and only secondarily on the external power of the law. The Pope speaks to the conscience of men, he counts upon the inner vitality of faith to make his word listened to; to enforce his doctrinal and moral directions in the Catholic people he has recourse to the spiritual sanctions of Canon Law but on comparatively infrequent occasions.

He has over the Church an authority that is supreme and sovereign.[38] But this supreme authority is exercised on a vast and infinitely variegated structure made up of all local Churches, which have their own particular life in the whole, and whose heads enjoy in their own sphere genuine and autonomous, though subordinate, authority. The bishops are not to the Pope as generals to a chief of supreme headquarters, or as civil servants to the central administration. According to the basic tenets on which

37. "La Fondazione della chiesa come società si e effettuata, contrariamente all'origine dello stato, non dal basso all'alto, ma dall'alto al basso" (address for the inauguration of the new juridical year of the Tribunal of the Rota, October 2, 1945, reported in *Osservatore romano,* October 3, 1945).

Cajetan, in 1511, had already made clear that difference between the origin of power in the Church and in civil society, in his opuscule *De Comparatione auctoritatis papae et concilii.*

38. Cf. supra (*Man and the State*), p. 49.

the constitution of the Catholic Church is grounded, they are invested with the fulness of priesthood; they are the successors to the Apostles; each one of them is the spouse of his local Church. The central government of the Church respects their rights and legitimate freedom of action. It takes into account, to a degree much more considerable than is ordinarily fancied, the various trends and initiatives, rooted in particular circumstances, of the episcopate and the faithful of each nation, and the *feeling of the Church*, who is not the ecclesiastical hierarchy only, but the whole body of Christ, laity and clergy together.

The Church in her very essence is an object of theological faith—belongs to the order of those realities hidden in divine life and made known by divine revelation which are called supernatural mysteries. As a result, between the believer, who thinks of the Church in terms of faith, and the unbeliever, who thinks of her in terms merely human, there is a kind of unavoidable mutual misapprehension. The first one knows that the life which animates her is the life of the God-given grace of Christ, which is received in deficient human beings, and from which these human beings slip away each time they do evil. He knows, therefore, that she is sinless while composed of sinful members. The unbeliever, on the contrary, ascribes to her all the faults of her members. He does not realize that even in the natural order a nation for instance is possessed of a life of its own which is, fortunately for those who cherish it, superior (though not come down from God) to the disheartening pettiness of a great many of its nationals. Those men of faith who have the truest and highest idea of the transcendent essence of the Church and her substantial holiness—tangibly manifested in her saints and all the fruits of sanctity that proceed from her—are best able to see without flinching the lapses of her members, and the way in which, to a greater or lesser extent, the behavior of Christians cannot help proving false to Christianity.

In the course of twenty centuries, by preaching the Gospel to the nations and by standing up to the flesh and blood powers in order to defend against them the liberties of the spirit, the Church has taught men freedom. Today the blind forces which for two hundred years attacked her in the name of freedom and of the human person deified, are at last dropping the mask. They appear as they are. They yearn to enslave man. Present times, however miserable they may be, have the wherewithal to elate those who love the Church and love freedom. The historical situation they are facing is definitely clear. The great drama of the present day is the confrontation of man with the totalitarian State, which is but the old spurious God of the lawless Empire bending everything to his adoration. The cause of freedom and the cause of the Church are one in the defense of man.

VI

Philosophy of History

Intimations of Maritain's philosophy of history appear as early as 1930 in his Religion et Culture, *and numerous diverse elements of it were expressed in 1933 in his* Du Régime Temporel et de la Liberté *and in 1936 in* Humanisme Intégral. *Indeed, his friend Monsignor Charles Journet [now Cardinal Journet] observed in the* Revue Thomiste *in 1948 that although Maritain as yet had no volume on the subject, a remarkable philosophy of history had already emerged in his works.*

As a matter of fact Maritain was in 1948 already showing signs of a growing interest in a more direct confrontation with the philosophy of history. In Existence and the Existent *he wrote: "Not only is everything present in the equipment of Thomism to allow it to find room for the historic dimension in the knowledge of Nature and the knowledge of Man, but its primary intuitions await, so to say, the introduction into it of that dimension; they are eager to welcome and to carry out the idea of development and evolution, and to complete the* opus philosophicum *by a philosophy of his-*

tory." His On the Philosophy of History *appeared in 1957, and it goes a long way towards opening up this area of the philosophy of history within the Thomist perspective.*

Central ideas for Maritain in this area are the philosophy of history's being the final return of the whole philosophical corpus *to the singular* par excellence, *that is, the movement, the very motion, of human history in time; the philosophy of history's belonging nevertheless to moral philosophy rather than to metaphysics or the philosophy of nature; man's passing under different historical climates or historical constellations, each of them expressing given intelligible structures and having therefore particular requirements (cf. the "Church and State" selection under "Politics" in this book); the analogical application of immutable principles in different existential conditions; the law of the two-fold simultaneous progress in good and in evil; and the ambivalence of history.*

Other sources for Maritain's philosophy of history are

> CHRISTIANITY AND DEMOCRACY
> MAN AND THE STATE
> MORAL PHILOSOPHY
> RANSOMING THE TIME

18

Spurious and Genuine
Philosophy of History *

1. The Hegelian system is the most brilliant, telling, and power-ful form, but it is far from being the only form of spurious philos-ophy of history.

Good historians—because they have personal experience of the contingencies, complexities, and uncertainties of historical work, nay more, of the element of relative non-intelligibility that is involved in history—have a natural distrust for the philosophy of history. This natural distrust becomes an all-too-justified loathing when they are confronted with the spurious philosophy of history which is, as a rule, to be found on the market.

What is it that makes them angry and unhappy when they con-cern themselves with the notion of a philosophy of history? They are incensed by the intolerable dogmatism of philosophies which pretend to be rational disciplines and which (whether they claim, with Hegel, to save religion by making it a mythical chrysalis of their own "absolute knowledge" or, with Marx, to sweep away religion in the name of the good tidings of atheism or, with Auguste Comte, to build up a new and definitive religion, the religion of Humanity) offer themselves to mankind as the mes-sengers of some messianic revelation, and use history as an instru-ment to validate their empty claims.

Furthermore, the historians (for instance, Henri Marrou in his book mentioned above**) reproach the philosophy of history

* On The Philosophy Of History (New York: Charles Scribner's Sons, 1957), pp. 29–37.
** Henri Marrou, De la connaissance historique (Paris: Ed. du Seuil, 1954) [Editors].

with four capital sins: first, its almost inevitably oversimplified, arbitrary, and wanton approach in regard to the choice of materials, the historical value of which is assumed for the sake of the cause; secondly, its self-deceptive ambition to get at an *a priori* explanation of the course of human history; thirdly, its self-deceptive ambition to get at an *all-inclusive* explanation of the meaning of human history; and fourthly, its self-deceptive ambition to get at a so-called *scientific* explanation of history, the word "scientific" being used here in this quite peculiar sense, which can be traced back to the sciences of nature, that with such an explanation our thought enjoys a kind of intellectual mastery over the subject-matter.

And yet, the historians of whom I am speaking cannot help recognizing that, once the problem "does the pilgrimage of mankind, triumphant and heart-rending by turns, through the duration of its history, have a value, a fecundity, a meaning?" has been posed, it cannot be eluded.[1]

What do all the previous observations point to? They tell us that the historian cannot help feeling the appeal of the philosophy of history, and that at the same time he thinks he must resist this appeal, given the spurious forms in which, as a rule, the philosophy of history greets his eyes. What he is loathing in reality is not genuine philosophy of history, but the *gnosticism of history*—that gnosticism of history which was carried by Hegel to supreme metaphysical heights, but which is to be found also, at quite another level, in a system as completely fascinated by positive sciences and as decidedly anti-metaphysical as Comte's system is.

2. Spurious philosophy of history, thus, is gnosticism of history in the most general sense of this expression, and insofar as it is characterized by the four "capital sins" that have just been mentioned.

Contrariwise, a genuine philosophy of history, to which we pointed in the first section of this chapter,* does not claim to dis-

---

1. Cf. Henri Marrou, *op. cit.*, p. 16.
* *On The Philosophy Of History*, Chapter I, pp. 1–6 [Editors].

mantle the cogs and gearwheels of human history so as to see how it works and master it intellectually. History, for it, is not a problem to be solved, but a mystery to be looked at: a mystery which is in some way supra-intelligible (insofar as it depends on the purposes of God) and in some way infra-intelligible (insofar as it involves matter and contingency, and depends on the nothingness injected into it by man when he does evil). The question, therefore, is only to perceive in such inexhaustible subject-matter certain intelligible aspects, which will always remain partial and somehow disconnected. Theology does not *explain* the divine Trinity. Analogically, the philosophy of history does not *explain* history. And so, any temptation to the first afore-mentioned "capital sin" is reduced for it to a minimum, and it is immune to the three others, for the simple reason that a genuine philosophy of history does not dream of being an explanation of history. And where there is no explanation, there can be neither *a priori* explanation, nor all-inclusive explanation, nor master explanation.

Let us, then, state as our first principle: history can be neither rationally *explained*[2] nor *reconstructed* according to necessitating laws.[3]

But history can be *characterized, interpreted,* or *deciphered in a certain measure and as to certain general aspects*—to the extent to which we succeed in disclosing in it meanings or intelligible directions, and laws which enlighten events, without necessitating them.

3. I have emphasized in another book[4] this basic truth that the laws of nature are necessary but that the course of events in nature is contingent. The necessity proper to *laws* does not make the *events* necessary, because the laws refer, in one way or another, to universal essences brought out from things by abstraction, while the events take place in existential, concrete, indi-

2. As against all philosophies of history of the Hegelian or dialectical type.
3. As against all philosophies of history of the Comtian or supposedly "scientific" type.
4. Cf. J. Maritain, *The Degrees of Knowledge* (New York: Charles Scribner's Sons, 1959), Chapter II.

vidual reality, which lies open to the mutual interference of independent lines of causation, and which is made of nature and adventure.

If this is true in the realm of nature, it is still more true in the realm of history, because in the course of the events of nature we have to do only with contingency, whereas in the course of the events of history we have to do also with the free will of man. The observations I have submitted above* on human freedom and history presupposed a certain metaphysics, which sees the problem of free will as a central problem to be thoroughly sifted, and which considers the existence of free will an essential characteristic of man. But the philosophy of history of Hegel, of Marx, or of Comte (not to speak of their persistence in confusing "necessary laws" with "necessitating laws") presupposes either a certain metaphysics or a certain anti-metaphysics which dreams of going beyond the alternative: freedom or determinism, and, as a result, disregards or ignores in practice the reality of free will in man. Hence, the awkward and silly way in which, while they depict—explain or reconstruct—human history as a self-development resulting, in each of its phases, from the inflexible requirements of necessitating laws, either dialectical or phenomenal, they try at the same time to make room for "human freedom" (in a most equivocal sense), human initiative and human energies in the shaping of events. Auguste Comte had at least the merit of frankly exposing such a self-contradictory position, when he prided himself on his bastard concept of *fatalité modifiable,* "modifiable inevitability."

At this point we have to make clear that no philosophy of history can be genuine if the general philosophy it presupposes, and of which it is a part, does not recognize the existence of human free will (together with the other properties of the human person) and the existence of God: the consequence of these two truths being that human history implies a double kind of contingency, on the one hand with respect to the transcendent freedom of God, and on the other hand with respect to human free will as well as to natural accidents and vicissitudes.

* *On The Philosophy Of History,* pp. 24–28 [Editors].

If we do not believe in the existence of human free will, we cannot understand how man can exert, as I mentioned above, a decisive influence on the mode or specific orientation of an historical change which is necessary in itself, or with regard to the accumulated needs it answers; and we cannot realize, either, that the historical necessity in question refers to a kind of general pattern which is, as a rule, undetermined and, so to speak, neutral with respect to what matters most to the hearts of men: whereas the mode, specific orientation, or specific inspiration which depends on human freedom has to do with what has, for good or ill, the most direct impact on human persons and human societies.

And if we do not believe in the existence of God, we shall not, of course, see history as governed by Him from above, and as continually modeled and remodeled by His eternal purposes, making up for the evil through which human free will spoils human history, and turning losses into greater gains. But then, if we do not look at history as at a tale told by an idiot, and if we try to work out a philosophy of history, we shall, in our effort to make history rational, transfer to it the very rationality which no longer belongs to transcendent divine purposes; in other words, we shall transform these formerly divine purposes either into history's own inner purposes and dialectical requirements, or into "scientific" laws which shape its development with sheer necessity. It was the misfortune of the philosophy of history to have been *advertised* in the modern world by philosophers who were either the greatest falsifier [Hegel] in divinity, or utter atheists. Only a spurious philosophy of history could be elicited by them.

4. Let us conclude this section with a few words about the structure of time.

The subject-matter of the philosophy of history is the unrolling of time, the very succession of time. Here we are confronted not only with the singularity of particular events, but with the singularity of the entire course of events. It is a story which is never repeated; it is unique. And the formal object of the philosophy of history is the intelligible meaning, as far as it can be perceived, of the unrolling, of the evolution in question.

Now I would merely observe that time, the time of human history, has an inner structure. Time is not simply a garbage can in which practical men would have to pick up more or less profitable opportunities. Time has a meaning and a direction. Human history is made up of periods each of which is possessed of a particular intelligible structure, and therefore of basic particular requirements. These periods are what I have proposed calling the various historical climates or historical constellations in human history. They express given intelligible structures, both as concerns the social, political, and juridical dominant characteristics, and as concerns the moral and ideological dominant characteristics, in the temporal life of the human community. . . .

With the question of the structure of time, which I just touched upon, the question of its irreversibility (or of its not cyclical, but "linear" or "vectorial" character) is closely connected. In this regard, I would like to bring to our attention some significant observations made by Mircea Eliade. In his book, *Le mythe de l'éternel retour*,[5] he stresses the fact that the *acceptance* of time—and of history—far from being matter-of-course for man, is for him a difficult and dearly paid achievement. Man is naturally frightened by the irreversibility of his own duration and the very newness of unpredictable events. He refuses to face them. Hence the negation of time by archaic civilizations. They defended themselves against the dire reality of history either by constructing mythical archetypes, or by assuming a periodic abolishment and regeneration of time, and a periodic recurrence of the same historical cycles. As I pointed out at the beginning of this chapter,* acceptance of time and of history was a conquest of Christianity and modern times. But this very acceptance would be of a nature to drive man to despair if he could not decipher some transhistorical meaning in the awful advance of time into the night of the unknown, thronged with perpetually new perils.

5. Paris: Gallimard, 1949 (English translation: *The Myth of the Eternal Return*, Bollingen Series, Pantheon Books, 1954).
* *On The Philosophy Of History*, Chapter I, p. 2 [Editors].

19

THE LAW OF TWO-FOLD CONTRASTING PROGRESS *

1. I mentioned in Chapter I** the law that history progresses both in the direction of good and in the direction of evil. By way of elucidating this further, we might meditate on a famous parable in the Gospel. Of course, the Gospel is not concerned with the philosophy of history, but we do find in it the most illuminating statements for the philosopher of history—statements which we may use from our own philosophical point of view, in applying them to this particular matter, the philosophy of history. I am thinking of the parable in Chapter XIII of the Gospel according to St. Matthew about the man who sowed good seed in his field, only to have his enemy come and oversow it with cockle:

> The kingdom of heaven is likened to a man that sowed good seed in his field.
> But while men were asleep, his enemy came and over-sowed cockle among the wheat and went his way.
> And when the blade was sprung up and had brought forth fruit, then appeared also the cockle.
> And the servants of the goodman of the house coming said to him: Sir, didst thou not sow good seed in thy field? whence then hath it cockle?
> And he said to them: An enemy hath done this. And the servants said to him: Wilt thou that we go and gather it up?
> And he said: No, lest perhaps gathering up the cockle, you root up the wheat also together with it.
> Suffer both to grow until the harvest, and in the time of

---

* *On The Philosophy Of History* (New York: Charles Scribner's Sons, 1957), pp. 43–52.
** *Ibid.*, pp. 1–42.

the harvest, I will say to the reapers: Gather up first the
cockle and bind it into bundles to burn, but the wheat
gather ye into my barn.

This parable is a quite striking expression of the law we are now
considering. It means that good is not divided from evil in human
history—they grow together. Let us first consider its primordial,
its religious meaning. Its proper object is the kingdom of grace;
it refers to the ultimate end beyond the world. The evil works
accumulated in time will burn in hell, and the good works accumulated will be gathered into the divine barn. But pending the
end, sinners and saints will grow together. Thus, from the point of
view of the history of the kingdom of grace, or of Christ's mystical
body, it may be said that two immanent movements cross each
other at each point of the evolution of mankind, and affect each
of its momentary complexes. One of these movements draws upward (toward final salvation) everything in mankind that participates in the divine life of the kingdom of grace, or the Church
(which is *in* the world but not *of* the world), and follows the
attraction of Christ, Head of the human race. The other movement draws downward (toward final doom) everything in mankind which belongs to the Prince of this world, head (as St.
Thomas says)[1] of all evildoers. It is in undergoing these two
internal movements that human history advances in time. The
Christian knows that, though constantly thwarted and constantly
concealed, the work of the spirit is carried out in spite of everything, as history goes on, and that thus from fall to fall, but also
from obscure gain to obscure gain, time marches toward the
resurrection.

A particular instance of this double movement is pointed out
by St. Thomas when he is considering the state of mankind during the time between the original sin and the coming of Christ.[2]
Briefly, St. Thomas says that with the development of time sin
began to make its impact felt more and more in the human race
in such a way that the instinct of natural law became insufficient
for man to act rightly, and it thus became necessary to have the

1. *Sum. theol.*, III, 8, 7.
2. See *ibid.*, III, 61, 3, ad 2.

precepts of written law. In this increase of the weight of sin we have the movement downward. But we have simultaneously the movement upward: there is the divine gift of the Decalogue; there are the sacraments of the Ancient Law; and there is the progressive increase in the knowledge of divine things; through the teaching of the prophets the elements of faith are disclosed bit by bit—until the full revelation achieved by Christ. This instance of the double movement concerns, of course, the kingdom of grace and the ultimate end beyond the world.

2. But what I would like to emphasize particularly now is that the parable of the wheat and the cockle has a universal meaning and bearing which is valid for the world as well as for the kingdom of grace. And we must say, from the philosophical point of view, that the movement of progression of societies in time depends on this law of the double movement—which might be called, in this instance, the law of the degradation, on the one hand, and the revitalization, on the other, of the energy of history, or of the mass of human activity on which the movement of history depends. While the wear and tear of time and the passivity of matter naturally dissipate and degrade the things of this world and the energy of history, the creative forces which are proper to the spirit and to liberty and which are their proof, and which normally have their point of application in the effort of the few, constantly revitalize the quality of this energy. Thus the life of human societies advances and progresses at the cost of many losses. It advances and progresses thanks to the vitalization or superelevation of the energy of history springing from the spirit and from human freedom. But, at the same time, this same energy of history is degraded and dissipated by reason of the passivity of matter. Moreover, what is spiritual is, to this very extent, above time and exempt from aging.

And, of course, in certain periods of history what prevails and is predominant is the movement of degradation, in other periods it is the movement of progress. My point is that both exist at the same time, *to one degree or another.*

We have here a notion of progress which is quite different both from the necessary, rectilinear, and indefinite progress which the eighteenth century dreamed of, and in which future things were supposed to be always and by right better than past ones; and, on the other hand, from that negation of any progress and that disregard for the God-given élan at work in us which prevail among those who despair of man and of freedom.

The deeper our knowledge of anthropology becomes, the more, I think, shall we become aware of the fact that the most telling instance of the law I am discussing took place in the ages when mankind passed from its childhood to its adult state. No progress upward was more important than this coming of human thought and human societies to rational knowledge (as contradistinguished from mythical knowledge) and to political life (as contradistinguished from tribal life). Yet the simultaneous downward movement cannot be overlooked. The concept of the *good savage,* as cherished by the eighteenth century, was a silly notion of over-civilized people; there was no more *innocence,* absolutely speaking, in the primitive man than in the child each one of us was. The fact remains, nevertheless, that there was a *kind* of innocence in both. There were in the myths of primitive man an obscure grasping of essential truths—in his approach to things a power of imaginative intuitivity and a vital participation in nature —in his tribal life a real and probably heartening, though slavish, communion with the group, which have been lost in the process.

Shall we look for another instance? Let us think of a few striking features of modern history. On the one hand we have, from the last decades of the eighteenth century on, an awareness of human rights and of the dignity of the human person, a longing for freedom and human fellowship, a recognition of the principle: government of the people, for the people, and by the people, a growing concern for civil liberties and for social justice, an assertion of man's power over nature which constitute an exceptionally significant progress upward. But, on the other hand, we are confronted, during the same space of time, with the subjection of all citizens to military service, with more and more destructive wars, with the growth of mercantile materialism, then of nationalist passions, then of communism, of fascism, of racism, and, in those years which will always be alive in our memory, with the mass murder of six million Jews by Hitler; the first half of the nineteenth century witnessed the enslaved conditions of life to which the industrial proletariat was then submitted; and our own times face the threat to human freedom raised by communist totalitarianism thriving in large regions of the earth.

May I now allude to the problem of the temporal mission of the Christian? As I indicated in Chapter I,* the philosophy of history has practical consequences, which shows that it pertains to the domain of practical or moral philosophy. From the genuine notion of progress, which I just emphasized, a practical consequence can be drawn with respect to the work of the Christian in the world. The work of the Christian in history does not aim to set the world up in a state from which all evil and all injustice would have disappeared. If it did, then it would be only too easy, considering human history, to condemn the Christian as a utopian, or to say, as some Protestant theologians do, that, given the corruption of human nature, the very notion of a Christian (that is, Christian-inspired) civilization, and of an effort to make Christian justice and brotherhood prevail in the world, is a contradiction in terms.[3] The work of the Christian is to maintain and augment in the world the internal tension and the movement of slow deliverance which are due to the invisible potencies of truth and justice and love, in action in the mass which goes counter to them. And this work cannot be in vain—it surely produces its fruit. We have no illusions about the misery of human nature. But we have no illusions, either, about the blindness of the pseudo-realists who cultivate and exalt evil in order to fight against evil, and who consider the Gospel a decorative myth which we could not take seriously without throwing the machinery of the world out of order.

Genuine Christianity does not forget the original greatness of man. It abhors the pessimism of inertia. It is pessimistic in the

---

* *On The Philosophy Of History*, pp. 1–42 [Editors].

3. I remember a discussion I once had with an eloquent and dynamic Protestant theologian, who was also a Socialist deputy of the French Parliament. "If you are so hopeless about any Christian possibility in the world," I asked him, "why, then, are you a Socialist? Do you not hope for some improvement in terrestrial justice?" And he answered: "I am a Socialist, a Protestant Socialist, only to *protest* against evil and injustice. But I don't hope for any truly Christian accomplishment in the terrestrial order, I don't believe that any Christian civilization will ever be possible."

sense that it knows that the creature comes from nothingness, and that everything that comes from nothingness tends of itself toward nothingness. But its optimism is incomparably more profound, because it knows that the creature comes from God, and that everything that comes from God tends toward God.

3. To conclude my remarks on the law of the double antagonistic movement, I would observe that we find a particular application of this law in what might be called the law of the parasitical part played by error in the progress of human speculative or theoretical knowledge, especially in the realm of our knowledge of nature and in the realm of philosophy. What I mean is that great discoveries are usually paid for in human history by the reinforcement that a given truth receives from error preying upon it, and from the emotional overtones that error provides. For instance, the mathematical knowledge of nature—that great scientific conquest which started in the sixteenth and seventeenth centuries—was stimulated and fortified by a mistaken philosophy (the mechanist philosophy) which preyed upon it and appeared for a long time as inseparable from it. And we may think that without the ambitions developed by mechanist philosophers the human mind would not have been sufficiently enflamed to make the progress that was this discovery of mathematical knowledge of nature. Similarly, we might say that the awareness of science as a knowledge of phenomena, distinct from philosophy, that is, from knowledge of intelligible being, took place at the same time as Kantian philosophy. It is, so to speak, thanks to the errors of Kant that this notion of science (our modern science) as knowledge of phenomena was recognized in human history. Also, we might say that the great psychological discoveries about the unconscious were reinforced and stimulated by the erroneous philosophy of life which prevailed in the mind of Freud.

20

MAGICAL AND RATIONAL STATES IN HUMAN THOUGHT AND CULTURE*

1. This distinction, which I simply indicated at the beginning of this chapter,** refers—at least, I think so—to a genuine philosophy of history. It is a philosophical distinction founded on, and interpreting, inductive data afforded by anthropology.[1] In an essay on *Sign and Symbol*,[2] written many years ago, I submitted that a distinction should be made between the *logical* sign, which speaks primarily to the intellect, and the *magical* sign, which speaks primarily to the imagination. My working hypothesis was the notion of functional condition or existential state, in the sense in which I have used the term "state" in this book. I was pointing to a fundamental distinction between the state of our developed cultures and another state or existential condition in which, for psychic and cultural life as a whole, the last word rests with the imagination, as the supreme and final law. In this latter state, the intellect is doubtless present, and with all its inherent principles and laws, but in a way it is not *free*—it is tied up, bound to the imagination. That is the state I am calling the *magical* regime or state of psychic and cultural life.

* On The Philosophy Of History (New York: Charles Scribner's Sons, 1957), pp. 96–104.
** Ibid., pp. 77–78.
1. I would stress that no philosophy of history can be complete without anthropology—anthropology is a basic consideration for the philosopher of history.
2. See Quatre essais sur l'esprit dans sa condition charnelle (Paris: Des-clée De Brouwer, 1939; new edition: Paris: Alsatia, 1956), Chapter II; Ransoming the Time (New York: Charles Scribner's Sons, 1941), Chapter IX.

I would note that this working hypothesis succeeded in reconciling opposed points of view in a particularly controversial field. A few years before his death, Professor Lévy-Bruhl was so kind as to write and express his agreement with me on this point: "as you put it quite rightly, primitive mentality is a *state* of human mentality, and I can accept the characteristics through which you define it."

Allow me to quote now the testimony of the great Polish anthropologist, Bronislaw Malinowski: "I have chosen to face the question of primitive man's rational knowledge directly: watching him at his principal occupations, seeing him pass from work to magic and back again, entering into his mind, listening to his opinions. The whole problem might have been approached through the avenue of language, but this would have led us too far into questions of logic, semasiology, and theory of primitive languages. Words which serve to express general ideas such as *existence, substance,* and *attribute, cause* and *effect,* the *fundamental* and the *secondary;* words and expressions used in complicated pursuits like sailing, construction, measuring and checking; numerals and quantitative descriptions, correct and detailed classifications of natural phenomena, plants and animals—all this would lead us exactly to the same conclusion: that primitive man can observe and think, and that he possesses, embodied in his language, systems of methodical though rudimentary knowledge."

And Malinowski continues: "Similar conclusions could be drawn from an examination of those mental schemes and physical contrivances which could be described as diagrams or formulas. Methods of indicating the main points of the compass, arrangements of stars into constellations, co-ordination of these with the seasons, naming of moons in the year, of quarters in the moon—all these accomplishments are known to the simplest savages. Also they are all able to draw diagrammatic maps in the sand or dust, indicate arrangements by placing small stones, shells, or sticks on the ground, plan expeditions or raids on such rudimentary charts. By co-ordinating space and time they are able to arrange big tribal gatherings and to combine vast tribal movements over extensive areas. . . . The use of leaves, notched sticks, and similar aids to memory is well known and seems to be almost universal. All such 'diagrams' are means of reducing a complex and unwieldy bit of reality to a simple and handy form. They give man a relatively easy mental control over it. As such are they not—in a very rudimentary form no doubt—fundamentally akin to developed scientific formulas and 'models,' which are also simple and handy paraphrases of a complex or abstract reality, giving the civilized physicist mental control over it?"[3]

The intellect in primitive man is of the same kind as ours. It may even be more alive in him than in some civilized men. But the question with which we are concerned is that of its existential conditions, the existential regime or state under which it operates. In primitive man the intellect is in a general way involved with, and dependent on, the imagination and its savage world. This kind of mental regime is one in which acquaintance with nature is experienced and lived through with an intensity and to an extent we cannot easily picture. I observed in the previous chapter[*] that in passing from the myths of the primitive man to our rational or logical regime there were surely losses, compensating for the greater gains achieved by such a progress.

The magical state is a state of inferiority, but it is by no means despicable. It is the state of mankind in its infancy, a fertile state through which we have had to pass. And I think that anthropologists should recognize that under this regime humanity enriched itself with many vital truths, which were known by way of dream or divinatory instinct, and by actual participation in the thing known—not in a conceptual, rational manner. It is extremely difficult for us to imagine now what can have been the functioning of the human mind in such a state. It is a difficulty analogous to that which we experience when we try to penetrate the mental life of animals. Whatever *we* picture to ourselves is in fact bathed in intelligence, and in intelligence which is free, which has the upper hand over imagination. Therefore we have great trouble in depicting to ourselves any state in which—in the case of primi-

---

3. Bronislaw Malinowski, *Magic, Science and Religion* (New York: Doubleday, Anchor Books, 1955), pp. 33–34. See also Pierre Lecomte du Noüy, *Human Destiny* (New York: New American Library, 1949), Book III, especially pp. 79–80.

* *On The Philosophy Of History*, Chapter 2, pp. 47–48 [Editors].

tive man—imagination had the upper hand over the intellect; or in which—in the case of the animal—there is knowledge, but merely sensitive knowledge: knowledge by way of the senses, which admittedly are capable, in superior vertebrates, of *resembling* intelligence to a great extent. It is really impossible for a man to imagine how a dog is "thinking." But nevertheless there is a dog-knowledge which exists as a matter of fact, and is the object of the psychology of animals. We experience a similar difficulty when it comes to the magical state proper to the mental activity of the primitive man, a state utterly different from our logical state, and in which the imagination was the queen of the human mind. We might call our present state a daylight or solar state because it is bound up with the luminous and regular life of the intellect. And the magical state might be called a nocturnal state, because it is bound up with the fluid and twilight life of the imagination.

2. Here I would like to propose some remarks on positivism and Comte's law of the three states. From the positivist point of view one is led to say that the mathematical and physico-mathematical sciences, and all the multifarious sciences of phenomena, constitute the only function of truth and real knowledge in human thought, and that, therefore, religion, mystical experience, metaphysics, and poetry are, in the civilized mind, an inheritance from the primitive and "pre-logical" mentality. This is a major tenet in the positivists' philosophy of history. These types of mental activity are but metamorphoses of ancient magic—perhaps justifiable in the practical and emotional order, but directly opposed, as is magic itself, to the line of science and truth.[4] The era of science has succeeded to the era of magic, and magic and science are essentially inimical and incompatible.

For Bergson, I may add, magic and science are similarly inimical and incompatible. "Magic is the reverse of science," he wrote

4. I remember that Lévy-Bruhl sent a copy of his first book on primitive mentality to a friend of his, the Belgian poet Verhaeren. Verhaeren wrote to Lévy-Bruhl that he was delighted to read the book because he found in it a complete description of his own mentality. Well, this was more of a criticism than a compliment.

in *The Two Sources* because, for Bergson, also, science consists entirely in the mathematical explanation of matter. Yet in Bergson's view, science, at least science in the process of being born, always co-existed with magic. And science does not exhaust the function of truth and real knowledge in human thought. Other functions—religion, mystical experience, metaphysics, and poetry—are also functions of truth, and more profound ones. But for Bergson, as for the positivists, these things are at right angles to the line of science, and they spring from the same vital center as magic. Magic and religion have a common origin, from which they developed in opposite directions—magic in the direction of illusion, myth-making, and laziness; and religion (what Bergson called "dynamic religion") in the direction of heroism and of truth.

Now the distinction which I have proposed between the magical and the rational states of the human mind and culture differs at once from the positivist and from the Bergsonian positions. To my mind, our modern science of phenomena is only one of the possible forms of science, only one of the degrees of knowledge. Moreover, science, philosophy, metaphysics, like religion and mysticism, and like poetry, are destined to grow up together. In the nocturnal state, the magical state of the primacy of the dream and of the imagination, they were inchoate, more or less fused or confused, but they were there. Once the threshold of the daylight state of the primacy of the intellect and the Logos was passed, they became more and more differentiated from each other. It is not true that "the era of science has succeeded the era of magic"—what is true is that the state of Logos has succeeded the state of Magic—for all the mental and cultural functions of the human being existed in the state of magic, and they now exist in the state of logical thought. Science, like religion, existed in the nocturnal state before it existed in the daylight state. So, one cannot say that there is nothing in common between magic and science, and that magic is the reverse of science. One can only say that the magical state of science—of that rudimentary science of the tribal man which was alluded to in Malinowski's remarks quoted above—is in opposition to the logical state of civilized man's science.

Thus my point is that all human thought, with its great and

at first undifferentiated primordial ramifications, passes through
a diversity of existential conditions or states. The science of the
primitive man was science, and it was such in the state of magic
—primitive man had a certain knowledge of nature, real and
workable, though different from ours. This knowledge made use
of certain connections of physical causality, and it formulated
them in an intelligibly manageable manner, all the while immers-
ing them in a kind of sacral empiricism, and in a general way of
thinking dominated by the magical sign. Science left this condition when it passed over the threshold of the Logos-dominated
regime of thought and of culture. Now, in our civilized times, the
residues of magical knowing are taken over, by virtue of a process of abnormal integration, by a pseudo-science—the occultism,
or the occult "sciences," of civilized man—utterly different from
the magic of primitive man, and which will carry with it certain
pathological characteristics for intellectual life (as happens for
affective life in certain cases of infantile retrogression among
adults).

Similar observations may be made with respect to religion.
Religion was at first in a magical or nocturnal state, and then it
passed under a new regime, the daylight state of human thought
and culture. The religion of civilized humanity crossed the threshold of this daylight state either by a transformation into more or
less rationalized mythology (as in Greece), or by a process of
metaphysical elaboration (as in India), or by forms of revelation adapted to such a state (as in Judaeo-Christian monotheism).
And, just as in certain forms of pseudo-knowledge, so in certain
pseudo-religious phenomena to which the civilized man is liable
to fall prey, residues of the magical state will appear, taken over,
by virtue of a process of abnormal integration, by superstitious
notions and imagery, wherein the part played by pathology is far
greater than in magical religion itself.

21

MAN AND THE HUMAN CONDITION*

1. The considerations that follow do not have to do with doctrines and systems, they bear on human conduct itself and on the most general options with which our attitude in life is linked. These considerations are connected however in an indirect way with the philosophical positions examined in the present work; every great moral system, indeed, is in reality an effort to ask man, in one manner or another and to one degree or another, to go beyond his natural condition in some way. But either these same great philosophical doctrines refuse to acknowledge the effort in question, or else they leave in a wholly implicit state the problem it envelops. To my mind, on the contrary, it is important to disengage the problem explicitly. One sees then that it concerns the moral life of each one of us in such a fundamental way, and involves so profoundly the individual subjectivity, that it depends, to tell the truth, on a sort of metaphysics of conduct which precedes moral theories and systematizations. If one tries to examine it in itself, reducing things to the essential, one is led, it seems to me, to distinguish the four different attitudes I am about to discuss, of which the first two, more or less outlined, in fact, in the lives of certain among us, but impossible to carry through, are too irrational to correspond to any definite doctrine; and of which the last two correspond, one to the thought of India, the other, inchoatively, to the Western philosophical tradition, and, under its perfected and really effective form, to Christian thought.

The fact is, I believe, that in the background of all our moral

---

* *Moral Philosophy* (New York: Charles Scribner's Sons, 1964), pp. 452–462.

difficulties there is a fundamental problem which is ineluctably posed for each of us, and which in practice is never fully resolved, except in those who have entered into the ways of perfection: the problem of the relation of man to the human condition, or of his attitude in the face of the human condition.

This condition is that of a spirit united in substance with flesh and engaged in the universe of matter. It is an unhappy condition. In itself it is such a miserable condition that man has always dreamed of a golden age when he was more or less freed of it, and so miserable that on the plane of revelation, the Christian religion teaches that mankind was created, with the grace of Adam, in a superior condition in which it was free of sin, of pain, of servitude, and of death, and from which it fell through its own fault. The Judaeo-Christian tradition also teaches that after the end of history and in a new world the human condition will be supernaturally transfigured. Those who believe neither in the state of innocence nor in original sin put the golden age at the end of history, not at the beginning, and fancy that man will attain it in the last stage of his terrestrial adventure, through his own liberating effort, thanks to science and to radical social transformations; others, who want no part of consoling illusions, try to escape the spectacle of this planet by surrendering to some powerful passion which distracts them day after day from themselves and from the world, or by the ardor of a despairing pity which in a way appeases their hearts while it corrodes them little by little.

Indeed, the tragic perplexity in which we are placed consists in the fact that we can neither refuse the human condition nor accept it purely and simply. I will explain later on in what sense I understand the expression "to accept *purely and simply* the human condition." As to refusing the human condition, it is clear that it is a question there only of a moral disposition. Such a refusal belongs to the world of dream; but man nourishes himself on dreams, and a dream which has its roots in the depths of the individual psychology of the subject can determine his fundamental attitude in life.

THE TEMPTATION TO REFUSE THE HUMAN CONDITION

2. It is solely in the perspective of nature that we shall consider things in this and the three following sections. We have just noted that the human condition is an unhappy condition. The state of intermediary species is in general a state little to be envied; and it is in a paradoxically eminent manner that the human species, at once flesh and spirit, is an intermediary species. The heavens tell of the glory of God, but the earth that He has made is dreadful to man. A "vale of tears," yes, and this is not a mere poetic image.

It is not a question here of any sort of Manichaeism. It is quite true that the material universe abounds in wonders and is resplendent with an inexhaustible beauty that makes apparent the mark of the Spirit Who created it; it is quite true that despite the cruelty and voracity which inhabit it the world of nature is penetrated with the goodness and the generosity of being, and embraces finally all things in the imperturbable peace of its great laws, and of its great rational necessities which superbly ignore us; it is quite true that in man himself the world of the senses, whatever bitterness it may harbor, is made first and above all to enchant us with its sweetness and its joys; it is quite true that human nature is good in its essence, and that for every living being, but eminently for man, to live is a marvellous gift. And yet, for all that, a spirit whose operations have need of matter surmounts matter only at a formidable price and by running immense risks, and is most often scoffed at by it. The spirit is immortal, and matter imposes the law of death on the body animated by it. Man has more grandeur than the Milky Way; but how easy evil is for him, how inevitable (if one considers the species collectively) it is, in a being in which sense and instinct, and the animal unconscious, ask only to elude or to twist the judgment of the mind. As for suffering, it is already a frightful thing to see an animal suffer, but the suffering of beasts is of small account in comparison with the suffering that pierces a flesh united to spirit, or spirit itself.

3. Thus we can understand that the temptation to refuse the human condition has a greater chance of worming its way into

us when man has in one manner or another become better aware of the natural exigencies of the spirit in him—of that spirit which is his soul, and which reveals itself to him in the highest powers of the soul. Such a temptation does not exist in the primitives. We may believe that in the collective history of mankind it is largely this temptation which, at work in us without our being aware of it, makes the very progress through which civilization advances go side by side with delusions which impair it or degradations which corrupt it.

To refuse—in one's innermost heart—the human condition, is either to dream of leaving our limits and to wish to enjoy a total liberty in which our nature would expand through its own powers; or else to play the pure spirit (what I once called the sin of angelism); or else to curse and try to disown all that presents an obstacle to the life of the intellect, and to live in a state of interior revolt against the fact that one is a man; or else to flee by no matter what frenzy, even if it be in the folly of the flesh, this situation of a reason everywhere at loggerheads with matter which is a permanent challenge to the demands of the spirit in us. It is hardly surprising that those who devote themselves to the life of the intelligence, the poet in particular, and the philosopher, are more or less exposed to this temptation. The ancient sages of Greece succumbed to it when they said that the best thing for man is not to have been born.

In the life of an individual the most frequent occasion for this temptation—which does not justify it for all that—is that the man who endeavors, as Aristotle said, "to live according to the intellect," is more conscious than those who live "according to the human" of everything we said above concerning the misery of the human condition. Often even the man dedicated to meditation forgets that the spirit finds, through the senses, the source of its life in the very matter that torments it; he forgets too that the evils that matter causes are made transitory to a certain extent by matter itself, since it is a root principle of change.

But above all, if he pays attention to the lessons of history and to the long cry of the poor and the abandoned, he understands that naked suffering, horror, anguish without consolation—all this is the true background of the world for us, however generous nature may be, and however admirable the victories won by human generations to make things less hostile to man and the structures of his own life more worthy of him, through the progress of civilization, of art, and of knowledge. It may be that for a long while we almost lose sight of this background of the world. But every now and then it re-appears to us.

The man who has passed the threshold of the life according to the intellect understands all that is offensive and humiliating— for that spirit in which his specific difference itself and his dignity consist—in the radical contingency linked with matter and the dependence with regard to matter which constitute the metaphysical infirmity of our existence. In the eyes of material nature is a man worth any more than the sound of the brook? To pursue its work there the spirit struggles ceaselessly against the fortuitous and the useless; its very movement depends not only on the absolute values in which it has its proper object, it depends also on chance, on good and bad encounters; it advances from generation to generation enduring a perpetual agony, only to have in the end what it has produced here on earth fall—I mean with regard to men, and unless it is divinely protected—under the law of decay and futility which is the law of matter, and only to have what is immortal in itself be received by our species only at the cost of equivocations and misunderstandings that are perpetuated throughout time.

The fact remains that all that must be accepted. Even when they do not repeat in their own way, and however pitifully, the story of Faust, there is no sadder and more fruitless distress than the distress of men who under the pretext of wanting to live according to the intellect allow themselves to be carried away by the temptation to refuse the human condition. They are vanquished beforehand, and their defeat aggravates their subjection.

THE TEMPTATION TO ACCEPT PURELY AND SIMPLY THE HUMAN CONDITION

4. Would the solution therefore be to accept *purely and simply* the human condition?—This pure and simple acceptance would

be just as costly, and is no less impossible. It would be a betrayal of human nature not to recognize the demands, which are consubstantial to it, of the superhuman in man, and this nature's need of the progressive movement of the spirit, with its torments and its dangers, in other words, its need of perpetually going beyond the presently given moment of our condition on earth. And if we want to go beyond it, it is because to that extent we do not accept it without reserve.

It is fitting moreover to see the whole import of the expressions one uses. To accept the human condition is to accept—with all that life offers of the good and the beautiful and the pure, and with all the grandeurs of the spirit, and with "the call of the hero"—the radical contingency, the failures, the servitudes, the immense part of sorrow and (as regards nature) of inevitable uselessness of our existence, sickness, death, the different kinds of tyranny and hypocrisy which prey on social life, the stench of gangrene and the stench of money, the power of stupidity and of the lie. But if it is a question for a man of accepting *purely and simply* the human condition, why then, after all, in accepting all the evil of suffering that our nature entails, should he not accept at the same stroke all the evil of sin to which it is inclined? He has been made as he is, with the weaknesses of his flesh and the covetousness that is in him, with the longing for pleasure and power and the rage of desires, of that obsessing desire especially which does not come from him but from his species, to which his individual person matters little but which has need of his chromosomes in order to perpetuate itself. All that also is part of the human condition. To accept *purely and simply* (if that were possible) the human condition, means to accept it in its entirety, with the misery of sin as well as with the misery of suffering.

This cannot be, moreover, without a fundamental contradiction and without additional torments. For the social groups—horde or society—and the state of culture without which the human species cannot endure on earth require rules and taboos guaranteed by terrifying sanctions; and it is essential to the human condition that the sense of moral obligation, and of the distinction between good and evil, which exists naturally in the soul of each one of us (and which is in itself contradictory to the acceptance of moral evil as supposedly required by our nature), exert itself at least under the wholly exteriorized form of obedience to tribal prohibitions, and according as good and evil appear only as what is permitted or forbidden by the social group. To accept *purely and simply* the human condition is therefore an intrinsically contradictory moral disposition (although more or less outlined in fact in a great number of human beings)—a disposition to accept not only subjection to Sin as well as subjection to Suffering, but also subjection to the law of Fear, which forbids certain definite faults as infractions of the general conduct and the rules of the closed society.

Supposing that it could be fully carried out, such an acceptance of the human condition would make man live on the edge of animality; it is, as we have noted, as impossible in reality as the refusal of the human condition, because to accept fully subjection to moral evil, in whatever manner one conceives it, is not possible for the human being. What we are calling *pure and simple* acceptance of the human condition is only a limit to which, even in its most primitive representatives, our species has never attained. Indeed, it is in more or less approaching this limit that many among us seem to accept purely and simply the human condition. They accept it *almost* purely and simply. They not only have the code of their gang, their class or their accustomed social group (which implies already, though under a very inferior form, the prohibition of wrongdoing), they have also an outline at least, and often a great deal more than an outline, of authentic moral life, by reason of which they do not love the evil that they do. But even if their conscience has in other respects firm convictions, there are a certain number of domains—notably the domain of sex, and, in certain periods, that of "honor" (duel), and that of war—in which to act without taking account of the moral law seems normal in their eyes: it's the human condition that requires it, they believe that at this point it imposes another code on them. Perhaps, however, they will repent one day of the actions thus committed in contempt of the moral law (not to speak of many others among us who violate the law only in the pangs of remorse). To do evil and to repent of the evil that one does is the minimum of what the human being is capable of to testify that it is impossible to give in completely to the temptation to accept *purely and simply* the human condition.

THE ANSWER OF INDIAN SPIRITUALITY

5. What is asked of man is neither to accept purely and simply nor to refuse the human condition—it is to transcend it.[1] Here too, however, two very different ways can be envisaged. It can be a question of transcending the human condition in a manner which implies a certain refusal of it (because in this case it is through his own forces that man has to transcend his condition, he must then engage himself in an effort against the grain of nature); or it can be a question of transcending the human condition while consenting to it (because in this case a "new nature," has been grafted on human nature, and permits man to transcend his condition by going, not against the grain of nature, but higher than nature). The first way corresponds to what we shall call, to be brief, the Hindu-Buddhist solution; the second, to what we shall call the Gospel solution.

By abolishing, by means of a sovereign concentration of the intellect and the will, every particular form and representation, the wisdom of India adheres, through the void, to an absolute which is the Self in its pure metaphysical act of existing—experience conceived as leading at the same stroke either to the Transcendence of Being (Atman) or to total indetermination (nirvâna). All the forms of illusion in the midst of which our life is spent have disappeared, everything is denied and annihilated, there remains only the Self in contact with itself.

It is clear that to attain such an end (not to speak even of the "powers" for which one is to search without pause), is to tran-

---

1. I am not speaking of the Hegelian-Marxist answer to the problem of the human condition. In this perspective it is not a question of transcending the human condition, but of transforming it and finally of deifying it, through the work of history and of man himself. Such a solution rests on a manifestly erroneous philosophical postulate, in which the notion of human nature gives way to that of process of self-creation of man by man.

scend the human condition by dint of spiritual energy. But it is also clear that it is to transcend it by the means of refusal. The living delivered-one gains a sort of interior omnipotence by falling back upon himself and separating himself from everything human; he enters into a solitariness incomparably more profound than the solitude of the hermit, for it is his soul itself which has broken with men and all the miseries of their terrestrial existence. To pass beyond illusion, and to deliver oneself from transmigration, or at least from all the sorrow that it carries with it and perpetuates, is at the same stroke to deliver oneself from the human condition. The refusal of this condition is there but a means of transcending it, it is not an act of revolt against it, a pure and simple refusal. It remains however essential to the spirituality of India. That is why, even when the sage, as in the Buddhism of the Great Vehicle (Mahayana), spreads his pity over men, it is as it were through the condescension of a being who no longer belongs to their species, and whose heart—by the very exigency of solitariness in nirvâna is not wounded by their trou bles and does not enter into participation with them.

How can we not see in the implicit refusal of the human condition of which I have just spoken one of the weak points of the spirituality of India? If one considers in itself (independently of the graces which in fact can supervene in a soul of good will) this effort to escape the state in which we are naturally placed by our coming into the world, it manifests, along with an exceptional courage, an exceptional pride of spirit. Moreover such a refusal is in reality doomed, whatever victories it may bring, to a final defeat. Courage and pride are precisely two of the most profound features of the human condition. The Hindu or Buddhist sage quits the human condition only by showing in spite of himself his belonging to it—I mean, by the very negations to which he is led and all the apparatus of exercises and techniques he needs, and by the kind of never-ending *tour de force* by means of which he comes to transcend this condition. And the living delivered-one still has to die like the others; he is not delivered from that which is the most tragically human in the human condition.

THE GOSPEL ANSWER

6. What of the Christian or Gospel solution? It takes us beyond pure philosophy and pure reason, and yet, by a strange paradox, it is in it and in the mystery that it proposes to us that an authentically rational attitude toward the human condition becomes possible for man.

I said above that every great moral system is in reality an effort to ask man, in one manner or another and to one degree or another, to go beyond his natural condition in some way. These systems in fact (let us mention here only those which have been examined in the present work) ask man—while he rejects moral evil but accepts the suffering to which the human condition is exposed—to go beyond the human condition: either, as with Plato, Aristotle, the Stoics, Epicurus, Kant, Sartre, or Bergson, by attaching himself to a good superior to human life, or to a happiness in which human life is achieved rationally, or to virtue, or to pleasure decanted to the point of indifference, or to duty, or to liberty, or to the sovereign love to which the great mystics call us; or, as with Hegel, Marx, Comte, or Dewey, by deifying nature. But even in those cases where the effort to go beyond the human condition is the most authentic, there is no question, except in Bergson (and, in the name of faith, in Kierkegaard) of truly transcending it. And the attempt to go beyond the human condition by the sole means of man remains in the last analysis doomed either to futility or to illusion. It is only with Christianity that the effort to go beyond the human condition comes to real fruition.

It is superfluous to remark that I am not speaking here of the average behavior of the mass of people of Christian denomination. I am speaking of the exigencies of Christianity such as they are proposed to every one—and almost completely realized only in saints.

The question for the Christian is to transcend the human condition but by the grace of God—not, as for the Indian sage, by a supreme concentration on oneself—and in consenting at the same time to this condition, in accepting it, although not purely and simply, without balking; for the Christian accepts it as to all that pertains to the evil of suffering proper to the human condition, not as to what pertains to moral evil and sin. Rupture with the human condition as to sin, acceptance of the human condition as to the radical contingency and as to the suffering as well as to the joys that it entails: that is demanded by reason, but is decidedly possible only by the configuration of grace to Him Who is sanctity itself because He is the Word incarnate. At the same stroke, the acceptance of the human condition ceases to be simple submission to necessity; it becomes active consent, and consent through love.

That in a certain measure every soul inhabited by the gifts of grace, and in a full measure the saint, the one who has entered into what we called in a previous chapter* the regime of supraethics, transcends the human condition—this is obvious to anyone who holds that grace is a participation in the divine life itself. It is the other aspect of the Gospel solution, the simultaneous acceptance (except as to sin) of the human condition that it is important for us to insist on here.

In the human condition thus transcended and accepted at the same time, everything, to tell the truth, remains the same and everything is transfigured. If grace makes man participate in the divine life and if it superelevates his nature in its own order, nevertheless it is a nature still wounded which is thus superelevated, it is a man still devoured by weakness who shares in eternal life and in God's friendship. The human condition has not changed. It was not changed because the Word of God assumed it such as it was and such as it will remain as long as history endures. In taking upon Himself all the sins of the world, He Who was without sin also took upon Himself all the languors of the world, and all the suffering that afflicts the human race, and all the humiliation of its dependence with regard to the contingent and the fortuitous. What matter henceforth the contingency and the metaphysical futility to which our existence is subjected, since the most insignificant of our acts, if it is vivified by charity, has an eternal value, and since the Son of God has accepted to undergo Himself the servitudes of our condition?

During His hidden life He was a poor village workman, and

---

* *Moral Philosophy*, Chapter XIV [Editors].

His activity as preacher and miracle-worker took place in an historical milieu which made weigh on Him all its circumstances of time and place and all its hazards. He willed to die as the most unfortunate of men died in His time. His passion was an atrocious condensation of all the agony and abjection attached to the human condition since the Fall.

Consequently, when what I called just now the true background of the world—the world of naked suffering, of horror, of anguish without consolation—reveals itself to the Christian and takes possession of him, this matter of accepting (as to the evil of suffering) the human condition takes on an entirely new sense for him, comes to enter into the redemptive work of the Cross, and to participate in the annihilations of Him Whom he loves.[2] No wonder the saints are desirous of suffering. Suffering, because it is for them a signature of their love, and cooperation in the work of their Beloved, has become for them the most precious of goods here on earth.

There they are, then, the saints, who by an apparent contradiction give thanks to God for all the goods He heaps upon them and for all the protections, consolations, and joys He dispenses to them, and give thanks to Him at the same time for all the evils and afflictions He sends them. We who are wicked, do we give a stone to our children when they ask for bread? And yet thanks be to God when He gives us bread, and thanks be to Him when He gives us a stone and worse than a stone. The evil of suffering, while remaining what it is, and while being fully experienced as such, is transvalued now in a superior good, one perfectly invisible besides, unless there appear for an instant some sign of the more than human peace that inhabits the tortured soul.

7. The unbeliever sees here only a ghastly facility that religion allows itself, playing on two boards at the same time. The believer sees here the supreme grandeur of a mystery accessible to faith alone, and which can—in faith—be attained in some fashion

---

2. "Our annihilation is the most powerful means we have of uniting ourselves to Jesus and of doing good to souls," wrote Father de Foucauld. Cf. Jean-François Six, *Itinéraire spirituel de Charles de Foucauld* (Paris: Seuil, 1958), p. 364.

and stammered by the intelligence, but which remains in itself as incomprehensible as God Himself.

It is doubtless for the philosopher that this mystery is the most incomprehensible, because the philosopher knows too well that essences do not change, and that in the ordinary course of things, suffering, unless the one that it visits undertakes bravely to surmount it, degrades and humiliates the human being. He would be a fool, however, if he did not bow before the testimony of the saints. But in his perspective as a philosopher the best he can say is that God's love is as transcendent as His being, which is as no thing is; and that it is more difficult still for the heart of man to apprehend the transcendence of Love subsisting by itself than it is for the human intelligence to apprehend the transcendence of Being subsisting by Itself. "Believe that God loves you *in a way that you cannot imagine,*" said Dostoevski.[3]

And here again can the philosopher refrain from asking some questions?

He is astonished by another apparent contradiction in the behavior of the saints. They desire suffering as the most precious of goods here below. After all, that's their affair, or rather an affair between God and them. But what about the others, those whom they love, and who comprise all men? Do they not desire for them also this most precious of goods here on earth? Yet this is not what they do, they spend their time trying to lessen the sufferings of men and to cure them of their wounds. The answer, to the extent that one can catch a glimpse of it, concerns the very structure of the spirit.

In itself suffering is an evil, and will always remain an evil. How then could one wish it for those one loves? The simple knowledge possessed by the Christian (and so frequently recalled to his attention by the commonplaces of pious literature) that suffering unites the soul inhabited by charity to the sacrifice of the Cross, superimposes on suffering, ideally and theoretically, a quality thanks to which this knowledge helps one to accept suffering; it cannot make it be loved or desired, it does not transvalue it. If there is real and practical transvaluation, it can only

3. Cf. Henri Troyat, *Sainte Russie* (Paris: Grasset, 1956), p. 149.

be in the fire of the actual and absolutely incommunicable love between the self of a man and the divine Self; and that remains a closed secret, valid only for the individual subjectivity. Thus the saints would keep for themselves alone what they consider to be the most precious of goods here on earth. Singular egoists! They want suffering for themselves, they do not want it for others. Jesus wept over the dead Lazarus, and over the sorrow of Martha and Mary.

But the philosopher has still other questions. What strikes him above all in the human condition is not the suffering of the saints, it is the suffering of the mass of men, the suffering they have not willed, the suffering that falls on them like a beast. How could he resign himself to the suffering of man?

He knows that the struggle against suffering is one of the aspects of the effort through which humanity goes forward, and that in this struggle the work of reason and the ferment of the Gospel, the progress of science and the progress of social justice, and the progress of the still so rudimentary knowledge that man has of himself, enable us constantly to gain ground. He is not tempted to adore the Great Being, but he renders thanks to the men—to the innumerable workers known and unknown who throughout the course of an immense history, by dint of inventive genius and sacrifice of self, have applied themselves and will always apply themselves to making the earth more habitable. But the philosopher also knows that as one gains ground in the struggle against suffering, new causes of suffering begin to abound, so that man, despite all his progress, will never have done with suffering just as he will never have done with sickness.[4] Modern man suffers in other ways than the cave man. On the whole, one can wonder whether he suffers less; one can wonder whether all the victories gained in the struggle against suffering do not result in maintaining, by compensating the progress in suffering, a kind of middle level at which life as a whole is almost tolerable. However this may be, there will always remain enough suffering to put the heart and the intelligence in anguish.

Thus the answers that the philosopher gives himself in think-

4. Cf. René Dubos, *Mirage of Health* (New York: Harper, 1959).

ing about the suffering of men are valid but insufficient. There is another answer still, one that not only concerns terrestrial history but also and above all eternal life. It was given in the Sermon on the Mount.

If there is in humanity an immense mass of suffering which is not redemptive like that of Christ and His saints, it is in order that it may be redeemed, and that everywhere at least where human liberty does not intrude its refusal, those who have wept in our valleys may be consoled forever.

Index of Names

385